Co [barcode: D0943651]

*The **Michelin maps** you will need with this Guide are:*

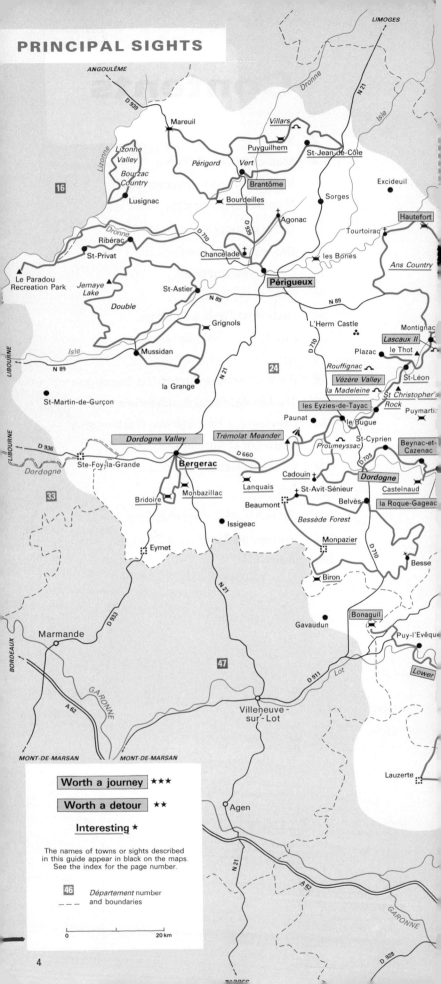

PRINCIPAL SIGHTS

Worth a journey ★★★

Worth a detour ★★

Interesting ★

The names of towns or sights described
in this guide appear in black on the maps.
See the index for the page number.

46 *Département* number
--- and boundaries

0   20 km

4

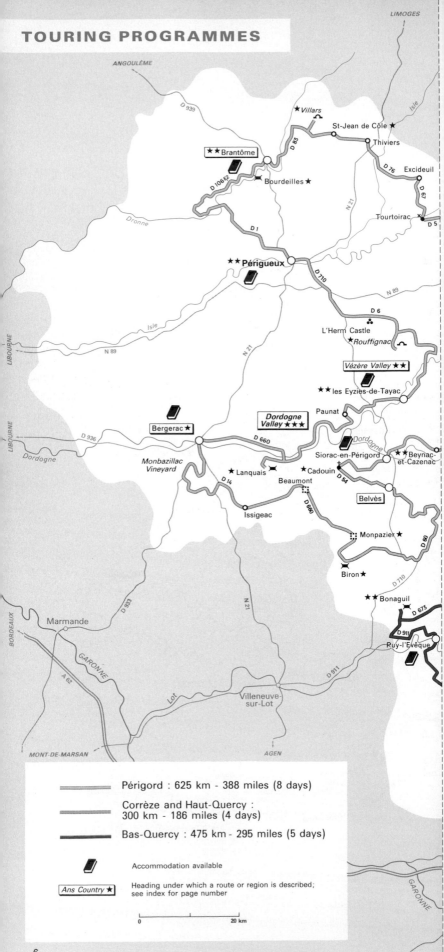

TOURING PROGRAMMES

LIMOGES

ANGOULÊME

★ *Villars*

St-Jean de Côle ★

Thiviers

Excideuil ×

★★ Brantôme

D 939

D 85

D 106 E²

★ Bourdeilles ★

Dronne

Tourtoirac ×

D 1

D 710

★★ Périgueux

N 89

D 6

L'Herm Castle
★ *Rouffignac*

Isle

N 21

Vézère Valley ★★

N 89

★★ les Eyzies-de-Tayac

Paunat

Dordogne
Valley ★★★

Dordogne

Bergerac ★

D 936

Siorac-en-Périgord

★★ Beynac-
et-Cazenac

Dordogne

Monbazillac
Vineyard

★ Lanquais ×

★ Cadouin

D 54

D 660

Belvès

Beaumont

D 14

Issigeac

D 660

Monpazier ★

D 60

Biron ★

D 710

★★ Bonaguil

D 673

D 903

N 21

D 911

Marmande

BORDEAUX

GARONNE

Puy-l'Evêque

A 62

Lot

D 911

Villeneuve-
sur-Lot

MONT-DE-MARSAN

AGEN

GARONNE

Legend

Périgord : 625 km - 388 miles (8 days)

Corrèze and Haut-Quercy :
300 km - 186 miles (4 days)

Bas-Quercy : 475 km - 295 miles (5 days)

Accommodation available

Ans Country ★   Heading under which a route or region is described;
see index for page number

0   20 km

6

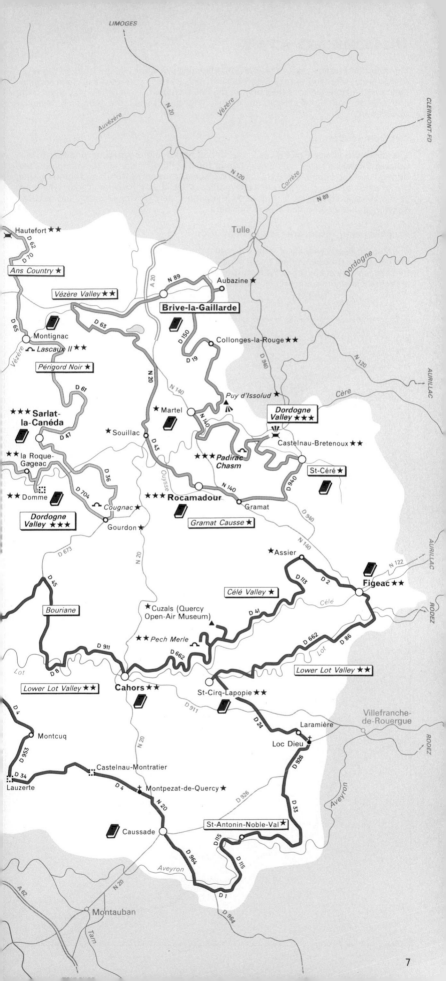

LIMOGES

Auvézère

Vézère

N 20

CLERMONT FD

N 120

Corrèze

N 89

Dordogne

Tulle

★ Hautefort ★★
D 62
D 70

Ans Country ★

A 20
N 89
Aubazine ★

Vézère Valley ★★

Brive-la-Gaillarde

D 63

D 150

Collonges-la-Rouge ★★

Montignac
D 19

⌂ Lascaux II ★★

N 20
N 140

D 940

AURILLAC

Vézère
D 65

Périgord Noir ★

D 61

Cère

★ Martel
Puy d'Issolud ★

Dordogne Valley ★★★

★★★ **Sarlat-la-Canéda**
D 47

N 140

Castelnau-Bretenoux ★★

★ Souillac
D 43

★★ la Roque-Gageac

D 36

Oysse

★★★ *Padirac Chasm*

St-Céré ★

D 940

★★ Domme
D 704

⌂ Cougnac ★

N 140

Gramat

D 940

Dordogne Valley ★★★

Gourdon ★

★★★ **Rocamadour**

Gramat Causse ★

D 673

N 20

★ Assier

N 140

AURILLAC

D 45

Célé Valley ★

D 113

D 2

Figeac ★★

N 122

RODEZ

Bouriane

★ Cuzals (Quercy Open-Air Museum)

Célé

D 41

Lower Lot Valley ★★

D 911

★★ *Pech Merle*

D 662

D 662

D 86

Lot

Lot
D 8

Lower Lot Valley ★★

Cahors ★★

St-Cirq-Lapopie ★★

Villefranche-de-Rouergue

D 911

Laramière

RODEZ

D 4

Montcuq

D 24

Loc Dieu ✝

D 953

Castelnau-Montratier

N 20

D 34

Lauzerte

D 4

✝ Montpezat-de-Quercy ★

D 926

D 926

D 33

Aveyron

N 20

St-Antonin-Noble-Val ★

Caussade

D 115

D 115

A 62

D 964

Aveyron

Montauban

Tarn

N 20

D 1

D 964

PLACES TO STAY

The mention **Facilities** under the individual headings or after place names in the body of the guide refers to the map below which indicates towns selected for the accommodation and leisure facilities they offer to the holidaymaker. To help you plan your route and choose your hotel, restaurant or camping site consult the following Michelin publications.

Accommodation

The **Michelin Red Guide France** gives a selection of hotels and restaurants, and the **Michelin Camping Caravaning France** lists a selection of the 11 000 officially graded camping sites. Both are revised annually and are based on inspectors' reports. Hotels and camping sites are graded according to the type and quality of facilities they offer. Those which are above average standards, by dint of their situation, staff, degree of peace and quiet, or the welcome they offer, are clearly indicated.

Planning your route, sports and recreation

The **Michelin Maps,** at a scale of 1:200 000, cover the whole of France. For those concerning the region see the layout diagram on page 3. In addition to a wealth of road information, these maps indicate beaches, bathing spots, swimming pools, golf courses, racecourses, air fields, panoramas and scenic routes.

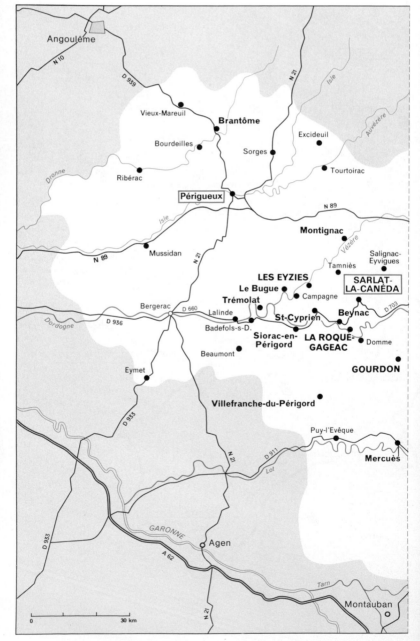

CLIMATE

The Dordogne has a temperate climate, characterised by bright sunshine, hot dry summers, on the whole gentle winds and the odd rainstorm. A wide variety of crops flourishes under these conditions.

The hot **summer** season lasts from June to September, during which there is generally some rainfall, much to the relief of the farmers who would otherwise have to resort to irrigation. The rainfall means that summer is not accompanied by the glaringly bright light and dusty dryness of a Mediterranean climate. However, since it usually follows in the wake of a strong hot wind which has been blowing steadily from the west for a few days and manifests itself as a violent storm with torrential hail accompanying thunder and lightning, it can have devastating effects on fruit and tobacco crops.

Happily, such outbursts are rare, and summer conditions are ideal for discovering the towns, villages and natural features of the region, either independently or on one of the several trips organised by local tourist authorities. There is also plenty of opportunity to indulge in favourite leisure activities, whether these be water sports, walking, horse-riding or pot-holing *(for further details see the Practical Information section: New Discoveries at the end of the guide).*

Autumn and winter are generally mild and fairly humid, with a minimal amount of snowfall in the winter. This is the best time of year to explore the regional markets with their tempting agricultural produce. Occasionally there is a cold, dry winter. A mild winter can give way to a cold **spring** with frosty nights and foggy mornings. The clear spring light reveals green buds and colourful flowers reappearing after the winter break.

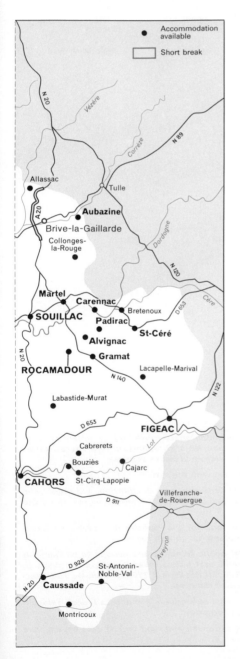

● Accommodation available

▭ Short break

LOCAL WORDS AND SPECIAL TERMS

Arcvôlt: a covered passage in the towns and villages of Quercy

Barri or **barry**: a settlement outside the town walls

Bastide: fortified town of the 13C

Bolet: porch-staircase characteristic of houses in Quercy *(illustration p 32)*

Borie: dry-stone hut

Cabecou: small goat cheese

Caselle: dry-stone hut

Causse: limestone plateau

Caveur: truffle hunter

Chabrol: soup with wine added

Chartreuse: 17 and 18C nobleman or bourgeois house with one storey

Cingle: meander (from the Latin word *cingula* meaning belt), loop or bend found in the Lot and Dordogne Valleys

Cloup: depression in the *causse (qv)*

Cluzeau: shelter dug into the cliff

Cornière or **couvert**: arcaded gallery

Gariotte: dry-stone shelter

Igue: wells or natural chasms in limestone countryside formed by the dissolving action of water or the caving-in of the roof of a cave; known as *edzes* or *eidges* in Périgord

Jarrissade (or garrissade): typical *causse* vegetation consisting of clumps of stunted oak trees and extensive open spaces

Lauzes: limestone stone slabs used as roofing material

Pech or puy: small hill topped by limestone cliffs

Ribeyre: a valley in Quercy

Segala: arid plateau with acidic soil which supports the cultivation only of rye *(seigle)*; opposite of ground suited to the cultivation of wheat *(fromental)*

Soleilho: open space under the eaves of houses in Quercy, used for drying laundry, storing wood etc.

Sotch: large hollow (enlarged *cloup*)

FRENCH WORDS APPEARING ON THE MAPS AND PLANS

For words and expressions used in hotels and restaurants see the annual Michelin Red Guide France.
See also art and architectural terms pp 26-27.

aéroport	**airport**	grotte	**cave**
ancien (ne)	**former**	halles	**covered market**
barrage	**dam**	hôtel	**mansion, town house**
belvédère	**viewpoint**	hôtel de ville	**town hall**
bureau de P.T.T.	**post office**	lycée	**secondary school**
calvaire	**wayside cross**	mont	**mount**
caserne	**barracks**	moulin	**mill**
cathédrale	**cathedral**	musée	**museum**
chapelle	**chapel**	parc des	**exhibition ground**
château	**castle, château**	expositions	
cirque	**amphitheatre**	police	**police**
cité administrative	**municipal or**	pont	**bridge**
	administrative centre	pont tournant	**swing bridge**
donjon	**keep**	remparts	**ramparts**
église	**church**	signal	**beacon**
esplanade	**esplanade**	site	**site, setting**
étang	**pool, lake**	stade	**stadium, sports ground**
foirail	**fair-ground, agricultural**	table d'orientation	**viewing table**
	market place	tour	**tower**
forêt	**forest**	usine	**factory, power station**
gare	**railway station**	vallée	**valley**
gare routière	**bus station**	vers	**towards**
gisement	**deposit**	vieux (vieille)	**old**
gorges	**gorge**	vélodrome	**cycle racing track**

3615 MICHELIN Minitel Service

Michelin Travel Assistance *(AMI)* is a computerised route finding system offering integrated information on roads, tourist sights, hotels and restaurants. *3615 MICHELIN* is one of the French Telecom videotex services.

3615 MICHELIN: *access code to connect with the service.*

Route planning: *give your point of departure and destination, stipulate your preference for motorways or local roads, indicate the sights to see along the way and it will do the rest.*

Lunchtime or overnight stops: *now look for that special restaurant, secluded country hotel or pleasant camp site along the chosen route.*

Where to find the Minitel terminals: *public terminals are usually to be found in all post offices, some petrol stations and hotels (over 6 million terminals in France). The cost of consulting 3615 MICHELIN is 1.27F per minute. This user-friendly travel service is available round the clock.*

Access for users outside France: *foreign subscribers can access French Telecom videotex services; consult your documentation.*

Field of operation: *this outstanding European and road tourist data base covers most European countries.*

Introduction

DESCRIPTION OF THE COUNTRY

FORMATION OF THE LAND

Primary Era – This began about 570 million years ago. It was towards the end of this era that an upheaval of the earth's crust took place. This upheaval or folding movement, known as the "Hercynian fold", the V-shaped appearance of which is shown by dotted lines on the map, resulted in the emergence of a number of high mountains; notably, the Massif Central, formed by crystalline rocks which were slowly worn down by erosion.

Secondary Era – This began about 260 million years ago. Towards the middle of this era, there was a slow folding of the Hercynian base and the seas then flooded the area. Sedimentary deposits, mainly calcareous, from the sea accumulated on the edge of the Massif Central, forming the Quercy *causses* (limestone plateaux) during the Jurassic period and then the beds of cretaceous limestone of the Périgord region.

Tertiary Era – This began about 65 million years ago. During this period siderolithic deposits (clay and gravel, rich in iron) originating from the Massif Central covered some parts of Quercy, such as the Bouriane region, whereas argillaceous sands accumulated to the west of Périgord, creating the heathlands dotted with lakes (Double and Landais regions).

Folded areas of the Tertiary Era
Regions submerged during the Secondary Era
Primary massifs (Hercynian folds)

Quaternary Era – This began about 2 million years ago. It is during this period that the evolution of man has taken place.

The effects of erosion had by now given the region its present appearance. Rivers emanating from the catchment area of the Massif Central had created the Vézère, Dordogne and Lot Valleys.

COUNTRYSIDE

Périgord

The Périgord is made up of porous and dry cretaceous limestone plateaux deeply cut by valleys which attract the essential economic activity of the region.

Périgord Vert – Between the area around Nontron and that around Excideuil is Périgord Vert (*vert* - green), made up of fragments of the old massif, small basins scoured out of the soft Lias marl and a few limestone tables. Its landscape of woodlands, areas of well-tended mixed farming and colourful patches of sunflowers anticipates that of the Limousin region. The handful of towns scattered across this lush green borderland provide the link between light industry and the commercialisation of agricultural products.

Périgord Blanc – Continuing the Saintonge westwards, the Périgord Blanc (*blanc* – white), aptly named because of its vast chalky, limestone area of white and grey soil, corresponds more or less in area with the Ribéracois region.

It is the cereal-producing area of Périgord, and to cereal crops is added the raising of dairy cows and calves for veal.

Ribérac, the capital of the region, is an important agricultural market.

Central Périgord – The countryside of hills and slopes around Périgueux consists of meadows interspersed with coppices of oak and chestnut trees. This region is drained by the rivers of Beauronne, Vern and Dronne, and the river valley bottoms are covered with pasture and arable land; the larger Isle Valley is scattered with small industrial towns and the alluvial soil is used as ley pasture, or for the cultivation of maize, tobacco or walnuts

South of Périgueux around Vergt and Rouffignac, the siderolithic deposits (rich in iron) which cover the limestone have proven to be an ideal soil for the cultivation of strawberries.

Northeast, Central Périgord meets the **Périgord Causse**. This block of Jurassic limestone, scored by the Isle, Auvézère and Loue Valleys, exhibits the sparse vegetation characteristic of the *causse*. It is at the foot of the stunted oaks, which are scattered about the countryside, that the most aromatic variety of truffle grows.

Double and Landais regions – South of Ribérac, covering the Tertiary deposits originating from the Massif Central, are vast forests of tall oak and chestnut trees and an increasing number of maritime pines.

The non-porous clay soil of the Double is dotted with lakes. This region, once an unhealthy marshy area, is now a source of timber and renowned as a good place for shooting.

The less primitive Landais region is covered with a forest of maritime pines, and at its boundaries there are vineyards and meadows.

Bergerac region – The region around Bergerac is divided into several sections all of which share a mild climate favourable to meridional crops.

The Dordogne Valley, very wide at this point, is divided into plots of land where tobacco, maize, sunflowers and cereals are cultivated, profiting from the fertility of the alluvial deposits.

West of Bergerac arboriculture predominates. The slopes are covered with the vineyards of Bergerac and Monbazillac.

Thanks to its environment, Bergerac plays an important role in the wine trade and tobacco industry.

Périgord Noir – Dissected by the Vézère and Dordogne Valleys, Périgord Noir (*noir* - black) owes its name to the greater density of trees to be found growing on the sandy soils covering the limestone areas and also to the presence of the holm-oak with its dark, dense foliage, which is prevalent in the Sarladais. The alluvial soil of the valleys, with screens of poplars or willows along the banks of their rivers, supports a variety of crops: wheat, maize, tobacco and walnuts.

The lively and prosperous markets sell excellent walnuts, mushrooms, truffles and *foies gras.* Such gastronomic riches attract tourists, who also appreciate the grottoes with marvellous concretions, and the caves and shelters with sculpted or painted walls bearing witness to the activity of prehistoric man.

Along the Dordogne and Vézère Rivers, gentle and harmonious landscapes are enhanced by solid golden-coloured limestone buildings with *lauzes* roofs, such as the superb examples in Sarlat-la-Canéda, capital of Périgord Noir.

Brive Basin – The depression of the Brive Basin is a sunken zone between the crystalline escarpments of the Uzerche plateau and the limestone ridges of the Quercy *causses.* It is an area made of sandstone and schists, drained by the rivers Vézère and Corrèze. In the green valleys segmented by screens of poplars, the gentle slopes facing the sun specialise in fruit growing. Today Brive is an important centre for the canning of fruit and vegetables.

South of Brive, the Corrèze *causse* is covered by large holdings which are used for sheep rearing, renewed exploitation of truffle oak plantations and the fattening of geese for the production of *foie gras.*

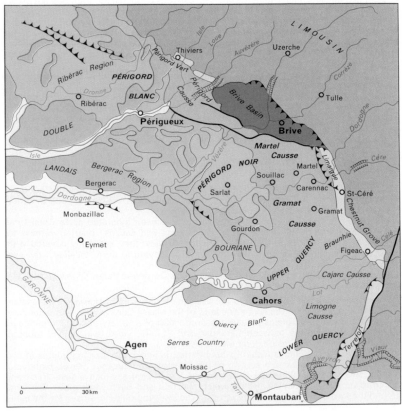

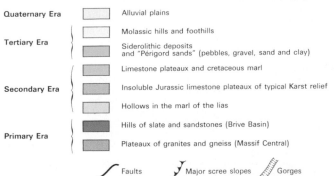

Quaternary Era		Alluvial plains
Tertiary Era		Molassic hills and foothills
		Siderolithic deposits and "Périgord sands" (pebbles, gravel, sand and clay)
Secondary Era		Limestone plateaux and cretaceous marl
		Insoluble Jurassic limestone plateaux of typical Karst relief
		Hollows in the marl of the lias
Primary Era		Hills of slate and sandstones (Brive Basin)
		Plateaux of granites and gneiss (Massif Central)

Faults   Major scree slopes   Gorges

South of the Dordogne – Vast stretches of gently undulating molassic hillside, with limestone outcrops forming terraces here and there, extend beyond the wine-producing slopes of Monbazillac. Small holdings interspersed with forest massifs are given over to the cultivation of cereals, vines (AOC Bergerac) and stock plum trees. Eymet, the main centre, is famous for the high quality of its canned food.

Towards the east, making the transition with the Bouriane region in Quercy, is the thick forest of **Bessède**, which flourishes on the millstone or siderolithic sands, hardly disturbed at all by the foundation of *bastides* and abbeys during the Middle Ages.

Quercy

Formed by a thick layer of Jurassic limestone, with an average height of 300m – 984ft, Quercy is gashed by the valleys of the Dordogne, Célé, Lot and Aveyron which delimit the *causses*. The *causses* as a group slope away from the southwestern edges of the Massif Central and down towards the Garonne Valley.

The causses – This dry land with no drainage is cut across by dry valleys (known locally as coombs), where ley pasture and a few small vineyards can be found. The vast area known as the *causses* is covered by juniper, oak and carob trees, and sheep graze in pastures separated by stone walls.

The Quercy *causses* are an important sheep rearing centre (with about 300 000 head). The plateau sheep or Gramat species is known as the "spectacled" breed, for it has white fleece and black rings round its eyes. It bears high quality wool but it is especially for its fine meat (with very little fat) that this hardy, prolific breed is known. A strict selection is maintained for the ewe-lambs and young rams.

The **Martel Causse**, between the Limousin and the Dordogne Valley, is richer than its neighbours in dry valleys and crops. It bears the name of its main town, Martel, a large agricultural town where sheep skins are sold.

The **Gramat Causse,** rising to 350m – 1 148ft, offers many natural phenomena (Padirac Chasm) and unusual landscapes. Magnificent canyons break the monotonous but grand horizons of this enormous block of striated limestone 50km – 31 miles wide; in the north lie the Ouysse and Alzou Canyons (with Rocamadour clinging to the cliff face of the latter); in the south lies the much longer Célé Canyon. Between the narrow gashes of the Alzou and the Célé lies the arid **Braunhie** (pronounced Brogne – rhyming with Dordogne), an arid region riddled with caves and ravines. The towns of Gramat and Labastide-Murat have suffered from the rural exodus.

The **Cajarc Causse**, a low-lying plateau, is hemmed in by the banks of the Célé and Lot Rivers, the meanders of which are richly cultivated.

The **Limogne Causse**, with its drier climate, has a very different appearance. Bordered by the valley of the Lot, the plateau is dotted with dolmens and megaliths, which appear amidst the clumps of white truffle oaks, the juniper shrubs and the fields of lavender.

Here and there *gariottes (qv)*, the curious shepherds' shelters built beside old vineyards, are to be found.

There are few big towns, although Limogne-en-Quercy and Lalbenque remain the busiest agricultural centres.

The valleys – Cutting deeply into the hard limestone, the rivers have carved out their valleys, shaping meanders which enlarge as the valley broadens, to the point that they become ever widening *cingles* – loops in the river.

These valleys of the Dordogne, Célé and Lot have been inhabited since prehistoric times. They are laid out with oppidums, châteaux and castles bearing witness to the role of these valleys in the region's history. Today, they are richly covered with crops such as maize, vineyards (with the Cahors vineyard in the Lot Valley – *qv*) and orchards.

Towns have established themselves: Souillac in the Dordogne Valley, Figeac in the Célé Valley and Cahors in a meander of the Lot.

The limits of Upper Quercy – To the east, the fertile area of **Limargue** and **Terrefort** divides the *causses* from the crystalline land of the Massif Central. The land extending in basins and over vast plains favours the production of a variety of crops: greengage plums and strawberries between Carennac and St-Céré, vines, walnut and tobacco plantations growing alongside great meadows.

Upper Quercy also includes within its boundaries, between the dizzying gorges of the Cère and the Lot, the eastern section of the **Châtaigneraie** (chestnut grove), high-lying country on a cold crystalline rock-base from the Massif Central which is never free from the constant trickle of water and on which chestnut and birch trees grow. The land around the farms and hamlets scattered over the lowering hilltops is used for the cultivation of spring cereals and the raising of pigs and calves for meat.

Elsewhere, west of the N 20 as far as Périgord, a layer of sand and clay supports heathlands, coppices and woodlands. This region, the **Bouriane**, resembles more its neighbouring Périgord than Quercy. The tapping of maritime pines for resin, the timber industry and the sale of livestock, chestnut and walnuts form the economic basis of the region, the capital of which is Gourdon.

Quercy Blanc – *Photograph p 165*. Southwest of the Lot Valley and Cahors, the Jurassic limestone disappears under the tertiary limestone creating unusual landscapes, *planhès*, vast undulating white areas which have given the region the name Quercy Blanc (*blanc* – white). These plateaux are cut into narrow ridges, *serres*, by the rivers. The crests of the *serres* are levelled off into plains which are covered with sheep-grazing grazing pastures and oak forests and, when the soil becomes argillaceous, rich crops. Between the *serres*, the valleys are fertile corridors, spreading between the sandstone as they get closer to the Garonne, pastures lined with poplars produce abundant crops of fruit, cereals and tobacco as well as supporting vineyards.

The towns of Montcuq, Lauzerte, Castelnau-Montratier, Montpezat-de-Quercy are all situated on *puechs*, rocky hilltops; they have animated market days.

CAVES AND CHASMS

Although dispersed throughout Périgord, the arid *causse* slices through an otherwise luxuriant landscape. The Quercy limestone plateaux roll away to the far horizon, stony, grey and deserted. The dryness of the soil is due to the calcareous nature of the rock which absorbs rain like a sponge.

Formation of the Padirac Great Dome

Water infiltration – Rainwater, charged with carbonic acid, dissolves the carbonate of lime to be found in the limestone. Depressions, known as **cloups**, which are usually circular in shape and small in size, are then formed. The dissolution of the limestone rocks containing in particular salt or gypsum produces a rich soil particularly suitable for growing crops; when the *cloups* increase in size they form large, closed depressions known as **sotchs**. Where rainwater infiltrates the countless fissures in the plateau more deeply, the hollowing out and dissolution of the calcareous layer produces wells or natural chasms which are called **igues**.

Underground rivers – The infiltrating waters finally produce underground galleries and collect to form a more or less swift-flowing river. The river widens its course and often changes level, falling in cascades. Where the rivers run slowly they form lakes, as at Padirac, above natural dams, known as **gours**, which are built up layer by layer by deposits of lime carbonate. Tourists are able to discover these lakes by boat. The dissolution of the limestone also continues above the water-level in these subterranean galleries: blocks of stone fall from the roof leaving domes to form, their tips pointing towards ground level above. Such is the case with the Great Dome of Padirac which lies only a few feet beneath the surface of the plateau *(see diagram)*. When the roof of the dome wears thin it may cave in, disclosing the cavity from above and opening the **chasm**.

Cave formation – As it circulates below ground, the water deposits the lime with which it has become charged, thus building up concretions in fantastic shapes which defy the laws of gravity and equilibrium. In some caverns, the seeping waters deposit calcite (lime carbonate) which forms pendants, pyramids and draperies. The best known formations are stalactites, stalagmites *(see diagram)* and eccentrics. **Stalactites** grow from the cave roof. Every droplet of water seeping through to the ceiling deposits upon it, before it drips down, some of the calcite with which it is charged. Gradually the concretion builds up layer by layer as the drops run down its length, depositing calcite particles before falling.

Stalagmites are formed in the same way but rise from the floor towards the roof. Drops of water, dripping constantly onto the same place, deposit their calcite particles, which build up to form a candle-like shape. This rises towards the stalactite above (source of the drips) with which it ultimately joins to form a pillar linking the cave floor with the ceiling.

Cave with concretions
① Stalactites – ② Stalagmites
③ Pillar in formation – ④ Completed pillar

Concretions form very slowly indeed; the rate of growth in a temperate climate is about 1cm – 0.4in every 100 years.

Eccentrics are very fine protuberances which seldom exceed 20cm – 8in in length. They emerge at any angle, either as slender spikes or in the shape of small, translucent fans. They are formed by crystallization and seem to disregard the laws of gravity.

Resurgent springs – Underground rivers form either by the disappearance of a water course into a rift *(igue)* of the *causse*, or by an accumulation of infiltrated water reaching non-porous strata (marl or clay). The water then finds a way through by following the line of the strata. When the impermeable layer breaks through on the side of a hill, the water emerges once more above ground and is known as a resurgent spring *(see diagram)*. The river at Padirac, for example, flows underground for some miles, disappearing roughly in the spot where the tour of the Hall of the Great Natural Dams ends, and reappearing some 11km – 7 miles away in the Montvalent Amphitheatre.

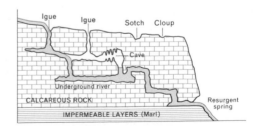

Development of a resurgent spring

From prehistory to modern exploration – The caves and grottoes, providing a natural protection against the cold, were initially inhabited by animals and then by man, who left these natural shelters about 10 000 years ago.

At the end of last century, the methodical and scientific exploration of the underground world, with which the name of E A Martel is associated, led to the discovery of a certain number of caves and their conversion into a tourist attraction. Knowledge of the underground system is still very incomplete.

ABC OF PREHISTORY

The Quarternary Era is relatively young, since it began only about two million years ago. Nevertheless, it is during this short period that the evolution of man has taken place.

There is no definitive evidence of life having existed on the earth in the Pre-Cambrian Age; reptiles, fish and tail-less amphibians appeared in the course of the Primary Era, mammals and birds during the Secondary Era. The primates, the most ancient ancestors of man, appeared at the end of the Tertiary Era and were followed in the Quarternary Era by ever more advanced species.

QUATERNARY ERA		Years BC
	Birth of Christ	
	Foundation of Rome	753
IRON		900
BRONZE		2 500
AGE OF METALS		
	The Pyramids	2 800
NEOLITHIC		7 500
MESOLITHIC		10 000
	UPPER	35 000
PALEOLITHIC	MIDDLE	150 000
STONE AGE	LOWER	2 000 000
	Appearance of Man	

The slow pace of human progress during the Palaeolithic Age stuns the imagination: it took people nearly two million years to learn to polish stone. But then the few thousand years that followed saw in the Middle and Far East the development of brilliant civilizations, which reached their climax in the construction of the pyramids in Egypt.

A few centuries later a new step was taken with the discovery of bronze and later still, in approximately 900BC, of iron.

The researchers – The study of prehistory is a science essentially French in origin which began in the early 19C. Until that time only the occasional allusion by a Greek or Latin author, a study by the Italian scholar Mercati (1541-93) in the 16C and a paper by Jussieu, published in 1723, gave any hint of the existence of ancient civilizations. In spite of the scepticism of most learned men – led by Cuvier (1769-1832) – the researchers pursued their investigations in Périgord, Lozère and in the Somme Valley. To Boucher de Perthes (1788-1868) falls the honour of having **prehistory** (the science of man before the invention of writing) recognised. His discoveries at St-Acheul and Abbeville were the starting-point for an important series of studies. Among the eminent pioneers who laid the foundations on which modern archaeology is based are: Edouard Lartet (1801-71), who undertook many excavations in the Vézère Valley and established a preliminary

UPPER PALAEOLITHIC

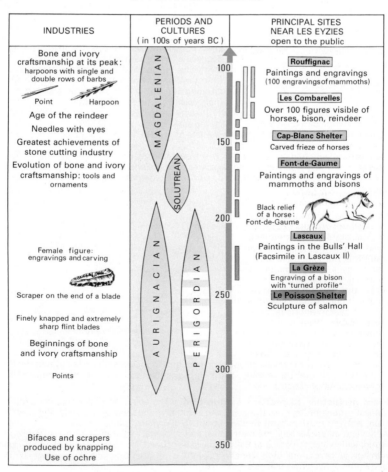

INDUSTRIES	PERIODS AND CULTURES (in 100s of years BC)		PRINCIPAL SITES NEAR LES EYZIES open to the public
Bone and ivory craftsmanship at its peak: harpoons with single and double rows of barbs	M A G D A L E N I A N		**Rouffignac** — Paintings and engravings (100 engravings of mammoths)
Point Harpoon			
Age of the reindeer			**Les Combarelles** — Over 100 figures visible of horses, bison, reindeer
Needles with eyes			
Greatest achievements of stone cutting industry			**Cap-Blanc Shelter** — Carved frieze of horses
Evolution of bone and ivory craftsmanship: tools and ornaments		SOLUTREAN	**Font-de-Gaume** — Paintings and engravings of mammoths and bisons
			Black relief of a horse: Font-de-Gaume
Female figure: engravings and carving	A U R I G N A C I A N	P E R I G O R D I A N	**Lascaux** — Paintings in the Bulls' Hall (Facsimile in Lascaux II)
			La Grèze — Engraving of a bison with "turned profile"
Scraper on the end of a blade			**Le Poisson Shelter** — Sculpture of salmon
Finely knapped and extremely sharp flint blades			
Beginnings of bone and ivory craftsmanship			
Points			
Bifaces and scrapers produced by knapping Use of ochre			

classification for the various eras of prehistory; Gabriel de Mortillet (1821-98), who took up and completed the classification adding the names Chellean, Mousterian, Aurignacian, Solutrean and Magdalenian to correspond with the places where the most prolific or most characteristic deposits were found: Chelles in Seine-et-Marne, Le Moustier in Dordogne, Aurignac in Haute-Garonne, Solutré in Saône-et-Loire and La Madeleine near Tursac in Dordogne.

Carving on antler found at La Madeleine Site

Since the end of the 19C the discovery of Palaeolithic tombs, tools, wall paintings and engravings has enabled researchers to reconstruct the life and activities of prehistoric man. The names associated with these studies in prehistory are the Abbés A and J Bouyssonie, Dr L Capitan, D Peyrony, Rivière, Abbé Lemozi, Cartailhac and R Lantier. Abbé Breuil (1877-1961), with his detailed accounts and graphic charts, made known the wonders of wall paintings and engravings in France and Spain. More recently, André Leroi-Gourhan (1912-86) specialised in the study of Palaeolithic art.

Excavations can only be performed by specialists with knowledge of the geological stratigraphy, the physics and chemistry of rock formations, the nature and form of stones and gravels, and of how to analyse pollen, possibly fossilised wood, coal and bone fragments.

In the rock shelters and cave mouths, prehistorians have discovered hearths (accumulations of charcoal and kitchen debris), tools, weapons, stone and bone furnishings and bone fragments. The vestiges have collected in layers; during excavations each of these different layers is uncovered and the civilisation or period is then reconstructed with the help of the different data unearthed.

Prehistory in Périgord – Périgord has been inhabited by man since Palaeolithic times. The names Tayacian (Les Eyzies-de-Tayac), Micoquean (La Micoque), Mousterian (Le Moustier), Perigordian and Magdalenian (La Madeleine) are evidence of the importance of these prehistoric sites.

Nearly 200 deposits have been discovered, of which more than half are in the Vézère Valley near Les Eyzies-de-Tayac *(qv)*.

The evolution of man in the Palaeolithic Age – Man's most distant ancestors (some 3 000 000 years ago) were the early hominids (i.e. the family of man) of East Africa, who, unlike their instinctive predecessors, were rational thinkers. They evolved into *Homo habilis* followed by *Homo erectus*, characterised by his upright walking (Java man or *Pithecanthropus erectus*, discovered by E Dubois in 1891, with a cranial capacity halfway in size between the most highly developed ape and the least developed man; and Peking man or *Sinanthropus*, identified by D Black in 1927), who made rough-hewn tools, tools for chopping from split pebbles and heavy bifaced implements.

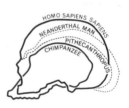

Neanderthal man appeared *c*150 000 years ago. In 1856, in the Düssel Valley (also known as the Neander Valley, east of Düsseldorf, Germany) portions of a human skeleton were discovered with the following characteristics: cranial capacity approximately 1 500cu cm – 91.5cu in, elongated cranium (dolichocephalus), sharply receding forehead, prominently developed jawbones and small stature (1.60m – 5ft 3in).

Skeletons with similar characteristics were found in France at La Chapelle-aux-Saints (Corrèze) in 1908, at Le Moustier (Dordogne) in 1909, at La Ferrassie (Dordogne) in 1909 and 1911, and at Le Régourdou (Dordogne) in 1957. Neanderthal man completely disappeared without descendants 35 000 years ago; at the same time the first burial sites were appearing.

Homo sapiens was flourishing in France about 40 000 years ago. His essential characteristics – perfect upright stance, cranial capacity of about 1 500 to 1 700cu cm – 91.5 to 104cu in, raised forehead, slightly projecting eyebrows – showed him to be highly developed and comparable to present man (*sapiens* = intelligent). Several races have been traced as belonging to this same family. Cro-Magnon man seems to have been quite similar in appearance, in fact, to the present *Homo sapiens*.

Cro-Magnon man (skeletons found in the rock shelters of Cro-Magnon in Dordogne and Solutré in Saône-et-Loire) was tall – about 1.80m – 5ft 11in – with long, robust limbs denoting considerable muscular strength; the skull was dolichocephalic in shape. This people lived from the Upper Palaeolithic to the Neolithic Age.

Chancelade man (skeleton discovered in 1889 at Chancelade, near Périgueux) appeared in the Magdalenian Period; he had a large cranium of dolichocephalic form, a long, wide face, pronounced cheek-bones and a height of not more than 1.55m – 5ft 1in.

Scraper on the end of a blade

Point-Harpoon

Necklace

CULTURE AND ART IN THE PALAEOLITHIC AGE

The oldest skeletons, belonging to Neanderthal man, found in Périgord and Quercy date from the Mousterian Culture (Middle Palaeolithic).

Later, during the Ice Age, tribes are thought to have come from eastern Europe and settled in the Vézère and Beune Valleys. Bordering these valleys were cliffs and slopes pitted with caves and shelters offering many natural advantages which flat country could not offer: protection from the cold, nearby springs and rivers abundant in fish and narrow ravines used for intercepting game as it passed through. There were, however, several dwelling huts found in the Isle Valley, upstream from Périgueux.

The Palaeolithic Age (*paleos* = ancient, *lithos* = stones) covers the period in which men knew only how to chip flints. An intermediate age, the Mesolithic (*mesos* = middle), separates it from the Neolithic Age (*neos* = new), when man learnt to polish stone. The first group were predators (hunting, fishing and gathering), whereas the last group were farmers and breeders. Skill in flint knapping evolved very slowly and, therefore, the Palaeolithic Age is subdivided into three periods: the Lower, Middle and Upper.

Lower Palaeolithic

This began about two million years ago. Men living in this period in Périgord knew how to use fire and hunted big game. The earth suffered three successive ice ages known as the Günz, the Mindel and the Riss Ice Ages (after the tributary valleys of the Danube where they have been studied). Between each ice age, France and Britain had a tropical climate.

Flint knapping began with a cut made by striking two stones violently one against the other, or by striking one against a rock which served as an anvil. These two methods gave rise to the two types of industry shown below.

Abbeville biface	Clacton flints (flakes)
Cleared of its flakes on two sides, the flint kernel is fined down and takes the form of an unevenly peeled fat almond. In the Acheulean Period better finished arrow-heads were obtained.	By using the flakes a relatively smooth or worked face could be obtained. This Clacton industry (it has been pinpointed to Clacton-on-Sea) existed in the Tayacian Period and produced smaller pieces (La Micoque Shelter at Les Eyzies).

Middle Palaeolithic

This began about 150 000 years ago. With Neanderthal man there appeared better finished and more specialised tools. Mousterian industry used both bifaced implements and flakes. New methods – the fashioning of flints with a bone or wooden striker – enabled triangular points to be produced, also scrapers, used probably for working skins, and flints adapted to take a wooden handle and serve as hunting clubs (bear skulls pierced by such weapons have been found).

During the Mousterian Culture some cave entrances were used as dwelling places, others were used as burial places. Man by this time possessed more sophisticated weapons with which to hunt big game and protected himself from the cold with animal skins. His intelligence was similar to ours. He was large and rugged in appearance.

Scraper-point

Points

Upper Palaeolithic

This began about 35 000 years ago. Cro-Magnon man and Chancelade man replaced Neanderthal man. There was a constant improvement in the production of tools; the life style was made easier with the perfection of new hunting methods (their stone industry was no longer based on flakes but rather on blades), resulting in more time for leisure and, therefore, for artistic expression.

Perigordian and Aurignacian Cultures – These two cultures, following the Mousterian and Levalloisian Cultures and preceding the Solutrean Culture, were contemporary but parallel.

The **Aurignacian** stone industry produced large blades, stone flake tools, burins (a sort of chisel) and points made from antlers (early ones have a split base). Cave decoration, applied on blocks of limestone (La Ferrassie near Le Bugue) and at times in tiny caves, consisted of engraved animals, painted or partially carved, or female figures.

At the end of the Perigordian Culture, Gravettians made burins and points; these people decorated their shelter walls (Le Poisson, Laussel) and carved "Venus" figurines, small female statues with exaggerated curves evoking fertility.

Laussel: Venus with
the horn of plenty

Lascaux:
horse pierced with lines

Lascaux:
charging bison

The burial places contain some ornaments and jewellery: shells and bead necklaces. The first examples of wall decoration appear as hands placed flat against the rock and outlined in black or red; these are to be found at Font-de-Gaume and at Le Pech Merle. The animals are only rudimentarily sketched. By the end of this period, man had become a true artist as may be seen by the sculptures at the Le Poisson (Fish) Shelter and the engravings and paintings found at Font-de-Gaume and Lascaux. La Grève Cave with its engraved bison in "turned profile" (as described by Abbé Breuil: an animal drawn in profile but given certain features as though seen full face) dates from between the late Perigordian and the early Solutrean.

Solutrean Culture – Very well represented in the Dordogne, this period is distinguished by exquisite low reliefs carved out of limestone slabs (such as the Devil's Oven, found near Bourdeilles and now exhibited in the National Museum of Prehistory at Les Eyzies).
The stone-cutting industry also underwent a brilliant period during the Solutrean Culture. Flint blades, following a method of splitting under pressure, became much slimmer, forming blades in the shape of laurel or willow leaves. Shouldered points were used as weapons, after they had been fitted with wooden shafts. It was during this period that the first needles with eyes appeared.

Magdalenian Culture – It was in this period that bone and ivory craftsmanship reached its peak. The existence of herds of reindeer, which is accounted for by the very cold climate that occurred at the end of the Würm Glacial Period, influenced man towards working with bone and antler, producing perforated batons, sometimes engraved, which were used as armatures for points and harpoon heads; projectile tips, sometimes engraved, used as spears; and decorated flattened points.
This is also the period when cave wall art, depicting essentially animal subjects, reached its peak. To protect themselves from the cold, the men of the Magdalenian culture lived in the shelter of overhanging rocks or at the mouths of caves; inside, these caves were underground sanctuaries, at times quite some distance from the cave entrance.
They used the shelter (as at the Cap-Blanc Shelter) and sanctuary walls to express their artistic or religious emotions by low-relief carving, engraving and painting. This period introduced a very sophisticated style compared to the more rudimentary outline drawings of the Perigordian and Aurignacian Cultures. However, due to the juxtaposition or superimposition of the figures drawn and deterioration (only a few Magdalenian caves are open to the public due to the difficulty in preserving these works of art), the study of these paintings is not easy.

Pech Merle: horses,
outlined hands and black spots

Bara-Bahau:
engraving of a horse

Font-de-Gaume:
black relief of a horse

After Lascaux, during the Middle and Upper Magdalenian, numerous cave-sanctuaries appeared. Portable art, manifested through smaller objects, is another form of expression developed in the shelters. Animals are much less stylised and increasingly realistic, whether it be in the details of their anatomy or their movements or faithful and detailed rendering of their physical aspects: coat, tail, eyes, ears, hoofs, antlers, tusks.
Nonetheless, the style is more ornamental. The perspective of the animals in profile, non-existent in the beginning, was pursued and even distorted during Lascaux's last period. New graphic techniques appeared: stencilling, areas left intentionally without colour, polychrome colours etc. Towards the end of the Magdalenian Culture, art became more schematic and human figures made their appearance. This great animal art then disappeared from France and Spain, as the herds of reindeer migrated northwards in search of the lichen which was disappearing during the warming-up at the end of the Würm Glacial Period.

Rouffignac: engraving of a mammoth and lines drawn with fingers

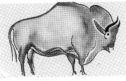

Font-de-Gaume:
multicoloured bison

Les Combarelles:
engraving of a reindeer

HISTORICAL TABLE AND NOTES

Events in italics indicate particular milestones in history.

Prehistory	As early as the Middle Palaeolithic Age, Périgord and Quercy are inhabited by man *(see Introduction: ABC of Prehistory)*.

Gauls and Romans

BC	Périgord is inhabited by Petrocorii and Quercy by Caduici.
59-51	Conquest of Gaul by Caesar. The last Gaulish resistance to Caesar is at Uxellodunum, which historians believe to be in Quercy *(see Martel: Excursion)*.
55	*Julius Caesar lands in Britain.*
16	Emperor Augustus creates the province of Aquitaine. The capital of the land of the Petrocorii is Vesunna (Périgueux) and of that of the Caduici, Divona Cadurcorum (Cahors).
AD	
1-3C	**Pax Romana.** For three centuries towns develop (several public buildings built). In the country around the towns new crops are introduced by the Romans: walnut, chestnut and cherry trees and above all vineyards.
235-284	Alemanni and Franks invade the region. In 276 several towns are razed. Vesunna defends itself behind fortifications hastily built from the stones taken from Roman public buildings.
313	*Edict of Milan. Emperor Constantine grants Christians the freedom of worship.*
476	*End of the Roman Empire.*

Merovingians and Carolingians

486-507	Campaign of Clovis, king of the Franks, to conquer Gaul, ending at the Battle of Vouillé (near Poitiers) in 507 where Clovis kills Alaric II, king of the Visigoths. Aquitaine falls into the hands of the Franks.
8C	Quercy and Périgord become counties under the kingdom of Aquitaine.
800	*Charlemagne crowned Emperor of the West in Rome.*
9C	The Dordogne and Isle Valleys and Périgueux are laid waste by Vikings.
10C	The four baronies of Périgord – Mareuil, Bourdeilles, Beynac and Biron – are formed as well as the overlordships of Ans, Auberoche, Gurson, etc.
	The Périgord County passes to the house of Talleyrand. Powerful families rule Quercy: the Gourdons, Cardaillacs, Castelnaus, Turennes and St-Sulpices.
c950	Beginning of the Pilgrimage to St James's shrine in Santiago de Compostela.
1066	*William the Conqueror lands in England.*
12C	Abbeys founded in Périgord include Cadouin, Dalon, Sarlat, Boschaud and Chancelade; and in Quercy: Rocamadour, Figeac, Souillac and Carennac.

Wars between England and France

1152	Eleanor of Aquitaine marries Henry Plantagenet, bringing as dowry all south-west France *(see Notes below)*. In 1154 Henry Plantagenet becomes King Henry II. Later on their sons Henry Short Coat and Richard the Lionheart occupy and pillage the region.
1190	Agreement between Philippe Auguste and Richard the Lionheart: Quercy is ceded to the English with the exception of the abbeys of Figeac and Souillac.
1191	Richard the Lionheart dies at Châlus.
early 13C	Albigensian Crusade. Simon de Montfort raids Quercy and Périgord.
1229	The Treaty of Meaux (also called Treaty of Paris) between the king of France and Raymond VII, Count of Toulouse, recognises that Quercy belongs to Raymond VII.
1259	By the **Treaty of Paris**, Saint Louis cedes Périgord and Quercy to the English. The treaty puts an end to the constant fighting and enables the people of the region to live in peace until the Hundred Years War.
1337	French king Philip VI declares the English-held duchy of Guyenne confiscated.
1340	Edward III of England proclaims himself king of France.
1345	Beginning of the Hundred Years War in Aquitaine; French king Jean II seeks to win back Aquitaine. The region becomes the battlefield of the war with the taking of Tulle (1346) and Domme (1347).

ENGLAND
Calais
County of Ponthieu
Rouen
Paris
Rennes
Orléans
Angers
Seine
Loire
Poitiers
Castillon-la-Bataille
Périgueux
le Puy
Bordeaux
Garonne
Cahors
Bayonne
Rhône
Toulouse

Lands held by the English

in 1253

at the beginning of the Hundred Years War (1338)

after the Treaty of Brétigny (1360)

after the reconquests by Charles V and Du Guesclin (1380)

1355	Edward the Black Prince lands in Bordeaux.
	Edward defeats and captures King Jean II (Battle of Poitiers 1356).
1360	The **Treaty of Brétigny** cedes Aquitaine to the English as part of the ransom for Jean II's liberty.
1369	Quercy and Périgord are won back by the king of France (Charles V). Du Guesclin, Constable of France, is active in the liberation of Périgord.
	During the period that follows the lords of the north of Périgord owe allegiance to the king of France; the lords of south of Périgord to the English. Many regularly swap sides in unashamed support of their own interests.
1405	French take towns in Saintonge and Périgord. Assassination of the Duke of Orléans, which results in the civil war between the Burgundians and Armagnacs. Both factions seek English aid.
1420	Henry V of England recognised as king of France under the Treaty of Troyes. France divided into three parts controlled by Henry V (Normandy, Guyenne, Paris area), Philip the Good, Duke of Burgundy (also Paris area, Burgundy) and the Dauphin (Central France and Languedoc).
1429-1439	Soldier gangs working indiscriminately for the warring factions devastate the region.
1444	Truce of Tours (Charles VII and Henry V); the English retain Maine, the Bordelais region, parts of Artois and Picardy and most of Normandy.
1449	French begin a campaign in Guyenne, but the people of the region are hostile to the French from years of loyalty to the English crown; Bergerac falls in 1450, Bordeaux in 1451.
1453	Defeat of John Talbot, Earl of Shrewsbury, at the **Battle of Castillon,** which marks the end of the Hundred Years War.
1492	*Christopher Columbus discovers America.*
2nd half of 15-early 16C	During this period of peace towns are rebuilt, and castles are either built or old ones remodelled. Literary life *(p 23)* blossoms: Clément Marot, La Boétie, Brantôme and Montaigne.
1509-47	*Henry VIII's reign.*
1558-1603	*Elizabeth I's reign.*

Wars of Religion

1562	Massacre of Protestants at Cahors.
1572	St Bartholomew's Day Massacre (20 000 Huguenots die).
1570-90	War is declared; Bergerac and Ste-Foy-la-Grande are Huguenot bastions while Périgueux and Cahors support the Catholic League.
	Vivans, the Huguenot leader, scours Périgord; Périgueux falls in 1575 and Domme in 1588.
1577	Peace of Bergerac anticipates the Edict of Nantes.
1580	Cahors taken by Henri de Navarre (Henri IV).
1588	*Defeat of the Spanish Armada.*
1589	Henri IV accedes to the throne and converts to Catholicism in 1593; is crowned in 1594.
	Under Henri IV, the County of Périgord becomes part of the royal domain.
1594-95	*Croquant (qv) revolt.*
1598	**Edict of Nantes** grants Huguenots freedom of worship and places of refuge.
1610	Henri IV assassinated; Louis XIII's reign begins.
1637	*Croquants* revolt against Louis XIII's government and Richelieu's taxes.
1643-1715	Louis XIV's reign.
1685	**Revocation of Edict of Nantes**. Huguenots flee France.

18 to 20C

1714-27	*George I's reign.*
1743-57	Tourny, administrator of the Treasury of Bordeaux, instigates a number of town planning projects in the southwest (Allées de Tourny in Périgueux).
1763	*Peace of Paris ends French and Indian War (1754-63); it marks the end of France's colonial empire in America.*
1775-83	*American Revolution.*
1789	*Storming of the Bastille and beginning of the French Revolution.*
	George Washington chosen as first President of the United States.
1790	Creation of Dordogne *département.*
1792	*Proclamation of French Republic after Battle of Valmy.*
1805	*Battle of Trafalgar.*
1812-14	Périgord is a Bonapartist fief; several of Napoleon's generals and marshals are natives of the region: Murat, Fournier-Sarlovèze, Daumesnil.
1815	*Battle of Waterloo.*
1837-1901	*Victoria's reign.*
1838	Birth of Léon Gambetta at Cahors.
1861-65	*American Civil War.*
1868	Phylloxera destroys the vineyards of Cahors and Bergerac, causing a rural exodus.
	Discovery of Cro-Magnon cave skeletons.
1870-71	*Franco-Prussian War.*
1914-18	*First World War.*
1939-45	*Second World War.*
1940	Discovery of Lascaux Cave.
20C	Marked by a continued rural exodus; the depopulated regions live essentially from agriculture and tourism.

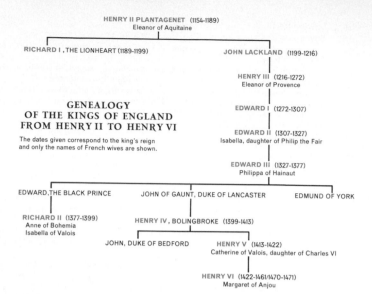

HENRY II PLANTAGENET (1154-1189)
Eleanor of Aquitaine

RICHARD I , THE LIONHEART (1189-1199)   JOHN LACKLAND (1199-1216)

HENRY III (1216-1272)
Eleanor of Provence

**GENEALOGY
OF THE KINGS OF ENGLAND
FROM HENRY II TO HENRY VI**

The dates given correspond to the king's reign
and only the names of French wives are shown.

EDWARD I (1272-1307)

EDWARD II (1307-1327)
Isabella, daughter of Philip the Fair

EDWARD III (1327-1377)
Philippa of Hainaut

EDWARD,THE BLACK PRINCE   JOHN OF GAUNT, DUKE OF LANCASTER   EDMUND OF YORK

RICHARD II (1377-1399)
Anne of Bohemia
Isabella of Valois

HENRY IV , BOLINGBROKE (1399-1413)

JOHN, DUKE OF BEDFORD   HENRY V (1413-1422)
Catherine of Valois, daughter of Charles VI

HENRY VI (1422-1461/1470-1471)
Margaret of Anjou

HISTORICAL NOTES

Eleanor's dowry – In 1137, Prince Louis, son of the king of France, married Eleanor, only daughter of Duke William of Aquitaine. She brought as her dowry the Duchy of Guyenne, Périgord, Limousin, Poitou, Angoumois, Saintonge, Gascony and the suzerainty of Auvergne and the County of Toulouse. But it was an ill-assorted marriage; Louis, who was crowned Louis VII, was a sort of royal monk, while his wife was frivolous in character. After 15 years of conjugal misunderstanding, the king had the Council of Beaugency (1152) pronounce his divorce on his return from a Crusade. Eleanor recovered not only her liberty but also her dowry.

Her marriage two months later with **Henry Plantagenet**, count of Anjou and lord of Maine, Touraine and Normandy, was a political disaster for the Capetian royal house of France. Eleanor's and Henry's joint domains were already as great as those of the king of France. Two years later Henry Plantagenet inherited the throne of England which he ruled as Henry II. The balance of power was destroyed and the Hundred Years War broke out. By building *bastides (qv)* in the 13C, the kings of France and England hoped to consolidate their positions and justify their territorial claims. The Capetians and Plantagenets each tried to get a foothold in the other's territories but the Dordogne acted as a dividing line between them *(see map p 20)*. The Treaty of Paris in 1259, between St Louis and Henry III of England, was in reality only a truce. From 1340, supported by the Flemish, Bretons and Normans, the English imposed their military supremacy over the whole of Aquitaine. Périgord and Quercy returned to French rule in 1369, but remained under threat of invasion by the English, who kept hold of Guyenne until the end of the Hundred Years War (1453).

Wars of Religion – As early as 1540 a first centre of Protestantism developed in Ste-Foy-la-Grande; the Reformation reached Bergerac in 1544. Protestantism was upheld in Périgord by the princes of Bourbon-Albret (Jeanne d'Albret, mother of Henri de Navarre) and Caumont-Laforce and in Quercy by Jeanne de Genouillac, the Gourdons and Cardaillacs. From 1570-90 skirmishes and massacres were rife.

The Huguenots, led by **Armand de Clermont**, lord of Piles, fought against the **Marshal of Montluc** and his army. After Clermont's death (a victim of the St Bartholomew's Day Massacre), **Geoffroi de Vivans** became leader and devastated the region. His best weapon was craftiness; he entered and captured Sarlat during Carnival celebrations and his strategy provoking the fall of Domme was famous. The Protestant towns of western Périgord were opposed by the Catholic towns of Périgueux and Cahors (the latter seized by Henri de Navarre in 1580). The Catholic Pierre de Bourdeille (Brantôme) denounced these religious wars in his writings. He was particularly shocked by the massacre at La Chapelle-Faucher, when the vengeful Huguenot leader Admiral Coligny rounded up 300 peasants in the castle and set it on fire.

Henri IV promulgated the Edict of Nantes; Protestantism was strengthened, but under Louis XIII and Richelieu fighting reoccurred. Louis XIV declared the Revocation of the Edict of Nantes, causing many of the people of Périgord to emigrate.

Peasant revolts – Peasant uprisings troubled the rural areas intermittently for 200 years. Poverty, famine and heavier taxes caused the uprisings. In 1594, the *Croquants* (a peasant movement against the nobility and all forms of oppression) revolted, uniting to form an army and refusing to work for their lords. The nobility joined forces, and skirmishes at St-Crépin-d'Auberoche (1595) and Condat-sur-Vézère quashed the *Croquant* army. Forty years later, in 1637, the peasants again revolted, voicing the same grievances as before. A gentleman, **La Mothe la Forêt**, led an army of several thousand peasants. They attempted to seize Périgueux, succeeded at Bergerac but were stopped at Ste-Foy-la-Grande. They were defeated at La Sauvetat. In spite of La Mothe's surrender and the dissolution of his army, the *Croquants* continued forays in the area and pushed back the royal troops. In 1642, the *Croquants* were once again quashed.

In 1707 a new tax provoked a new uprising, the *Tard-Avisés* (name already given to rebels in 1594). It broke out in Périgord and Quercy but was rapidly quashed. Peasant revolts continued throughout the Revolution of 1789.

INTELLECTUAL AND LITERARY LIFE

The courts of love – There appeared in 12C Périgord an original type of lyric poetry: the poetry of the **troubadours.** This poetic form, which soon spread to Quercy, developed and flowered in the feudal courts where idle but educated nobles and their ladies enjoyed singing, music and poetry. Troubadours were inventors (*trobar* is occitan for "find") of musical airs – both melodies and words in the Oc language. Under the protection and encouragement of their lords, they created new poetic forms: love poems (songs and romances) in which lyrical homage to the lady of the castle illustrated the theme of courtly love; songs of war and satirical ballads. The courts of love each had several troubadours who would vie in wit with one another on a set subject. **Bertrand de Born** (*c*1140-*c*1215), author of the politically and moralistically inspired *Sirventès,* Bertrand de Gourdon, Aimeric de Sarlat, Giraut de Borneil, native of Excideuil, and Arnaut Daniel of Ribérac were the most famous of these troubadours. In this male-dominated art form one woman, Dormunda de Cahors, nonetheless managed to shine. This formal poetry had disappeared by the end of the 12C as the conditions under which it flourished deteriorated during wars and the crusades.

The humanists – After the Hundred Years War, during the 15C, intellectual life continued, centering on its new universities – Cahors was founded in 1331 by Jacques Duèze, who had become Pope John XXII. In the early 16C printing houses were established in Périgueux, Cahors and Bergerac. But it was the Renaissance, which was marked by an important intellectual movement known as humanism, which restored respect for classical languages and poetic forms. A native of Cahors, **Clément Marot** (1496-1544), one of the great poets of the French Renaissance, excelled at composing epigrams and sonnets. He was valet to Marguerite d'Alençon, future Queen of Navarre, and to François I before being named official court poet. His brilliant life at court was interrupted by several prison sentences due to his penchant for the Reformation. During one of his detentions,

he wrote a poetic epistle to the king begging for his freedom and was released. Also from Cahors, **Olivier de Magny** (1529-65) was influenced by the Pléiade; after becoming friends with the poet Du Bellay (who wrote of Magny in one of his sonnets compiled in *Regrets*), he wrote verse of considerable lyric quality.

At the same time **Etienne de la Boétie** (1530-63) was born in Sarlat. A humanist and friend of Montaigne, he denounced tyranny in his *Discourse on Voluntary Subjection* and *Contre' un (Against One).*

In addition there was Pierre de Bourdeille (1535-1614), who wrote under the pseudonym of **Brantôme** (name of the abbey of which he was abbot), a talented chronicler, who described the lives of great captains and soldiers as well as giving accounts of life at the French court.

Jean Tarde (1561-1636) born at La Roque-Gageac was one of the most learned men of his time. This canon of Sarlat was a historian, cartographer, astronomer and mathematician.

17C – Born in Toulouse, **François Maynard** (1582-1646) spent the greater part of his life at St-Céré in Quercy. He was a follower of Malherbe and produced some charming odes, letters, sonnets and epigrams.

Portrait of Pierre de Bourdeille pseudonym
Brantôme

Fénelon who was born at Fénelon Castle near Ste-Mondane in 1631 (d 1715) was no less a man of letters than he was a man of the church. He was famous for his *Télémaque*, a tract for the edification of his student the Duke of Burgundy, dauphin of France. He wrote it at Carennac, on the banks of the Dordogne, where he was senior prior for 15 years.

Age of Enlightenment – Both from Périgord, **Joseph Joubert** (1754-1824) from Montignac and **Maine de Biran** (1766-1824) from Bergerac were philosophers and moralists of considerable sensitivity: Joubert's *Pensées* are so precise and delicate in style as to make them near perfect; Maine de Biran was a metaphysician and psychologist whose deep introspection heralded the movement of spiritualistic philosophy.

Regional writers – **Eugène Le Roy** (1836-1907) is Périgord's own novelist. In *Jacquou le Croquant*, which is set at L'Herm Castle, Le Roy describes the peasant uprisings *(Croquants)* which ravaged the region in a very vivid style.
Among the more contemporary authors is **Claude Michelet**, who describes peasant life in Corrèze in his novels, two of which have been adapted for French television.

ART

ABC OF ARCHITECTURE

To assist readers unfamiliar with the terminology employed in architecture, we describe below the most commonly used terms, which we hope will make their visits to ecclesiastical, military and civil buildings more interesting.

Ecclesiastical architecture

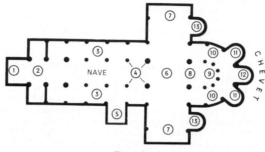

illustration I

Ground plan. – The more usual Catholic form is based on the outline of a cross with the two arms of the cross forming the transept: ① Porch – ② Narthex – ③ Side aisles (sometimes double) – ④ Bay (transverse section of the nave between 2 pillars) – ⑤ Side chapel (often predates the church) – ⑥ Transept crossing – ⑦ Arms of the transept, sometimes with a side doorway – ⑧ Chancel, nearly always facing east towards Jerusalem; the chancel often vast in size was reserved for the monks in abbatial churches – ⑨ High altar – ⑩ Ambulatory: in pilgrimage churches the aisles were extended round the chancel, forming the ambulatory, to allow the faithful to file past the relics – ⑪ Radiating or apsidal chapel – ⑫ Axial chapel. In churches which are not dedicated to the Virgin this chapel, in the main axis of the building is often consecrated to the Virgin (Lady Chapel) – ⑬ Transept chapel.

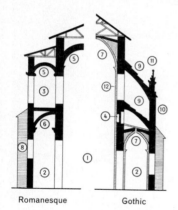

Romanesque   Gothic

◄ illustration II

Cross-section: ① Nave – ② Aisle – ③ Tribune or Gallery – ④ Triforium – ⑤ Barrel vault – ⑥ Half-barrel vault – ⑦ Pointed vault – ⑧ Buttress – ⑨ Flying buttress – ⑩ Pier of a flying buttress – ⑪ Pinnacle – ⑫ Clerestory window.

illustration III ►

Gothic cathedral: ① Porch – ② Gallery – ③ Rose window – ④ Belfry (sometimes with a spire) – ⑤ Gargoyle acting as a waterspout for the roof gutter – ⑥ Buttress – ⑦ Pier of a flying buttress (abutment) – ⑧ Flight or span of flying buttress – ⑨ Double-course flying buttress – ⑩ Pinnacle – ⑪ Side chapel – ⑫ Radiating or apsidal chapel – ⑬ Clerestory windows – ⑭ Side doorway – ⑮ Gable – ⑯ Pinnacle – ⑰ Spire over the transept crossing.

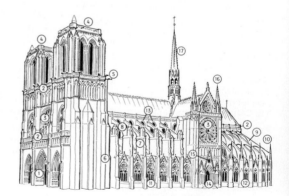

illustration IV

Groined vaulting:
① Main arch – ② Groin
③ Transverse arch

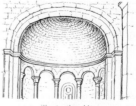

illustration V

Oven vault:
termination of a barrel
vaulted nave

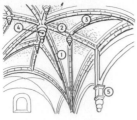

illustration VI

Lierne and tierceron vaulting:
① Diagonal – ② Lierne
③ Tierceron – ④ Pendant
⑤ Corbel

illustration VII

Quadripartite vaulting:
① Diagonal – ② Transverse
③ Stringer – ④ Flying buttress
⑤ Keystone

▼ illustration VIII

Doorway: ① Archivolt. Depending on the architectural style of the building this can be rounded, pointed, basket-handled, ogee or even adorned by a gable – ② Arching, covings (with string courses, mouldings, carvings or adorned with statues). Recessed arches or orders form the archivolt – ③ Tympanum – ④ Lintel – ⑤ Archshafts – ⑥ Embrasures. Arch shafts, splaying sometimes adorned with statues or columns – ⑦ Pier (often adorned by a statue) – ⑧ Hinges and other ironwork.

illustration IX ▶

Arches and pillars: ① Ribs or ribbed vaulting – ② Abacus – ③ Capital – ④ Shaft – ⑤ Base – ⑥ Engaged column – ⑦ Pier of arch wall – ⑧ Lintel – ⑨ Discharging or relieving arch – ⑩ Frieze.

Military architecture

illustration X

Fortified enclosure: ① Hoarding (projecting timber gallery) – ② Machicolations (corbelled crenellations) – ③ Barbican – ④ Keep or donjon – ⑤ Covered watchpath – ⑥ Curtain wall – ⑦ Outer curtain wall – ⑧ Postern.

illustration XI

Towers and curtain walls: ① Hoarding – ② Crenellations – ③ Merlon – ④ Loophole or arrow slit – ⑤ Curtain wall – ⑥ Bridge or drawbridge.

◀ illustration XII

Fortified gatehouse: ① Machicolations – ② Watch turrets or bartizan – ③ Slots for the arms of the drawbridge – ④ Postern.

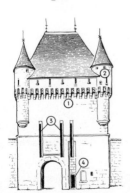

illustration XIII ▶

Star fortress: ① Entrance – ② Drawbridge – ③ Glacis – ④ Ravelin or half-moon – ⑤ Moat – ⑥ Bastion – ⑦ Watch turret – ⑧ Town – ⑨ Assembly area.

ART AND ARCHITECTURAL TERMS USED IN THE GUIDE

Aisle: illustration I.
Altarpiece: see retable and illustration XV.

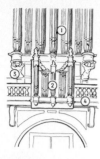

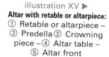

◀ illustration XIV
Organ:
① Great organ case –② Little organ case – ③ Caryatids ④ Loft

illustration XV ▶
Altar with retable or altarpiece:
① Retable or altarpiece –
② Predella③ Crowning piece –④ Altar table –
⑤ Altar front

Ambulatory: illustration I.
Apse: semicircular or semipolygonal end to church axis, housing an altar.
Apsidal chapel: illustration I.
Arcade: a range of arches within a larger arch.
Archivolt: illustration VIII.
Atlantes: supports in the form of carved male figures.
Axial or Lady Chapel: illustration I.
Bailey: open space or court of stone built castle.
Barrel vaulting: illustration XVIII.
Bartizan: illustration XII.
Basket-handled arch: depressed arch.
Bastion: illustration XIII.
Bay: illustration I.
Billet: a moulding made up of several bands of raised short cylinders or square pieces set at intervals and used as decoration (such as around an archivolt).
Bracket: small supporting piece of stone or timber to carry a beam or cornice.
Buttress: illustration II.
Capital: illustration IX.
Caryatids: supports in the form of carved female figures.
Cenotaph: a monument to a person buried elsewhere.
Chevet: French term for the east end of a church: illustration I.
Chicane: zig-zag passageway.
Coffered ceiling: vault or ceiling decorated with sunken panels.
Corbel: see bracket: illustration VI.
Credence: side table, shelf or niche for eucharistic elements.
Crypt: underground chamber or chapel.
Curtain wall: illustration X.
Depressed arch: three-centred arch sometimes called a basket-handled arch.
Diagonal ribs: illustrations VI and VII.
Dome: illustrations XVI and XVII.

◀ illustration XVI
Dome on squinches:
① Octagonal dome –
② Squinch –③ Arches of transept crossing

illustration XVII ▶
Dome on pendentives:
① Circular dome –
② Pendentive – ③ Arches of transept crossing

Engaged column: illustration IX.
Flamboyant: last phase (15C) of French Gothic architecture; name taken from the undulating (flame-like) lines of the window tracery.
Fresco: mural painting executed on wet plaster.
Frieze: decorated band either in relief or painted.
Gable: triangular part of an end wall carrying a sloping roof; the term is also applied to the steeply pitched ornamental pediments of Gothic architecture: illustration III
Gallery: illustration II.
Gargoyle: illustration III.
Glacis: illustration XIII.
Groined vaulting: illustration IV.
Half-timbered: timber-framed construction.
High relief: sculpted relief figures which are proud of their background by more than half their thickness.
Horseshoe arch: can either be pointed or rounded.
Hood-mould: a projected moulding above a window or decorative unit to protect it from the rain.

Impost: a member in wall formed of a bracket-like moulding on which the end of an arch rests.

Jetty: overhanging upper storey.

Keel vaulting: resembling an inverted ship's hull.

Keep or donjon: illustration X.

Keystone: middle and topmost stone in an arch or vault.

Lintel: illustration VIII.

Loophole or **arrow slit:** illustration XI.

Low relief: bas-relief (carved or sculpted figures which are slightly proud of their background).

Machicolations: illustration X.

Maze: a complex geometric design of tiles, which the faithful followed crawling on their hands and knees; and where the master craftsman signed his name.

Merlon: illustration XI.

Misericord: illustration XIX.

Moat: generally water-filled.

Modillion: small console supporting a cornice.

Mullion: a vertical post dividing a window.

Oculus: round window.

Organ case: illustration XIV.

Oven vaulting: illustration V.

Overhang: jetty or overhanging upper storey.

Parapet wall: see watchpath: illustration X.

Parclose screen: screen separating a chapel or the choir from the rest of the church.

Pendant: illustration VI.

Peristyle: a range of columns surrounding or on the façade of a building.

Pier: illustration VIII.

Pietà: Italian term designating the Virgin Mary with the dead Christ on her knees.

Pilaster: engaged rectangular column.

Pinnacle: illustrations II and III.

Piscina: basin for washing the sacred vessels.

Polyptych: a painted or carved work consisting of more than 3 leaves or panels folded together.

Porch: covered area before the entrance to a building.

Postern: illustrations X and XII.

Putti: naked cupids or cherubim represented in painting or sculpture.

Quadripartite vaulting: illustration VII.

Ravelin: illustration XIII.

Recessed arches: illustration VIII.

Recessed tomb: funerary niche.

Retable: illustration XV.

Rose window: illustration III.

Semicircular arch: round-headed arch.

Spire: illustration III.

Squinch: a support, often arched, across the corners of a bay to carry some superstructure: illustration XVI.

Stalls: illustration XIX.

illustration XVIII
Semicircular or barrel vaulting:
① Vault
② Transverse arch

illustration XIX ▶
Stalls: ① High back
② Elbow rest – ③ Cheek-piece
④ Misericord

Torus: large convex moulding semicircular in shape at the base of a column or pedestal.

Tracery: intersecting stone ribwork in the upper part of a window.

Transept: illustration I.

Transverse arch: illustration XVIII.

Triforium: illustration II.

Triptych: three panels hinged together, chiefly used as an altarpiece.

Tunnel vaulting: see barrel vaulting.

Twinned: columns, pilasters, windows, arches... grouped in twos.

Voussoir: one of the stones forming an arch.

Wall walk: see watchpath.

Watchpath: illustration X.

Watch turrets: see bartizan.

Wheel window: see rose window.

ART AND ARCHITECTURE
IN THE DORDOGNE

The Vézère Valley, the prehistoric sites of Les Eyzies and the caves of Quercy contain the finest examples of the artistic endeavours of prehistoric man, the first known manifestations of art in France. Since then art and architecture have evolved in close connection with the region's turbulent history. The large periods of construction correspond with periods of calm: the Pax Romana, the 12C, which was a time when a number of monasteries were built, as well as the period which spans the end of the 14 to 16C. During times of war – Hundred Years War, Wars of Religion – the peoples' main concern was their protection, hence the fortification of their towns, castles and churches.

Bonaguil Castle

Gallo-Roman Art

Of all the buildings constructed by the Gauls and the Romans only a few have withstood the test of time. Souvenirs of the period of the Gauls do survive in several sites in Quercy – Capdenac-le-Vieux, Murcens, Impernal and Puy d'Issolud – which argue over which had the honour of being the site of the battle of **Uxellodunum,** last site of Gaulish resistance to Caesar. During the Roman occupation, Vesunna (Périgueux), the capital of the Petrocorii, and Divona Cadurcorum (Cahors) capital of the Caduici, were important towns, and numerous public buildings were erected.
Roman remains uncovered in Périgueux suggest the magnificence of the ancient city of Vesunna: Vesunna's Tower, the excavations of a large 1 and 2C *domus* (town house), the arena ruins as well as the mosaics, steles and altars exhibited in the Périgord Museum. In Cahors, the grid-like town plan shows Gallo-Roman influence: the arch of Diana, all that is left of the baths, is the only Gallo-Roman architectural still standing. The Cahors Museum of Henri Martin houses a 3C sarcophagus and a carved lintel.

Romanesque Art

After the troubled times of the early Middle Ages, marked by the Viking invasions, the decadence of the Carolingian dynasty and the struggles between the great feudal barons, the year 1000 marks the beginning of a new era in the art of building.
Simultaneously with the affirmation of the royal power, came a vast surge of faith throughout France: Carolingian buildings, which were too cramped and no longer suited to the needs of the times, were replaced by churches of much greater size built with more robust methods.

Religious architecture

In Périgord – Périgord is rich in Romanesque churches. Their plain, almost severe appearance was enhanced by the use of a fine golden limestone with warm overtones. The exteriors were startling for the extreme simplicity of their decoration: the doorways without tympana were embellished with recessed orders carved with tori and festoons in a saw-tooth pattern. The church's inside plan was simple as well; apsidal chapels opened off the chancel (St-Jean-de-Côle, Tourtoirac, Montagrier) and most of the east ends were flat. The predominance of a nave only is a custom in this area; only four churches have been built with side aisles. The originality of the Périgord Romanesque style is in its vaulting – the **dome.** Some specialists believe this was brought back from the Orient, others that it is a French invention. The dome offers several advantages over cradle vaulting, which necessitates powerful buttresses. The dome on pendentives allows the support of the weight of the vault to be divided between the side walls and the transverse arches of the nave. Often used over the transept crossing, the domes also vault the nave when they follow one right after another as shown in Périgueux at St Stephen's Church (St-Étienne-de-la-Cité), where this type of "doming" was first employed (followed by Trémolat, Agonac, Grand-Brassac, Cherval). The nave is thus divided into several square bays vaulted with a dome on pendentives; the role of the pendentives is to serve as transition from a square to a circular base. St Front's Cathedral in Périgueux with its Greek-cross plan covered with five domes is unique *(photograph p 128).*

If these characteristics are to be found in many Romanesque buildings in Périgord, some churches have a different design: the nave is lined on either side by aisles (St-Privat-des-Prés, Cadouin) with rounded and pointed barrel-vaulting. A number of façades are adorned with rows of arcades showing the relation with the art styles of the Saintonge and Angoumois regions.

Tympanum of Carennac Church (Église St-Pierre)

In Quercy – Quercy Romanesque style displays a number of similarities with that of Périgord Romanesque: same simple plan, same use of the dome (St Stephen's in Cahors, Souillac) same material – limestone. And yet the Quercy churches are much richer in sculptural decoration showing the influence of Moissac and the Languedoc School, the centre of which was at Toulouse. The school's workshops drew inspiration from Byzantine art, illuminations and Antiquity and created carved doorways which were among the most beautiful in France at that time: the remains of the Souillac doorway with its admirable Prophet Isaiah, the tympana of Cahors, Carennac, Martel and Collonges-La-Rouge, on the boundary between Quercy and Limousin.

Civil and military architecture – There are few traces left of civil architecture of the Romanesque period. The former town hall of St-Antonin-Noble-Val in Quercy, although it has been considerably restored, is an interesting example of municipal Romanesque architecture of the 12C, with its sculptured gallery, arcaded portico and tall square belfry. The feudal fortresses erected in the 10 and 11C were greatly altered in later centuries and can scarcely be said to have withstood the warfare and destruction of the times. The only remaining buildings of this period are the keeps, last refuge of the defence systems, which were usually square in shape. Castelnau-Bretenoux Castle in Quercy, with its strongly fortified keep, is a good example of a feudal construction built on a hilltop site. In Périgord, parts of the castles of Biron and Beynac, Bourdeilles, Commarque and Castelnaud, date back to the Romanesque period.

Gothic Art

Gothic art was born in the first half of the 12C, apparently in the Ile-de-France and very gradually superseded the Romanesque style. It arrived quite late in Périgord and Quercy, but once there remained until the 16C.

Religious art

Architecture – The essential elements of Gothic art – quadripartite vaulting, based on diagonal ribs, and the systematic use of the pointed arch – were to undergo changes according to the different geographical regions.
The south did not adopt the Gothic elements of the north and this new art style – Gothic – stayed closely linked to Romanesque traditions. Therefore, specifically southern Gothic art, known as the Languedoc School, is characterized by the construction of wide naves without side-aisles, many-sided apses and the use of massive buttresses, between which have been erected chapels, to support the thrust of the vaulting (in the north, flying buttresses play this role).
Due to their geographical position, Périgord and Quercy were influenced by the north and south, as seen at times in the same building. Sarlat cathedral, for example, has a nave with side-aisles and soaring flying buttresses typical of northern Gothic, whereas the side chapels are influenced by southern Gothic. In Quercy, the Languedoc School inspired the church plans – a nave almost as wide as it is high, without side-aisles, but with side chapels – at Gourdon, Martel, Montpezat-du-Quercy and St-Cirq-Lapopie.

Monasteries – Monastic architecture produced some remarkable groups of buildings which have not always been able to withstand the ravages of time: of the former Cistercian Abbey of Beaulieu-en-Rouergue only the abbey church (13C), remarkable for its pointed vaulting and its elegant heptagonal apse, remains. On the other hand, at Cadouin and Cahors there are still cloisters built in the Flamboyant style, and at Périgueux the cloisters which took from the 12 to the 16C to build.

Fortified churches – During the 13 and 14C, while Gothic churches were being built in other regions, the insecurity that reigned throughout southwest France was the reason why churches were fortified and fortresses themselves with crenellated towers, watchpaths etc. were used as sanctuaries (churches at Rudelle and St-Pierre-Toirac). These churches constituted the most secure refuge against the violence of marauding armed bands.

Sculpture and painting – From the second half of the 13 to the 15C several remarkable works of art were produced: the tomb of St Stephen at Aubazine, Entombment (15C) at Carennac, tomb of the Cardaillacs at Espagnac-Ste-Eulalie and the recumbent figures of Cardinal Pierre des Prés and his nephew Jean des Prés in the collegiate church at Montpezat-du-Quercy.

Thonac Virgin

Frescoes, mural paintings done with water-based pigments on fresh plaster, allowing the colours to sink in, were used to decorate numerous chapels and churches. The west dome in Cahors cathedral is entirely covered with 14C frescoes. In Rocamadour the chapels are painted with frescoes both inside and on the exterior façades. In the chapels of St-André-des-Arques, Martignac, Soulomès (Quercy), Cheylard (St-Geniès) and Montferrand-du-Périgord churchyard, naïve 14 and 15C frescoes of the Holy Scriptures are a fine example of how peasants and nobility were clothed at the time.

Civil and military architecture – A number of **castles** in Périgord and Quercy were constructed during the Gothic period, as can be seen in the architectural details found at Bourdeilles, Château-l'Évêque, Beynac-et-Cazenac, Castelnaud, Castelnau-Bretenoux and Cabrerets. Bonaguil is in a class of its own, for although it was built at the end of the 15C and early part of the 16C it has all the features of a medieval fortress *(photograph p 28)*.

In the **towns** an important burst of construction occurred after the Hundred Years War. This building boom hit Sarlat, Périgueux and Bergerac as well as Cahors, Figeac, Gourdon and Martel. The façades of the town houses are decorated by large pointed arches on the ground floor – where the small shop was set up – depressed arched or rose windows on the upper floors and the whole ornamented with turrets. Among the finest examples of this period note Hôtel de la Raymondie in Martel, the Mint in Figeac, Hôtel Plamon in Sarlat and the famous Valentré Bridge in Cahors.

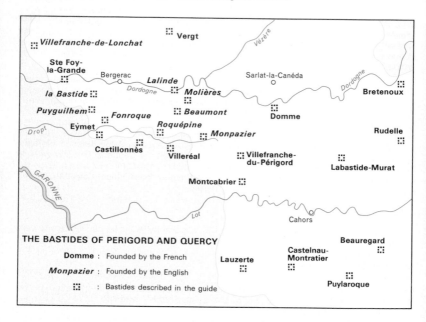

THE BASTIDES OF PERIGORD AND QUERCY

Domme : Founded by the French
Monpazier : Founded by the English
::: : Bastides described in the guide

The bastides – These new, more or less fortified towns (in the Oc language: *bastidas)* appeared in the 13C, and in the 14C their fortified aspect was further developed.

The founders – The principal founders were Alphonse de Poitiers (1249-71) – Count of Toulouse and brother to Saint Louis – and from 1272 on, the seneschal lords under Philip the Bold, Philip the Fair and King Edward I of England, also Duke of Aquitaine.

Development – Their construction satisfied economic, military and political needs. The founders took advantage of the growth of the population and encouraged people to settle on their land, which had previously been divided up in equal plots. In return for the land (land to live on and land to cultivate) they were granted a charter, guaranteed protection, exempted from military service and given the right to inherit.
The bailiff represented the king, dispensed justice and collected taxes, whereas the consuls, elected by the people, administered the town; under this system, the town flourished. After the Albigensian Crusade when the Count of Toulouse, Raymond VII, built about 40 *bastides* and with the outbreak of hostilities between the French and English over the Périgord, Quercy and Agenais borders, the political and military advantages of the *bastide* were confirmed. Alphonse de Poitiers had built Eymet, Castillonès and Villeréal along the Dropt River as well as Villefranche-du-Périgord and Ste-Foy-la-Grande. The king of England responded with the construction of Beaumont (1272), Molières, Lalinde and Monpazier (1285), while in 1281 Philip the Bold founded Domme.

Urbanism – All the *bastides,* whether French or English, were built to an identical plan – a chequered square or rectangular plan (Ste-Foy-la-Grande, Monpazier) – and yet they differed either because of the terrain and type of site needed or because of the potential for population growth and defence purposes (Domme). Furthermore, the *bastide* was at times built around a pre-existing building – a fortified church, as in Beaumont, or a castle. The design of Monpazier is the most characteristic; it is on a quadrilateral plan with straight streets crossed at right angles by alleys known as **carreyrous**; narrow spaces or **andro" nes** divided the house and served as fire breaks, drains or even latrines; in the centre of town the "square" was surrounded with covered arcades or **couverts**, also known as **cornières**, and contained a wooden covered market *(halle)*. The church and cemetery stood either near the main square or its periphery; the outer walls were punctuated with towers and gateways and enclosed the *bastides*. The names of new towns sometimes referred to their founder (Villeréal = royal town), their privileges (Villefranche) or their link to a castle (Castelnau). Most of the *bastides* no longer look as they did 500 years ago; the best preserved are Monpazier, Domme and Eymet.

Renaissance Art

The Golden Age of the château – At the beginning of the 16C, the artistic movement in France was revitalized by the influence of Italy. Artistic treasures in Italy awoke in the king, François I, and his noblemen the desire to copy the architecture and sculpture and introduce it to their native land, which they did by employing Italian artists. Keeping up to date with the times, pleasing their ladies who were often more aware of the evolution of fashion, promoting authority and national heritage, these were just some of the reasons motivating the plethora of noblemen and some richer members of the merchant class to build or restore hundreds of châteaux within the space of a century. Financial resources boomed after the end of the Hundred Years War: improved returns on estates after the development of share-cropping; freedom of trade in Dordogne; exploitation of iron ore; compensation and remunerative duties for emeriti. Extremely low labour costs and the possibility of spreading repayments across several successive generations meant that even those of average means could afford such undertakings.

Architecture – In Périgord and Quercy, the new style flowered at Assier where the château and church were built at the beginning of the 16C by Galiot de Genouillac, Grand Master of the Artillery under François I, who had participated in the campaign in Italy. This château, a remarkable achievement comparable to the finest châteaux of the Loire Valley, was unfortunately three-quarters destroyed. The châteaux of Montal and Puyguilhem, with their grace and style, are also very similar to the Loire Valley châteaux. Most of the other châteaux built in the 16C incorporate significant defensive features besides the windows, dormers, chimneys and other purely Renaissance architectural elements. This is the case in the châteaux of Monbazillac, Losse and Bannes, while the châteaux of Cénevières, Bourdeilles, Lanquais and Les Bories and the church at Rouffignac were partially transformed by the Renaissance; Biron Castle is graced by a marvellous Renaissance chapel.
Civil architecture was also influenced by the graceful Italian style: Roaldès Mansion in Cahors, Cayla House (or Consul's House) in Périgueux, Hôtel de Maleville in Sarlat, and Hôtel de Labenche in Brive.

Sculpture – In Quercy, the remarkable friezes carved with militaristic attributes, which decorate the outside of the church and the interior façade of the château at Assier, are among the most original works of the Renaissance. Inside the church, the tomb of Galiot de Genouillac completes this unit.
The inner court of Montal Castle is an outstanding example of the Italian style with its busts in high relief, superb works of art of realism and refined taste; inside, the remarkable staircase rivals those of the châteaux of the Loire. In the chapel at Biron Castle, the recumbent figures of the Gontaut-Birons are decorated with carvings influenced by the Italian Quattrocento (15C).

Classical Art

The classical period (17-18C) did not produce much in the region. The Château de Hautefort and its hospital with a central plan, on the borders of Limousin and Périgord, are very good examples of classical architecture, while the Château de Rastignac, built in the early 19C, is an almost exact copy of the White House in Washington, D.C.
Architectural elements such as staircases and door frames are more frequent. The wood sculpture that remains is interesting: for example, the monumental altarpiece in the baroque style located in St Front's in Périgueux.

A window of La Boétie's House in Sarlat

TRADITIONAL RURAL ARCHITECTURE

Périgord house

The solid and elegant rural architecture of Périgord and Quercy is among the finest in France. Many houses doomed to ruin, due to the rural exodus, have been saved by lovers of old stones who have restored these houses and established them as their holiday homes (more than half of the houses in Lot are holiday homes).

Périgord houses – The most typical house in **Périgord Noir** is a sturdy block-like construction in golden limestone topped with a steeply pitched roof covered with flat brown tiles or *lauzes*; Périgord *lauzes* are neither slate nor layered schistlike tiles but small limestone slabs. Set horizontally, their weight is such (500kg/m² - about 102lb/ft²) that they require a strong, steeply pitched timberwork roof to distribute the weight. In the wealthier houses, small towers or dovecots adjoin the house.

In Périgord Blanc or the **Ribéracois** region, the low houses in grey or white limestone are lit through windows topped by bull's-eyes (*œils-de-bœuf*). The flat roof covered with Roman-style terracotta tiles already reflects a more meridional style.

In the **Double**, a forest region, the houses were traditionally built of clay and half-timbering.

In the vineyards of **Bergerac** the wine-growers' houses are distinguishable by their wine-making plants, which are either built in a U-shape or across two adjoining courtyards. The tumble-down cottages of the vineyard labourers *(bordiers)* can be seen amidst the vines.

Chartreuse

Chartreuses – This kind of manor-house first appeared in the 17C, became more widespread during the 18C and remained popular until the end of the 19C. It is not a château, although its size might make it seem like one. It is a one-storey country mansion, often the residence of a winegrower.

Its exterior architectural features (symmetry, mouldings, balustraded terraces) as well as the high quality finishing touches of its interior distinguish it from a farmhouse. Inside, a series of rooms leads off a north-facing corridor.

Most *chartreuses* were built between 1650-1850 and reflect a way of life more than any social rank or pretension. They are very numerous in the southwest of France, and more than 200 of them have been counted in Périgord alone.

Quercy houses – Built in blocks of white limestone mortared in lime, the solid Quercy houses display a range of shapes, additions, towers and openings which makes for a charming country building.

Traditionally, the ground floor, in fact slightly below ground level and called the *cave,* contains the stable, sheds and store rooms. The first floor was used as the living quarters; access is via an outside staircase which overlooks a terrace protected by a porch or *bolet* held up by stone or wood columns.

Quercy house

Two types of roofing are found: the steeply pitched roof with flat tiles or sometimes *lauzes* and the shallower pitched roof covered with Roman-style terracotta tiles.

Outbuildings – The farm outbuildings often include (especially in **Upper Quercy**) a baking house, a low building with a rounded, apse-like end containing the oven.
The most attractive wells are covered with an arch with joggled joints or by a roof with pyramidal masonry.
Dotted along the narrow ridges of **Lower Quercy** are tower mills with rotating caps.
The **Périgord Vert** and the Quercy **Châtaigneraie** still have a few "*clédiers*" (chestnut drying sheds, *see the Musée Éclaté at Cardaillac*).
The borderland between Périgord and Quercy and the Auvergne contains a number of "horse-block" -style stable-barns (around Espédaillac in the Braunhie, for example), built on an inclined plane to enable hay to be stored on the first floor, leaving the ground floor free to stable the animals.

Dovecots – There are numerous dovecots in the area, many of which look quite elegant. Some are small towers attached to the main building, others stand alone, either resting

on a porch or supported on columns. Before 1789, the right to keep pigeons was reserved essentially for large landowners, but Quercy and to a lesser degree Périgord (where the right could be bought for a fee) were exceptions. Dovecots were built mainly for collecting pigeon droppings. The esteem in which these droppings was held is shown by the fact that when a property was divided up on the death of its owner the pigeon-dung was shared out between the heirs in the same way as the land and livestock. Not only was it an excellent manure, but it was also prized by bakers (for the aroma it gave to their rolls) and by chemists (as a relief for goitre, among other things). The appearance of chemical fertilisers after 1850 led to a decline in production.
The oldest types of freestanding dovecot were arcaded (known as "*suspendu*" - hanging), built on small columns to protect them from the damp. The stubby capitals (*capels*) created overhangs to deter would-be predators from climbing up the

A dovecot

columns (*see illustration right*). Those dovecots with a square or circular design and a fully concave base, as if for storing grain, appear to have been built more recently. However, it never does to generalise too much; the seigneurial dovecot at Assier belongs to the second category, but was built in 1537. Its roof capped with a flight turret can be clearly seen on the approach from the Garonne Valley.

Dry-stone huts – Here and there, isolated in a field or, more rarely, grouped in hamlets (*see Breuil hamlet under Sarlat: Excursions*), can be seen small constructions built entirely of dry stones, with conical roofs of stones supported by joggles (notches in each new layer are fitted into notches in the layer below to stop the roof slipping, and the whole roof is fixed at the top by a sort of keystone). They are known as *gariottes*, *caselles* or *bories*, but it is not known precisely what their function used to be, or when they were first built. Some are still in use as barns or toolsheds.

Kitchen in a dry-stone hut

DORDOGNE'S HOMEGROWN GASTRONOMY

The region of Périgord and Quercy is a kingdom of gastronomic delight. Its very name conjures up images of truffles, *foies gras* and *confits* - specialities which rank high among the culinary marvels of France. Périgueux restaurant owners and their *pâtés* have been famous since the 15C. The Périgord chef Villereynier, who with royal approval was known as "Villereynier de la Gâtine, Pastrycook to the King", was raised to a peerage by Louis XV. During the Revolution the master-chefs Lafon and Courtois continued to supply both England and France with their partridge *pâtés*. Périgord *pâté* had until then been made from partridges stuffed with chicken livers and chopped truffles, but was made from then with truffled goose livers following 1726 precepts by Close, chef to the Marquis de Contades, Governor of Strasbourg. Talleyrand had strong connections with Périgord and won some of his toughest diplomatic battles around a sumptuously laden table; his most reliable allies were truffles and Monbazillac.

The rich dishes of Périgord use local delicacies, exploiting to the full the variety of produce which can be grown in the region: truffles, *cèpes* (mushrooms), walnuts, strawberries, vines, and of course the geese, ducks and pigs which are the pride of every local farm.

Menu – The meal always begins with a *tourain blanchi* - a white soup made from garlic, goose fat and eggs, sometimes with sorrel or tomato added for a richer flavour. This is followed by *foie gras* or *pâté de foie* (general term for liver *pâté*), and then by a *cèpe* or truffle omelette. Now comes the main course, perhaps a *confit d'oie aux pommes sarladaises* (goose preserved in its own fat, fried until brown, with potatoes fried in goose fat with garlic, garnished with *cèpes* or some other wild mushroom). Then a refreshing salad in a walnut oil dressing follows, and after this the cheese course - try Cabecou (Quercy goats' cheese) - and finally, for those with any room left, a slice of walnut gâteau or a local tart made from flaky pastry with a prune filling.

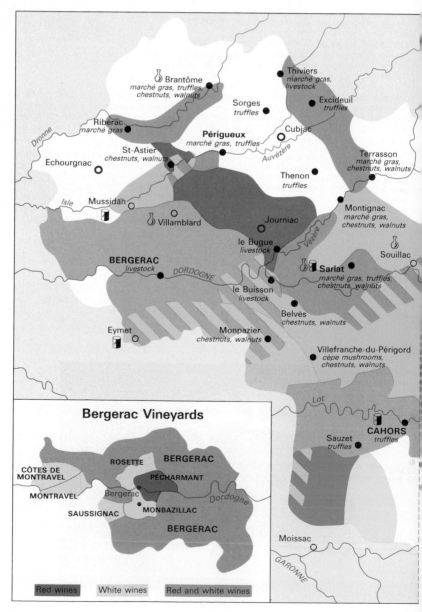

Foies gras – This regional speciality has resulted in a massive increase in the number of geese (nearly 200 000) and ducks (about 250 000) raised in Périgord and Quercy. They are raised primarily for the production of *foies gras* and *confits*, but numbers are still not high enough to satisfy local production demands, which have to be met in part by importing livers from Hungary or Israel.

The fat, heavy livers are obtained by force-feeding geese or ducks. After three months free-range in the fields on a diet of grass, the ducks and geese are put on a transitional diet of flour, meat and corn, before undergoing a three-week force-feeding programme. During this period they are made to ingurgitate 30-40kg - 66-88lb of maize mash three times a day through a funnel. On such a diet their livers reach enormous weights of 600-1 500g - 21-53oz.

These livers can be served in a variety of ways. *Foie d'oie* (goose liver) preserves well and is sold in a block (*en bloc*), as *pâté* or as a *terrine*. It is also found as *mousse de foie gras* (minimum liver content 75%), as *mousse de foie d'oie* (minimum liver content 50%) or included in the *ballottine*.

Duck livers, which have a more subtle flavour, are usually eaten as they are. If fried, split second timing is needed to prevent them melting away to nothing in the pan.

Confits – Traditionally the basis of Périgord and Quercy cooking, the *confit* was a method enabling farmers to preserve the various parts of the goose, having removed its liver, before the advent of the freezer. Now regarded as a speciality, it is nonetheless still prepared using traditional methods. The pieces of goose are cooked in their own fat for three hours and then preserved in large earthenware pots (*tupins*). This procedure is also used to preserve duck, turkey and pork (pork *confit* is called *enchauds*). Goose grease is used instead of butter in all local cooking (prompting Curnonsky to make the pun on the French saying "sans peur et sans reproche" - fearless and above reproach - by describing Périgord cuisine as "sans beurre et sans reproche" - butterless and above reproach), for example in *pommes de terre sarladaises*.

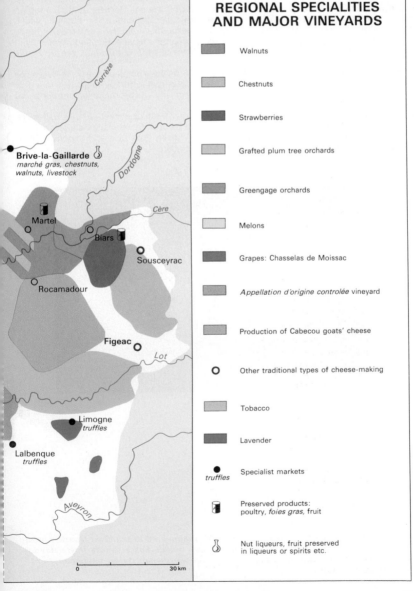

REGIONAL SPECIALITIES AND MAJOR VINEYARDS

Walnuts

Chestnuts

Strawberries

Grafted plum tree orchards

Greengage orchards

Melons

Grapes: Chasselas de Moissac

Appellation d'origine controlée vineyard

Production of Cabecou goats' cheese

O Other traditional types of cheese-making

Tobacco

Lavender

● Specialist markets
truffles

Preserved products: poultry, foies gras, fruit

Nut liqueurs, fruit preserved in liqueurs or spirits etc.

Brive-la-Gaillarde
marché gras, chestnuts, walnuts, livestock

Corrèze

Dordogne

Cère

Martel

Biars

Sousceyrac

Rocamadour

Figeac

Lot

Limogne
truffles

Lalbenque
truffles

Aveyron

0   30 km

Stuffings and sauces – Stuffing, moist and tasty, flavoured with liver and truffles, is also frequently used to garnish poultry, game, suckling pigs and in the famous *cou d'oie farci* (stuffed goose neck).

The most commonly used sauces are the *rouilleuse*, which is used to give colour to and accompany *fricassée de volaille* (fricassee of poultry), and *sauce Périgueux*, a Madeira sauce made from a base of chicken stock, to which fresh truffles are added.

Truffles – This underground mushroom, which when fully grown can weigh up to 100g - 3.5oz, is considered by the reputed gastronome Curnonsky to be the "perfumed soul of Périgord". It develops around the mycelium, a network of filaments invisible to the naked eye, and lives symbiotically around the roots of hazel, lime and in particular oak trees. It likes dry chalky soil, good exposure and clearly differentiated seasons. Wherever the truffle is growing underground, other vegetation dies above. Between December and February the truffle hunter (*caveur*), accompanied by a sow or more often nowadays a dog specially trained to hunt truffles,

Geese from Périgord

digs down into the soil where the animal has smelled truffles to harvest them at their most ripe and fragrant.

There are about thirty different types of truffle, but the best is the variety known as the Périgord truffle.

The main centres of production and sale in the Dordogne are Brantôme, Thiviers, Excideuil, Périgueux, Thenon, Terrasson, Sarlat, Domme and Sorges; in the Lot region they are Cahors, Limogne, Sauzet and in particular Lalbenque. Production, which reached hundreds of tonnes a century ago, has dropped a great deal, and the Dordogne at present produces approximately 4 tonnes. Truffle oaks have been planted recently in the hope of increasing production (*for further details on truffle cultivation, see the Truffle Centre at Sorges*).

The black diamond of gastronomy, the truffle can be seen as black specks in delicacies such as *foies gras*, *pâtés*, poultry dishes, *ballottines* (white turkey meat and *foie gras* moulded in aspic) and *galantines* (cold meat cuts in jelly). Its aromatic flavour enhances every dish it graces.

For the best results the truffle should be eaten either fresh or conserved by small-scale, skilled enterprises (*en conserve artisanale*). It can be used in salads, omelettes, or even wrapped and cooked whole over an open fire - given how rare and expensive it is, however, this latter must be the supreme extravagance.

Truffle hunting

The English truffle (tuber aestivum) has reappeared in the West Country after several years absence. This white-fleshed truffle has a faintly nutty flavour and is milder than its pungent black French cousin (tuber melanosporum) - and a lot cheaper!

Wine – The vineyards of Bergerac and Cahors, famous already in Gallo-Roman times, have been struck by a number of catastrophes, not least the devastation (complete destruction in the case of the Lot region) of the vineyards by the phylloxera aphid in the 19C. They are now enjoying renewed expansion, producing quality wines which have earned the *appellation d'origine contrôlée* (AOC).

Cahors wine – Well-known and much sought after in the Middle Ages, Cahors wine was transported by barges (*gabares*) to Bordeaux and from there by ship to various European capitals.

In 1868 the prosperous vineyards were completely wiped out by phylloxera. The land was abandoned, and the wine-growers emigrated. After the Second World War, it was decided to replant the Cahors vineyards with the Auxerrois grape variety on the sunny slopes of the Lot Valley and the pebbly terraces of the plateaux. The real rebirth of these vineyards occurred during the Sixties, and growth has continued since. Between 1962 and 1984 the surface area of the vineyard had grown from 208 to 2 600ha - 514 to 6 425 acres. The vineyards were classified AOC in 1971.

The Cahors vineyards produce a wine characterised by its dark red colour and robust, full-bodied flavour. Wine from the plateaux is more austere and tannic than wine from the valleys. Cahors wine improves if left to mature for 2-3 years in the cask and 10 years in the bottle where it acquires body and nose. It may be drunk with poultry, game, roasts and cheese.

Bergerac wines – The Bergerac vineyards cover an area of 11 000ha - 27 181 acres divided into 93 *communes* and producing an average 200 000hl - 4 400 000gal (UK) of white wine and 150 000hl - 3 300 000gal (UK) of red wine. Spread over the terraces above the Dordogne Valley, the vineyard is divided into several zones, which produce different types of wine: Bergerac, Côtes de Bergerac, Monbazillac, Montravel, Côtes de Montravel, Pécharmant (this name derives from Pech Armand), Côtes de Saussignac and Rosette. The most widely grown grape in the region is the Sauvignon.

The Bergerac Regional Wine Council, which is located in Bergerac, monitors the quality of the wines and awards them the AOC.

Among the white Bergerac wines, **Monbazillac** stands out in particular. It is golden, unctuous and fragrant, a heavy wine that can be served as an *apéritif* or with *foie gras* or dessert. It owes its distinctive bouquet to the *pourriture noble* (noble rot) which reduces the acidity of the grape. This process dates from the Renaissance. The grapes are harvested in several batches, as for Sauternes; in each harvesting session the only grapes picked are those which have reached the desired state of maturity. Monbazillac develops its full flavour after 2-3 years and will keep for up to 30 years.

Dry white wines such as Montravel and Bergerac, which are vigorous and fruity, are the perfect accompaniment to seafood and fish; sweeter white wines such as Côtes de Bergerac, Côtes de Montravel, Rosette and Saussignac are good served as *apéritifs* or with white meat.

Red wines such as Bergerac or Côtes de Bergerac are well-rounded and fruity and can be drunk while still young, whereas **Pécharmant**, an excellent full-bodied and generous wine, does not reveal its full charms until after quite a lengthy period of maturation.

MORE LOCAL AGRICULTURE

Strawberries – Thanks to recent efforts the Dordogne *département* is ranked number one producer of strawberries (level with Lot-et-Garonne) in France with a production of almost 20 000 tonnes.

Initially cultivated in the Lot and Dordogne valleys, strawberries have gradually spread across the plateaux and are now to be found all over the Vergt and Rouffignac regions in Central Périgord. So that the strawberries are protected from bad weather and enabled to flower and grow in a constant environment, they are placed under plastic sheets, which bedeck the countryside in long silvery ribbons during the spring. The fruit is left to ripen under these sheets before being picked and sent to large markets in the Paris region or the north of France, where the Périgord strawberry is particularly appreciated.

Walnuts – Walnuts are one of the four main agricultural products associated with the Périgord and Quercy region (along with truffles, tobacco and *foie gras*). They are still harvested in large quantities (5-7 000 tonnes per year in Dordogne) in spite of the fact that their production is tending to decline.

The Marbot walnut, an early-ripening variety most common in the Lot region, is often sold fresh. The Grandjean walnut, produced in the Sarlat and Gourdon areas, accounts for most of the green walnuts (*cerneaux*) from Périgord and Quercy. The Corne walnut grows best in the Hautefort area and the better soils of the *causses*; it is a good quality nut, but there have been problems marketing it, as it is often small in size. The Franquette walnut is found on the new plantations.

The Dordogne is the second largest producer of walnuts of all the *départements* in France, the largest being Isère. Walnuts are cultivated in the north of the Dordogne, in the south of the Corrèze and over a large part of the Lot *départements*.

Tobacco – Conditions in Périgord and Quercy, and in all of southwest France, are highly favourable for the cultivation of tobacco. It is a vigorous plant, which was imported from America in the 16C and used initially for medicinal purposes, before becoming appreciated by those who smoke it (*for the history of tobacco see the Tobacco Museum at Bergerac*).

Tobacco growing – The traditional varieties of brown tobacco in this area are strictly controlled by the Régie nationale, S.E.I.T.A (state tobacco monopoly), whereas light tobacco is treated in the Sarlat factory.

The plant requires assiduous care and a large labour force, but it assures substantial cash income per acre. It is grown particularly on the alluvial soils of the valleys of the Dordogne and the Lot and on the mud terraces of the Périgord and Quercy hills; sowing takes place at the end of March; during the end of spring and the summer, work goes on pricking and planting out seedlings, land dressing, topping plants and disbudding. Harvesting is done stem by stem, each stem being covered with 10 to 12 leaves 60 to 90cm - 24 to 32ins long. Curing takes place in ventilated sheds, which can be seen throughout the region, and the air curing lasts about six weeks. Before being sent to the cooperative's warehouses, the leaves are sorted with a great deal of precision. The principal buyer, the S.E.I.T.A., prepares tobacco for smoking. The Lot has the greatest proportion of tobacco grown for snuff.

Tobacco market – The demand for products with American tobacco taste made from light tobacco increases constantly. This situation has brought about the creation of a research and development programme of the different types of American tobacco: Virginia or Burley. The production of the Virginia demands special machines (flue-curing) but these varieties are, nevertheless, in constant growth. For example, in Dordogne, it has been recorded that in 1989 800 tonnes of light tobacco were produced.

There are some 4 300 planters in the Dordogne, Lot and Lot-et-Garonne *départements*; it is essentially a family business, although mechanisation is increasing.

The Dordogne *département* ranks number one in France for tobacco production. About 2 000 planters produce approximately 20% of French production.

BOOKS TO READ

Fact

A Guide to the Dordogne, J. Bentley (Penguin)

A Little Tour in France, H. James (Macmillan Publishers Ltd)

Cave of Lascaux, M. Ruspoli (Thames and Hudson)

France Telegraph, a quarterly journal with articles and special features covering all regions of France which can be bought at most major bookshops and newsagents

French Farmhouses and Cottages, Walshe and Miller (Weidenfeld & Nicholson)

Goose Fat and Garlic (Country recipes from southwest France), J. Strang (Kyle Cathie)

Le Lot, H. Martin (Columbus)

Nouveau Guide du Périgord-Quercy, J.-L. Aubardier, M. Binet and G. Mandon (Ouest-France, Rennes)

Périgord, M. Blancpain (Nathan, Paris)

The Cave Artists, A. Sieveking (Thames and Hudson)

The Dordogne, S. Brook (George Philip)

The Dordogne, D. Gallant and S. Cobley (Weidenfeld & Nicolson)

The Dordogne and Lot, B. Eperon (Helm/A & C. Black)

The Dordogne Region of France, I. Scargill (David & Charles (Holdings) Ltd)

The Generous Earth, P. Oyler (Penguin)

The Most Beautiful Villages of France, D. Repérant (Thames and Hudson)

Three Rivers of France: Dordogne, Lot, Tarn, F. White (Faber & Faber)

The Way of St James, J. Bentley (Pavilion Books)

Walking in Wine Country, R. Carrier (Weidenfeld & Nicholson)

What to see in Dordogne Périgord (Pierre Fanlac, Périgueux)

Fiction (in French) set in the Dordogne region

Des grives aux loups, C. Michelet (Presses Pocket, Paris)

Jacquou le Croquant, E. Le Roy (Collection le Livre de Poche, Paris)

Le déjeuner de Sousceyrac, P. Benoit (Albin Michel, Paris)

Le fou de Bergerac, G. Simenon (Presses Pocket, Paris)

L'ennemi de la mort, E. Le Roy (Presses Pocket, Paris)

Sights

Rocamadour

AGONAC

Michelin map **75** fold 5 or **233** fold 42

This Périgord Blanc (White Périgord) town lies in a pleasant setting in a wooded, hilly region.

Church (Église St-Martin) ⊙ – The squat outline of the church stands erect in the Beauronne Valley, beside the D 3ᴱ, south of the town.
The great square belltower and the buttresses (16C) were added after the destruction caused by the Protestants during the Wars of Religion.
The interior has all the characteristics of the Romanesque style often seen in Périgord: an arched nave, domes above the pre-chancel and the sanctuary and a flat east end. The nave has three late-11C bays; the main dome, which is on pendentives and supports the belltower, was built in the 12C; the system of two-storey high defence chambers encircling the dome recalls the troubled times when churches were turned into fortresses.
The chancel is decorated with archaic-style capitals of monsters spewing leaves.

ALLASSAC
Pop 3 379

Michelin map **75** fold 8 or **239** fold 26 – Facilities

The houses of this small town have roofs of slate and walls of black schist, decorated here and there with red sandstone quoins (in the Rue L Boucharel for example). The **church** of the Beheading of St John the Baptist is also built of black schist, with the exception of its elegant **south porch**★ for which contrasting shades of sandstone have been used. Nearby, the 30m-98ft high Caesar Tower is all that remains of the medieval fortifications.
The period before the First World War was one of affluence for the slate-workers of Allassac and Donzenac; many of the farmers replaced their thatched roofs with slate ones. The last quarries closed down in 1982.

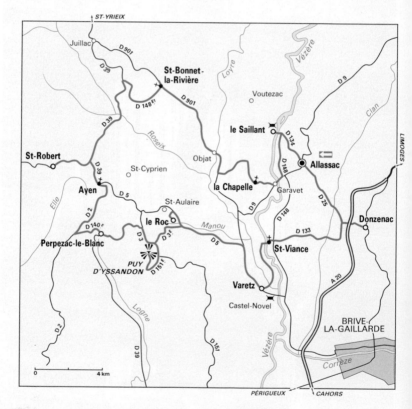

DISCOVER THE YSSANDON REGION
Round tour of 70 km – 43.5 miles leaving from Allassac – allow half a day

The **Yssandon region** extends over the west part of the Brive basin. During the Middle Ages its territorial boundaries formed a *pagus* (the origin of the French word for country, *pays*) with Yssandon as the main regional town. The region's varied geology, including the black schists of the Corrèze plateau and red sandstone knolls overshadowed by limestone outcrops known locally as puys, is one explanation for the enchanting variety of material used in the building of the towns and villages. The undulating countryside conceals pastureland with lines of poplars in the valleys, fields of tobacco and maize, walnut groves and fruit trees on the more exposed soil, and oak forests crowning the limestone plateaux. The vineyards around Voutezac and St Cyprien have a reputation dating back to the time of Henri IV's court.

Le Saillant – This hamlet is pleasantly situated at the mouth of the Vézère Gorge (*qv*). From the pretty **bridge** that spans the river, there is a view of the much-restored Lasteyrie du Saillant manor-house on the west bank. This was home for a time to the Marquis of Saillant's brother Mirabeau, the revolutionary orator.

La Chapelle – *Go south on the D 148, turn right onto the D 9 to cross the Vézère at Garavet, and take the road to the right towards St Aulaire.*
Commanding a full view of the Vézère valley from its ledge, this attractive Romanesque **chapel** is built in red sandstone and has a pentice gallery along its outside wall.

St-Bonnet-la-Rivière – Pop 327. The Romanesque church is built of red sandstone, circular in shape, with a belfry-porch. Legend has it that the local squire, a knight, vowed to build a church in the form of the Holy Sepulchre on his return from captivity in the Holy Land. Inside, the ambulatory is separated from the circular nave by ten columns.

St-Robert – *See St-Robert.*

Ayen – Pop 682. Former castellany of the viscounty of Limoges, Ayen is renowned for the 12C tombs enclosed in the outside walls of its church.

Perpezac-le-Blanc ⊙ – Pop 404. The houses of yellow limestone are characteristic of this lovely village, which is also home to an **Astropole**, a centre of astronomy and other space-related activities. A planetarium and a computer workshop have been built in the old school building. A field (called *le champ du châtel*) has been made into a shooting range for 1m-3ft miniature rockets, and there is also an observatory equipped for studying sunspots by day, as well as observing the night sky with the aid of powerful telescopes.

The Puy d'Yssandon – This site has been inhabited for many centuries; vestiges of the structural elements of a Gallic oppidum have been discovered here, as have some Gallo-Roman remains. In the 7C the inhabitants had joint control of the land that now constitutes the Yssandon region. This was then taken over by the very powerful families of Pompadour and Noailles. All that is now left of the medieval fortress is a ruined tower. Two orientation tables give details of the views of the Limoges mountains, the Périgord hills, the Brignac plain and the Brive basin.

Le Roc – *Take the D 3ᵉ towards Objat.*
This rural hamlet, built entirely of red sandstone, perches above the Manou valley, overlooked by St Aulaire castle.

Varetz – Pop 1 851. Castel Novel castle, now a hotel, is to be found on the road towards Brive, as you leave this market town. The French writers Henri de Jouvenel and his wife Colette drafted a number of novels while living there between 1912 and 1923.

St Viance – Pop 1 407. In this charming village with its red sandstone buildings on the banks of the Vézère, an outstanding example of Limoges enamel work is to be found in the church: a 13C champlevé enamel **reliquary★** kept in an alcove in the chancel.

Donzenac – Pop 2 050. Built on the side of a hillside on the edge of the Brive basin, Donzenac's strategic position has been the object of fierce dispute in the past, particularly during the Hundred Years War. Set amidst ancient houses, the church has a belltower which dates from the 14C. The Penitents' chapel has a well-proportioned Renaissance façade.

★ ANS COUNTRY

Michelin map 🎰 fold 7 or 🎰🎰🎰 folds 43 and 44 and 🎰🎰🎰 fold 25

The Ans Country, limited by Limousin and Périgord, was the most important overlordship of the Limoges viscounty. Many of the villages in the area still have as part of their name the word "d'Ans": Badefols-d'Ans, Ste-Eulalie-d'Ans, Granges-d'Ans, etc. In 1607 the overlordship was united with the crown under the reign of Henri IV. The countryside is lovely; the rolling hills are covered with a patchwork of woods, fields planted with crops and walnut trees. One of the major agricultural activities is the raising of sucking calves.

ROUND TOUR STARTING FROM MONTIGNAC

86km – 53.5 miles – allow 4 hours

Montignac – *See Montignac.*
Take the D 704 northwards and turn left into the D 67.

Auriac-du-Périgord – Pop 377. This charming village has a Romanesque church, which was transformed in the 15C. It is linked to the presbytery by a bridge with a handrail.
Turn back and then take a left onto the D 65.

Bee Museum (Écomusée de l'Abeille) ⊙ – *2km – 1.2 miles north of Auriac on the D 65.* Visitors are introduced to the workings of a family bee-keeping concern.
Continue along the D 65; at La Bachellerie turn left to Château de Rastignac.

Château de Rastignac – Designed by a native of Périgord, the architect Mathurin Blanchard, the château was built between 1811 and 1817 by the Marquis of Rastignac. This handsome neo-classical building bears a striking resemblance to the White House in Washington DC (*see Michelin Green Guide to Washington DC*). It comprises a rectangular main building surmounted by a terrace adorned with a pillared balustrade. A semicircular peristyle with eight Ionic columns forms the façade on the garden side. Burnt down by the Germans in 1944, the château has since been restored.
Join the N 89 and drive westwards, just after Thenon turn right onto the D 68.

Ajat – Pop 276. In this village, the Romanesque church, which has an oven-vaulted apse roofed with *lauzes* (*qv*), and the machicolated castle walls, make an attractive sight.
Take the road to Bauzens.

Bauzens – The **church**'s west front superimposes two decorative styles: below, a doorway with pointed annular archivolts; and above, a blind arcade in the Saintonge style. The first two bays in the nave form a kind of atrium which used to serve as a cemetery. The rest of the building is covered with *lauzes (qv)*. Behind the church there is a circular dovecot with flight holes in the little turret at the top.

After Gabillou the road *(via Chourgnac)* crosses a plateau fairly bereft of vegetation apart from some oak trees, juniper bushes and pines, with here and there a dip filled with red earth.

Tourtoirac – See *Tourtoirac*.

Take the D 5 then the D 62 to Hautefort.

★★ Hautefort Château – See *Hautefort Château*.

Continue along the D 62.

Badefols-d'Ans – Pop 451. The lordship of Badefols was the property of the Born family. One of the members of the family, Bertrand de Born *(qv)*, a soldier and poet, was mentioned in Dante's *Divine Comedy*.

A sturdy square keep, the oldest part of the castle, was once linked to a 15C main building. The 18C wing, on a right angle, serves as living quarters. The castle has been restored since being burned by the Germans in 1944.

Continue along the D 62.

After Beauregard-de-Terrasson **Peyraux Castle** appears on the left, clinging to its wooded hillside. The main building is flanked by two round feudal towers.

Condat-sur-Vézère – Pop 907. Built near the large paper mills of Le Lardin-St-Lazare, the old village of Condat, once a commandery of the Knights Templars, then of the Hospitallers, still has a well-preserved group of conventual buildings dating from the 15C and 16C. The Coly waterfall and watermill add further to the charms of the village.

Pick up the D 704 which takes you back to Montignac.

★ LES ARQUES
Pop 160

Michelin map **79** fold 7 or **235** fold 10 – 6km – 3.5 miles south of Cazals – Local map under BOURIANE

In this tranquil Bouriane *(qv)* village are two interesting churches both of which have undergone extensive restoration.

Ossip Zadkine – Russian by birth and French by adoption, the sculptor Zadkine (1890-1967) arrived in Paris in 1909. He was first influenced by Cubism, a style which he subsequently abandoned.

In 1934 he bought the house at Les Arques where he realised his most important works (*Diana, Pietà, Christ*); their monumental expression and well-constructed forms give them a widespread and longlasting appeal.

Zadkine Museum ⊙ – Three rooms display examples of the artist's work: lithographs, tapestries, bronzes (*Musical Trio*, 1928) and monumental wood sculptures (*Diana*). There is an audio-visual presentation of an interview with Zadkine.

★**Church (Église St-Laurent)** ⊙ – Located in the centre of the village, this church is all that is left of a priory-deanery founded in the 11C by Marcilhac Abbey *(qv)*. When the nave was restored in the 19C, it was narrowed and shortened; yet the apse and apsidal chapels have kept the purity of the Romanesque style. Certain archaisms have been preserved such as the oculus in the south arm of the transept, a characteristic of the Carolingean style, and the tori at the base of the columns supporting the transverse arches. The most original part of the interior is the shape of the arches: round horseshoe-shaped arches onto which open the apsidal chapels and rampant arches which adorn the passageway between the apse and apsidal chapels.

Two moving works by Zadkine enhance the church's interior: the monumental **Christ★** (on the back of the façade) and the **Pietà★** (in the crypt).

Church (Église St-André-des-Arques) ⊙ – *Go down towards the Masse River, cross the D 45.*

Set in a clearing, this church presents a remarkable series of **frescoes★** of the late 15C, discovered in 1954 by Zadkine.

The chancel window is framed by the Annunciation and on either side by the apostles with either the instruments of their punishment – St Andrew and the X-shaped cross and St Matthew and the halberd – or the instruments with which they are symbolised in art: St Peter with his keys, St James with his pilgrim's staff and St Thomas with his architect's set square. On the vault, spangled with red stars, is Christ in Majesty seated on a rainbow-shaped throne with one hand held up in blessing and the other holding the globe. He is surrounded by the symbols of the four Evangelists. On the pillars of the apse, which are holding up a triumphal arch, are St Christopher and, on the other side, the Infant Jesus waiting for Christopher to help him cross the river.

Admission times and charges
for the sights described
are listed at the end of the Guide.

Every sight for which there are times and charges
is indicated by the symbol ⊙ in the text describing the sight
in the main part of the Guide.

This Quercy village, due to the generosity of Galiot de Genouillac, possesses two remarkable Renaissance monuments.

Galiot de Genouillac (1465-1545) – Page under Charles VIII, then First Gentleman of the Bedchamber under Louis XII and finally Grand Master of the Artillery under François I, Jacques Galiot de Genouillac enjoyed announcing that he had served under three kings. This captain – a military man and a brilliant tactician – possessed many titles: Master of the Horse, Knight of the Order of St Michael, Seneschal of Quercy, Superintendent of Finances and Grand Master of the Artillery. He also organised the camp of the Field of Cloth of Gold near Calais in 1520 when François I met Henry VIII. Proud of his accomplishments, Galiot de Genouillac had them recounted for all to see on a frieze on both the castle and church.

His ambiguous motto – *J'aime Fortune* (I love fortune) or *J'aime Fort Une* (I love one greatly) – can also be found on both buildings.

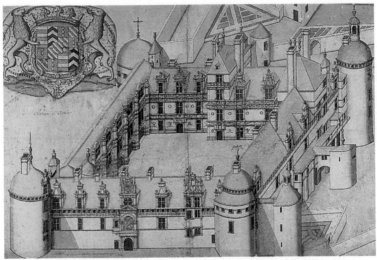

Gaignières's ink and watercolour rendering of the castle in 1680

Castle ⊙ – "Although built in a very ugly setting, in rough, ugly and mountainous country," Brantôme (historian and biographer, 1540-1614) maintained, "the Castle of Assier equals in splendour the palaces of the Loire Valley," and he went on to say it was "the best furnished house in France with its quantities of silver, tapestries and silks." Galiot de Genouillac wanted a sumptuous residence displaying his wealth and glory, a wish which was fulfilled to judge by Gaignières's ink and watercolour rendering of the castle in 1680 *(illustration above)*.

Unfortunately, as early as 1766 the castle was sold by his descendants and broken up. Only the guards' wing was saved; it is much plainer than the other three wings which were decorated in the more grandiose Renaissance style. The castle was saved from total abandonment when Prosper Mérimée had it classed as a historical monument in 1841.

The exterior façade still has machicolations between its two round towers. In the centre above the monumental entrance, framed by two Doric columns, is a niche which contained the equestrian statue of Galiot de Genouillac. The roof, once in the form of an upturned ship's keel and covered with *lauzes (qv)*, was pierced by several dormer windows, like those which can still be seen.

The **interior façade**★ has none of the severity of its counterpart. On the contrary, it shows a classical purity. It is decorated with friezes divided into sections running above each storey. The many scenes from the legend of Hercules symbolise the captain's omnipotence; cannons spurting flames recall his office of Grand Master of the Artillery. Between each window medallions with busts were placed – only the bust of a Roman emperor remains.

Inside, in the lower rooms with pointed arched vaulting, architectural elements of the castle can be seen as well as a remarkable 17C recumbent figure of Anne de Genouillac, who was a Maltese prioress.

A fine staircase in the transitional Gothic-Renaissance style leads to the first floor. On the landing is a finely carved limestone **pillar**★. It depicts on one side Fortune, on the second side Galiot de Genouillac's trophies and on the third side Hercules fighting the Nemean Lion. In one of the rooms on the first floor is a display of 17C *grisailles*.

★**Church (Église)** – This was built between 1540 and 1549 and is the original structure. The decoration on the outside is a long panegyric of Galiot de Genouillac's exploits and claims to fame.

A **frieze** goes right round the church. The subjects depicted include: sieges, battles, knights, foot-soldiers and artillerymen, which may surprise the visitor who will hardly expect to see such warlike motifs ornamenting a religious building. The frieze is a useful document on 16C arms and costume.

The **doorway** has a classical air: on the tympanum two cherubim proffer to the Virgin the captain's insignia, his sword as the Master of the Horse and St Michael's chain. The portico, formed by two columns surmounted by a triangular pediment, supports a domed niche.

Inside, the first chapel on the north side contains the great captain's **tomb**: the recumbent figure in court dress lies on a marble sarcophagus; above in high relief, Galiot de Genouillac is shown surrounded by his military emblems and two gunners who would appear to be waiting for his orders to fire.

The **stellar vaulting** of this chapel, which forms a dome supported on squinches, is an outstanding and very unusual feature.

★ AUBAZINE   Pop 788

Michelin map **75** fold 9 or **239** fold 26 – Local map under BRIVE-LA-GAILLARDE: Excursions – Facilities

Aubazine is pleasantly situated between the rivers Corrèze and Coiroux, on a promontory set back from the main roads.

A Dual Monastery – During the first few months of the 12C a group of men and women, united by a common desire to lead a life of fasting and prayer, gathered together in the forest of Aubazine to join the hermit St Stephen who had come from the nearby Xaintrie district in the Corrèze valley. Having adopted the rule of St Benedict, this small community built a monastery at Aubazine, and then a convent only 600m-656yds away from this in the Coiroux valley. In 1147, although the existence of a community of women proved to be a severe handicap, St Stephen nevertheless gained admittance for his communities into the Cistercian Order. This distinction of a dual monastery was preserved until the Revolution. The founder had decreed that the women take vows of complete enclosure, so they were totally dependent, both spiritually and materially, on the monastery. This no doubt gave rise to the local joke that anyone with a daughter at Coiroux gained a son-in-law at Aubazine.

The Monastery – The **abbey★** was built in the second half of the 12C and dedicated to the Blessed Virgin, as were most Cistercian churches. In the 18C it was truncated, losing six of its nine bays, so it is easy to imagine how large the original must have been. The west façade was built during that period.

The **belltower★** crowning the transept crossing is of a very original design; the transition from a square shape to an octagonal one is made by a system of stone tiers, which form a geometrically regulated surface, a technical achievement unique to that time.

Inside, the central nave has a barrel-vault and the huge square of the transept is topped by an elegant dome on pendentives. Three radiating chapels, with flat apses, open from each side of the choir which itself ends in a five-sided apse. The stained-glass windows in grisaille are the only ones to have been permitted in a Cistercian Church.

Furnishings★ – In the south arm of the transept there is the remarkable **tomb of St Stephen★★** made from limestone between 1250 and 1260, probably by artists from a studio in the Paris area. The face of the recumbent figure has been disfigured by the faithful flock (who believed that the dust they obtained by scraping at the stone held miraculous powers). A blind arcade cuts across the height of the alcove in which the figure lies, and the canopy above has two sloping sides which are decorated with scenes in relief. On the side that can be seen, the Virgin holding the Child Jesus greets St Stephen and his communities on earth. Opposite the tomb, the Coiroux **Entombment** is on display. This piece of stonework was originally polychrome and is of an exceptional quality; it was rediscovered in 1985 during the excavation of the convent.

In the first chapel in the north arm of the transept a 15C stone Pietà, with traces of polychrome, has a striking expression of immense spirituality.

At the foot of the great staircase which led to the dormitory there is the oldest **liturgical cupboard★** in France. Made in the 12C from oak beams, it is decorated with blind arcades on its sides.

The choir stalls date from the 18C, when the abbey was chosen as the noviciate for the whole of western Aquitaine. On the misericords of the stalls, now dispersed around the building, there are some very expressive carved figures.

Conventual Buildings – These are occupied by a community of Catholic nuns who follow the Oriental rite. Visitors are admitted ⊘ to the small library, the chapter-house with its groined vaulting resting on two columns, the nuns' common room, the kitchen and the large fish-breeding pond, fed by the "nuns' canal". This was built in the 12C, starting from a capture on the river Coiroux, partly hollowed out of the rock itself and partly cantilevered above a sheer drop of over 50m - 164ft, and it is a technical work of art of an exceptional standard. It is possible to follow the whole of its course (*see route indicated to the right along the course of the Coiroux river; distance: 1.5km - 1 mile*).

Convent – *600m - 656yds from the market town; to get there take the road towards Palazinges.*

All that remains standing of the convent, which was abandoned in 1791, is the church walls. However, recent excavation work has unearthed the irrigation system for drinking water and, beneath the embankment of the modern road, the arched doorway by which the monks and nuns communicated. This is designed like a lock chamber; one of the communities had the key to the outside door and the other the key to the inside door.

EXCURSION

★Puy de Pauliac – *Take the D 48 along the Coiroux Gorges and bear left onto a smaller road to the summit.*
A path (*15 min on foot Rtn*) through heather and chestnut trees leads up to the top (520m – 1 760ft) from where there is a wide **view★** (viewing table) southeast onto Vic Rock and northwards onto Monédières Massif.
Continue along the D 48 to the **Coiroux Tourist Centre** (Centre Touristique du Coiroux) where facilities (swimming, sailing, windsurfing and golf) have been set up around a lake.

★ BEAULIEU-EN-ROUERGUE ABBEY

Michelin map 79 fold 19 or 235 fold 19 – 10km – 6 miles southeast of Caylus – Local map under ST-ANTONIN-NOBLE-VAL

On the border of Quercy and Rouergue, the charming Seye Valley was the place where, in 1144, several monks sent by St Bernard founded an **abbey** ⊘ which was called Beaulieu (*Belloc* in Occitanian).
After the Revolution, the abbey was partly demolished and became a farm. It was not until 1960 that restoration was started by the abbey's new owners and continued when it was donated to the *Caisse des Monuments Historiques* (Historic Buildings Commission) in 1973. The result is remarkable, especially in the case of the church, which is an excellent example of Cistercian architecture.
The abbey is now a **Contemporary Art Centre** (Centre d'Art Contemporain) which holds exhibitions and concerts in the summer.

★Church (Église) – This fine building erected in the mid-13C is a good example of the pure Gothic style with its pointed vaulted nave lit by rose and lancet windows.
The transept ends in an elegant heptagonal apse and has, above its crossing, an octagonal **dome** on squinches. A square chapel opens off each transept.

Abbey buildings (Bâtiments abbatiaux) – The **chapter-house**, the oldest part of the abbey, opened onto the cloisters (no longer standing) with three pointed arches. It is made up of two bays each covered with three pointed vaults supported by two mighty columns.
The **cellar**, on the ground floor of the Laymen's Building (Bâtiment des Convers), has ten cross-ribbed vaults resting on four columns, the capitals of which are adorned with leaves in very low relief. The beauty of the room and the refinement in the detail used, as shown in the unadorned pendants, demonstrate the careful attention that the Cistercians paid in the construction of each building, even an annexe.

EXCURSION

St Igne – Near the village there is an unusual and striking monument dating from 1882, the "Phylloxera cross", in memory of the devastating effects of the phylloxera aphid on the local vines. The inscription means "We are struck down by the hand of God."

BEAUMONT   Pop 1 166

Michelin map 75 fold 15 or 235 fold 5 – Facilities

Beaumont was built as a *bastide* in 1272 by the Seneschal of Guyenne in the name of Edward I, king of England, and today retains only traces of the fortifications but still has many houses with angle irons.

Church (Église St-Front) – Built after 1272 in the Early Gothic style and cantoned by four huge towers connected by a rampart walk, this church was the last place of refuge for the inhabitants of the town during periods of siege. The asymmetry of the towers on the main façade reflects their different functions; the lower was a bell-tower until 1789, and the higher a crenellated keep armed with machicolations. The towers frame a doorway, which has five archivolts and which is supported by clustered columns, and a **gallery★** with a beautifully decorated balustrade and an illuminated frieze underneath it. The elegant south porch has a trifoil arcade dominated by a lancet dais. It is protected by a brattice. Major restoration work during the last century has significantly altered the church's originally military character.

Interior – In the belltower to the left, the enormous arch-stone (weighing 450kg – 992lb!) to the chancel vault can be seen. It is decorated with carved figures of faces, including that of the church's patron, St Front. In the same side aisle towards the middle of the nave there is the chapel of St Joseph, almost certainly the remainder of a much older church. Notice in between two tombs the little piscina in which the priests used to perform their ritual ablutions.

Rampart ruins – A good view of the curtain walls, the 13C fortified Luzier Gate (Porte de Luzier) and the impressive outline of the church can be seen by going westwards, beyond the line of ramparts.

EXCURSION

Château de Bannes – *5km – 3 miles northwest on the D 660 and then up a road on the left.* Perched on a rocky spur, the château was built at the end of the 15C by the bishop of Sarlat, Armand de Gontaud-Biron. What is so incongruous in this château is that the military features – machicolated towers – are tempered by the carved doorway and richly decorated dormer windows surmounted by finials and pinnacles in the Early Renaissance style.

BELVÈS

Pop 1 663

Michelin map **75** fold 16 or **235** fold 5 – Local map under DORDOGNE VALLEY **3**

Perched as it is on a limestone promontory on the site of a Gallo-Roman castrum, Belvès has a marvellous position overlooking the Nauze valley. Approach from the southeast on the D 52 or the south on the D 710 to get a charming view of the whole town with its old turreted houses, belltowers and terraces arranged as gardens and covered with greenery.
Plaques attached to the major monuments make these easy to identify.

Place d'Armes – The belltower and the 15C covered market *(halle)* with stone and wooden supports have been preserved. In a small window on one of the pillars, the pillory chain can still be seen. All around the square, the façades are embellished with pretty wrought-iron balconies. Take the covered passage to the right of the Archbishop's House.

Rue Rubigan – This attractive little street leads to the Consuls' House (Maison des Consuls), which houses the **Castrum Museum** ⊙ and its collection of art and traditional objects. The Auditor's Tower, which may date from as early as the 13C, was once part of a magnificent house.

Rue des Filhols – On the right there is the lovely Renaissance façade of the Hôtel Bontemps. Cross the Place d'Armes once again.

Rue Jacques Manchotte – Stop and admire the half-timbered house at no 40; its roughcast walls are decorated with herringbone pattern brickwork. Several alleyways leading off to the left have pretty old houses along them. The road opens into Croix-des-Frères square, in which the most noticeable feature is the belltower of the old Dominican monastery, capped with an octagonal turret. This building now houses the tourist office (syndicat d'initiative).

In another outlying district of the town are the remains of the medieval fortress; the 12C castle keep and the Gothic church of Notre Dame de Montcuq, which used to be a Benedictine priory.

FORTIFIED TOWNS OF BESSÈDE FOREST: THE BASTIDES

Round tour of 105 km – 65 miles leaving from Belvès – allow a whole day – local map above

The small town of Belvès is surrounded by the forbidding forest of Bessède, which is an extension eastwards of the Belvès forest country *(Pays au Bois)*, antechamber of the Bouriane *(qv)* region. A thick layer of clay covers most of the limestone plateau, and this results in acidic soils which are hardly ideal for cultivation. The area was not really inhabited until after a number of *bastides* (fortified towns) *(qv)* had been built there. Trees now far outnumber any other occupants of the area, and the forest is an important natural resource. Just how important is shown by the large number of sawmills, which can be seen along the route, the quantities of chestnuts and the rich smell of *cèpes* (mushrooms) in the autumn.

Montferrand-du-Périgord – Pop 197. *Take the D 53 southwest from Belvès, then turn right onto the D 26.* The main feature of this pretty terraced village above the Couze is the semi-ruined château with its 12C keep.
The covered market with its beautiful columns, the old houses and the dovecots all contribute to the charm of the scene.
In the cemetery above the village, the Romanesque chapel is decorated with a lovely collection of mural frescoes dating from between the 12C and the 15C.

Ste-Croix – Pop 94. This village has a charming Romanesque church surrounded by the half-ruined buildings of what used to be a priory. This 12C church has a clear, uncluttered outline. The nave is covered in round tiles, in contrast to the apse and side chapel which are covered in *lauzes (qv)*. A gabled belfry adorns the top of the façade.

St-Avit-Sénieur – *See St-Avit-Sénieur.*

The route along the D 25 as far as Beaumont goes past many attractive manor-farmhouses.

Beaumont – *See Beaumont.*

At the top of the area known as **Petit Brassac** *(5 km – 3 miles south of Beaumont on the D 660)* opposite a signpost advertising guestrooms *(chambres d'hôte)* is a splendid dovecot supported on pillars of wood- and brickwork.

★**Monpazier** – *See Monpazier.*

★**Biron Castle** – *See Biron Castle.*

Villefranche-du-Périgord – *See Besse: Excursion.*

Besse – *See Besse.*

After leaving Besse, the road enters a thick forest of pines and chestnut trees, one of the most sombre parts of the Périgord. Just before St-Pompont this gives way to a coppice of scattered oak trees with stones here and there on the ground. There is some cultivation, of maize and tobacco in particular, confined to the dry valleys.

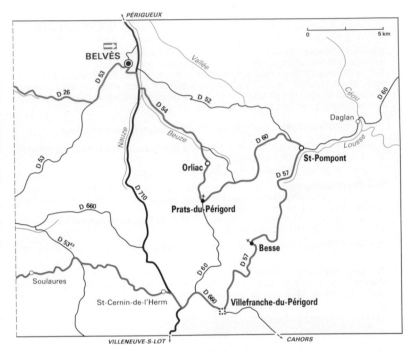

St-Pompont – Pop 452. This old village contains many houses typical of the Périgord region. There are pretty dormer windows surmounted with shell ornamentation and framed with spiral scrolls. A **fortified doorway**★ is all that remains of a fortress built here by the English in the 15C, albeit on the back of a hoarding of wood- and brickwork. On leaving the village in the direction of Prats-du-Périgord, a footpath goes along an unusual Cyclopean wall and then climbs the Gillous hill, leading to a "Gallic fort" *(300 m – 328 yds)*, a cairn which has been said to be a megalithic burial place.

Prats-du-Périgord – Pop 199. The Romanesque **church**★, fortified in the 15C, has an unusual appearance, with its nave being framed by the tall apse and the graceful belfry wall.

Orliac – Pop 72. This tiny village, buried in the hollow of a valley which is otherwise occupied by a pine forest, has a fortified church, a real nave-cum-keep which the Renaissance porch does little to brighten up. Notice the typical positioning of the gutter-stone on one of the houses.

★ **BERGERAC**   Pop 26 899

Michelin map **75** folds 14 and 15 or **234** folds 4 and 8 or **235** fold 5 – Local maps under BERGERAC: Excursions and DORDOGNE VALLEY **5**

Spread out on both banks of the Dordogne where the river tends to be calmer and the valley widens and forms an alluvial plain, Bergerac is surrounded by prestigious vineyards and fields of tobacco, cereals and maize.

In the heart of this town, which evokes all the charm of the southern towns, the restoration of the old quarter brought about the renovation of 15 and 16C houses.

An intellectual and commercial crossroads – The town's expansion began as early as the 12C. Benefiting from the town's situation as a port and bridging point, the local middle class developed rapidly, profiting from successful trade between the central provinces of Auvergne and Limousin and Bordeaux on the coast.

In the 16C, this Navarre fief became one of the bastions of Protestantism. The city flourished. The town's printing presses published pamphlets which circulated throughout the Protestant world. In August 1577 the *Peace of Bergerac* was signed between the king of Navarre and the representatives of King Henri III; this was a preliminary to the *Edict of Nantes* (1598). But in 1620, Louis XIII's army took over the town and destroyed the ramparts. After the *Revocation of the Edict of Nantes* (1685), the Jesuits and Recollects tried to win back their Protestant disciples. A certain number of Bergerac citizens, faithful to their Calvinist beliefs, emigrated to Holland, a country where they had maintained commercial contacts.

Bergerac was the capital of Périgord until the Revolution, when the regional capital was transferred to Périgueux, which also became *Préfecture* of the *département*.

In the 19C, wine growing and shipping prospered until the onslaught of phylloxera and the arrival of the railway respectively.

Bergerac today – Essentially an agricultural centre, Bergerac is the capital of tobacco in France, and as a result the Experimental Institute of Tobacco and the Tobacco Planters Centre of Advanced and Refresher Training are located here.

In addition the 11 000ha – 27 170 acres of vineyards surrounding the town produce wine with an *appellation d'origine contrôlée* (which means it is of an officially recognized vintage) including: Bergerac, Côtes de Bergerac, Monbazillac, Montravel and Pécharmant *(qv)*. The Regional Wine Council, which establishes the *appellation* of the wines, is located in the Recollects' Cloisters *(see Old Bergerac below)*.

The main industrial enterprise of the town is the powder factory producing nitro-cellulose for use in such industries as film-making, paint, varnish and plastics.

Famous citizens – Oddly enough, the "Cyrano" of Edmond Rostand's play was inspired by the 17C philosopher Cyrano de Bergerac whose name had nothing to do with the Périgord town. Not discouraged in the slightest, the townspeople took it upon themselves to "adopt" this wayward son and erect a statue in his honour in Place de la Myrpe. The philosopher Maine de Biran, on the other hand, was a native son of Bergerac; he was born here in 1766.

★OLD BERGERAC *time: 30 min (4 hours including the museums)*

A pleasant stroll through this maze of streets and shaded squares can be enhanced by a visit to the various museums.

Start at the car park which is located at the old port.

Old Port (Ancien port) (C) – Try to imagine the *gabares (qv)* mooring here to drop off goods and wood, which came from the upper valley, and load on the barrels of wine bound for England and Holland via Bordeaux.

Leaning against the house, at the bottom of Rue du Port, is an interesting metre bar, which gauges the Dordogne's floods.

Rue du Château (C 5) – An unusual balustraded balcony overhangs a sharp bend in the street.

★★Tobacco Museum (Musée du Tabac) (C) ⊘ – The museum is located in the **Peyrarède Mansion★** (Maison Peyrarède), also known as the French Kings' House, an elegant building built in 1603 and ornamented with a corbelled turret. This remarkable and beautifully presented collection traces the history and evolution of tobacco through the centuries.

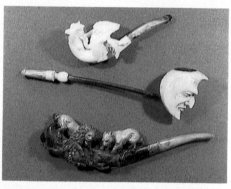

Two cigarette holders and a pipe in the Tobacco Museum

On the **first floor** the origin and evolution of the plant is described. Until the 15C tobacco was used only by the American Indians, who believed it possessed medicinal properties. On display are tobacco pouches, **calumets** or peace pipes and Indian pipes. After the discovery of the New World, tobacco was introduced to Europe. Jean Nicot brought it into France in *c*1560; he sent snuff to Catherine de' Medici to cure her migraines.

Smoking became such a craze that Pope Urbain VIII went so far as to excommunicate the smokers and Louis XIII forbade the sale of tobacco before proceeding to levy a tax. At this time tobacco was presented in the form of a carrot which then had to be grated to form powder. The **graters** exhibited are amazing works of art carved in wood or ivory. At the end of the 18C snuff was sold directly in powder form, which was preserved in large handpainted **porcelain jars.** Each smoker carried his own snuffbox. Exhibited alongside the jars are a number of these **snuffboxes,** some of which were decorated with portraits of Louis XVIII, Napoleon or Charles X. This was a way for the smoker to express his political views.

The next step in the art of smoking was the pipe. The pipe had been in use in Holland since the early 17C, but its use was considered vulgar and common. Officers of the First Empire started the fashion and were quickly followed by the Romantics, including George Sand. There are 19C **satirical engravings** depicting the art of consuming tobacco. In the display cabinets, **pipes** in porcelain, meerschaum and wood have been decorated with comic subject matters and portraits of famous people.

Finally in the mid-19C, the cigarette arrived on the scene and with it its accessories, including the elegant ivory **cigarette holders.**

On the **second floor** works of art depicting tobacco and smokers are displayed. *Two Smokers* from the 17C northern French School, *Three Smokers* by Meissonier and the charming *Interior of the Tobacconist's Shop* by David II Teniers, known as Teniers the Younger, are among the works exhibited.

Nearby is a pedestal table made by the Mexican Indians. It is fascinating to see how many cigar bands have been used to make the table's marquetry.

A section is devoted to the cultivation of tobacco (planting, harvesting, drying, etc.) with special reference to the Bergerac region.

Museum of Urban History (Musée d'Histoire Urbaine) ⊘ – In a house adjoining the Peyrarède Mansion there is a display of various objects – maps, documents, architectural remains, furnishings – evoking Bergerac's history.

Also worth noting are old town plans and glazed earthenware *(faïences)*, made in Bergerac in the 18C.

After leaving Peyrarède Mansion on the left, walk to Place du Feu and then the crossroads of Rue d'Albret.

Rue d'Albret (C 2) – At the end of this street to the right is the town hall, the former convent of the Sisters of Faith.

On the left, on the corner of Place du Feu, is a vast building with pointed arched doorways.

Place du Docteur-Cayla and Place de la Myrpe (C) – This large, charming shaded square is lined with half-timbered houses. In the middle of Place de la Myrpe stands the statue of Cyrano de Bergerac swathed in his cape.

Recollects' Cloisters (Cloître des Récollets) (C) ⊘ – Located between Place du Docteur-Cayla and the quays, the old Recollects' monastery houses the Regional Wine Council. The brick and stone building was built between the 12 and 17C. The interior courtyard has a 16C Renaissance gallery beside an 18C gallery. In the southeast corner is the monks' small oven.

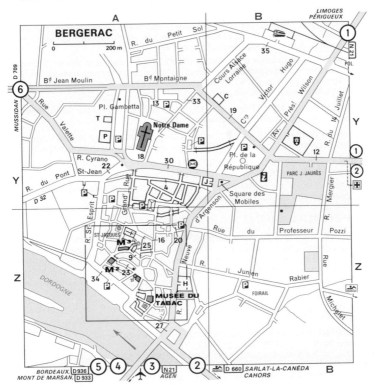

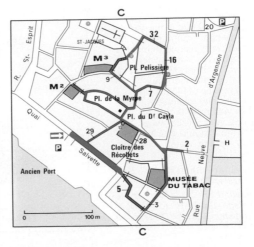

Go down the steps into the vaulted wine cellar where the meetings of the Bergerac wine society, Conférence des Consuls de la Vinée, are held. There is an audio-visual presentation on the Bergerac vineyards.

There is a fine view of the Monbazillac vineyards from the sumptuously decorated great hall on the first floor.

The wine-testing laboratory is in the eastern part of the building. The wine-tasting room can be visited; it is here that all the Bergerac wines are tasted annually to determine whether they are worthy of the *appellation d'origine contrôlée.*

The tour ends at the **Wine Centre** (Maison du Vin) at the corner of Place de la Myrpe. The chapel attached to the Recollects' monastery is now a Protestant church.

★**Wine, Shipping and Cooperage Museum** (Musée du Vin, de la Batellerie et de la Tonnellerie) (**C M²**) ⊘ – Located in a lovely brick and half-timbered house at the end of Place de la Myrpe, this museum is divided into three sections.

On the first floor, the importance of barrel-making to the Bergerac economy is explained. The coopers had to submit to strict control standards of barrel capacity, type of wood used and so on.

The section on wine shows the evolution of the Bergerac vineyards over the centuries and the type of houses the winegrowers lived in.

The second floor concerns the river boats. There are models of the various kinds of river boats, *gabares,* flat-bottomed boats sometimes with sails, which transported the different kinds of goods on the Dordogne River. They did not go above Bergerac, which was the port where the goods were transshipped. Photos show the bustling port of Bergerac in the 19C, as well as scenes of fishing with cast-nets strong enough to bring in enormous catches during the spawning season of fish such as salmon or shad.

Place Pélissière (**C**) – This large square was opened up after the demolition of some run-down houses. Spread on different levels around a fountain it is overlooked by St-Jacques church, once a centre for pilgrims on their way to Santiago de Compostela; near it is the Museum of Sacred Art.

Museum of Sacred Art (Musée d'Art Sacré) (**C M³**) ⊘ – Displayed in the small mission station are religious works of art: paintings, sculptures and sacred vases of different styles. Note the Lauzerte stone, an unusual archaic statue discovered in a chapel in Lauzerte (in Tarn-et-Garonne *département*).

Rue St-James (**C 32**) – There are 15, 16 and 17C half-timbered houses with mullioned windows all along this street.

Rue des Fontaines (**C 16**) – The Vieille Auberge at the corner of Rue Gaudra has well-preserved moulded arcades, 14C capitals, and pointed arched windows.

Rue des Conférences (**C 7**) – The name of this street calls to mind the conferences held before the *Peace of Bergerac (qv).* It is bordered by half-timbered houses.

Cross the Place de la Myrpe and Place du Docteur-Cayla and take Rue des Récollets to the old port (and car park).

ADDITIONAL SIGHT

Church of Our Lady (Église Notre-Dame) (**AY**) – Built in the Gothic style this 19C church has a slender belltower. There are two fine paintings in the east chapel: an *Adoration of the Magi* attributed to Pordenone, a Venetian painter and student of Giorgione, and more especially an *Adoration of the Shepherds* attributed to the Milanese, Ferrari, student of Leonardo da Vinci. In the west chapel is an immense Aubusson tapestry portraying the Bergerac coat of arms.

EXCURSIONS

Monbazillac Vineyard – *Round tour of 27km – 16.5 miles – about 1 hour 30 min. Leave Bergerac southwards on the D 13.*

This road crosses a market-garden area and then the meadowlands of the Dordogne's wide alluvial plain before reaching the first slopes of the hill on which the vineyards are situated *(the vineyard area is marked in green on the local map below).*

The famous vineyard of Monbazillac has a reputation that goes back hundreds of years. There is a story that in the Middle Ages, when pilgrims from Bergerac were visiting Rome, the pope asked, "And where is Bergerac?" "Near Monbazillac", replied their chamberlain.

The white wine of Monbazillac is a sweet wine and is served with *foie gras* as well as with dessert. The bunches are picked when the "noble rot" mould attacks them (drying up the water) – a guarantee of quality.

★**Monbazillac Château** – *See Monbazillac Château.*

Beyond the castle take, in the village, the D 14ᴱ to the right and soon after the D 107 to the left.

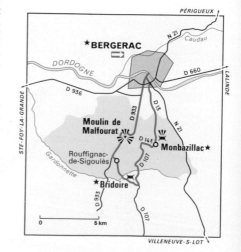

The road winds its way through carefully cultivated vineyards.

★**Bridoire Castle** (Château de Bridoire) – This Protestant fortress was partly destroyed by Montluc in 1568 and rebuilt under Henri IV. It was restored in the 19 and 20C. The castle is made up of two large main buildings set at right angles flanked by round towers facing an inside courtyard which is closed by a crescent-shaped curtain wall. Its grey stone, its roof of brown tiles and massive round machicolated towers are reminiscent of the Château de Monbazillac.

The road goes through **Rouffignac-de-Sigoulès,** a wine growers' village, where many of the houses have been roofed with round tiles.

Take the D 933 to the right which runs alongside the vineyards. A road climbs up to Malfourat Mill.

Malfourat Mill (Moulin de Malfourat) – Viewing table. The mill, now without its sails, stands on top of a hillock. From the bar terrace there is a **panorama**★ of the Monbazillac vineyard and Bergerac and the Dordogne Plain to the north.

The D 933 is picturesque as it drops down through the vineyards to Bergerac.

Caudau Valley – *38km – 23.5 miles. Allow 1 hour. Leave Bergerac by* ① *on the town plan, N 21, then turn right on the D 21 which follows the Caudau Valley.*

Lamonzie-Montastruc – Pop 407. Perched on a rock to the left of the road is Château de Montastruc, a handsome building in the classical style. Its main building is 16C, flanked by 15C circular corner towers, while another façade is 18C.

Continue along the D 21 then at Clermont-de-Beauregard take a path to the left.

La Gaubertie Castle (Château de la Gaubertie) – Built in the 15C, this castle was completely restored in the early 20C. The large main building, its façade overlooking the Caudau Valley, is flanked by a square tower on one side and a round corbelled tower on the other side. A machicolated rampart walk runs right around the castle. The 17C chapel stands not far from the castle.

At Clermont-de-Beauregard, take a small road along the Caudau Valley towards St-Laurent-des-Bâtons.

St-Maurice Castle (Château de St-Maurice) – The castle is partly hidden by the trees in its grounds, but its 14 and 15C buildings crowned with machicolations are nonetheless an attractive sight.

After the castle turn left onto another small road.

Go through St-Armand-de-Vergt, which has a pretty Romanesque church.

Turn left on the D 42, then right towards Lac de Neuf Font.

The road skirts **Neuf Font Lake** where there are swimming facilities and pedal boats.

From the lake take the D 8 to Vergt.

Vergt – Pop 1 422. This large agricultural town has become one of the main strawberry centres ⊙. The soil (ferrugineous sand) of the region is perfect for the cultivation of this fruit. This explains why at certain times during the year great plastic sheets can be seen protecting the strawberries.

BESSE   Pop 171

Michelin map **75** fold 17 or **235** fold 9-10

Standing in the centre of the forest that covers much of Quercy between the Lot and the Dordogne is the little village of Besse. Its interesting Romanesque church roofed with *lauzes (qv)* makes an attractive picture with the 16 and 17C château.

Church (**Église**) – An ogive doorway and a double flight of stairs lead into the remarkable carved **doorway**★ in the west front, dating most probably from the 11C. Such features are rare in the architecture of the Périgord region, and this particular example is exceptional. The sculptures on the archivolt depict the Redemption, including images of Adam and Eve before and after the Original Sin, St Michael slaying the dragon and Isaiah being purified by a glowing coal. The arch moulding is surmounted by a triangular pediment with lozenge patterning, supported by two free-standing columns and six illuminated corbels which, together with the capitals and parts of the door, depict Sin and Damnation; monsters devouring human souls, headless contortionists etc.

EXCURSION

Villefranche-du-Périgord – Pop 827. Facilities. *8km – 5 miles to the south on the D 57.*

This *bastide (qv),* was founded in 1261 by Alphonse de Poitiers. An enormous covered market with heavy pillars and part of the covered arcades are still to be seen. In the high street the **Chestnut Tree, Chestnut and Mushroom Centre** (Maison du Chataignier, Marrons et Champignons) ⊙ offers a display and a "Mushroom Nature Trail".

Doorway

Michelin map **75** fold 17 or **235** fold 6 – Local map under DORDOGNE VALLEY **3** – Facilities

Beynac Castle *(photograph p 74)* stands on a remarkable **site★★**, rising from the top of a rock; it overlooks the beautiful Dordogne Valley winding between hills crowned with castles. The village tucked at the foot of the cliff by the river is where the poet Paul Éluard chose to end his days.

A formidable stronghold – In the Middle Ages Beynac, Biron, Bourdeilles and Mareuil were the four baronies of Périgord. When the Capetians and the Plantagenets were at war, the castle, which had been captured by Richard the Lionheart, was used as a base by the sinister **Mercadier,** master-at-arms, whose bands of men pillaged the countryside on behalf of the king of England. In 1214, during the Albigensian Crusade, Simon de Montfort seized the castle and demolished it. The castle was later rebuilt, as we see it today, by a lord of Beynac.

During the Hundred Years War, the Dordogne marked the front between the English and the French, and there were constant skirmishes and raids between Beynac under the English in 1360, then the French in 1368, and Castelnaud under the English *(see Castelnaud Castle)*. Once peace had returned, Beynac Castle was left once more to watch over the village.

Frescoes in the Hall of State, Beynac Castle

★★ Castle ⊙ – *Access by car: take the D 703 on leaving the village to the west (3km – 2 miles) or on foot via the village.*
The castle is in the form of an irregular quadrilateral extended on the south side to form a bastion. The austere crenellated keep dates from the 13C. A double curtain wall protected the castle from attack from the plateau; on all the other sides there is a sheer drop of 150m – 492ft to the Dordogne. The main building, dating from the 13 and 14C, is extended by the 15C seigneurial manor-house to which a bartizan was added in the 16C.

Interior – The great Hall of State, where once the nobles of Périgord used to assemble, has fine broken barrel vaulting; the oratory is decorated with Gothic frescoes, naïve in style, with lively draughtsmanship depicting the Last Supper, a Christ of Pity at the foot of His Cross (as He appeared to St Gregory according to the medieval legend), and members of the Beynac family.
From the watchpath and the south bastion, which overlook the Dordogne and are reached by the main staircase (17C), there is a wonderful **panorama★★** of the valley and from left to right, of the "threshold" to Domme and the castles of Marqueyssac, Castelnaud and Fayrac.

Wayside cross (Calvaire) – This stands on the cliff edge 150m – 492ft to the east of the castle. A **panorama★★** as wide as the one from the castle watchpath can be seen from this point.

★ Village – A steeply sloping footpath known locally as the **Caminal del Panieraires★** (basketmakers' path) leads from the bottom of the village, through rows of houses dating from the 15C to the 17C, to the castle and the church. All along the climb the architectural décor exudes elegance and the prosperity of Renaissance Beynac. There are gabled doorways, façades decorated with coats-of-arms or discs, ornate dormer windows, and small, beautifully laid out squares.

Museum of Proto-History ⊙ – Objects (originals and facsimiles) assembled by theme introduce the civilisation (2000/1000BC) and techniques of the region's first farmers and iron workers.
Once through the pointed-arched gateway in the village's curtain wall, the footpath continues to the **church,** the former castle chapel, remodelled in the 15C.

Archaeological Park ⊙ – This includes about ten reconstructions based on the discoveries of archaeological research, mainly living quarters from the end of the Neolithic period, a fortified gateway and an oven made of Gallic earthenware. The display is further enhanced by demonstrations of flint-stone carving, the making and firing of earthenware and so forth.

Cazenac – *3km – 2 miles west.* This hamlet possesses a 15C Gothic church from which there is a lovely view of the valley.

Michelin map **75** fold 16 or **235** fold 9

From its perch at the top of a puy, Biron Castle commands an impressive view, the massive bulk of its towers and walls towering over the borders of the Périgord and Agenais regions.

From the Capitol to the Tarpeian Rock – Among the many celebrated men of the Biron family, **Charles de Gontaut** met with a particularly memorable fate.
Friend of Henri IV and one of his first lieutenants, he was appointed first Admiral and then Marshal of France. In 1598 the Barony of Biron was created and conferred as a dukedom on Charles de Gontaut who was next promoted to Lieutenant-General of the French Army and then Governor of Burgundy. Even these honours did not satisfy him and, in league with the Duke of Savoy and the Spanish Governor of the state of Milan, he laid a plot which would have led to the breaking up of the kingdom of France. Biron, his treason exposed, was pardoned. But the mercy of Henri IV did nothing to halt his ambitions. Once more he plotted against his lord. Once again he was exposed and was taken before the king, who agreed to pardon him if he would confess his crime. The proud Biron refused. He was beheaded in the Bastille on 31 July 1602.

From medieval fortress to the present building – This castle is made up of buildings of very different styles, the work of fourteen generations of Gontaut-Birons, who owned the castle from the 12 to 20C.
As early as the 11C a medieval fortress existed here. Razed by Simon de Montfort in the 13C, the castle was reconstructed. During the Hundred Years War, the castle changed hands constantly between the English and the French, getting badly damaged in the process.
In the late 15C and during the 16C, Pons de Gontaut-Biron, former Chamberlain of Charles VIII, decided to transform his castle into a lovely Renaissance château like those he had seen in the Loire Valley. He altered the buildings east of the main courtyard and had the Renaissance chapel and colonnaded arcade built. It was planned that a great staircase would lead from this arcade down to the bottom of the slope. Work was interrupted, however, and not resumed until the 18C.
This mass of buildings and the 10 000m² – 107 600sq ft of roof have made it exceedingly difficult for individual owners to maintain the castle. The Dordogne *département* bought it in 1978 and began a massive restoration programme. It also set up an art centre, which organises exhibitions every summer.

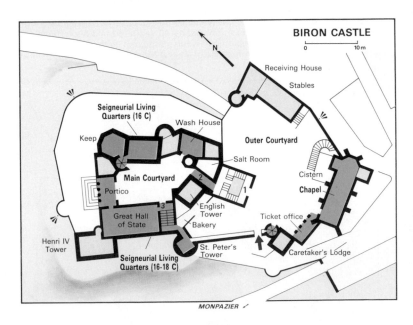

MONPAZIER

TOUR ⊘

Outer courtyard – Surrounding the castle's living quarters on three sides, the outer courtyard includes the caretaker's lodge, chapel, the receiving house and the bakery. The guards' tower, now the **caretaker's lodge,** is an elegant building in which crenellations, a watchpath and Renaissance decoration are happily juxtaposed.
The **chapel** was built in the Renaissance style in the 16C. A pierced balustrade runs round the base of the roof. The lower chamber once served as a parish church for the village; the upper chamber or seigneurial chapel, which opens directly onto the courtyard has remarkable pointed vaulting. It shelters **two tombs with recumbent figures,** the sculptures showing the influence of the Italian Quattrocento (15C) period. The recumbent figure of Armand de Gontaut-Biron, bishop of Sarlat, is decorated with three seated figures of the virtues, while the recumbent figure of his brother Pons (d 1524) is carved in low relief and recounts the life of Christ in a macabre frieze. Both figures were damaged during the Revolution. The chapel also contained a *Pietà* and an *Entombment,* two remarkable works of art, which were sold to the Metropolitan Museum of Art in New York City *(see Michelin Green Guide to New York City).*

From the terrace between the chapel and the receiving house, an imposing building with a turret, there is a bird's-eye view of the town.

The salt room is a larder where salt provisions were stored.

Main Courtyard – Access is by a staircase (**1**) and a pointed vaulted corridor (**2**). Opening onto this inner main courtyard *(cour d'honneur)* is a portico. On the right, the 16C seigneurial living quarters, with Renaissance windows, contain elegant restored galleries now used for art exhibitions. On the left, the 16 to 18C main building has an elegant remodelled staircase (**3**), which goes up to the Great Hall of State, the timberwork roof of which is in the form of a ship's keel and has just been rebuilt.

In the basement, the kitchen, the former garrison's refectory, is a vast room (22 x 9m – 72 x 30ft) with pointed barrel vaulting. The large 13C polygonal keep was redesigned in the 15C and made part of the other buildings.

From the castle terraces, the **view*** extends over the rolling countryside and the Birons' other fief, the *bastide* of Monpazier *(qv)*.

★★ BONAGUIL CASTLE

Michelin map **79** fold 6 or **235** fold 9 – Local map under LOT VALLEY: Meanders of the Lower Reaches.

This majestic fortress *(photograph p 28)*, which stands on the borders of Périgord Noir and Quercy, is one of the most perfect examples of military architecture from the late 15 and 16C. Its uniqueness is that, although it appears to be the traditional defensive stronghold able to hold off any attack, its conception was also adapted to the use of firearms new at that time: loopholes, harquebuses etc.

Furthermore, Bonaguil, which was built neither as a lookout post nor as a fortress but as a secure place of refuge, able to withstand attack of any kind, was a pioneer in 1480-1520 in its use of firearms essentially for defensive purposes. This is, after all, what forts are designed to do.

A strange character – It was a strange quirk of character that made **Bérenger de Roquefeuil** enjoy proclaiming himself the "noble, magnificent and most powerful lord of the baronies of Roquefeuil, Blanquefort, Castelnau, Combret, Roquefère, Count of Naut". He belonged to one of the oldest families of Languedoc and was a brutal and vindictive man who, in his determination to be obeyed, did not hesitate to use force. But extortion and other outrages he perpetrated incited revolt. In order to crush this, Bérenger transformed Bonaguil Castle, which had been built in the 13C, into an impregnable fortress from which he would be able to observe and quell any signs of an uprising without delay. It took him nearly 40 years to build his fortified eagle's eyrie, which looked an anachronism when compared with the châteaux being erected by his contemporaries for a life of ease at Montal, Assier and along the Loire.

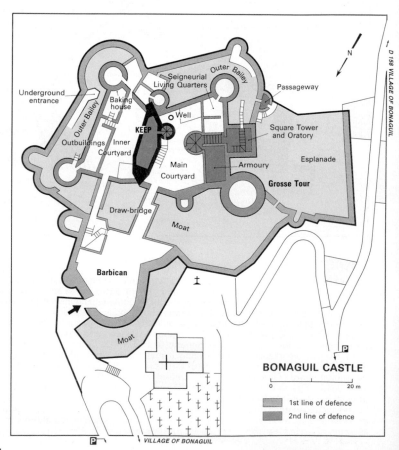

BONAGUIL CASTLE

1st line of defence
2nd line of defence

However, his castle was never attacked and was intact until the eve of the Revolution. Although demolished during the Revolution in the prevailing urge to destroy all signs of the old feudal system, this colossus, notwithstanding its mutilations, still evokes the absolute power it once represented.

This masterpiece of military architecture, while still keeping the traditional defences against attack by escalade or sapping, was also designed to make use of artillery and other new battle equipment.

Castle ⊙ – Time: 1 hour 30 min.

After passing through the outer wall, the visitor comes to the barbican. This was an enormous bastion on its own with its own garrison, powder store, armouries and way of escape. The barbican formed part of the 350m – 380yds long first line of defence; its bastions, thanks to the embrasures, permitted cross-firing.

The second line of defence consisted of five towers of which one, known as the Grosse Tour, is among the strongest round towers ever to have been built in France. The tower is 35m – 115ft high and is crowned with corbels; the upper storeys served as living quarters, the lower contained weapons, such as muskets, culverins and harquebuses, etc.

The keep overlooked both lines of defences; it served, with its cant walls, not only as a watch tower but also as a command-post. Shaped like a vessel with its prow, the most vulnerable point, turned towards the north, it was the last bastion of the defence. Inside, a room houses arms and objects found during the excavation of the moats.

With a well sunk through the rock, outbuildings (baking house) where provisions could be stored, monumental chimneys and drainage systems, dry internal ditches, and vaulted tunnels which enabled the troops to move about quickly, the castle garrison of about a hundred men could easily withstand a siege provided they were not betrayed or starved out.

LES BORIES CASTLE

Michelin map 𝟟𝟧 fold 6 or 𝟤𝟥𝟥 fold 43 – 12km – 7.5 miles northeast of Périgueux

Les Bories castle ⊙, built in the 16C by the St-Astier family, stands in a pleasant site on the bank of the Isle River.

The castle comprises the main building, flanked by two round towers and a massive, square tower with battlements.

The **interior architecture★** is outstanding. A monumental staircase leads up inside the square tower with a small room occupying the space in the centre on each floor; this was a Gothic chapel on the top floor. The **beautiful kitchen** has Gothic vaulting decorated with discus arch-stones; it has two huge chimneypieces with basket-handled arches.

In the guard room there is an unusual vault on squinches resting on pointed ribs starting from a central column.

The great hall contains Louis XIII furnishings, a fine Renaissance chimney and a Flemish *verdure* (tapestry in shades of green).

★ BOURDEILLES   Pop 811

Michelin map 𝟟𝟧 fold 5 or 𝟤𝟥𝟥 fold 42 – Facilities

The impressive castle of Bourdeilles, with the village clustered at its foot, makes a delightful picture as it stands on the rocks that rise up sheer above the Dronne River. It was here that the famous chronicler, Brantôme *(qv)*, was born in 1540.

A coveted spot – In 1259 Saint Louis ceded Périgord and Bourdeilles, his most important barony, to the English. This incredible desertion made the country rise in revolt and divided the Bourdeille family: the elder branch supported the Plantagenets, and the Maumonts, the younger branch, the Capetians. A while later, after plots and lawsuits, Géraud de Maumont, Counsellor to King Philip the Fair, who urged him on, seized the castle of his forebears. He turned it into a fortress. Then, to show his strength in Périgord, Philip the Fair exchanged land in Auvergne for Bourdeilles and, during a period of peace, set up a strong garrison within the fief of his enemies, the English.

The smile of the Renaissance – Credit for the plans for the 16C château must go to Jacquette de Montbron, wife of André de Bourdeille and sister-in-law to Pierre de Brantôme, with her active and informed interest in geometry and architecture.

Building was started in haste at the promise of a visit by Catherine de' Medici, but was abandoned when the visit was cancelled. The Renaissance part of the castle, nevertheless, is an interesting example of the architecture of that period and adds a lighter note to the group of 13C buildings.

★CASTLE ⊙ *time: 1 hour 30 min*

Cross the first fortified curtain wall, pass under the watchpath to get inside the second wall and enter the outer courtyard, in which there is a fine cedar. Continue to the esplanade, on which the two castles were built, one in the 13C, the other in the 16C.

Medieval castle – The 13C castle, built by Géraud de Maumont on older foundations and hence given the name New Castle, is an austere building surrounded by a quadrangular curtain wall. Inside the main building, exhibitions are held in a great hall.

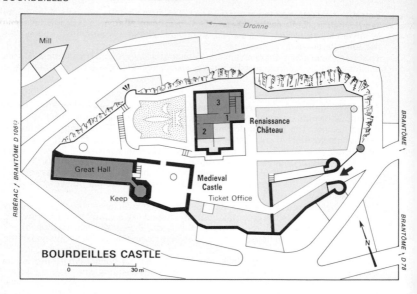

This is surmounted by an octagonal keep dating from the early 14C topped by machicolations; its walls are 2.40m – 7ft thick. From the upper platform of the keep there is a good overall view of the castle and a sweeping, bird's-eye **view** of the river Dronne.

Renaissance château – Sober and elegant in appearance, the château consists of a rectangular main building with a wing at right angles to it. It houses remarkable **furnishings★★** collected by two patrons who donated their collection to the Dordogne *département*.

On the ground floor, a gallery (**1**) houses 15 and 16C wooden chests, an interesting Limoges granite salt mill and a splendid 16C carved panel of the German School portraying the Dormition of the Virgin. In an adjoining room (**2**) note the recumbent figure of Jean de Chabannes and a replica of the Holy Sepulchre, which came from Montgé Priory (16C Burgundy School). The hall of armour (**3**), with its fine old tiling, contains metal chests in which gunpowder was kept and a magnificent Renaissance table.

On the first floor visit the dining hall with its 16C carved **chimneypiece★★** decorated with palm leaves and the Gothic room preceding the **gold salon★**. This sumptuously decorated room was built to accommodate Catherine de' Medici; it has a painted ceiling, woodwork and monumental chimneypieces by Ambroise Le Noble of the Fontainebleau School. Note the magnificent tapestry, based on a cartoon by Laurent Guyot, showing François I and his falconers.

In three rooms on the second floor there is a bright 15C **Catalan primitive painting** of *St Bartholomew exorcizing a demon from an Armenian princess*, cabinets with secret drawers, a 16C canopied bed, armchairs in Cordoba leather, a fine 17C octagonal table and especially the heavily carved and gilded **bedroom of Emperor Charles V**.

From the rampart walk at the far (east) end of the promontory overhanging the river Dronne, there is a lovely **view★** of the castle and its setting; a Gothic bridge with cutwaters, a very attractive 17C seigneurial mill in the shape of a boat roofed with round tiles and the green waters of the river lapping at the rocks below.

Emperor Charles V's bedroom

EXCURSION

Boulou Valley – *Round tour of 22km-14 miles-about 1 hour 15 min. Leave Bourdeilles northwards on the C 301.*

St-Julien-de-Bourdeilles – Pop 109. In this modest hamlet is a small Gothic church with two lovely statues in polychrome wood and parts of a 17C altarpiece.

Take the C 5 towards La Gonterie-Boulouneix; at the intersection, turn left.

Boulouneix – A Romanesque chapel with a domed belltower stands in the middle of a cemetery. In the chancel, 17C mural paintings represent Mary Magdalene and St Jerome. The façade with two storeys of arcades is of Saintonge influence.

About 100m-109yds after the church, bear left towards Au Bernard.

The road descends through the woods (hornbeam and filbert) to the marshy Boulou Valley. Several prehistoric sites have been discovered in the region.

Turn right on the C 2.

Paussac-et-St-Vivien – Pop 398. Several 16C houses and an interesting fortified **church** are of interest in this village.

The church's defensive areas, built above the three domes covering the nave and chancel, can still be seen. The south wall is decorated with arcades. Inside, note the capitals decorated in vey low relief with naïve carvings, a large Christ in polychrome wood and a Louis XV-style pulpit.

Take the C 2 towards Brantôme; at Les Guichards turn right towards Les Chauses, leaving the road to Puy-Fromage on the left.

From the road you will soon see Bourdeilles and its tall keep.

BOURIANE

Michelin map **79** folds 6 and 7 or **235** folds 9, 10 and 14

The Bouriane extends from Gourdon to the Lot Valley and west of the N 20. It is a region where the limestone formation disappears under a bed of sideritic sand (iron carbonate bearing), which is a lovely red and ochre colour. This rather unfertile soil nevertheless allows the cultivation of chestnut, pine and walnut. There are vineyards on the more exposed slopes.

A great number of rivers carve through the plateau creating a hilly, wooded countryside scattered with farms.

ROUND TOUR FROM GOURDON

94km – 58 miles – allow 3 hours – local map below

★**Gourdon** – *See Gourdon. Facilities.*

Salviac – Pop 1 003. The Gothic church has some lovely 14C stained-glass windows depicting scenes from the life of St Eutrope.

Cazals – Pop 538. This old *bastide* built by English kings is designed around a large central square. A moat was dug around the castle mound.

Montcléra Castle – The fortified entrance gate dates from the 15C. Behind it is a square keep and residential quarters flanked by round, machicolated towers.

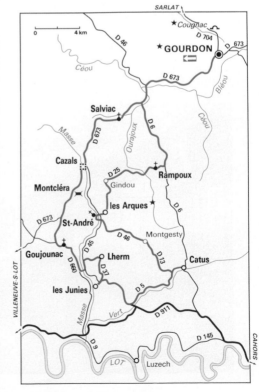

Goujounac – Pop 174. There used to be a Romanesque priory around the church, but there are now only a few vestiges of this. On the south wall of the church, the Romanesque tympanum, depicting Christ in Glory giving the sign of God's blessing surrounded by the symbols of the four Evangelists, is the work of a Quercy artist who was probably influenced by the tympanum at Beaulieu-sur-Dordogne.

Lherm – Pop 232. This little village of white limestone houses with steeply-pitched roofs covered with small brown tiles is dominated by a belltower, a turret and several dovecots. In a small isolated, wooded valley, the church, once a priory, has a Romanesque apse and a plain barrel-vaulted nave of ashlar-stone. The chancel contains a profusely decorated altarpiece of gold and carvings against a blue background, a rather grandiose, local interpretation of the Baroque style. The building was altered in the 16C; there is a fine Renaissance-style door.

Continue along the D 37.

Les Junies – Pop 255. The 15C castle flanked by round towers is decorated with elegant Renaissance windows.
Set apart from the village, the 14C church, an austere building, is of massive proportions. It was part of a priory, which was attached to the Dominican order in 1345 and which had been founded by one of the local lords, Gaucelin des Junies, Cardinal of Albano.

Take the D 660. At Rostassac, turn left onto the D 5.

Catus – Pop 807. The **priory chapter-house** (salle capitulaire) ⊙ adjoining the church contains some very beautiful Romanesque capitals, one of which shows Christ's appearance to the Apostles, and also some fragments of sculpture.

Take the D 13. At Montgesty, turn left onto the D 46.

Church (Église St-André-des-Arques) – *See Les Arques.*

★**Les Arques** – *See Les Arques.*

Rampoux – Pop 81. There is an interesting 12C Romanesque church here, made of red and white stone, which used to be a Benedictine priory. Inside, the 15C frescoes illustrate the Life of Christ in naïve style.

★★ BRANTÔME
Pop 2 080

Michelin map 📕 fold 5 or 📗 fold 31 – Facilities

Brantôme lies in the charming valley of the Dronne. Its old abbey and picturesque **setting**★ make it one of the most delightful places in Périgord.

HISTORICAL NOTES

The chronicler Brantôme – The literary fame of **Pierre de Bourdeille** *(illustration p 23)*, better known as Brantôme, brought renown to the abbey of which he was commendatory abbot.
Born the third son of the Baron of Bourdeilles in 1540, Brantôme spent the first years of his life at the court of Marguerite of Valois, queen of Navarre, since both his mother and maternal grandmother were members of the royal household. In 1549 he went to Paris to continue his education, which he completed in 1555 at the University of Poitiers. He began life as a soldier of fortune and courtier, went with Mary Stuart to Scotland, travelled in Spain, Portugal, Italy and the British Isles and even to Africa. Wild adventures brought him into contact with the great and famous in an era rich in scandal.
After fighting at Jarnac in 1569, he withdrew to his abbey and began his famous chronicles. The Huguenots twice threatened to destroy the abbey during the Wars of Religion and he had to use all his diplomatic skill with Coligny, one of the leaders of the Protestants, to save it from being pillaged. He left the abbey to return to court as Chamberlain to Charles IX. In 1584 a fall from his horse crippled him, and he left the restless and impetuous Valois court to retreat to the peace of his monastery and finish his chronicles.
Brantôme's posthumous fame lies in his *Les vies des hommes illustres et grands capitaines* ("Lives of Illustrious Men and Great Leaders") and *Les vies des dames galantes* ("Lives of Court Mistresses") in which morality and historical facts are sometimes confused. He was a lively, witty and sometimes cynical historian, who knew Ronsard, the poet, and other great writers of his time personally; he told a good tale well with many a spicy detail; his style was simple and has served as a model to many writers.

Abbey

SIGHTS

★★ Banks of the River Dronne – To get a complete picture of this romantic spot amble along the banks of the Dronne; the old houses with their flower-covered balconies and trellises and the lovely gardens near the abbey are reflected in the tranquil mirror of water. The charm lies in the harmony, serenity and calm of the scene and the softness of the light.

A 16C elbow bridge with asymmetrical arches, a Renaissance house with mullioned windows and the abbey, clinging to the limestone cliffs, make an attractive sight.

Abbey (Ancienne abbaye) – Brantôme Abbey, which was founded by Charlemagne in 769, under the Benedictine rule, to house the relics of St Sicaire, attracted a multitude of pilgrims. Sacked by the Normans, it was rebuilt in the 11C by Abbé Guillaume. In the 16C, it became *in commendam* with Pierre de Mareuil as commendatory abbot (he had constructed the most interesting of the buildings) followed by his nephew, Pierre de Bourdeille.

The present buildings are those built in the 18C by Bertin, administrator of Périgord.

Abbey church (Église abbatiale) – Angevin vaulting, a compromise between crossribbed vaulting and a dome, replaced the two original domes in the 15C. The nave is plain and elegant; a bay in the form of a cross and three depressed-arched windows below it illuminate the flat east end.

The baptistry is adorned with a 14C low relief in stone of the Baptism of Christ. Another low relief, this time dating from the 13C and showing the Massacre of the Innocents, may be seen underneath the porch above the font, which rests on a fine Romanesque capital decorated with strapwork.

Near the main doorway go into one of the cloistral galleries from where it is possible to get a glimpse of the former chapter-house; its palm tree vaulting is supported by a central column.

★★ Belltower (Clocher) ⊙ – The belltower was built apart from the church upon a sharp rock towering 12m – 39ft high, beneath which are vast caves. It was erected in the 11C and is the oldest gabled Romanesque belltower in Limousin. It was made of four storeys, each stepped back and slightly smaller than the one below, and topped by a stone pyramid. The ground floor storey is roofed with an archaic dome where the evolution from the square to the ellipse is obtained by triangular ribs held up by marble columns, an architectural element most likely recovered from a Merovingian construction. The three other storeys are opened by round arched bays supported on columns with simply decorated capitals.

Conventual Buildings – These now house the town hall and the **Fernand-Desmoulin Museum** ⊙ which displays prehistoric art and works by local painters. There are temporary exhibitions held in what used to be the monks' dormitory.

Troglodytic tour ("Du Creusé au Construit") ⊙ – The hermits who had converted the "fountain of the rock", originally a place of pagan worship, to Christianity were succeeded by monks, who initially occupied the caves in the rock face. Later on they continued to use the caves as outbuildings, or as refuges when the abbey buildings came under attack (in the 11C, the 12C, the 14C and the 17C). The tour circuit shows the monks' calefactory and the lavacrum, the remains of the abbey mill and the troglodytic dovecot. The "fountain of the rock", dedicated to St Sicaire, is still believed to have life-giving properties and the power to cure infant diseases in particular. The awesome atmosphere of the **Cave of the Last Judgment**, decorated with an epigrammatic Triumph of Death and an Italianate crucifixion sculpted in the 15C, is indication of the sort of spirituality that pervaded the monastic community of Brantôme for a thousand years.

The final cave contains a breeding ground for young trout, which are eventually used to restock the river Dronne.

THE HEART OF PÉRIGORD VERT

Round tour of 117km – 73 miles – allow about 6 hours – local map overleaf

A long swathe of Limoges-Périgord borderland stretches between the Nontron and Terrasson regions. On the last fragments of the crystalline shelf to the north, as on the limestone embankments around Brantôme, the waters of the Périgord Vert are subject to the west winds, which affect the dense network of streams, the myriad lakes full of carp and the lush, green undergrowth. A great number of isolated farms and hamlets add a touch of cheer in the midst of tiny patches of cultivation, areas of well-tended mixed farming and dairy production.

La Chapelle-Faucher – Towering over the Côle valley from the top of its cliff, the **castle** ⊙ was largely destroyed by fire when it was struck by lightning in 1916. The entrance postern and curtain wall are still standing however.

The main part of the building dates from the 15C and is crowned with a crenellated rampart walk. The living quarters adjoining the castle were built in the 18C. The lovely vaulted stables around the courtyard were added in the 17C. In 1569, during the Wars of Religion, the Huguenot leader Admiral Coligny laid siege to the castle with an army of 3 000 men. The chronicler Brantôme claims that 260 peasants were killed in cold blood.

Shortly after St-Pierre-de-Côle the outlines of the two ruined castles of **Bruzac** (11C and 15C) come into view on the hill to the left of the road.

★ St-Jean-de-Côle – *See St-Jean-de-Côle*

Thiviers – Pop 3 590. This small, lively town is well-known for its fairs and markets. The towers and turrets of Vaucocourt castle, built in a Renaissance-Gothic style and restored on countless occasions, overlook the church. The **Goose and Duck Centre** ⊙ (Maison de l'Oie et du Canard), to the right of the tourist office, contains a small *foie gras* museum – a product for which Thiviers is one of the centres of production.

★Villars Caves (Grottes de Villars) ⊙ – A winding passage leads to these caverns decorated with beautiful stone masses, including draperies of yellow ochre, two small natural limestone dams *(gours)* and, best of all, delicate white stalactites hanging from the ceiling.

In the first few galleries, the incredibly white stone masses are formed from a calcite which is almost pure and quite dazzling. The walls of some of the caverns are decorated with prehistoric paintings in manganese oxide which probably date from the same period as the Lascaux Cave *(qv)*, that is 17 000 years ago. The calcite deposit covering some of the paintings proves their authenticity.

★Puyguilhem Château – *See Puyguilhem Château.*

Boschaud Abbey – This Cistercian abbey was founded in 1163 in the wooded valley of *Bosco Cavo* ("hollow wood"), which gave rise to the name Boschaud.

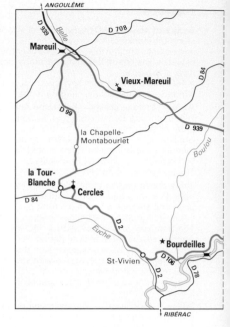

Destroyed during the Hundred Years War and the Wars of Religion, the abbey was partially rebuilt in the 17C. Restoration was begun again in 1950 by the Historic Building Commission and the *Club du Vieux Manoir* association. Traces of monastic buildings make it possible to reconstruct the plan of the abbey with its gatehouse, monks' living quarters, cellar and so on. The chapter-house still has five windows looking out onto the cloisters.

The very plain church is the only church of the Cistercian Order as yet known to have had a nave vaulted with a series of domes. Sadly, hardly anything now remains of the nave. Note the interesting, and rare, architectural cross-section of the pendentives and the cupola, now partially collapsed, of the nave's first dome.

Château de Richemont ⊙ – This bulky château, composed of two perpendicularly placed buildings, was built by the chronicler Brantôme in the 16C. On his death in 1614, he was interred in the chapel on the ground floor of the great, square tower. This was where he had inscribed his epitaph.

On the first floor of the entrance building there is Brantôme's bedroom with beautiful decorative woodwork.

Vieux Mareuil – Pop 360. Facilities. Although built in 13C, the church has all the characteristics of the Périgord Romanesque style: three domes on pendentives above the nave and pointed barrel-vaulting above the two bays of the nave, which has a flat east end.

The crenellations added in the 16C give the church a military air.

Mareuil – Pop 1 194. Tucked between the vast open spaces of the Ribérac region and the more rugged, higher-lying land to the north, the old baronial village of Mareuil, one of four in Périgord, has preserved its 15C castle intact. Having been the property of the Mareuil family, this passed into the hands of the Talleyrands of Périgord, then into those of the Montebellos, descended from Maréchal Lannes. The fortress was built on a plain, but protected by an impressive system of defences, of which the towers and the fortified wall still remain.

From the castle, walk up the main street, noting on the right through the openings in the wall an unusual neo-classical-style building. Two austere wings jut out, flanking a portico supported by six Tuscan columns. Completed in *c*1811, the house is almost certainly the work of Mathurin Blanchard, the architect of Rastignac *(qv)*.

La Tour-Blanche – Pop 408. The road to Cercles passes the foot of a mound overshadowed by a 13C keep and the ruins of a fortress which used to be the fief of the Counts of Angoulême before passing into the hands of the La Tour and then the Bourdeille families. The castle overlooks the village, which still has some lovely old houses and the Renaissance manor-house of Nanchapt.

Cercles – Pop 207. The Romanesque priory has become the **church** of St-Cybard. The nave dates back to the 13C. The doorway beneath the crenellated belfry wall has six beautifully carved capitals. The Renaissance section of the old cemetery is surmounted by an antifix cross. There is a good view of the whole church building from the cemetery.

★Bourdeilles – *See Bourdeilles.*

All along the D 106^{E2} and the D 78, which lead back to Brantôme, the cliff is undercut by spectacular rock shelters.

Stalactites, stalagmites and eccentrics are all extremely delicate; tourists can help to protect their fragile beauty by not touching them.

(Map area)

NONTRON

D 675

Dronne

Trincou

D 82   D 707   St-Martin-de-Fressengeas

St-Crépin-de-Richemont

D 98   ★ Puyguilhem   Grottes de Villars ★

Abb. de Boschaud   Villars   St-Jean-de-Côle ★

D 98

Richemont   D 82   D 78   D 707   Thiviers

D 939   Ch aux de Bruzac

BRANTÔME ★★   Côle   St-Pierre-de-Côle   N 21

D 78   D 78   la Chapelle-Faucher

D 106 62

Dronne

D 939

Sorges

0   5 km

PÉRIGUEUX   PÉRIGUEUX

BRIVE-LA-GAILLARDE   Pop 49 714

Michelin map **75** fold 8 or **239** fold 26 – Local map under BRIVE-LA-GAILLARDE: Excursions below

Brive, which owes its nickname *La Gaillarde* – the bold – to the courage displayed by its citizens on the many occasions when it was besieged, is an active town in the Corrèze alluvial plain. It is in the middle of the rich Brive Basin, where market gardening and orchards prosper.

Located at the crossroads of Bas-Limousin (Lower Limousin), Périgord and the Quercy *causses* (limestone plateaux), Brive is an important railway junction and is seeking to become the economic capital of the region.

Its main industries concern the canning of food, especially fruit and vegetables picked in the area.

A famous book fair has taken place annually in the Georges Brassens hall since 1982. Prizes are awarded mainly to books on tourism.

The plan of Brive is an excellent example of how a town can expand concentrically, with as its centre the old quarter and St Martin's Collegiate Church.

The "King of Brive" – The assassination of Chilgéric in 584 plunged Merovingian France into anarchy. A meeting of towns and villages at Brive proclaimed Gondowald, grandson of Clovis, king. Following Frankish custom, he was raised up on a shield and carried three times round the fortress. However the reign of the "King of Brive" was but brief; he was assassinated almost immediately, and for good measure his assassins also razed the basilica of St Martin to the ground.

A brilliant career – Guillaume Dubois (1656-1723), the son of an apothecary from Brive, took the Orders and became tutor to Philip of Orléans. He became Prime Minister when Philip was appointed Regent during the minority of Louis XV. Offices and honours were heaped upon him; he became Archbishop of Cambrai and then a cardinal. He made an alliance with England, which thus ensured a long period of peace in France.

A glorious soldier – Guillaume-Marie-Anne Brune enlisted in the army in 1791 and rose to become a general commanding the army in Italy in 1798. Following victories in Holland and Italy he was appointed ambassador at Constantinople. Elected Maréchal de France in 1804, he was banished by Napoleon soon afterwards for his "republican attitude". He became the symbol of the Revolution and died, a victim of a Royalist mob, in 1815 at Avignon.

OLD TOWN *time: 1 hour 30 min*

The old town located in the heart of the city, bounded by a first ring of boulevards, has been successfully restored. The buildings, old and new, create a harmonious ensemble of warm beige sandstone and bluish tinted rooftops.

St Martin's Collegiate Church (**Collégiale St-Martin**) (**BZ**) – Only the transept, apse and a few of the capitals are Romanesque, the traces of a 12C monastic community. Inside, over the transept crossing, is an octagonal dome on flat pendentives, characteristic of the Limousin style. The nave and side aisles are 14C. The chancel was faithfully rebuilt by Cardinal Dubois in the 18C; note the 12C baptismal font, decorated with the symbols of the Evangelists. From the outside admire the historiated capitals and modillioned cornice of the apsidal chapels.

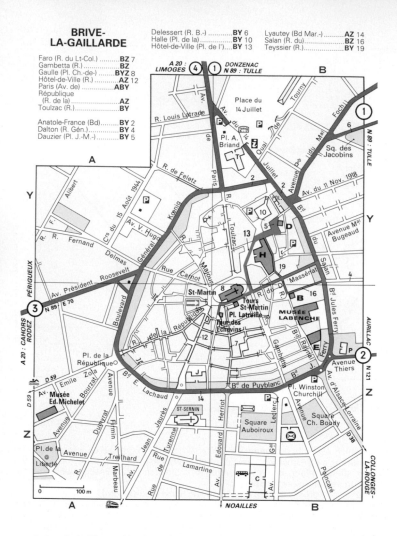

Archaeological Crypt – Vestiges of previous churches have been uncovered beneath the chancel, including the primitive construction dating from the 5C over the tomb of St Martin the Spaniard, who brought the Gospel to the town but was massacred by its inhabitants.

Échevins Tower (**Tour des Échevins**) (**BZ**) – In the narrow Rue des Échevins stands a town house with a fine corbelled Renaissance tower pierced by mullioned windows.

Place Latreille – This square was once the spiritual and commercial heart of the city and is still surrounded by old houses. That known as Tours St-Martin dates from the 15C and 16C.
Positioned at the corner of Rue Raynal and Rue du Salan is the 18C Hôtel des Bruslys (**BZ B**).

Turn right into Boulevard Jules-Ferry.

★**Labenche Museum** (**BZ**) ⊘ – Built in 1540 by Jean II de Calvimont, lord of Labenche and the king's keeper of the seals for the Bas-Limousin, this town house (Hôtel de Labenche) is a magnificent example of Renaissance architecture in Toulouse style and is the most remarkable secular building in town. From the inside courtyard the two main buildings can be seen set at right angles, above which are large arches. The roseate hue of the stone enhances the beauty of the building's decorative elements: mullioned windows adorned with festoons and slender columns and surmounted by busts of men and women set in niches.
Inside, it has been converted into a museum. The Roman-style main **staircase** with brackets carved as busts of warriors and ladies exudes the same exuberance as the outside.

Mortlake tapestry

Museum – The Counts of Cosinac room is decorated with a marvellous collection of **tapestries**, known as the Mortlake tapestries, made in the 17C using the widely renowned techniques of English high-warp tapestry. In the Cardinal Dubois room, there is the tomb of the pilgrim to Santiago di Compostela and a wonderful 11C silver and bronze **eucharistic dove** hanging above the altar, in which the sacred Host used to be kept. One of the main attributes of this museum is the successful reconstruction of the various series of excavations.

Residence of the Mother Superior of the Order of St Clare (Logis de l'Abbesse des Clarisses) **(BZ E)** – This Louis XIII building is distinguished by its dormer windows with semi-circular pediments decorated with keel-shaped spheres.

Former College of the Doctrinaires (Ancien collège des doctrinaires) **(BY H)** – Today these 17C buildings house the town hall. The façade on Rue Teyssier is of fine classical arrangement and the wall decorated with a colonnade overlooks an inner courtyard.
This college was maintained by the Brothers of Christian Doctrine, who were as much open-minded humanists as men of faith, and its prosperity increased up until the Revolution.

Place de l'Hôtel de Ville (BY 13) – On this large square, modern buildings (Crédit Agricole bank) and old turreted mansions form a harmonious architectural unit.
The 16C **Treilhard Town House (D)** consists of two main buildings joined by a round tower, decorated by a turret.

ADDITIONAL SIGHT

Museum of the Resistance and of Deportation (Musée Edmond-Michelet) **(AZ)** ⊙ – The museum traces the history of the Resistance movement and deportation with paintings, photographs, posters and original documents relating to the camps, especially Dachau, where Edmond Michelet, former Minister under General De Gaulle, was interned.

EXCURSIONS

★**1** **Aubazine** – *14km – 9 miles to the east by the N 89 and the D 48. Local map overleaf. See Aubazine.*

★**2** **Tour of the Lord of Turenne's Grounds** – *Round trip of 54km - 34 miles via Collonges-la-Rouge and Turenne – allow 4 hours – local map overleaf.*
This trip crosses the central area of the old viscounty of Turenne, which was not united with the French crown until 1738 *(see Turenne)*. After Turenne, the wooded hills of the Limoges region give way to the first limestone plateaux of the Quercy region.

Lacoste Castle (Château de Lacoste) – This former stronghold, built of local sandstone, has a main building flanked by three 13C towers. It was completed in the 15C with an elegant turret with a polygonal staircase.
At Noailhac you enter the region of red sandstone, which is used to build the lovely warm-coloured villages of the area. Soon Collonges-la-Rouge, perhaps the best known, can be seen against a backdrop of greenery.

★★**Collonges-la-Rouge** – *See Collonges-la-Rouge.*

Meyssac – Pop 1 124. Meyssac is in the centre of hilly countryside where walnut and poplar trees, vineyards and orchards prosper. Like Collonges-la-Rouge, the town is built in red sandstone.
The **church** is an unusual mixture of architectural elements: a Gothic interior, a belfry-porch fortified by hoarding and a limestone doorway in the Romanesque Limousin style, adorned with small capitals decorated with animals and foliage.
Near the church, the 18C **covered market,** which has a timberwork roof resting on alternating pillars and columns, is set in the middle of a square surrounded by elegant town houses, some of which have towers.
The picturesque nature of this village is confirmed by some of the houses, which are half-timbered with overhanging storeys and porch roofs.
The red earth, known as Collonges clay, is also used in pottery manufacture, which has developed in Meyssac.

For Saillac take the D 14, the D 28 and then right onto the D 28ᴱ.

Saillac – Pop 163. The village nestles amidst walnut trees and fields of maize. Inside the small Romanesque **church** is a doorway, preceded by a narthex, with a remarkable **tympanum★** in polychrome stone, relatively rare in the 12C. On the tympanum there is a representation of the Adoration of the Magi; the upper register depicts the Virgin Mary and Infant Jesus surrounded by Saint Joseph and the three kings; the lower register shows a winged leopard and an angel overcoming Leviathan. The tympanum is held up by a pier, composed of twisted columns adorned with foliage and hunting scenes, which probably came from a pagan monument.
In the chancel, topped by a dome on pendentives, are elegant historiated capitals.

Once on the D 19, turn left, then right on the D 8.

★**Turenne** – *See Turenne.*

Continue along the D 8, and turn left towards La Gleyjolle.

★**La Fage Chasm** – *See Turenne: Excursion.*

Turn around, turn left onto the D 73, then turn right.

Jugeals-Nazareth – Pop 604. The village of Nazareth was founded by Raymond I of Turenne on his return from the First Crusade. He built a leper-house which he entrusted to the care of the Knights Templars. Beneath the town hall there are several vaulted chambers, each equipped with a well and closed off with a railing, in which the lepers used to stay.

The D 8 and the D 38 go back to Brive-la-Gaillarde.

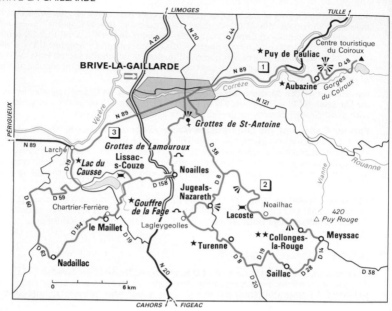

★ ③ **The Corrèze Causse** – *Round trip of 47km – 29 miles – allow 3 hours – local map above.* The road rises immediately above the Brive Basin.

St Antony's Caves (Grottes de St-Antoine) – These caves, hollowed out of sandstone, were used as a retreat by St Antony of Padua while he was living at Brive. They form an open-air sanctuary. Franciscans still provide hospitality for today's pilgrims. Follow the Stations of the Cross to the top of a hill to get a good view of Brive.

Take the small signposted road to the left.

Lamouroux Caves (Grottes de Lamouroux) – This picturesque group of caves arranged in five tiers was used by man in times of danger.

Noailles – Pop 648. Noailles, lying in a pleasant setting of green hills, is overlooked by its castle and church perched on a hill.
The **church** ⊘, topped by a Limousin style bell gable, has a Romanesque apse and chancel with realistic historiated capitals (cripples on crutches) on slender columns. In the pointed-vaulted nave are memorial plates of the De Noailles family. There is a painting by Watteau's teacher Claude Gillot (*Accessories of the Crucifixion*).
The Renaissance **château,** seat of the De Noailles family, is decorated with pinnacled windows, which have pediments ornamented with angels bearing the De Noailles coat of arms.

From Noailles, go west on the D 158.

The road climbs towards the lake and Corrèze Causse, an area of white limestone and with here and there a dip filled with red clay and covered with juniper bushes and stunted oak trees.

★ **Causse Lake** (Lac du Causse) – Also called Chasteaux Lake, this superb stretch of water (90ha – 222 acres), set in lush green countryside in the lovely Couze Valley, is a **leisure centre** ⊘ (swimming, sailing, water-skiing, windsurfing, sculling etc.).

The D 158 goes to Lissac-sur-Couze.

Lissac-sur-Couze – Pop 475. Set back from the lake, this elegant manor, flanked by battlemented turrets, was a military tower in the 13 and 14C. The church beside it has a bell gable.

Take the D 154 to Chartrier-Ferrière and Le Maillet.

Le Maillet – The limestone walls of the houses in this hamlet are constructed in a traditional way using "house martin" mortar, that is lumps of clay pressed into cracks. The vivid red of the clay gives a lot of character to the scene.

Nadaillac – Pop 285. This charming country village is famous for its high-quality truffles. Some of the medieval houses have roofs of *lauzes (qv)*. The fortified church is entered through a deepset doorway preceded by a vaulted passageway. The pre-chancel is covered by a dome on pendentives.

Take the D 63, then the D 60 to Larche. Join the N 89 to return to Brive-La-Gaillarde.

★ **BRUNIQUEL**   Pop 469

Michelin map 79 fold 19 or 235 fold 22 – Local map under ST-ANTONIN-NOBLE-VAL

Bruniquel, the bold outline of its castle set like a crown above the town, lies in a picturesque **setting★** at the mouth of the great gorges that the Aveyron has cut through the Limogne Causse (limestone plateau).
According to Gregory of Tours (bishop, theologian and historian, 538-594), Bruniquel originated from the founding of a fortress on this spot by **Brunhilda**. The memory of this princess, who was the daughter of the king of the Visigoths and the wife of Sigebert, king of Austrasia, is kept alive by the castle tower that bears her name.

Cruelties perpetrated on account of her rivalry with Fredegund, her sister-in-law, caused war between Austrasia and Neustria in the 6C. The death of the princess herself was so macabre that it has become famous: she was bound by her hair, an arm and a leg to the tail of an unbroken horse and smashed to pieces.

★Old Town – Bruniquel is a pleasant place for a stroll, with its fortifications, town gateways, old belfry and sloping alleys, with old houses roofed in round tiles. Rues de Mazel, Droite de Trauc and Droite de la Peyre are particularly pretty.

Castle ⊙ – The castle, built in lovely yellow stone on foundations dating, it is said, from the 6C, has parts still standing that were built from the 12 to 18C. The barbican, which defended the approaches to the castle from the village side, stands on the esplanade in front of the main building. The massive 12C square tower bears the name of Queen Brunhilda. Inside, the 12-13C Knight's Hall is decorated with small pillars and capitals.
There is a good view of the valley from a terrace near the chapel. Stairs lead to the first floor where a beautiful 17C chimneypiece with Baroque decoration may be seen in the Guard Room.
In the seigneurial part of the castle, a Renaissance gallery looks straight down over the cliff hollowed out with rock shelters, to give a wide **view★** of the river below.

Maison Payrol ⊙ – This town house belonged to the influential Payrol family. Building lasted from the 13C to the 17C. Upstairs, the impressive Renaissance ceiling is supported by relieving arches and carved brackets. Collections of regional objects on display include; cards, candlesticks, glassware and glazed earthenware.

EXCURSION

Montricoux – Pop 909. Facilities. *6km – 3.5 miles to the northwest.* Montricoux was built up on terraces above the right bank of the River Aveyron where it broadens out in a wide plain. The old curtain walls are still standing. Place Marcel-Lenoir and certain alleys contain picturesque half-timbered houses with medieval overhanging storeys (13-16C).

Marcel Lenoir Museum ⊙ – The château at Montricoux displays most of the work of the painter Marcel Lenoir, born in 1872 at Montauban, who became one of the great personalities of Montparnasse after the First World War, admired by Giacometti, Braque and Matisse. However, he espoused marginalisation, threw critics into utter confusion and refused to adhere to any one style. As a result, he did not achieve the same degree of fame as those who admired him and ended his days in obscurity at Montricoux. His original and powerful work deserves to be rediscovered.

LE BUGUE
Pop 2 764

Michelin map ⏸️ fold 16 or ⏸️ fold 1 – Local map under VÉZÈRE VALLEY – Facilities

This active commercial centre, where locally grown products are marketed, is situated at the gateway of the Périgord Noir *(qv)*, on the north bank of the Vézère, near its confluence with the Dordogne.

Périgord Noir Aquarium ⊙ – This has been designed to make visitors feel as if they are moving under water, like divers. The open-topped aquariums have natural lighting and open onto large windows. They contain fresh water fish, crustaceans and invertebrates from various parts of Europe. Of particularly impressive dimensions are the gleaning catfish, originating from the centre and east of the continent (some of the larger specimens are over 1.5m- 5ft long), white and silver grass carp and sturgeons. There is a separate display on the breeding cycle of the salmon.

Fossil Site (Le Gîte à fossiles) ⊙ – The palaeontology collection of about 3 000 exhibits comes, for the most part, from deposits in the region.

Bara-Bahau Cave (Caverne de Bara-Bahau) ⊙ – The cave, which is about 100m- 300ft long, ends in a chamber blocked by a rock fall. On the roof of the chamber, amid the protrusions in the rock face, may be seen drawings made with sharpened flints and fingers (Magdalenian Culture) and by scratching with bears' claws (Mousterian Culture). The finger drawings were discovered in 1951 by the Casterets and depict horses, aurochs, bison, bears and deer.

EXCURSION

★Proumeyssac Chasm (Gouffre de Proumeyssac) ⊙ – *3km – 2 miles to the south.* A tunnel drilled into a hill, overlooking the Vézère, leads to a platform built half-way up the chasm. This platform offers a view of this underground dome which is decorated, particularly at the base of the walls, with fine yellow and white concretions. Water seeps through abundantly, adding to the stalactites which, in some places, are very numerous and form draperies, pure coloured stalagmites and fantastic shapes such as the eccentrics and triangular crystallisations that are building up from the floor of the caves. Various objects subjected to encrustation with lime which lie scattered over the floor of the cave do not really fit in with the splendid natural décor.
The minute basket suspended in mid-air was until 1952 the only way of getting into the chasm. The 52m- 171ft descent in complete darkness at the mercy of the fluctuations in temperament of the mule which was working the winch must have been an unforgettable experience for the three tourists allowed down each time with their guide. In the little museum by the entrance, a display of photographs records this pioneering phase of visiting the chasm.
The use of construction materials which contrasted in tone, ranging from yellow to purple-red, gives a very attractive, patchwork appearance to the church of **Audrix** and some of the farms surrounding it.

Michelin map **75** fold 16 or **235** fold 5 – Local map under DORDOGNE VALLEY **3**

The Abbey of Cadouin, founded in a narrow valley near the Bessède Forest in 1115 by Robert d'Arbrissel, was taken over soon after by the Cistercians and was extremely prosperous during the Middle Ages.

The church and cloisters, restored after the Revolution, constitute an interesting architectural group around which has grown a small village, with an old covered market.

On 14 October 1890, the cinematographer Louis Delluc, founder of film criticism and cinema clubs, was born here in a house on the market square.

The Holy Shroud of Cadouin – The first written mention of the Holy Shroud appeared in 1214 in an act decreed by Simon de Montfort. This linen cloth adorned with bands of embroidery had been brought from Antioch by a priest from Périgord and was believed to be the cloth that had been wrapped around Christ's head.

The shroud became an object of deep veneration and attracted large pilgrimages, bringing great renown to Cadouin. It is said that Richard the Lionheart, St Louis and Charles V came to kneel before it in reverence. Charles VII had it brought to Paris and Louis XI to Poitiers. When the abbey was threatened by the English during the Hundred Years War – the Romanesque cloisters and many of the outbuildings were destroyed – the Holy Shroud was first entrusted to the care of the monks at Toulouse and then later to those at Aubazine. It was only returned to Cadouin, at the end of the 15C, after endless lawsuits and the intervention of the Pope and Louis XI. Restoration was undertaken and new buildings were built, but they in turn were damaged during the Wars of Religion.

Tradition vs. science – In 1934, two experts attributed the Holy Shroud of Cadouin to the 11C, as the embroidered bands bore kufic inscriptions citing an emir and a caliph who had ruled in Egypt in 1094 and 1101. The bishop of Périgueux therefore had the pilgrimage to Cadouin discontinued.

In 1982 two researchers from the C.N.R.S. went over the study from the beginning and added further details to the 1934 conclusions: only the embroidered bands, characteristic of the art work produced during the Fatimid dynasty, date from the late 11C; after all, it was quite unlikely that an Egyptian craftsman in the late 11C would have embroidered a cloth that was said to have been wrapped around Christ's head 1 000 years before.

★Church (Église) – The building, completed in 1154, presents a massive, powerful west front divided horizontally into three sections, where the influence of the Saintonge style is evident: the middle section, opened by three round-arched windows which light the church's interior, divides upper and lower arcaded sections. Tall buttresses running vertically cut the façade into three, showing precisely the church's interior plan: one nave with side aisles.

This austere architectural plan, where decoration is limited virtually to the play of light on the stone, emphassies the ornamental effect brought about by the gold colour of the Molières stone.

The finely proportioned building broke away from Cistercian architecture with its interior plan: a chancel with an apse between two apsidal chapels, a dome at the transept crossing capped by a pyramidal belltower roofed with chestnut shingles, and a more elaborate interior decoration (windows surrounded by mouldings, capitals with foliage and stylised animals and, in the two arms of the transept, elegant capitals decorated with interlacing and palm fronds). Nonetheless, the harmonious proportions and the grandeur of the construction emanate a spirituality entirely in keeping with Cistercian sanctuaries.

★★Cloisters (Cloître) ⊙ – Thanks to the generosity of Louis XI, the cloisters were built at the end of the 15C in the Flamboyant Gothic style. The work, in fact, continued to the middle of the 16C, as the Renaissance capitals of some of the columns bear witness. Despite the damage suffered during the Wars of Religion and the Revolution, the cloisters were saved and restored in the 19C, owing to the enthusiastic attention they were given by historians and archaeologists alike.

At each corner there is a fine door; the royal door is adorned with the arms of France and Brittany as both Charles VIII and Louis XII had been married to Anne of Brittany, the benefactress of Cadouin. The pendants are carved into people and lively little scenes. In the north gallery, facing the reader's lectern, the abbot's throne can be seen emblazoned with the abbey arms: the many scenes illustrated in low relief on either side end in a large fresco of the Annunciation. Four small columns cast in the form of towers are decorated with themes from the Old and New Testaments (Samson and Delilah, Job, etc).

Cloisters

The chapter-house and two other rooms have been set up as a **Shroud Museum** (Musée du Suaire) ⊘, where the restored relic is on display, forming the centrepiece of an exhibition to mark the eight centuries of pilgrimage and religious fervour that it provoked.

Bicycle Museum (Musée du Vélocipède) ⊘ – This is the most significant of its type in France. It occupies an outbuilding of the convent with a display of about one hundred models. Huge pennyfarthings, other old bicycles and tricycles represent the finest hours of technology and inventions in this field since the middle of the 19C. There are the pedals invented by the Michaux brothers, brake rod systems, the chainless bicycle produced by the Acatène company, the first tyres with inner tubes and the "hammock saddle". The beginnings of competitive cycling are represented by the model from the Paris-Brest return race of 1891 and a bicycle from the first ever Tour de France in 1903. The British postie's quadricycle bears witness to the long-standing relationship between the bicycle and the postal service. The two World Wars are also recorded by the folding "Gérard" bicycle used by French soldiers in the First World War and the towing tricycle that came to symbolize the exodus of 1940.

EXCURSION

Molières – Pop 315. This unfinished English *bastide (qv)* has a Gothic church with a façade flanked by a tall two-storey square defensive tower.

If you are puzzled by an abbreviation
or a symbol in the text or on the maps, look at the key.

★★ CAHORS

Michelin map **79** fold 8 or **235** fold 14 – Local maps under GRAMAT CAUSSE and LOT VALLEY – Facilities

Cahors, enclosed by a meander in the Lot River and overlooked by rocky hills, was a flourishing commercial and university city in the Middle Ages and still retains precious vestiges of its past. The city, which for centuries occupied only the eastern section of the peninsula, has slowly spread to cover the entire tongue of land and has now reached the neighbouring hills. **Boulevard Gambetta (BYZ)**, a typical southern town promenade lined with plane trees, cafés and shops, is the great north-south thoroughfare of the city; its busy, bustling atmosphere reflects the fact that Cahors is an important commercial centre. As *Préfecture* of the Lot *département,* the city has expanded its administrative and public services, which employ many local residents. As a tourist centre, the former capital of Quercy is an excellent starting point for tours of the Célé and Lot Valleys.

The sacred spring – A spring, discovered by Carthusian monks, led to the founding of Divona Cadurcorum, later known as Cadurca and later still as Cahors. First the Gauls and then the Romans worshipped the spring with a devotion which was confirmed by the discovery in 1991 of about a thousand coins dating from the beginning of Christianity, which had been thrown into the fountain as offerings. The town grew rapidly in size: a forum, a theatre, temples, baths and ramparts were built. This spring still supplies the town with drinking water.

The golden age – In the 13C Cahors became one of the great towns of France and experienced considerable economic prosperity due in no small part to the arrival of Lombard merchants and bankers. The Lombards were brilliant businessmen and bankers, but also operated somewhat less reputedly as usurers.
The Templars, in turn, came to Cahors; gold fever spread to the townspeople and Cahors became the leading banking city of Europe. Money was lent to the Pope and to kings, and Cahors counting houses were internationally widespread. The word *cahorsin*, which was what the people of Cahors were called, became synonymous with the word usurer.

The loyal city and the ungrateful king – At the beginning of the Hundred Years War, the English seized all the towns in Quercy. Cahors alone remained impregnable, in spite of the Black Death which killed half the population.
In 1360, under the *Treaty of Brétigny (qv),* Cahors was ceded to the English, but the town, still unbeaten, refused to be handed over. The king of France then ordered the keys of the city to be delivered up despite the consuls' protests: "It is not we who are abandoning the king, but the king who is abandoning us to a foreign master." By 1450, when the English left Quercy, Cahors was a ruined city.

Cahors and the Reformation – After several decades of peace, Cahors was able to regain some of its past prosperity; unfortunately in 1540 the Reformation reached the city and rapidly caused dissension among the population. In 1560 the Protestants were massacred. Twenty years later the town was besieged by the Huguenots, led by Henri de Navarre. The assault lasted three days and ended in the ransacking of the city.

Gambetta's childhood – Léon Gambetta has a special place among the famous men of Cahors, who included Pope John XXII (1316-34), founder of the successful university in Cahors in 1332 (which was combined with that of Toulouse in the 18C), and the poets Clément Marot (1496-1544) and Olivier de Magny (1529-61) *(qv).*
Born the son of a grocer in 1838 – his father was of Genoese extraction and his mother the daughter of a chemist from Molières – young Gambetta played truant from school, dreamed of wild adventures and hoped to sail the seven seas.

However, after a short spell at boarding school, he suddenly developed a passion for learning, reading and translating Greek and Latin on sight and winning prizes.

One day the young student went to watch a case at the Assize Court and became fascinated with the drama of the courtroom: the die had been cast, Gambetta gave up all ideas of going to sea to become a barrister.

In 1856 Gambetta left Cahors for Paris to enrol in the Faculty of Law. His outstanding career as a lawyer and statesman had begun. This ardent patriot, member of the Legislative Assembly, played an active part in the downfall of Napoleon III, in the proclamation of the Third Republic on 4 September 1870, and in the forming of a provisional government (he became Minister of the Interior).

Gambetta escaped from Paris, under enemy siege, in a balloon in October 1870, floating over the German lines and landing in Tours where he was able (in his capacity as War Minister) to organise the country's defence against the Prussian Army; an armistice was signed in 1871.

He became head of the Republican Union, then President of the Chamber of Deputies in 1879 and Prime Minister from November 1881 until January 1882. He died at the age of 44 on December 31, 1882.

There is scarcely a town or city in France which has not paid homage to this republican statesman by naming a street or square after him.

★★ VALENTRÉ BRIDGE (PONT VALENTRÉ) (AZ) ⊘ *time: 30 min*

The Valentré Bridge is a remarkable example of French medieval military architecture. The three towers, with machicolations and crenellated parapets, and the pointed cutwaters breaking the line of the seven pointed arches, give it a bold and proud appearance.

The best view of the Valentré Bridge and its towers, which rise 40m – 130ft above the river, is from a little way upstream on the north bank of the Lot.

A legend in which the Devil plays an important part, although he loses in the end, is linked to the construction work which began in 1308 and went on for more than fifty years. The architect was in despair at the slow progress of the bridge and agreed to sign a pact by which the Devil would bring all the materials necessary to the site and the architect, in his turn, would hand over his soul on successful execution of all his requests. The bridge grew quickly and work neared completion. The architect did not relish the idea of eternal torment, however, and had the brainwave of asking the Devil to bring him water in a sieve. After a few vain attempts the Devil confessed himself beaten but, in revenge, he broke off the topmost stone of the central tower, which has been known ever since as Devil's Tower. Every time the stone was replaced, it fell off. When the bridge was restored last century, the architect had the stone firmly fixed and on the corner he had carved the little figure of a devil trying to dislodge it.

The original appearance of Valentré Bridge was considerably modified in 1879 when the bridge was restored; the barbican, which reinforced the defences from the town side, was replaced by the present-day gate.

The bridge was originally an isolated fortress commanding the river; the central tower served as an observation post, the outer towers were closed by gates and portcullises. A guard house and outwork on the south bank of the Lot provided additional protection. The fortress defied the English during the Hundred Years War, and Henri de Navarre at the time of the siege of Cahors (1580); it has never even been attacked.

A restored **millboat** ⊘ has been moored near the bridge. From its position in the very middle of the river, it used the force of the current to drive a millwheel in its keel to crush the grain. Boats like this used to provoke arguments with sailors of other boats, as they impeded navigation; one such small craft was once deliberately capsized by a larger vessel in the middle of the night.

Valentré Bridge

★ST STEPHEN'S CATHEDRAL AND ITS PRECINCTS

time: 1 hour

★**St Stephen's Cathedral** (Cathédrale St-Etienne) (BY) – The clergy built this church as a fortress to provide a place of safety in troubled times, as well as to bolster prestige. At the end of the 11C, Bishop Géraud of Cardaillac began to build a church on the site of a former 6C church. Much of Bishop Géraud's church remains standing to this day. The trefoiled south door dates from 1119. The north door is 12C, the restoration work on the original east end dates from the 13C. The west front was built early in the 14C, and the paintings inside the domes and in the chancel were completed at the same time. The Flamboyant-style cloisters and some of the outbuildings were commissioned at the beginning of the 16C by Bishop Antoine de Luzech.

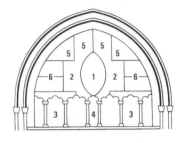

Exterior – The west front is made of three adjoining towers. The central one has a belfry above it and opens with double doors. On the first floor, the rose window is surrounded by blind arcades. In spite of windows with twin bays completing the decoration, the appearance of the façade remains austere and military.

★★**North Door** (Portail Nord) – This Romanesque door was once part of the west front; it was transferred to the north side of the cathedral before the present façade was built. The **tympanum** depicts the Ascension. It was carved in about 1135 and from its style and technique belongs to the Languedoc School.

A mandorla (almond-shaped glory) is the centrepiece of the composition; the haloed figure of Christ (**1**) stands with the right hand upraised and the left clasping a closed book. On either side an angel (**2**) explains the miracle to the Apostles who are seen below in the trefoiled blind arcades (**3**); beneath the central arch is the Virgin Mary (**4**) raising her hand to point to her Son. Above Christ, four cherubim (**5**) fly out from the clouds to greet Him and take His halo. On either side of Christ and the angels the sculptor has depicted scenes from the life of St Stephen (**6**): his sermon, his arrest by the Jews, his stoning, and the vision of the hand of God appearing in the sky to protect the martyr.

The cathedral apse, with its two balustrades on the upper register, gives an overwhelming impression of power without interfering with the building's overall harmony.

Interior – Enter by the west door and cross the narthex which is slightly raised; the nave is roofed with two huge domes on pendentives. There is a striking contrast between the nave, in pale-coloured stone, and the chancel, adorned with stained glass and paintings. The frescoes of the first dome were uncovered in 1872; these show the stoning of St Stephen in the central medallion, the saint's executioners around the frieze and eight giant-sized figures of prophets in the niches.

The chancel and the apse have Gothic vaulting. Among the radiating chapels, which were added in the 15C, is the Chapel of St Antony, which opens onto the chancel through a beautiful Flamboyant door.

★**Cloisters** (Cloître) (BY E) – Dating from 1509, these Renaissance cloisters were built after those of Carennac (*qv*) and Cadouin (*qv*), with which they have a number of stylistic similarities. Access to the cloisters is through a door on the right of the chancel. They are still rich in carved ornamentation in spite of considerable damage. The galleries are roofed with stellar vaulting; of the decorated pendants, only one remains above the northwest door, showing Jesus surrounded by angels. The jambs are decorated with niches which used to contain statues. Near the chancel door is a spiral staircase, and on the northwest corner pillar a graceful carving of the Virgin of the Annunciation, wrapped in a fine cloak, her hair falling to her shoulders.

In the **Chapelle St-Gausbert** ⊙ a fresco of the Last Judgment and 16C paintings on the ceiling have been discovered.

The chapel also contains ecclesiastical objects: church vestments, statues and portraits of 93 Bishops of Cahors from the 3 to the 19C.

Enter the inner court of the former arch-deaconry of St John through the door in the northeast corner of the cloisters. Note the lovely Renaissance decoration.

Pass in front of the covered market and take Rue Nationale.

Rue Nationale (BZ) – This was the main thoroughfare of the active Badernes Quarter. At no 16, the panels of a lovely 17C **door** are decorated with fruit and foliage.

Across the way, the narrow Rue St-Priest (BZ 28) has kept its medieval appearance.

Rue du Docteur-Bergounioux (BZ 13) – At no 40 a 16C town-house has an interesting Renaissance façade opened by windows influenced by the Italian Renaissance style.

Turn around, walk back and cross Rue Nationale.

Rue Lastié (BZ 20) – At no 35 note the Rayonnant-style windows.

On Place St-Priest a wooden staircase (Louis XIII style) can be seen; it served two buildings. At no 117, a 16C house has kept its small shop on the ground floor above which are twin bays on the first floor.

At no 156 half-timbered brick houses have been restored.

Rue St-Urcisse (BZ 30) – The late 12C St-Urcisse Church is entered through a 14C doorway. Inside, the two chancel pillars are decorated with elegant historiated capitals.

In this street there are several half-timbered houses with *soleilhos,* open attics, in which laundry was hung out to dry *(see Figeac).*

Roaldès Mansion (Maison de Roaldès) **(BY L)** ⊙ – The mansion is also known as Henri IV's Mansion because it is said that the king of Navarre stayed there during the siege of Cahors in 1580.

The house dates from the end of the 15C and was restored in 1912. In the 17C it became the property of the Roaldès, a well-known Quercy family.

The half-timbered south side is surmounted by a balcony and topped by a massive round tower.

The north side, overlooking the square, has mullioned doors and windows and different ornamental motifs – Quercy roses, flaming suns, lopped off trees – used by the Quercy School of the early 16C.

Inside, a spiral staircase gives access to the rooms, which are furnished with interesting pieces of furniture and, more especially, lovely carved chimneys where the decorative motifs – Quercy rose, lopped tree – of the Quercy School have been used.

Go along Quai Champollion to the Cabessut Bridge.

Cabessut Bridge (**Pont Cabessut**) **(BY)** – From the bridge there is a good **view★** of the upper part of the city, the Soubirous district. The towers bristling in the distance are: Tower of the Hanged Men or St John's Tower, the belltower of St-Bartholomew's, John XXII's Tower, Royal Castle Tower and the Pélegry College Tower.

Pélegry College Tower (**Tour du Collège Pélegry**) **(BY S)** – The College was founded in 1368 and at first took in thirteen poor university students; until the 18C, it was one of the town's most important establishments. The fine hexagonal tower above the main building was constructed in the 15C.

Royal Castle Tower (**Tour du Château du Roi**) **(BY)** – Near Pélegry College stands what is today the prison and was once the governor's residence. Of the two towers and two main buildings erected in the 14C, there remains the massive tower called the Royal Castle tower.

Ilôt Fouillac **(BY)** – This area, which used to be rather insalubrious, has undergone an extensive programme of redevelopment. By getting rid of the most run-down buildings, a square has been cleared. Its sides are decorated with **murals**, and it is endowed with the particularly interesting feature of a **musical fountain** to brighten it up. This is a real "aquatic-musical instrument", on which passers-by can produce their own sounds while at the same time controlling the pressure of the water jets.

La Daurade **(BY)** – This varied set of old residences around the Olivier-de-Magny square includes the Dolive house (17C), the Heretié house (14C to 16C) and the so-called Hangman's House (Maison du Bourreau), with windows decorated with small columns (13C).

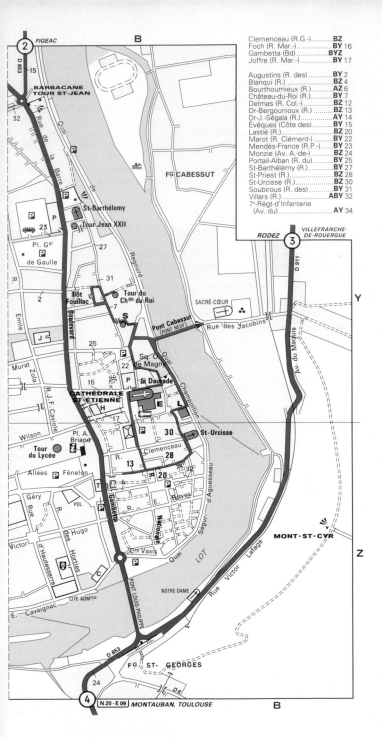

ADDITIONAL SIGHTS

★Barbican and St John's Tower (Barbacane et Tour St-Jean) (**BY**) – The ramparts, constructed in the 14C, completely cut the isthmus formed by the meander of the Lot River off from the surrounding countryside. Remains of these fortifications can still be seen and include a massive tower at the west end, which sheltered the powder magazine, and the old gateway of St-Michel, which now serves as entrance to the cemetery. It is on the east side, however, where the N 20 enters the town, that the two most impressive fortified buildings remain: the barbican and St John's Tower. The barbican is an elegant guard house which defended the Barre Gateway; St John's Tower or the Tower of the Hanged Men (Tour des Pendus), was built on a rock overlooking the Lot River.

St Bartholomew's Church (Église St-Barthélémy) (**BY**) ⊘ – This church was built in the highest part of the old town, and was known until the 13C as St-Etienne de Soubiroux, "*Sancti Stephani de superioribus*" (St Stephen of the Upper Quarter), in contrast to the cathedral built in the lower part of the town. The church was rebuilt to its present design in several stages. It now contains a rectangular belfry-porch with three lines of bays of depressed arches one above the other. The belfry, the base of which dates from the 14C, has no spire, and it is built almost entirely of brick.

The nave, with its ogive vaulting, was designed in the Languedoc style. In the chapel nearest the entrance, on the left, a marble slab and bust call to mind that John XXII was baptised in this church.

The *cloisonné* enamels on the cover of the modern baptismal font depict the main events in the life of this famous Cahors citizen.

The terrace near the church affords a good view of the Cabessut suburb and the Lot Valley.

John XXII's Tower (Tour de Jean XXII) (BY) – This tower is all that remains of the palace of Pierre Duèze, brother of John XXII. It is 34m – 112ft high and was originally covered in tiles. Twin windows pierce the walls on five storeys.

Lycée Tower (Tour du Lycée) (BZ) – From the Lycée Gambetta building, which was once a Jesuit college, rises a graceful 17C octagonal tower built of rose-coloured brick.

EXCURSIONS

★**Mount St-Cyr Viewpoint** (Point de vue du Mont-St-Cyr) (BZ) – *7km – 4 miles via the Louis-Philippe Bridge south of the plan and the D 6 which you leave after 1.5km – 1 mile to reach the mount, keeping to the left.* From the top *(viewing table)* there is a good **view★** of Cahors; the contrast between the old and the new quarters of the town, which are separated by the Boulevard Gambetta, Cahors' main artery, is striking. In the background the distinctive shape of Valentré Bridge can be seen.

Château de Cieurac ⊘ – *12km – 7.5 miles south on the D 6.*
This castle was built in the 16C. Its seigneurial mill and dovecot are still standing.

★**Croix de Magne Viewpoint** (Point de vue de la Croix de Magne) – *5km – 3 miles. At the exit west of Valentré Bridge, turn right and immediately left; just after the agricultural school (école d'agriculture) turn left, and left again at the top.* From near the cross the **view★** encompasses the *causse,* the Lot meander, Cahors and Valentré Bridge.

★**Viewpoint north of Cahors** – *5km – 3 miles. Take Rue du Dr. J.-Ségala* (AY 14) *which branches off the N 20 to the right just after St John's Tower.*
This pleasant road runs along the tops of the hills and affords good views of the Lot Valley, and Cahors in its setting. The old town appears to be stepped like an amphitheatre, bristling with belfries and battlemented towers and lines of fortifications and bridges, the most distinctive of these being Valentré Bridge.

Roussillon Castle ⊘ – *9km – 5 miles north on the N 20.*
The massive round towers of this medieval fortress owned by the Gontaut-Biron family can be seen rising from the bottom of the valley.

CAPDENAC
Pop 932

Michelin map **79** fold 10 or **235** fold 11 – Local map under LOT VALLEY: Cliffs and Promontories

Capdenac-le-Haut, perched on a promontory and enclosed by a meander in the Lot River, occupies a remarkable **site★**. This small town, which still looks much the way it did centuries ago, overlooks Capdenac-Gare, a busy railway junction which has developed in the valley.

Uxellodunum – Some historians claim Capdenac-le-Haut to be the site of the stronghold of Uxellodunum, the last site of Gaulish resistance to Caesar (the majority claims it to be at Puy d'Issolud *(qv)*, near Martel). Important excavations, especially those in 1815 headed by the Champollion *(qv)* brothers (including the famous Egyptologist), uncovered the necessary data which proved that the stronghold was a Gallo-Roman town.

The besieged town – When was Capdenac not under siege? It was besieged at least eleven times! There are two reasons for this: it played a major role during the Middle Ages, and it held a key position in Quercy.

In the beginning of the 8C, King Pepin the Short seized a fortress built on this site. Later, at the time of the Albigensian Crusade, Simon de Montfort *(qv)* occupied Capdenac in 1209 and in 1214. During the Hundred Years War, the English besieged the town, settled in it and were then ousted by the future King Louis XI. At the beginning of the 16C, Galiot de Genouillac *(qv)*, Grand Master of the Artillery under François I, took over the castle. During the Wars of Religion it became one of the main Protestant strongholds. After the death of Henri IV, Sully came to live in it and stayed for some time.

Ramparts (Remparts) – These are vestiges of the 13C and 14C outer walls and the citadel as well as the Northern Gate (Comtale), the village entrance, and the Southern Gate (Vijane).

Keep (Donjon) – This powerful square tower, flanked by battlemented watch turrets (13-14C) houses the tourist information centre and a small **museum** ⊘ which recounts Capdenac's history.

From the square, overlooked by the keep, Rue de la Peyrolie and Rue de la Commanderie lead off; along both streets there are half-timbered houses with overhanging storeys and pointed arches.

Fountain of a Hundred Steps (Fontaine des cents marches) ⊘ – Also known as the English Fountain. The steep staircase of 135 steps carved into the cliff face above Capdenac-Gare leads to two pools set in a cave. Champollion, inspired by the site, wrote that it seemed like the revered spot of an oracle, where one goes to seek one's destiny.

Caesar's Fountain (Fontaine de César) – Also known as the Roman Fountain, this Gallo-Roman fountain is to be found next to the north road into the village, along with another even older spring now run dry, which is thought to have been dried up by Caesar *(see Martel: Excursion).*

Viewpoints – Around the promontory there are several viewpoints. From a terrace near the church, the **view★** extends as for as the loop in the Lot River and its valley, a patchwork of cultivated fields. On the eastern side a terrace looks down onto Capdenac-Gare.

★ CARENNAC   Pop 370

Michelin map **75** fold 19 or **239** northeast of fold 38 – Local map under DORDOGNE VALLEY **1** – Facilities

One of the most attractive sights to be found along the Dordogne is the village of Carennac, where the picturesque houses of the Quercy, with their brown tile roofs, and the manor-houses, flanked with turrets, cluster round the old priory in which Fénelon once lived.

Fénelon at Carennac – The priory-deanery at Carennac, which was founded in the 10C and attached to the famous abbey at Cluny in the following century, owes its fame to the length of time spent there by François de Salignac de la Mothe-Fénelon before he became Archbishop of Cambrai.

While he was still a student at Cahors, Fénelon used to enjoy spending his holidays at the house of his uncle, senior prior of Carennac. In 1681 Fénelon's uncle died and was succeeded by the young abbot, who remained at the priory for fifteen years. Fénelon was greatly revered at Carennac; he enjoyed describing the ceremonies and general rejoicing that greeted his arrival by boat and his installation as commendatory prior.

Tradition has it that Fénelon wrote *Télémaque* while living at Carennac. The description of the adventures of Ulysses' son was at first only a literary exercise, but was subsequently turned into a tract for the edification of the Duke of Burgundy, Louis XIV's grandson, when Fénelon was appointed his tutor.

The Ile Barrade, in the Dordogne, was renamed Calypso's Island, and visitors will still be shown a tower in the village which is called Telemachus's Tower in which, it is maintained, Fénelon wrote his masterpiece.

THE VILLAGE *time: 30 min*

This charming village, where some of the houses date from the 16C, has barely changed since Fénelon's day, although the deanery and its outbuildings suffered considerable damage at the time of the Revolution. The deanery was suppressed by order of the Royal Council in 1788, and put up for auction and sold in 1791.

Of the old ramparts there remains only a fortified gateway, and of the buildings, only the castle and the priory tower are left. Go through the fortified gateway.

Church (Église St-Pierre) – In front of this Romanesque church, which is dedicated to St Peter, stands a porch with a beautiful 12C carved **doorway★**. It is well preserved and from its style would appear to belong to the same school as the tympana of Beaulieu, Moissac, Collonges and Cahors. In a mandorla (almond-shaped glory) in the centre of the composition *(photograph p 29)*, is Christ in Majesty. His right hand is raised in blessing. He is surrounded by the symbols of the four Evangelists. On either side are the Apostles on two superimposed registers, and there are two prostrate angels on the upper register. The tympanum is framed with a foliated scroll in the Oriental style. Its base is decorated with a frieze of small animals. The continuation of the animals was pursued on a protruding band which doubled the doorway arch, of which a dog and bear can still be seen on the left.

Inside, the interesting archaic capitals in the nave are decorated with fantastic animals, foliage and historiated scenes.

Cloisters (Cloître) ⊘ – The restored cloisters consist of a Romanesque gallery adjoining the church and three Flamboyant galleries. Stairs lead to the terrace.

The chapter-house, which opens onto the cloisters, shelters a remarkable **Entombment★** (15C). Christ lies on a shroud carried by two disciples: Joseph of Arimathaea and Nicodemus. Behind these figures, two holy women accompany the Virgin and the Apostle John; on the right, Mary Magdalene is wiping away a tear. The faces seem quite rustic in character.

★★ CASTELNAU-BRETENOUX CASTLE

Michelin map **75** fold 19 or **239** fold 39 – Local maps under DORDOGNE VALLEY **1** and ST-CÉRÉ: Excursions

On the northern border of Quercy stands Castelnau-Bretenoux Castle with the village of Prudhomat tucked beneath it. The great mass of the castle's red stone ramparts and the towers rise up from a spur overlooking the confluence of the Cère and the Dordogne. The scale on which the castle defence system was built makes it one of the finest examples of medieval military architecture.

For more than three miles round, the castle, as Pierre Loti (Julien Viaud 1850-1923) wrote, "is the beacon... the thing you cannot help looking at all the time from wherever you are. It's a cock's comb of blood-red stone rising from a tangle of trees, this ruin poised like a crown on a pedestal dressed with a beautiful greenery of chestnut and oak trees".

Turenne's egg – From the 11C onwards the barons of Castelnau were the strongest in Quercy; they paid homage only to the counts of Toulouse and proudly styled themselves the Second Barons of Christendom. In 1184 Raymond de Toulouse gave the suzerainty of Castelnau to the viscount of Turenne. The baron of Castelnau refused to accept the insult and paid homage instead to Philip Augustus, King of France. Bitter warfare broke out between Turenne and Castelnau; King Louis VIII intervened and decided in favour of Turenne. Whether he liked it or not the baron had to accept the verdict. The fief, however, was only symbolic: Castelnau had to present his overlord with... an egg. Every year, with great pomp and ceremony a yoke of four oxen bore a freshly laid egg to Turenne.

Castle ⊘ – Round the strong keep built in the 13C, there grew up during the Hundred Years War a huge fortress with a fortified curtain wall. The castle was abandoned in the 18C and suffered depredations at the time of Revolution. It caught fire in 1851 but was skilfully restored between 1896 and 1932.

The ground plan is that of an irregular triangle flanked by three round towers and by three other towers partially projecting from each side. Three parallel curtain walls still defend the approaches, but the former ramparts have been replaced by an avenue of trees.

From along the ramparts there is a far-reaching **view**★ of the Cère and Dordogne Valleys to the north; of Turenne Castle set against the horizon to the northwest; of the Montvalent Amphitheatre to the west; and of Loubressac Castle and the Autoire Valley to the southwest and south.

A tall square tower and the seigneurial residence, a rectangular building still known as the *auditoire* (auditorium), are to be found in the main courtyard, giving one an idea of the vast scale of this fortress, the garrison of which numbered 1 500 men and 100 horses.

Interior – In addition to the lapidary depositary, containing the Romanesque capitals of Ste-Croix-du-Mont in Gironde, many other rooms should be visited on account of their decoration and furnishings done by the former proprietor, a singer of comic opera, Jean Moulierat, who bought the castle in 1896. The former Chamber of the Quercy Estates General is lit by large windows; the pewter hall and the Grand Salon contain Aubusson and Beauvais tapestries; the oratory has stained-glass windows dating from the 15C and two 15C Spanish altarpieces.

St Louis' Collegiate Church (**Collégiale St-Louis**) ⊘ – The collegiate church was built by the lords of Castelnau in red ferruginous stone, at the foot of the castle. A few canons' residences can be seen nearby.

Enter the church. The lords' chapel has lovely quadripartite vaulting, the pendant of which is emblazoned with the Castelnau coat of arms. The furnishings include 15C stalls, a 17C retable and 18C altars; one of which is surmounted by a multicoloured wood Virgin with bird (15C), quite naïve in style. The chancel houses two 15C works of art in polychrome stone; a Virgin in Majesty and a depiction of the Baptism of Christ.

★ CASTELNAUD CASTLE

Michelin map **75** fold 17 or **235** fold 6 – Local map under DORDOGNE VALLEY **3**

The impressive ruins of Castelnaud Castle stand on a wonderful **site**★★ commanding the valleys of the Céou and the Dordogne. Right opposite stands Beynac Castle *(qv)*, Castelnaud's implacable rival throughout the conflicts of the Middle Ages.

An eventful history – In 1214 Simon de Montfort (*c*1165-1218, father of the English statesman and soldier) took possession of the castle, whose occupants had taken the side of the Cathars. In 1259 Saint Louis ceded the castle to the king of England who held it for several years.

Castelnaud Castle with Beynac Castle in the background

During the Hundred Years War the castle constantly changed hands between the French and the English. When at last peace was declared the castle was in terrible condition. During the whole of the second half of the 15C the castle was under reconstruction. Only the keep and curtain wall have kept their 13C appearance. In the 16C the castle was once again transformed in various ways, and the artillery tower was added.

After the Revolution it was abandoned and later used as a stone-pit.

In 1969 a major restoration program was undertaken which has enabled most of the buildings to be rebuilt.

Castle ⊙ – The castle is a typical example of a medieval fortress with its powerful machicolated keep, curtain wall, living quarters and inner bailey. Nonetheless, certain parts of the castle – artillery tower, loopholes – which were added later reflect the evolution of weapons in siege warfare. In the artillery tower, reconstructed scenes demonstrate artillerymen in action. Primitive cannon, stone balls, and a number of other weapons complete the display. The main part of the building contains the Middle Ages Siege Warfare Museum.

There are two audio-visual presentations: one explains the history of the castle and the other a history of fortifications and siege warfare tactics in the Middle Ages.

The barbican, the bailey and the reconstruction of siege apparatus, including a 12C mangonel, or ballista, and other stone-casting devices and a 15C mortar are in the castle grounds.

From the ward the view extends southwards over the Céou Valley. From the east end of the terrace there is an exceptional **panorama**★★★ of one of the most lovely views of the Dordogne Valley: in the foreground the patchwork of fields with screens of poplars encircled by a wide loop in the river; further off Beynac with its castle, Marqueyssac Castle and, at the foot of the cliffs, La Roque-Gageac and in the far distance a line of wooded and rocky hills skirting the Dordogne Valley.

CASTELNAU-MONTRATIER
Pop 1 820

Michelin map **79** folds 17 and 18 or **235** fold 18

This hilltop *bastide (qv)* was founded in the 13C by Ratier, lord of Castelnau, who gave it his name. It replaced a small village, Castelnau-de-Vaux, built at the foot of the hill, which was destroyed by Simon de Montfort *(qv)* in 1214 at the time of the Albigensian Crusade.

Square (Place) – Triangular in shape, this shaded square still contains some covered arcades and old houses.

Windmills (Moulins) – North of the promontory stand three windmills, one of which is still in working order.

In the past tower mills with rotating caps like these were widespread throughout Quercy.

CAUSSADE
Pop 6 009

Michelin map **79** fold 18 or **235** fold 18 – Facilities

Caussade, at the southern edge of the Limogne Causse, was a Protestant stronghold during the Wars of Religion.

At the beginning of the 20C, it was a centre of the straw-hat making industry, but fashions change, and today the factories turn out canvas hats and miscellaneous items for seaside resorts.

Church (Église) – The original octagonal church belfry, built in rose-coloured bricks, can still be seen in all its elegance, its three storeys topped by a crocketed spire. The remainder of the building was rebuilt in 1882 in the Gothic style.

There are some old houses in the older part of the town near the church.

EXCURSIONS

Chapel (Chapelle Notre-Dame-des-Misères) – *13km – 8 miles to the southwest on the N 20 and at Réalville turning right on the D 40.*
The pleasantly situated chapel was founded in 1150 and is crowned by an octagonal Romanesque belfry, two storeys high with double arcades.

Puylaroque – Pop 580. *14km – 8.5 miles to the northeast on the D 17.*
Puylaroque was once a *bastide* of Lower Quercy; its flat-roofed houses are grouped on the top of a hill overlooking the valleys of the Cande and the Lère. A few corbelled houses with half-timbered walls can still be seen in the narrow streets near the church, which has a massive square belfry adjoining the main doorway. There are views far over the rolling Quercy countryside and the plains of Caussade and Montauban from several of the town's esplanades, especially from the one near the church.

Saintonge Romanesque style architecture is characterised by a west front featuring one or more tiers of blind arcades around an ornately sculpted central doorway.

CAYLUS

This little village of Lower Quercy is set in a picturesque spot above the right bank of the Bonnette, a tributary of the Aveyron. The best view of the old town, closely grouped round the church with its tall belltower and overlooked by the ruins of the 14C fortress, is from the southwest along the D 926.

At the foot of the old town lies a small artificial lake.

Covered Market (Halle) – The great size of the market is evidence of Caylus's long-standing commercial importance. The old grain measures may still be seen cut into the stone.

Church (Église) – This was once a fortified church as the buttresses topped by machicolations suggest.

Inside, near the chancel, on the north side of the 14C nave, stands a gigantic figure of **Christ★** carved in wood in 1954 by Zadkine *(qv)*. The work is very striking and at the same time deeply moving. The 15C stained-glass windows (restored) in the chancel are worth a closer look.

Rue Droite – In Rue Droite, starting from the church, there are several medieval houses, in particular the 13C gable-fronted house, known as the **Wolves' Lair** (Maison des Loups), adorned with corbels and gargoyles in the form of wolves, from which the house derives its name.

EXCURSIONS

Lacapelle-Livron – *Round tour of 20km – 12 miles – allow 1 hour. Leave Caylus to the north.*

There are good views of the Bonnette River from the road, which soon passes, on the left, a path that leads to the pilgrimage chapel of Notre-Dame-de-Livron. The road becomes a picturesque cliff-top route overlooking the valley.

Notre-Dame-des-Grâces – This little pilgrimage chapel with its *lauze* roof is Gothic in style with a finely sculptured doorway.

From nearby, at the tip of the promontory on which the chapel is built, there is a wide view of the Bonnette Valley in its setting of hills dotted with woods and meadows and, in particular, of the St-Pierre-Livron waterfall.

Lacapelle-Livron – Pop 166. This old village with its *lauze*-roofed houses has a group of buildings, mostly in ruins, which used to be a commandery of the Order of Knights Templars. After 1307 it passed to the Order of St John with the Knights of Malta until the Revolution. There remains a fortified manor-house, overlooking the Bonnette, with a central courtyard, preserving the original layout of the commandery. To the south, beside the small Romanesque fortified church, is a powerful belltower-keep with a few remaining brackets left of the watchpath. The church is opposite the refectory, which is now the guard room.

Cornusson Castle – *8km – 5 miles east on the road to Cornusson.*

This castle which was largely rebuilt in the 16C, is flanked by numerous towers and is well situated on a wooded hill overlooking the Seye.

★ CÉLÉ VALLEY

The Célé, which owes its name to its swiftness (*celer* = rapid), is a delightful Quercy river which has cut a steep-sided valley through the *causse* (qv). The Célé Valley, in addition to passing through beautiful countryside, contains important prehistoric sites and archaeological remains.

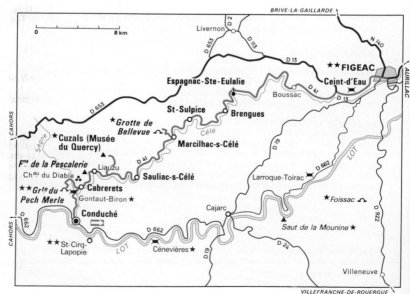

Valley of Paradise (Le Val Paradis) – The Célé rises in the chestnut woods that grow on the granite soil of Cantal; it enters Quercy and makes directly for the Lot River, but within 5km – 3 miles its course is blocked by Capdenac Hill. The Célé gets round its obstacle by turning westwards and cutting through 40km – 25 miles of limestone. This has resulted in a series of picturesque defiles, where the river can be seen winding along, still undermining the bases of the steep and many-hued rock walls. Adding to the beauty of the valley are the old mills built beside the river, and the archaic villages that stand perched on cliff ledges or half-hidden in the greenery; it is not surprising that the former priory at Espagnac (qv) was called the Valley of Paradise.

The "Hébrardie" – Throughout the Middle Ages the greater part of the Célé Valley was under the control of the Hébrard family of St-Sulpice, so that it virtually constituted a feudal benefice. The period of influence of the Hébrards was known locally as the "Hébrardie". The family, which lived at St-Sulpice (qv), enlarged or rebuilt the priories of Espagnac and Marcilhac and protected the local inhabitants, particularly at the time of the Hundred Years War. This great family numbered not only soldiers among its members; one of them was appointed seneschal of Quercy and others included such eminent ecclesiastics as Aymeric, Bishop of Coïmbra in Portugal and Anthony, Bishop of Cahors.

FROM CONDUCHÉ TO FIGEAC

65km – 40 miles – about half a day – local map opposite

The D 41 starts at Conduché, where the Célé flows into the Lot, and goes up the valley. The road is squeezed between the river bed and the cliff face, which rises on one side like a wall and at times even overhangs the road below. Many crops grow in the valley with maize tending to replace tobacco. A characteristic line of poplars marks the course of the river.

Cabrerets – Pop 191. Facilities. Cabrerets, set in a rocky amphitheatre, occupies a commanding position at the confluence of the Sagne and Célé Rivers.
There is a good overall **view**★ of Cabrerets and its setting from the left bank of the Célé, which is reached by crossing the bridge. Opposite stand the ruins of the **Devil's Castle** (Château du Diable), or Castle of the English, clinging to the formidable Rochecourbe cliff. This eagle's eyrie, a typical cliff-top castle, served as a base from which the English could pillage the countryside during the Hundred Years War.
On the far left is the impressive mass of the 14 and 15C **Gontaut-Biron Castle**★ overlooking the valley. A big corner tower flanks the buildings that surround an inner courtyard. One of the façade's mullioned windows opens onto a terrace with ornamental balustrades which juts out 25m - 82ft above the road.

The D 13 then the D 198 lead up the valley of the Sagne to Pech Merle Cave.

★★**Pech Merle Cave** – *See Pech Merle Cave.*

Return to Cabrerets.

Shortly after Cabrerets the cliff road crosses the face of high stone cliffs.

Pescalerie Fountain (Fontaine de la Pescalerie) – This is one of the most attractive sights of the Célé Valley; a beautiful waterfall pours out of the rock just near the road. It marks the surfacing of an underground river that has cut its way through the Gramat Causse. Beside the waterfall stands an ivy-covered mill, half-hidden by trees. By the exit to a tunnel, spectacular overhanging rock formations frame the **Liauzu sailing base**.

Take the small road left to Cuzals.

★**Cuzals (Quercy Open-Air Museum)** – *See Cuzals.*

Sauliac-sur-Célé – Pop 85. This old village clings to an awe-inspiring cliff of coloured rock. In the cliff face can be seen the openings to the fortified caves used in time of war as refuges by the local inhabitants. The more agile climbed up by way of ladders; invalids and animals were hoisted up in great baskets.
Beyond Sauliac the valley widens out. Crops and pasture land grow well on the alluvial soil of the valley bottom, and several round dry-stone shelters can be seen.

Marcilhac-sur-Célé – *See Marcilhac-sur-Célé.*

★**Bellevue Cave** – *See Marcilhac-sur-Célé.*

Between Marcilhac-sur-Célé and Brengues the contrast intensifies between the rocks with their sparse vegetation and the valley, which is densely cultivated with maize, sunflowers, vineyards and tobacco plantations.

St-Sulpice – Pop 126. The houses and gardens of this old village lie within the shadow of an overhanging cliff. The approach is guarded by a 12C castle which was rebuilt in the 14 and 15C. It is still the property of the Hébrard family of St-Sulpice.

Brengues – Pop 159. This small village is in a pleasant setting, perched on a ledge overlooked by a vertiginous bluff.
As far as Boussac the valley at times opens out and at others closes in; farmhouses stand here and there, their nearby, cylindrical dovecots (qv) roofed with *lauzes*.

Espagnac-Ste-Eulalie – *See Espagnac-Ste-Eulalie.*

Above Boussac the cliffs finally disappear, giving way to wooded hillsides, while the Célé spreads out over a wide alluvial bed.

Ceint d'Eau – This 15 and 16C castle, flanked by massive machicolated towers, rises above the D 13 and overlooks the Célé Valley, which is quite wide at this spot.

★★**Figeac** – *See Figeac.*

★ CÉNEVIÈRES CASTLE

Michelin map ⑦⑨ fold 9 or ②③⑤ fold 15 – 7km – 4 miles east of St-Cirq-Lapopie – Local map under LOT VALLEY: Cliffs and Promontories

This imposing **castle** ⊘ perches on a sheer rock face overlooking the Lot Valley from a height of more than 70m – 230ft. As early as the 7C the Dukes of Aquitaine had a stronghold built here. In the 13C the lords of Gourdon had the keep built. During the Renaissance, Flottard de Gourdon, who had participated in the campaigns in Italy with François I, completely rearranged the castle. His son, Antoine de Gourdon, converted to Protestantism and participated alongside Henri IV at the siege of Cahors (qv) in 1580. He pillaged the cathedral of Cahors and loaded the high altar and altar of the Holy Shroud onto boats returning to Cénevières Castle. The boat carrying the high altar sank in a chasm along the way. Before his death Antoine built a small Protestant church, which is in the outer bailey. He died childless, his widow remarried a La Tour du Pin and a new lineage took over Cénevières.

From the outside, the 13C keep and the 15C main wings joined by a 16C Renaissance gallery can be seen. The gallery is held up by Tuscan columns and above it are dormer windows. The moat which was crossed by a drawbridge has been filled in. Inside, the ground floor includes the vaulted salt room and kitchen. The keep has a trap door, which permits a glimpse of the three floors below which include the cellar, prison and dungeons.

On the first floor the great drawing room with a lovely Renaissance painted ceiling contains 15 and 16C Flemish tapestries and the shrine of the Holy Shroud brought back from Cahors. The small alchemy room is decorated with fascinating 16C naive frescoes illustrating Greek mythology. The alchemist's oven has a representation of the philosopher's stone.

Finally, from the terrace there are commanding **views** of the Lot Valley and the hanging village of Calvignac.

★ CHANCELADE ABBEY

Michelin map ⑦⑤ fold 5 or ②③③ fold 42 – 7km – 4 miles northwest of Périgueux

The abbey appears as a peaceful haven tucked at the foot of the green slopes overlooking the Beauronne. Founded in the 12C by a monk who adopted the rule of St Augustine, the abbey was protected by the bishops of Périgueux and later answered directly to the Holy See. It therefore prospered and was accorded considerable privileges: asylum, safety and franchises. From the 14C the abbey's fortunes declined; the English captured it, sent the monks away and installed a garrison. Du Guesclin freed it, but not for long as the English recaptured it and held it until the mid-15C. During the Wars of Religion, the abbey buildings were partly destroyed by the Protestants from Périgueux.

In 1623 Alain de Solminihac, the new abbot, undertook the reformation and restoration of Chancelade. He was so successful that he was named Bishop of Cahors by Louis XIII. The abbey was able to function calmly until the Revolution, when it became national property.

Church (**Église**) – The Romanesque doorway has recessed orders with nailhead moulding and is surmounted by an elegant arcade, showing Saintonge influence, underlined by a modillioned cornice. The square, Romanesque belltower is made up of three tiers of arcades, some of which are rounded while others are pointed.

Inside, few elements are left of the original 12C church: the nave was re-vaulted with pointed vaulting and the east end was demolished. The 17C stalls, in walnut, still have misericords carved with motifs of palm leaves, roses, shells, etc.

Conventual Buildings (**Bâtiments conventuels**) ⊘ – These include the abbot's lodgings and the outbuildings around the courtyard and garden, which comprise the 15C pointed barrel-vaulted laundry room (now an exhibition hall), stables, workshops and a fortified mill. Adjoining the courtyard is the garden. The north façade (called Bourdeilles's lodgings) is flanked by two turrets, one of which is opened by a finely decorated door (late 15C). To the east is the elegant building which used to be the abbot's residence, built at the beginning of the 17C, with a terrace surrounded by pavilions.

Chapel (**Chapelle St-Jean**) – This small, charming parish church was consecrated in 1147. Its façade is opened by an unusually small semicircular doorway with three barely perceptible pointed-recessed arches, surmounted by a bay framed by slender columns, and above that, a low relief of a lamb carrying a cross (the Benedictine Pax). There is a fine rounded apse with buttress-columns.

EXCURSION

Merlande Priory (**Prieuré de Merlande**) – 8km – 5 miles northwest on the D 1.
The road between Chancelade and Merlande rises through a wood of chestnut and oak trees. In a deserted clearing in Feytaud Forest stand a small fortified chapel and a prior's house, as solitary reminders of the Merlande Priory founded here in the 12C by the monks of Chancelade. Both have been restored. The chapel appears to be a fortress-like structure with its 4-sided plan and the little fort protecting its east end. It is a Romanesque building with two bays; the first has a transverse arch and pointed-barrel vaulting replacing the original dome, the second is roofed with an attractive dome on pendentives. The chancel, the oldest part, is slightly above the level of the nave and preceded by a rounded triumphal arch. It has barrel vaulting and a flat east end and is bordered by a series of blind arcades adorned with finely carved archaic **capitals**★; tangled-up monsters and lions devouring palm-leaf scrolls make up a bizarre but striking fauna.

Michelin map 75 fold 9 or 239 fold 26 – Local map under BRIVE-LA-GAILLARDE:
Excursions – Facilities

Cars are not allowed in the village during the summer. Use the car park by the old station. Collonges "the Red", built of red sandstone, is set with its small manor-houses, old houses and Romanesque church in a countryside already characteristic of the Quercy region, with juniper bushes, walnut plantations and vineyards very much in evidence. A historic atmosphere pervades the streets of this lovely old town. The village grew up in the 8C around its church and priory, a dependency of the powerful Charroux Abbey in the Poitou region. In the 13C, Collonges was a part of the viscounty of Turenne *(qv)* and thus received franchises and liberties. Much later on, in the 16C, Collonges was the place chosen by the leaders of the viscounty for their holidays. To accommodate themselves, they had constructed charming manors and mansions flanked with towers and turrets, which are what makes this town unique.

The old centre exudes a definite sense of harmony, probably due in part to the use of exclusively traditional materials for construction work, and to the interplay and correspondence of proportions between the different types of building.

TOUR *time: 1 hour*

> *Start near the old station (ancienne gare).*

Mermaid's House (Maison de la Sirène) ⊘ – This 16C corbelled house, with a porch and beautiful *lauze* roof, is adorned with a mermaid holding a comb in one hand and a mirror in the other. The **interior** has been reconstructed as the inside of a Collonges house of olden days.
Further along, the pointed gateway arch (Porte du Prieuré) marks the entrance of the former Benedictine priory, which was destroyed during the Revolution.

Hôtel des Ramade de Friac (B) – The *hôtel*, crowned by two turrets, was once the town house of the powerful Ramade de Friac family.
Go past the Relais de St-Jacques-de-Compostelle – the name recalls that Collonges was a pilgrims' stopping place along the famous route to Santiago de Compostela – and through a covered passageway and soon afterwards in an alley, on the right, there is an old turreted house.

Château de Benge – Set against a backdrop of poplars and walnuts is this proud towered and turreted manor-house with its lovely Renaissance window. The lords of Benge were top of the league of the famous Collonges vineyards, until these were decimated by phylloxera.

Flattened Gateway (Porte Plate) – This gateway, so named because it has lost its towers, was part of the town walls protecting the church, cloisters and priory buildings.

Covered market (Halle) (D) – The grain market, its timberwork supported by thick pillars, contains a village oven.

Church (Église) – The church, which dates from the 11 and 12C, was fortified during the Wars of Religion in the 16C. It was at this time that the great square keep was strengthened by a defence chamber communicating with the watchpath, and that the tympanum was placed in the new gable out of harm's way.

★**Tympanum** – Carved in the white limestone of Turenne, the 12C tympanum stands out among all the red sandstone. It depicts the Ascension (or perhaps the second coming of Christ) and was apparently carved by sculptors of the Toulouse School. The upper register shows the figure of Christ surrounded by angels, holding the Gospels in one hand, the other raised in benediction. The lower register shows the saddened Virgin surrounded by the eleven Apostles. The whole tympanum is outlined by a pointed arch ornamented with a fine border of carved animals.

Church

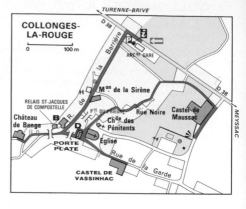

★ Belltower – The 12C belltower is in the Limousin style: two lower square tiers pierced with round-arched bays are surmounted by two octagonal tiers flanked by gables. The belfry is built onto the transept crossing.

Interior – In the 12C, the church had a cruciform plan around the transept crossing. The dome above the transept crossing rests on 11C pillars. Modifications were made in the 14 and 15C, when side chapels were added as well as a second nave in the Flamboyant style.

★ Vassinhac Manor-house (Castel de Vassinhac) – This elegant house was owned by Gédéor de Vassinhac, lord of Collonges, captain-governor of the viscounty of Turenne. Built in 1583, the manor-house bristles with large towers and turrets with pepper-pot roofs. Despite a large number of mullioned windows, its defensive role is obvious from its many loopholes and battlemented turrets.

Former Penitents' Chapel (Ancienne Chapelle des Pénitents) – The chapel was built in the 13C and modified by the Maussac family at the time of the Counter-Reformation.

Rue Noire – This street cuts through the oldest part of Collonges, where old houses can be seen set back one from the other, ornamented with turrets and towers and adorned with wisteria and climbing vines.

Maussac Manor-house (Castel de Maussac) – This building is embellished with a turret and a porch roof above the main door. A battlemented turret projects from the square tower, which is overlooked by a dormer window.

Before the Revolution this manor-house was the refuge of the last member of the Maussac family, who emigrated to Italy where he became the chaplain to Napoleon's sister, Princess Pauline Borghese.

Continue further south along the street to enjoy a pretty **view★** of Collonges, Vassinhac Manor-house and the belltower.

★ COUGNAC CAVES (Grottes de COUGNAC)

Michelin map **75** fold 18 or **235** fold 6 – 3km – 2 miles north of Gourdon

These caves are fascinating for two reasons: their natural rock formations and their Palaeolithic paintings similar to those of Pech-Merle *(qv)*.

Tour ⊘ – The caves, consisting of two chasms about 200m – 300yds apart, spread their network of galleries beneath a limestone plateau.

The first cave consists of three small chambers with roofs from which closely packed and sometimes extremely delicate stalactites hang in profusion.

The second cave is bigger and has two remarkable chambers: the **Pillar Chamber★** (Salle des Colonnes) is made particularly striking by the perspectives offered by columns reaching from floor to ceiling, and the **Hall of Prehistoric Paintings** (Salle des Peintures Préhistoriques) contains designs in ochre and black featuring deer, mammoths and human figures.

★ CUZALS

Michelin map 79 fold 9 or 235 fold 14 (40km – 25 miles east of Cahors)

Quercy Open-Air Museum (Musée de plein air de Quercy) ⊘.
To do justice to this interesting exhibition, visitors should allow at least half a day.

All the aspects of life in the Quercy region, from before the Revolution until the Second World War, are reproduced here in an area of 50ha-124 acres. The museum administrators set themselves the objective of "not embalming anything dead". Visitors are offered an authentic, scientific approach, which takes the area's cultural heritage very much into account.

Furniture in the two farmhouses has been reconstructed down to the very last detail. There is an exhibition of machinery and other objects, in connection with water; the mechanical washing machines from the beginning of this

Traction engine

century are particularly interesting. Other displays include a rather perturbing dentist's surgery from 1900, the milliner's and baker's shops, and of course examples of Quercy architecture, regional crop specialities and a collection of pieces of improbable-looking agricultural machinery featuring a splendid 1910 model of the Clayton traction engine. In the summer people from local communities gather together to operate all the exhibits; the thresher threshes, the mill mills, the bread bakes in the oven and teams of oxen untiringly take endless children for rides.

★★ DOMME Pop 1 030

Michelin map **75** fold 17 or **235** fold 6 – Local map under DORDOGNE VALLEY **3** – Facilities

Domme, the "Acropolis of the Dordogne", is remarkably situated on a rocky crag overlooking the Dordogne Valley.

Captain Vivans's exploit – While the struggles of the Reformation were inflaming France, Domme kept up resistance against the Huguenots who were overrunning Périgord. Yet, in 1588, the famous Protestant Captain **Geoffroi de Vivans** *(qv)* captured the town by cunning.

One night he and thirty of his men climbed along the rocks of the cliff face (the *Barre*), a place so precipitous that it had not been thought necessary to fortify it, and entered the sleeping town. Vivans and his men created an infernal racket and during the ensuing confusion opened the tower doors to their waiting army. The inhabitants were not sufficiently wide awake to resist. Vivans thereupon became master of the town (for four years), installed a garrison there, burned down both the church and the Augustine priory and established the Protestant faith. However, noting the increasing success of the Catholics in Périgord, he eventually sold them the *bastide* without a fight, careful to leave nothing but ruins for them at the appointed time on 10 January 1592.

His name was carved on the inside of one of the rampart towers.

★★★ PANORAMA

From the promontory, the view embraces the Dordogne Valley from the Montfort Meander to the east, to Beynac to the west.

Flowing east to west from the undulating countryside of Périgord Noir, the Dordogne River widens at the foot of Domme, in a fertile valley scattered with villages and farms, and continues its way below the cliffs of La Roque-Gageac and Beynac.

Changing with the time of day – hazy in the early morning mist, bright blue between lines of green poplars in the noonday sun, a silver ribbon in the evening light – the Dordogne winds its way through the carefully cultivated fields (maize, tobacco, cereals) against a backdrop of wooded hills. Of all the creative artists who have come here seeking inspiration, the writer Henry Miller was perhaps the most affected, describing the area as perhaps the nearest thing to Paradise on earth.

Barre Viewpoint (Belvédère de la Barre) – The esplanade at the end of the Grand'Rue offers a panorama of the valley below. The bust represents **Jacques de Maleville** (1741-1824) one of the authors of the *Code Civil* (Common Law).

Cliff Walk (Promenade des Falaises) – Continue along the promontory eastwards, passing below the gardens. The view is more extensive than at the Barre Viewpoint.

Jubilee Gardens (Jardin public du Jubilé) – These attractive gardens, in which there is an **orientation table**, are situated at the tip of the promontory, on the site of the entrenched camp installed here in 1214 by Simon de Montfort. He had just beaten the Cathars and razed their fortress **Domme-Vieille**, of which there are only a few remains left standing. To visit these, leave the gardens and go past the old Roy mill.

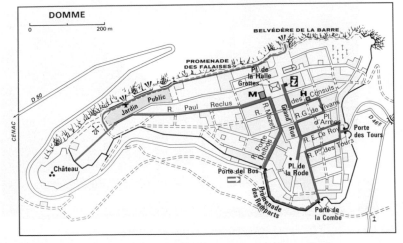

★THE BASTIDE

Founded by Philip the Bold in 1283, this *bastide* is far from presenting the perfect rectangular plan of the *bastide* as such – it is more in the form of a trapezium. The surrounding fortifications have been adapted to the terrain; inside the fortified town, the streets follow a geometric plan, as far as possible.

The *bastide* played an important role in the Hundred Years War. Its pivotal position made it the ideal headquarters for the Périgord-Quercy seneschalsy. After the Wars of Religion, the Domme area entered a period of relative wealth, thanks to the quality of its vines, river trade on the Dordogne and the quarrying of millstone.

Rampart Walk (Promenade des Remparts) ⊘ – When you come to the **Del Bos Gateway** (Porte del Bos), which has a pointed arch and was once closed with a portcullis, bear left to walk inside the ramparts. Opposite the **La Combe Gateway** (Porte de la Combe), turn left towards the town where there are many fine houses to be seen. The beauty of the gold stone and the flat brown tiles is often enhanced by the addition of elegant wrought-iron balconies and brightened by climbing vines and flower-decked terraces. Go through the late 13C **Towers' Gateway** (Porte des Tours) ⊘, the most impressive and best preserved of the town's gateways. On the side of Place des Armes, the wall is rectilinear but on the outside, the gateway is flanked by two massive semicircular rusticated towers, which were once defended by a brattice, of which one can still see the machicolations. The towers were built by Philip the Fair and originally served as guard rooms. Between 1307 and 1318 Knights Templars were imprisoned there and left their mark with graffiti.

Rue Eugène-le-Roy – During the period he spent in a house along this street, Eugène le Roy wrote two of his masters-works: *L'ennemi de la mort* (The Enemy of Death) and *Le moulin du Frau* (Frau Mill).

Place de la Rode – This is the place where the condemned were broken on the wheel. The **House of the Money Minter** is decorated with fine Gothic apertures.

Grand'Rue – This shopping street is lined with shops displaying gastronomic specialities of Périgord.

Rue Geoffroy-de-Vivans – The house on the corner of the Grand'Rue has a lovely Renaissance window.

Rue des Consuls – The Hôtel de Ville (town hall) is located in a 13C building, which was once the Seneschal law courts.

Place de la Halle – In this large square *(photograph below)* stands an elegant 17C **covered market** (halle). Facing it is the 16C **Governors' House** (Maison des Gouverneurs) flanked by an elegant turret. It now houses the tourist information centre.

ADDITIONAL SIGHTS

Caves (Grottes) ⊘ – *The entrance is in the covered market.*
These caves served as refuge for the townspeople of Domme during the Hundred Years War and the Wars of Religion.
So far about 450m – 490yds of galleries have been cleared for the public to visit; the chambers are generally small and are sometimes separated by low passages. The ceilings in certain chambers are embellished with slender white stalactites. There are also places where stalactites and stalagmites join to form columns or pillars. The Red Chamber (Salle Rouge) contains some eccentrics *(qv)*.
Bison and rhinoceros bones, discovered when the caves were being prepared for tourists, are displayed in the exact place where they were found.

Museum of Folk Arts and Traditions (Musée d'Art et de Traditions populaires) (M) ⊘ – In an old house on Place de la Halle, this museum presents a retrospective of Domme life through reconstructed interiors and displays of furnishings, clothing and husbandry. Archives and photographs also help to recapture the village's past.

Covered market and Governors' House

The Dordogne is one of the longest rivers in France and is said to be the most beautiful. The variety and beauty of the countryside through which the river flows and the architectural glories that mark its banks make the valley a first-class tourist attraction.

A lovely journey – The Dordogne begins where the Dore and the Dogne meet at the foot of the Sancy, the highest peak in the Massif Central. Swift flowing and speckled with foam, it crosses the Mont-Dore and Bourboule Basins and soon leaves the volcanic rocks of Auvergne for the granite of Limousin. Between Bort and Argentat, where the river once flowed between narrow ravines, there is now a series of reservoirs and great dams. The river calms down for a short while after Beaulieu as it crosses the rich plain, where it is joined by the Cère River, which rises in Cantal. From this point the Dordogne is a truly majestic river, though it nonetheless remains swift and temperamental. The *causses* (limestone plateaux) of Quercy bar its way and so in true Herculean style it cuts a path through the Montvalent Amphitheatre. Having reached the Périgord plateaux beyond Souillac, the river begins to flow past

great castles, washing the bases of the rocks on which they perch. Starting at Limeuil, where the river is joined by the Vézère, the valley widens out and, after crossing some rapids, reaches Bergerac and then the Guyenne Plains with their vineyards. At the Ambès Spit, the Dordogne completes its 500km – 310 mile journey; it joins the Garonne, which it almost equals in size, and the two flow on together as the Gironde.

Château de la Treyne

The capricious Dordogne – The Dordogne flows swiftly through both the mountains and the plains, but its volume is far from constant. Winter and spring rain storms and the melting of the snows on the Millevaches Plateau and in the mountains of Auvergne bring floods almost every year which are sudden, violent and at times devasta-

ting. Dam construction and other civil engineering projects – Bort, Marèges, L'Aigle, Le Chastang, Argentat – in the upper valley have enabled the flow to be controlled.

The days of the gabares – For a long time there was river traffic on the Dordogne. Until the last century a world of sailors and craft lived on the river in spite of the dangers and the river's uneven flow. The boatmen used flat-bottomed boats known as *gabares* or *argentats*, after the town with the largest boat-building yards. These big barges, sailing downstream, carried passengers and cargo, especially oak for cooperage in Bordeaux; sailing upstream they loaded salt at Libourne and continued their journey up to Souillac *(qv)* where it was sold. The journey was full of the unexpected and the *gabariers* had to be skilled to get their boats through. When they arrived, the boats were broken up and sold for timber. Today river traffic plies solely on the lower Dordogne; upstream the only boats to be seen are those of anglers or canoeists.

★★THE QUERCY STRETCH OF THE DORDOGNE

① From Bretenoux to Souillac

56km – 35 miles – allow 3 hours – local map overleaf

Bretenoux – Pop 1 211. Facilities. In its leafy riverside setting, this former *bastide*, founded in 1277 by a powerful lord of Castelnau, has kept its grid plan, its central square, covered arcades and parts of the ramparts.

After visiting the picturesque **Place des Consuls** with its 15C turreted town house, go through a covered alley to the old manor at the corner of the pretty Rue du Manoir de Cère. Turn right and right again returning via the charming quay along the Cère. Having collected the waters of the Cère, the river passes within sight of the impressive mass of Castelnau-Bretenoux Castle.

★★ **Castelnau-Bretenoux Castle** – *See Castelnau-Bretenoux Castle*.

Downstream from Castelnau, the Bave tributary *(qv)* joins the Dordogne, which divides into several streams flowing in a wide valley bounded to the south by the cliffs of the *causses*.

★ **Carennac** – *See Carennac*.

Beyond Carennac, the Dordogne cuts a channel between the Martel and Gramat *causses* before entering the beautiful area of the Montvalent Amphitheatre.

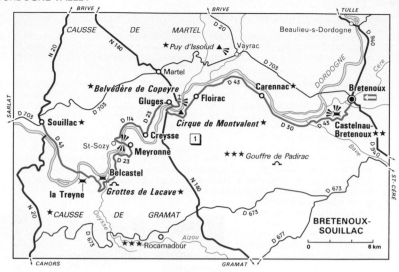

Floirac – Pop 296. A 14C keep is all that remains of the old fortifications.

★ Montvalent Amphitheatre (Cirque de Montvalent) – The road is very picturesque, running for the most part beside the river, though sometimes running along a ledge above it. There are attractive views of the valley and the *causse* cliffs from every bend.

> *Cross the Dordogne, take the D 140 towards Martel and then turn right on the D 32 to the Copeyre Viewpoint.*

★ Copeyre Viewpoint (Belvédère de Copeyre) – There is a good **view★** of the Dordogne and the Montvalent Amphitheatre from a rock beside the D 32 on which there is a wayside cross. At the foot of the cliffs, the Dordogne can be seen flowing in a wide arc through pastures divided by lines of poplars; on the left, to one side of the river, is the Puy d'Issolud and on the right, to the other side, the village of Floirac.

> *Turn back and follow the north bank of the Dordogne.*

Gluges – This village (with old houses) lies in a beautiful **setting★** beside the river at the foot of the cliffs.

The road then winds upwards around a tall overhanging ochre-coloured cliff, hidden in places by a thick carpet of ivy. At times the road carves a route out of the cliff.

Creysse – Pop 227. The charming village of Creysse with pleasant, narrow streets, brown-tiled roofs, houses bedecked with climbing vines and with flights of steps leading to their doors, lies at the foot of the rocky spur, on which stands a pre-Romanesque church, the former castle chapel, with its curious twin apses. The church and the remains of the nearby castle are reached by a stony alleyway, which climbs sharply to a terrace. It is from a little square shaded by plane trees, near the war memorial, that you get the best overall view of the village.

After Creysse the road follows the willow-bordered bank as far as St-Sozy and then crosses the river over the bridge at Meyronne.

Meyronne – Pop 210. From the bridge over the Dordogne, there is a pretty **view★** of the river and the village – former home of the bishops of Tulle – with its charming Quercy houses built attractively into the cliffs.

The road subsequently follows the course of the Dordogne through beautiful countryside of rocks and cliffs, then crosses the Ouysse River near Lacave.

★ Lacave Caves – *See Lacave Caves.*

Belcastel Castle (Château de Belcastel) ⊘ – A vertical cliff dropping down to the confluence of the Ouysse and the Dordogne is crowned by a castle standing proudly in a remarkable **setting★** *(photograph p 170).* Only the eastern part of the main wing and the chapel date from the Middle Ages; most of the other buildings were reconstructed later.

The chapel and terraces are open to the public. From the terraces there is a bird's-eye view of the Ouysse and the Dordogne.

> *Follow the D 43 to the next bridge.*

Château de la Treyne ⊘ – The château *(photograph p 83)* stands perched on a cliff, which on one side overlooks the east bank of the Dordogne and on the other side a vast park. Burned by the Catholics during the Wars of Religion, the château was rebuilt in the 17C; only the square tower is 14C.

The buildings are now a hotel. The park (French gardens) and chapel (where exhibitions are held) are open to the public.

The road then crosses the Dordogne, to run along the north bank to Souillac.

★ Souillac – *See Souillac. Facilities.*

Don't leave anything to chance!
Consult Minitel 3615 MICHELIN to choose
your route, the sights to see, a hotel and restaurant.

***THE PÉRIGORD STRETCH OF THE DORDOGNE

② From Souillac to Sarlat
32km – 20 miles – allow 1 hour 30 min – local map below

★**Souillac** – *See Souillac. Facilities.*
Leave Souillac to the west by the D 703.

The countryside of Quercy is only very slightly different from that of Périgord Noir, through which the Dordogne flows below Souillac. The river is calmer and its meanders, separated only by narrow rock channels, form a series of rich basins. Mountain peaks crowned with dark trees ring the horizon.

The road crosses the well cultivated alluvial plains surrounded by wooded hills and follows the river bordered with poplars — a typical Périgord Valley scene.

A couple of miles after Viviers, leave the D 703 and turn right towards Carlux.

Carlux – Pop 594. Overlooking the valley from its commanding position, the village still has some old houses and a small covered market. A rare Gothic chimney, jutting out from a gabled wall, adds a touch of the unexpected to the scene. Two towers and an imposing curtain wall are all that remains of the lárge castle, which once belonged to the viscounty of Turenne. From the castle terrace, there is a lovely view of the valley and the cliffs, which were used as the castle foundations.

The crossing of the Dordogne is guarded by **Rouffillac castle**; its attractive outline can be seen rising out of the green oak trees.

Fénelon castle ⊘ – François de Salignac de Lamothe-Fénelon, later to become the Duke of Burgundy's mentor and author of Télémaque (qv), was born here on

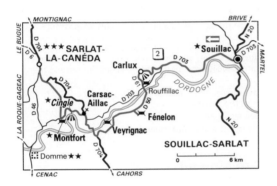

6 August 1651 and spent his early childhood within these walls. His family had been feudal lords since the 14C and remained so until 1780. Built near Ste-Mondane village, on a hill overlooking the Dordogne and the Bouriane forest, Fénelon castle underwent substantial alterations in the 17C, although its foundations actually date back to the 15C and 16C. Its triple enceinte gives it the appearance of being a very powerful fortress. The residential buildings and towers are still covered with *lauzes (qv)*. A beautiful **staircase** with two bends gives access into the main courtyard. Inside, the Fénelon bedroom, the chapel, the kitchen hollowed out of the rock and a collection of medieval military miscellania are all open to visitors.

Château de Veyrignac ⊘ – This large palace was built in the 18C on a terrace on the banks of the Dordogne. It is classical in design with well-balanced proportions. Interest is added to the main façade of the residence by a slightly protruding avant-corps flanked by two pavilions. One of the cellars contains a spectacular collection of **instruments of torture**. Also open to visitors are the Historama d'Aquitaine, an exhibition of figures dressed in reproduced period costume, and a museum of vintage cars.

Return to the D 703.

Carsac-Aillac – Pop 1 219. The modest but delightful church of Carsac, built in a lovely golden stone, stands in a country setting not far from the Dordogne. The porch in the façade has five recessed arches resting on small columns. The massive Romanesque belltower and the apse are roofed with *lauzes*.

The nave and the lower aisles had stellar vaulting decorated with elegant discs or bosses added to them in the 16C. A small dome on pendentives rises above the transept crossing; the chancel ends in a Romanesque apse with oven vaulting and is adorned with interesting archaic oriental-style capitals. Gothic chapels are situated on either side of the nave and at the entrance to the chancel.

There are strikingly modern **stained-glass windows** and a **Stations of the Cross** by Zack. The Stations are arresting for their robust style and the austerity of their design; the texts are taken from the writings of Paul Claudel (diplomat and author: 1868-1955).

★**Montfort Meander and ★Castle** (Cingle et Château) – *See Montfort.*

★★★**Sarlat** – *See Sarlat-la-Canéda. Facilities.*

③ From Sarlat to St-Cyprien
60km – 37 miles – allow 4 hours – local map overleaf

This trip is the most attractive in Périgord. Great rocks rise up at every step, golden in colour and crowned with old castles and picturesque villages.

★★★**Sarlat** – *See Sarlat-la-Canéda. Facilities.*

Soon after Vitrac, Domme comes into view on its rocky promontory on the left.

Cénac – Pop 993. The only remaining evidence of the large priory built in Cénac in the 11C is the small Romanesque **church** ⊘, which stands outside the village. Even the church did not escape the Wars of Religion, and only the east end escaped the depredations of the Protestants serving under Captain Vivans (qv) in 1589. The short nave and transept were rebuilt in the 19C.

Go into the churchyard to get an overall view of the east end with its fine stone roof and its column-buttresses topped by foliated capitals. A cornice, decorated with modillions bearing small carved figures, runs round the base of the roof of the apsidal chapels.

Inside, in the chancel and the apse, there is a series of interesting **historiated capitals**, which date from 1130. A very varied and realistic animal art enlivens these capitals; the scenes depicted include Daniel in the Lions' Den and Jonah and the Whale.

★★ Domme – *See Domme.*

This is the most beautiful part of the whole valley; in between lines of poplars the Dordogne spreads its course to flow calmly through a mosaic of farmland and meadows. A succession of increasingly spellbinding settings for towns and castles unfolds to view.

★★ La Roque-Gageac – *See La Roque-Gageac. Facilities.*

★ Castelnaud Castle – *See Castelnaud Castle.*

A short stretch of road between Castelnaud and Les Milandes Castle passes below Fayrac Castle.

Fayrac Castle – A double curtain wall surrounds the interior courtyard, which is reached by two drawbridges. The 16C buildings bristling with pepper-pot roofs form a complex yet harmonious unit in spite of the 19C restorations (note the pseudo-keep). The castle is tucked amidst the greenery on the south bank of the Dordogne opposite Beynac-et-Cazenac.

Les Milandes – Built en 1489 by François de Caumont, the **castle** ⊘ remained the property of this family until the Revolution. In the past the castle was associated with the well-known American singer, Josephine Baker or *La Perle Noire* as she was known in her Paris cabaret heyday in the Twenties and Thirties. It was here that she achieved her dream of a "village of the world", gathering together children of different races, religions and nationalities and bringing them up to promote mutual understanding.

A spiral staircase gives access to the various floors. In addition to the possessions of the De Caumont family are furniture and effects belonging to Josephine Baker. The castle is surrounded by an attractively arranged garden. From the terrace there is a view of the park.

> *Return by the same road and cross the river by the Castelnaud bridge to join the D 703 on the north bank of the Dordogne.*

★★ Beynac-et-Cazenac – *See Beynac-et-Cazenac.*

Beyond Beynac, the valley does not widen out much before St-Cyprien.

St-Cyprien – *See St-Cyprien.*

④ From St-Cyprien to Limeuil

34km – 21 miles – about 1 hour 30 min – local map below

St-Cyprien – *See St-Cyprien.*

Below St-Cyprien, the Dordogne runs through an area where meadows and arable fields spread out to the cliffs and wooded slopes, marking the edge of the valley.

Siorac-en-Périgord – Pop 904. Facilities. This small village, sought after for its beach, has a 17C castle and a small Romanesque church.

> *From Siorac take the D 25, then turn left to Urval.*

Urval – This village set in a small valley nestles in the shadow of its massive 12C church. The walls of the rectangular chancel are covered with blind arcading held up by archaic capitals. The grey marble column has been taken from an earlier construction. Next to the church is the medieval **communal oven★** (still in use) in which the baron allowed villagers to bake their bread for a nominal fee.

> *Take the small road, southwest of Urval, to Cadouin.*

★ Cadouin – *See Cadouin.*

From Cadouin the D 25 continues northeast to Le Buisson through rolling hills covered with underbrush and chestnut trees.

> *Cross over the Dordogne towards Périgueux (D 51). Continue along the D 51 towards Limeuil, after crossing the Vézère turn right onto the D 31.*

Chapelle St-Martin – Henry II Plantagenet funded the construction of this chapel as penance for the murder of Thomas à Becket, Archbishop of Canterbury. It was completed after his death at the request of his son, Richard the Lionheart. His name and the date of consecraton of the chapel, 1194, are inscribed on the **foundation stone** set in the left wall of the nave (it is rare to find churches with their foundation stone). The transept crossing is topped by a crude dome.

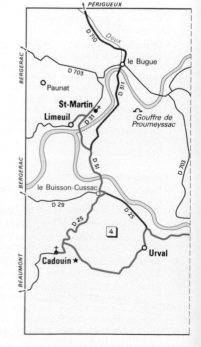

Limeuil – Pop 336. *Walk up the main street*. Built on a steep promontory, this old village, arranged in tiers overlooking the confluence of the Dordogne and Vézère Rivers, occupies a picturesque **site***. Its two bridges, unusually set at right angles and spanning each of the rivers, mark the confluence. Traces of its past as a fortress town can be seen on climbing up the ancient narrow streets to the site of the old castle and church.

Limeuil's role as "arsenal and watchtower" established itself quite early on, thanks mainly to its strategic position, which aroused desire and envy in those who saw it. At one point the Croquants *(qv)* gained control of the town. Limeuil was also for many centuries a port and "safe haven" for heavy barges.

⑤ From Limeuil to Bergerac

53km – 33 miles – about 2 hours 30 min – local map overleaf

Limeuil – *Description above.*

Take the D 31 on the north bank of the Dordogne.

Soon after the confluence of the Dordogne and the Vézère, the very picturesque road overlooks the Dordogne at Roches Blanches (viewpoint) across from Sors Plain.

Trémolat – Pop 625. Facilities. Built on a meander in the Dordogne, this charming village was made famous by the shooting of Claude Chabrol's film *The Butcher*. It has a 12C Romanesque church which represents a condensed version of all the religious architectural features of the Périgord region.

In it, heavy fortifications are combined with a vaulting system which sets off the dome favourably. The massive belltower-keep and the high walls with buttresses pierced by narrow loop-holes make it every inch a fortress. The huge defensive chamber covering the whole of the interior was a refuge for the entire village.

Inside, the unusual nave is vaulted with a **row of three domes** resting on pendentives. A fourth, more graceful dome sits atop the transept crossing.

In the churchyard, the **Chapelle St-Hilaire** is a small Romanesque chapel reached by a lovely doorway, above which runs a modillioned cornice.

When you get to Trémolat head north on the road to the Trémolat Meander: "Route du Cingle de Trémolat".

Racamadou Viewpoint (Belvédère de Racamadou) – From the water-tower platform there is an outstanding **panorama**** of the well-known Trémolat Meander.

**Trémolat Meander (Cingle de Trémolat) – At the foot of a semicircle of high, bare, white cliffs intersected by greenery coils the river in a large loop, spanned by bridges of golden stone and reflecting lines of poplars. Beyond the wonderful stretch of water, which is often used for rowing regattas, on the convex bank lies a vast mosaic of arable fields and meadows; far away on the horizon, one can see the hills of Bergerac, Issigeac and Monpazier.

Return to Trémolat and cross the south bank of the Dordogne.

The valley is dotted with tobacco-drying sheds.

Badefols-sur-Dordogne – Pop 150. Facilities. The village occupies a pleasant site beside the Dordogne. The country church stands close to the foot of the castle ruins perched on the cliff. This fortress served as the hide-out for the local thieves and robbers who used to ransack the *gabares (qv)* as they sailed downstream.

Take the D 29 towards Lalinde; turn left to St-Front by the bridge to Lalinde.

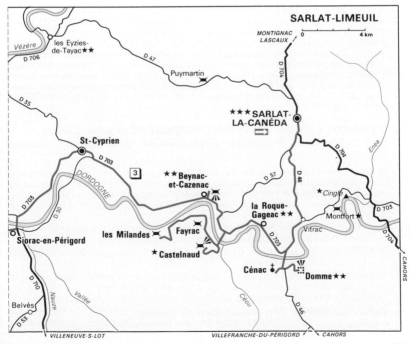

SARLAT-LIMEUIL

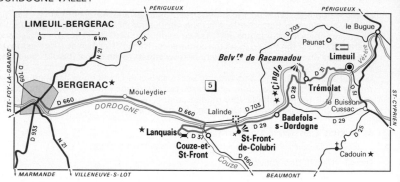

Chapelle St-Front-de-Colubri – Built in the 12C on top of a cliff overlooking the Dordogne, this chapel sheltered sailors who were venturing along the Saut de la Gratusse rapids. This passage was the most difficult of the river's middle section; specialised pilots were needed to guide sailors through it until the mid-19C, when the Lalinde canal was dug, enabling them to bypass it.

There is a marveillous **view**★ of the valley and the rapids up-river.

Return towards the river and turn left onto the D 8.

Couze-et-St-Front – Pop 831. Located at the mouth of the small Couze Valley, this active little town has specialised since the 16C in the manufacture of Dutch paper, which was sold as far away as Russia. It was the most important papermaking centre of Aquitaine, and, at its peak, thirteen mills were functioning. Only two mills remain from those prosperous times; at the **Larroque Mill** ⊙ (Moulin de Larroque) one can see the making of filigreed paper using traditional methods.

Several old mills can be seen one after the other along the banks of the river Couze, by taking the D 660 *(south)* for about 1km - 0.6 miles. On the top floor of these are large, window-like openings with wooden shutters; this was where the finished paper was unloaded.

Turn round and take the D 37 to the village and Lanquais Château.

★**Lanquais Château** – *See Lanquais Château.*

Turn back, take the D 37 on the left and cross the Dordogne once again.

The D 660 follows the wide alluvial valley down to Bergerac.

★**Bergerac** – *See Bergerac.*

DOUBLE

Michelin map **75** folds 3, 4 and 5 or **233** folds 41 and 42

During the Tertiary Era waterways came down from Massif Central spreading deposits of argillaceous sands which formed, notably, the Sologne, Brenne and Double regions.

The Double, in the west of the Périgord between the rivers Dronne to the north and Isle to the south, has a wild landscape of forest, sprinkled with lakes and dotted with half-timbered and clay houses.

It was a poor, desolate area; fever was rife near its waters, and thieves and wolves alike roamed its forests. This all changed for the better under the Second Empire (1852-70), when roads were built, lakes drained, soils improved and maritime pines planted. These pines, together with oak and chestnut trees, now constitute the major part of the forest cover. The people of the Double region have always bred fish, draining the networks of lakes and reed-infested channels (*nauves*) every two years to gather the fish for sale or consumption. 60 % of the area is now overrun by the forest; the wood is used for timber and the area is a paradise for hunters. The remaining 40 % is for medium-sized farms which concentrate on dairy farming and fattening up livestock.

FOREST, LAKES AND HALF-TIMBERED HOUSES

Round tour of 80km – 50 miles starting from St-Astier – allow half a day - local map opposite

St-Astier – Pop 4 780. Lying on the banks of the river Isle, the old town centre contains a few remaining Renaissance houses. It is overlooked by the church, supported by massive buttresses, and a magnificent **belltower** adorned with two tiers of blind arcades. The cement works near the river Isle give St-Astier the appearance of an industrial town.

On leaving St-Astier by the D 43, the steeply climbing hairpin-bends of the road reveal beautiful views of the town, before disappearing into the forest.

St-Aquilin – Pop 387. The church, built in a transitional Romanesque Gothic style, ends in a chancel with a flat east end.

Le Bellet Castle (Château du Bellet) – The fine tiled roofs and massive round towers of this castle, built on the side of a hill, come into view on the right.

Nearby, the lake of Garennes has facilities for swimming and other recreation.

Château de la Martinie – *Turn right off the D 43.* This enormous 15C and Renaissance building, with a balustrade above the carriage gateway, has been converted into a farm.

Segonzac – The Romanesque church (11-12C) was altered and enlarged in the 16C. The **apse** is remarkable for its ribbed half-dome and the capitals with enormous, richly sculpted abaci on its blind arcades.

Return to the D 43.

The road along the crest offers fine views of the Dronne Valley and Ribérac area; the undulating countryside is given over to cereal crops and dotted with clumps of trees.

Siorac-de-Ribérac – Pop 227. Overlooking a small valley, the fortified Romanesque **church** has a single nave roofed at the end with a dome.

Turn left onto the D 13, then right onto the D 44 towards St-Aulaye.

Creyssac – Surrounded by the waters of a small lake, the tall square dovecot and the hen houses tucked alongside it make a pleasant sight.

200m – 220yds further on take the left fork towards Grand Étang de la Jemaye.

Jemaye Lake (Grand Étang de la Jemaye) – In the middle of Jemaye Forest, the lake has been set up as a water sports centre with a beach and facilities for fishing, windsurfing and other activities.

St-André-de-Double – Pop 176. The small church with a lopsided tower-façade is built in local speckled sandstone.

Echourgnac – Pop 411. Not far from this village *(along the D 38)* stands a **Trappist Monastery** (Trappe de Bonne-Espérance). The monastery was founded in 1868 by Trappist monks from Port-du-Salut in Normandy. They set up a model cheesemaking farm, collecting milk from the neighbouring farms. Their "Trappe" cheese is very similar to Port Salut. The monks had to leave the monastery in 1910 and were replaced in 1923 by Trappistine nuns, who continued the cheese-making industry.

Towards the south, the D 38 takes a route through the forest, skirting a network of pools and reedy channels. In the clearings, farms are beginning to cultivate kiwi fruit.

St-Laurent-des-Hommes – Pop 938. Opposite the Gothic church, the 17C half-timbered house with a decorated balcony is widely held to be the "most attractive house in the Double region".

Return towards St-Astier on the D 3.

Gamanson – Set back slightly from the road, this hamlet constitutes the richest collection of traditional half-timbered and clay-walled houses of the Double region.

St-Martin-l'Astier – Pop 152. The unusual outline of the Romanesque **church** in the middle of the cemetery is right at the extremes of most Double architecture. The great octagonal belltower, its corners reinforced by buttressed columns, houses on ground level a **chancel**, also octagonal, which is covered by a dome supported on eight engaged columns. It is connected to a simple timber-frame nave by an opening in one of the panels of a narrow doorway. The nave leads to the outside through a porch with five arch mouldings.

Douzillac – Pop 628. A memorial has been built in honour of Corporal Louis Maine, one of the very few survivors of the memorable battle fought by the Foreign Legion in the Cameroon in 1863.

After Douzillac, the great round towers of the Renaissance château of **Mauriac**, which belonged to the Talleyrand family, can be seen on the right.

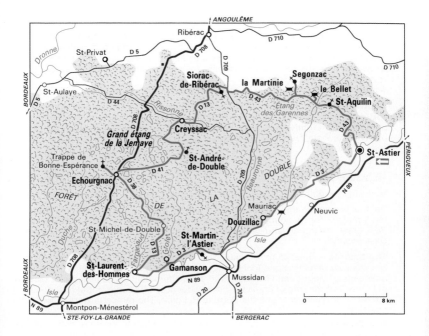

Michelin Maps, Red Guides and Green Guides are complementary publications. Use them together.

ESPAGNAC-STE-EULALIE

Michelin map 🟦 fold 9 or 🟦 fold 11 – 18km – 11 miles west of Figeac – Local map under CÉLÉ VALLEY

In this delightful village built in the picturesque setting of a series of cliffs, the houses with their turrets and pointed roofs are grouped round the former priory known as "Notre-Dame du Val-Paradis" (Our Lady of the Valley of Paradise, see Célé Valley).

Priory of Our Lady (Ancien Prieu-ré Notre-Dame) – Founded in the 12C by Bertrand de Grifeuille, a monk of the Augustinian Order, the priory was attached to the Abbey of La Couronne (near Angoulême). In 1212 the priory became a convent for the Augustinian canonesses and expanded considerably under the ægis of Aymeric Hébrard (see below), Bishop of Coïmbra. In 1283 the convent was moved to avoid its being flooded by the Célé River. During the Hundred Years War the convent suffered considerably; the cloisters were destroyed and the church was partly demolished. It was rebuilt in the 15C, however, and the community carried on until the Revolution. The conventual buildings are occupied by a rural centre and flats (gîtes communaux), which are let for the holidays by the commune.

Priory Church's belltower

Church (Église) ⊙ – The present Flamboyant-style church has replaced a 13C building of which there still remain the walls of the nave, a doorway and, jutting out beyond the walls, the ruins of bays which were destroyed during fires in the 15C. The exterior is peculiar for several reasons: the pentagonal chevet is higher than the nave and, on the south side, the belltower is surmounted by a square brick and timber chamber, topped by an octagonal roof of lauzes. Inside, the three tombs with recumbent figures placed in funerary niches are those of Aymeric Hébrard de St-Sulpice (d 1295) and of a knight, Hugues de Cardaillac-Brengues (buried here in 1342) and his wife, Bernarde de Trian. On the high altar, which has a 17C gilded wood predella, stands an 18C retable framing a picture of the Assumption, based on a painting by Simon Vouet.

EXCIDEUIL

Michelin map 🟦 folds 6 and 7 or 🟦 fold 44 – Facilities

The ruins of Excideuil Castle, harking back to times when there were viscounts of Limoges and counts of Périgord, crown a hill overlooking the Loue Valley.

Castle – A curtain wall, one-time façade of the feudal castle, links the two dismantled keeps, built respectively in the late 11C and the 12C. Beside the medieval fortress stands a Renaissance mansion with recently added turrets and mullioned windows. It once belonged to the Talleyrand family, for whom Louis XIII raised Excideuil to the status of marquisate in 1613.

A good view of the castle can be enjoyed from the banks of the river.

Church (Église) ⊙ – The former 12C Benedictine priory was very much altered in the 15C, which explains why the church has a fine Flamboyant doorway on its south side. Inside are a 17C gilded altarpiece (from the neighbouring Franciscan church) and a polychrome Pietà, Our Lady of Excideuil, which is surrounded by ex-voto.

EYMET

Michelin map 🟦 fold 14 or 🟦 fold 8 – Facilities

On the border of the Bergerac and Agen regions, Eymet is a small Périgord town famous for its gourmet food factories which preserve goose and duck liver (foie gras), galantines and ballottines (See Introduction: Dordogne's Homegrown Gastronomy).

The bastide – Time: 45 min. Founded in 1271 by Alphonse de Poitiers, the bastide was ruled by several seigneurial families – even though it was granted a charter guaranteeing privileges and liberties – who were alternately in allegiance with the king of France and the king of England. In consequence, it had an eventful history during the Hundred Years War and the Wars of Religion. The ramparts were razed under Louis XIII.

Place Centrale – The arcaded square is lined with old half-timbered or stone houses, some of which have mullioned windows. In its centre is a 17C fountain.

Keep (Donjon) – This 14C tower is all that remains of the castle.

A small **museum** ⊙ has been set up inside and displays regional art and folklore (clothes, tools etc.) as well as prehistoric objects.

Michelin map **75** folds 16 and 17 or **235** fold 1 – Local map overleaf – Facilities

The village of Les Eyzies is attractively placed in a grandiose setting of steep cliffs crowned with evergreen oaks and junipers, at the confluence of the Vézère and Beune Rivers. The Vézère River, lined on either side by poplars, at times winds between meadows and farmland, and at other times narrows to flow between walls of rock 50 to 80m — 164 to 262ft high. Shelters cut out of the bases of these limestone piles served as dwelling places for prehistoric man, whereas the caves, which generally appear half-way up the cliffs, were used as sanctuaries. The discovery within the last hundred years of these dwellings all within a limited radius of Les Eyzies has made the village the capital of prehistory.

On the outskirts of town, on the road to Tursac, stand the old ironworks which bring to mind the town's and region's industrial past (from the Middle Ages to the Second Empire of 1852-70). Although the present buildings (warehouse and workers' accommodations) date from the 18C, the forge's origin goes back to the 16C, when its main livelihood came from supplying iron to the merchants of Bordeaux.

THE CAPITAL OF PREHISTORY *local map overleaf*

The lower Vézère during the caveman era – During the Second Ice Age and at the time when the volcanoes of Auvergne were active, in the wake of the animals he hunted for food, prehistoric man abandoned the northern plains, where the Acheulean and Abbevillian civilizations had already evolved, and headed for the warmer areas to the south. The bed of the lower Vézère was then some ninety feet above its present level, and the river attracted the migrants because of its forested massifs, its easily accessible natural caves and the rocks overhanging it, which could be hollowed out into shelters more easily than the friable and fissured limestone of the Dordogne Valley.

People inhabited these cave dwellings for tens of thousands of years and left in them traces of their daily tasks and passage such as bones, ashes from their fires, tools, weapons, utensils and ornaments. Their civilization evolved simultaneously with the world around them. Animal species evolved into those we know today: after elephants and cave bears came bisons, aurochs, mammoths and, later still, musk-oxen, reindeer, ibex, stags and horses.

When the climate grew warmer and rainfall became more abundant at the end of the Magdalenian Period, man abandoned the caves for the hillsides facing the sun.

The archaeologists' paradise – Methodical study of the deposits in the Les Eyzies region has considerably increased our knowledge of prehistory *(see Introduction: ABC of Prehistory)*. The Dordogne *département* has greatly contributed to the study of prehistory with more than 200 deposits discovered there, of which more than half are in the lower Vézère Valley. In 1863 work began at the Laugerie and La Madeleine Deposits; the discovery of objects such as flints, carved bones and ivory, tombs (in which the skeletons had been coloured with ochre) greatly encouraged early research workers. In 1868 workmen levelling soil unearthed the skeletons of the Cro-Magnon shelter. Soon afterwards, more thorough research in the Le Moustier and La Madeleine Caves enabled two great periods of the Palaeolithic Age to be defined: the periods were called after the cave deposits – Mousterian and Magdalenian. Discoveries followed thicker and faster as Les Eyzies proved to be one of the richest prehistoric sites in the world with its **deposits**: La Micoque, Upper Laugerie, Lower Laugerie, La Ferrassie (south of Savignac-de-Miremont), Laussel and the Pataud Shelter; with its **shelters and caves** containing hidden carvings and drawings: Le Cap Blanc, Le Poisson, La Mouthe, Les Combarelles, Bernifal and Commarque; and with its caves containing polychrome **wall paintings**: Font-de-Gaume and Lascaux. The study of the engravings on bone, ivory and stone, as well as of low reliefs, wall carvings and paintings has made it possible to establish the beliefs, rituals, way of life and artistic evolution of Palaeolithic man.

Associated with the excavations and research are: L Capitan, D Peyrony, Abbé H Breuil, H Bordes, A Leroi-Gourhan, H L Movius and H de Lumley.

SIGHTS

Les Eyzies

★**National Museum of Prehistory (Musée National de la Préhistoire)** ☉ – The museum is in the old castle of the barons of Beynac. The 13C fortress, restored in the 16C, clings to the cliff half-way up, beneath a rocky outcrop, overlooking the village. From the terrace, on which there is a statue of Neanderthal man as interpreted by the sculptor Dardé, there is a good view of Les Eyzies and the valleys of Vézère and Beune. Part of the rich collection of prehistoric objects and works of art discovered locally over the last eighty years is on display in two buildings, in connection with castings of tombs and equipment which have contributed to the fame of other important prehistorical sites. This display is completed by diagrams showing the chronology of prehistoric eras, sections through the earth's strata and photographs. A gallery on the first floor is devoted to different stone-chipping techniques and a synthesis of prehistory. Prehistoric art is represented by wall paintings and rock carvings as well as domestic objects.

The second floor contains objects from all the prehistoric periods combined. The Breuil Gallery displays castings of prehistoric works of art from other museums. One gallery has assembled an impressive collection of carved limestone slabs dating from between 30 000 and 15 000 years BC and representing animals, female silhouettes and so on. Nearby ornaments made in stone, teeth or bone and weapons (spears, pierced bone implements, harpoons) are exhibited alongside castings of the most important female figurines of Europe.

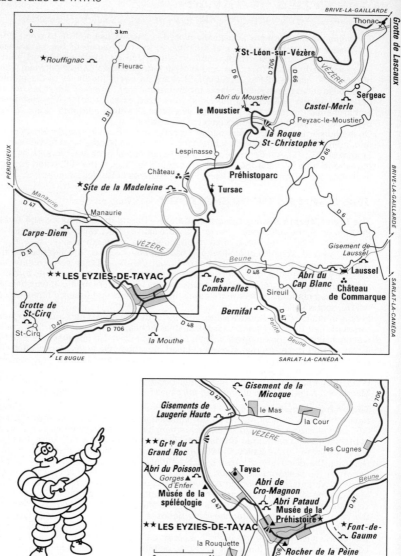

On the top floor in a large gallery is a display explaining the evolution of flint knapping as long as 2.5 million years ago.

In another building the Magdalenian tomb of a woman from St-Germain-la-Rivière, complete with its skeleton and a skeleton from Roc de Marsal, has been reconstructed.

Cro-Magnon Shelter (Abri de Cro-Magnon) – This cave was discovered in 1868 and it revealed, in addition to flints and carved bones of the Aurignacian and Gravettian Cultures, three adult skeletons which were studied by Paul Broca (qv), the surgeon and anthropologist who founded the School of Anthropology in France. The discoveries made in this cave were of prime importance in prehistoric studies, since they enabled the characteristics of Cro-Magnon man (qv) to be defined.

★Font-de-Gaume Cave (Grotte de Font-de-Gaume) ⊘ – *Leave the car by the road to St-Cyprien opposite a cliff-spur. A path takes you up 400m-440yds to the cave entrance.*

The cave runs back in the form of a passage 120m-130yds long with chambers and other ramifications leading off it. The cave has been public knowledge for some time, and since the 18C, visitors have regrettably left their mark, not recognising the importance of the wall paintings. Detailed examination and study of the paintings date them as belonging to the Magdalenian Period. Beyond a narrow passage, known as the Rubicon, are many multi-coloured paintings, often superimposed on one another; all the drawings of horses, bison, mammoths, reindeer and other deer indicate great artistic skill and, after Lascaux, form the finest group of polychrome paintings in France. The frieze of bison, painted in brown on a white calcite background, is remarkable.

Pataud Shelter (Abri Pataud) ⊘ – A museum on site shows objects and bones discovered during excavation work, and a video recording introduces visitors to the tour of the Pataud shelter. This is in fact a cavity 90m by 15m - 295ft by 49ft, in which a 9m - 30ft deep mound conceals the remains of civilizations dating from the beginning of the Upper Palaeolithic era (Aurignacian, Gravettian and Solutrean) between 35 000 and 20 000 years BC. In two large stratigraphic sections, bones, flints and the remains of fireplaces can be seen in situ, as well as a carved Venus in the most recent Gravettian layer. A three-minute film projected onto the rock face portrays a deer-hunters' camp of 25 000 years ago.

La Peine Rock (Rocher de la Peine) – This great rock, worn jagged by erosion, partially overhangs the road. A Magdalenian deposit was discovered within it.

Church (Église de Tayac) ⊘ – The warm, gold-coloured stone enhances this 12C fortified church. Two crenellated towers, arranged as keep-like structures and roofed with *lauzes*, frame the main body of the church. The tower above the doorway serves as the belltower.
The doorway is intriguing with the first recessed arch, which is multifoil, giving an oriental air while the two reused blue marble columns, with Corinthian capitals, show Gallo-Roman influence.
Inside, the arrangement of the three naves, divided by large arcades resting on piers, and the timberwork ceiling are features rarely found in the Périgord.

Along the D 47

Museum of Speleology (Musée de la Spéléologie) ⊘ – The museum is installed in the rock fortress of Tayac, which overlooks the Vézère Valley. The four chambers, cut out of the living rock, contain a selection of items pertaining to speleology: pot holing equipment, exhibits describing the geological formation and natural life of the pot holes and various models.

Le Poisson Shelter (Abri du Poisson) ⊘ – A 1.05m - 3.3ft long fish (*poisson*) has been carved on the roof of a small hollow. It is a salmon, one of a species which was very common in the Vézère until quite recently. It dates from the Gravettian period (about 20 000 years BC), and, with the Laussel Venus (*qv*), it is the oldest cave sculpture yet discovered.

★★ **Grand Roc Cave (Grotte du Grand Roc)** ⊘ – There is a good **view**★ of the Vézère Valley from the stairs leading up to the cave and the platform at its mouth. The length (40m - 45yds) of tunnel enables one to see, within chambers that are generally small in size, an extraordinary display of stalactites, stalagmites and eccentrics resembling coral formations, as well as a wonderful variety of pendants and crystallisations.

Upper Laugerie Deposit (Gisement de Laugerie Haute) ⊘ – Scientific excavations going on for over a century in a picturesque spot at the foot of high cliffs have revealed examples of the work and art of the cavemen at different degrees of civilization.
The excavations begun in 1863 were subsequently conducted in stages: 1911, 1921, 1936-39 and again over the past couplé of years. The work has enabled several sections to be made, which demonstrate the importance of this area, inhabited continuously by man from the middle of the Perigordian to the middle of the Magdalenian Period; that is to say, during the some 25 000 years of the Upper Palaeolithic Age.
The sections confound the imagination as they make one all too aware of how painfully slowly man progressed through these millennia. Two human skeletons have been discovered beneath masses of fallen earth in the western part of the deposits. Note the drip stones or channels cut in the rock in the Middle Ages to prevent water from running along the walls and entering the dwellings.

La Micoque Deposit (Gisement de la Micoque) – This deposit revealed many items belonging to periods known as the Tayacian and Micoquian Ages, which fall between the end of the Acheulean and the beginning of the Mousterian Ages. The finds are exhibited at Les Eyzies National Museum of Prehistory.

Carpe-Diem Cave (Grotte de Carpe-Diem) ⊘ – Following this 180m - 200yds long passage as it winds through the rock, stalagmites and different coloured stalactites can be seen here and there.

St-Cirq Cave (Grotte de St-Cirq) ⊘ – *Access via the road which extends the D 47 southwards*.
In a small cave underneath an overhanging rock engravings from the Magdalenian Period, representing horses, bison and ibex, have been discovered. However, the cave is best known for the painting of the **Man of St-Cirq** (at times inappropriately called the Sorcerer of St-Cirq), one of the most remarkable representations of a human figure found in a prehistoric cave.
A small museum exhibits fossils and prehistoric tools.

Along the Vézère River

The sights are described from north to south so that they might be included in the itinerary of the Vézère Valley (see Vézère Valley).

Castel-Merle – *See Vézère Valley.*

Le Moustier – This village, at the foot of a hill, contains a famous **prehistoric shelter** (Abri du Moustier). The prehistoric finds made here include a human skeleton and many flint implements. A culture in the Middle Palaeolithic Age was named Mousterian after the finds.
An interesting 17C carved confessional can be seen in the village church.

★ **St Christopher's Rock (La Roque St-Christophe)** ⊘ – For more than 900m - half a mile this long and majestic cliff rises vertically (80m - 262ft) above the Vézère Valley. It is like a huge hive with about a hundred caves hollowed out of the rock on five tiers. Excavations are underway along its foot, revealing that man lived here from the Upper Palaeolithic Age onwards.

In the 10C the cliff terraces served as the foundation for a fortress which was used against the Vikings and during the Hundred Years War, and then subsequently destroyed during the Wars of Religion, at the end of 16C. The many holes for posts, the drainage channels and water tanks, the fireplaces, the stairways and passages hollowed out of the rock all show that St Christopher's Rock was the site of continued, lively human activity. From the **Pas du Miroir**, it was once possible to see one's reflection in the Vézère, for the river at one time flowed at the foot (30m - 99ft below) of the cliff.

The terrace affords a good bird's-eye **view★** of the valley.

Tursac Préhistoparc

Tursac Préhistoparc ⊘ – In a small cliff-lined valley, carpeted with undergrowth, a discovery trail reveals about twenty reconstituted scenes of Neanderthal and Cro-Magnon man's daily life: mammoth hunting, cutting-up of reindeer, cave painting, burial customs etc.

Tursac church is dominated by a huge, forbidding belltower. There is a series of domes, characteristic of the Romanesque Périgord style, covering the church.

The road once more scales the cliff, giving good views of Tursac village and the Vézère Valley.

Beune Valley

Les Combarelles Cave (Grotte des Combarelles) ⊘ – A winding passage 250m-275yds long has many markings on its walls for the last 130m-140yds of its length, some of which are superimposed one upon another. The drawings include nearly 300 animals: horses, bison, bears, reindeer and mammoths can be seen at rest or in full gallop. This cave was discovered in 1901 at about the same time as Font-de-Gaume Cave and demonstrated the importance of Magdalenian art at a time when some scholars were still sceptical about the worth of prehistoric studies.

A second passage with similar cave drawings was the backdrop against which prehistoric man acted out his life as can be seen from the traces of domestic settlement and the tools of Magdalenian men which have been discovered.

Bernifal Cave (Grotte de Bernifal) ⊘ – *10 minutes walk.*

Cave paintings and delicate carvings from the Magdalenian period are spread over about a hundred metres (330ft). They include mammoths, asinine figures and tectiform shapes (suggesting dwellings).

Cap-Blanc Shelter (Abri du Cap-Blanc) ⊘ – Excavation of a small Magdalenian deposit in 1909 led to the discovery of **carvings★** in high relief on the walls of the rock shelter. Two bisons and in particular a frieze of horses were carved in such a way as to use to full advantage the relief and contour of the rock itself. A human grave was discovered at the foot of the frieze.

Commarque Castle (Château de Commarque) – The impressive castle ruins on the south bank of the Beune River stand opposite Château de Laussel. Commarque was built as a stronghold in the 12 and 13C and for a long time it belonged to the Beynac family. As a result of treachery, it fell into English hands, but was later retaken by the lord of Périgord, who then returned it to the baron of Beynac. Considerable parts of the fortifications are still standing. The keep, crowned with machicolations, the chapel and the various living quarters are set romantically amidst a mass of greenery.

Château de Laussel – This 15 to 16C château (redesigned in the 19C) is perched on a cliff which drops sheer into the Beune Valley. The building is small but elegant. A few hundred yards further along the valley a large prehistoric deposit (Gisement de Laussel) was discovered, which contained several human-like forms in low relief and the famous Venus with the horn of plenty *(illustration p 19)* from the Gravettian Culture; this is now exhibited in the Aquitaine Museum in Bordeaux.

** **FIGEAC** ⊂┃▲━┃▼⊃ Pop 9 549

Michelin map **79** fold 10 or **235** fold 11 – Local maps under CÉLÉ VALLEY and LOT VALLEY: Cliffs and Promontories – Facilities

Sprawled along the north bank of the Célé, Figeac's development began at the point where the Auvergne meets Upper Quercy. A commercial town, it had a prestigious past as is shown in the architecture of its tall sandstone town houses.

The small city's main industrial concern is Ratier, a company which specialises in aeronautical construction.

From abbots to king – Figeac began developing in the 9C around a monastery, which itself began expanding in the 11 and 12C.

The abbot was the town's lord and governed it with the aid of seven consuls. All administrative services were located inside the monastery. Because Figeac was on the pilgrimage route running from Le Puy and Conques and onto Santiago de Compostela *(see Michelin Green Guide to Spain)*, crowds of pilgrims and travellers flocked through it.

Benefiting from the town's geographical situation between Auvergne, Quercy and Rouergue, local craftsmen and shopkeepers were prosperous.

In 1302, following a disagreement between the abbot and the consuls, Philip the Fair took control of the town, represented by a provost. He won back the inhabitants' favour by allowing them the rare privilege of minting money.

The Hundred Years War and the Wars of Religion had an adverse effect on the town's development. From 1598 to 1622 Figeac was a safe stronghold for the Calvinists, until Richelieu broke up their fortifications.

Jean-François Champollion – Champollion, the outstanding Orientalist, whose brilliance enabled Egyptology to make such great strides, was born at Figeac in December 1790. At the beginning of the 19C, Ancient Egyptian civilization was still a mystery, since the meaning of hieroglyphics (the word means "sacred carving") had not yet been deciphered.

By the time Champollion was 14, he had a command of Greek, Latin, Hebrew, Arabic, Chaldean and Syrian. After his studies in Paris, he lectured in history, at the youthful age of 19, at Grenoble University.

He set himself the task of deciphering a polished basalt tablet, showing three different inscriptions (Egyptian hieroglyphics, demotic – simplified Egyptian script which appeared around 650 BC – and Greek), which had been discovered in 1799 by members of Napoleon's expedition to Egypt near Rosetta in the northwest Nile delta, from which it derives its name – the Rosetta Stone.

However he was not able to carry out his research on the stone itself, which had been seized by the English while at war with France (*it is now in the British Museum, London*), but had to make do with copies. Drawing on the work of a predecessor, the English physicist **Thomas Young** (1773-1829), who had succeeded in identifying genders and proper nouns, Champollion gradually unravelled the mystery of hieroglyphics.

He was harrassed for his Bonapartist views during the Restoration, and for several years progress with his work was slow; then in 1822, by illustrating that hieroglyphics are "a complex system of writing which is at once figurative, symbolic and phonetic", he hit upon the essential discovery that, while the Egyptians used their signs as letters for proper names, these same signs could be used to represent ideas, words and syllables the rest of the time.

Champollion left for Egypt to put his theory to the test and deciphered many texts while he was there.

In 1826, he founded the Egyptology Museum at the Louvre Palace, Paris, and became its first curator. In 1831, he was appointed Professor of Archaeology at the Collège de France, however he gave only three lecture courses before dying a year later, worn out by all his hard work.

The Rosetta Stone

During the reigns of the first nine Ptolomaic kings (332-80 BC), Egyptian priests recorded the decrees issued at the end of their synods on basalt tablets which were then displayed in the main temples. The Rosetta Stone is one of these tablets, carved in 196 BC. By this time, the members of the clergy were the only people to be taught hieroglyphics, hence the need for a translation into three languages so that the decrees would be understood also by those people who used demotic script in Memphis and Greek in Alexandria. The content of these decrees was both political and economic, defining the respective powers of the clergy and the monarch, the extent of fiscal privileges and the nature of laws and taxes among other things. This is illustrated by the following extracts from the Rosetta Stone:

"...The pharaoh Ptolemy, son of the pharaoh Ptolemy and of the pharaoh's wife Arsinoe, these gods-who love-their-father, undertakes much in the service of the temples of Egypt and of all those under his authority as pharaoh, indeed, he is...someone who has in the past given large amounts of money and grain to the temples of Egypt and to the continuing security of the temples, and someone who has rewarded the entire army under his supreme command. All duties and taxes imposed in Egypt have been reduced, or even abolished, at his command, so that the army and the rest of the people should be contented during his reign as pharaoh... in view of all this, he has decreed that the gods' estate revenue, the sums of money or quantities of grain that have to be paid in tax to the temple each year and the gods' share of vines, fruit trees and other things that were allotted to them by his father, be now submitted.

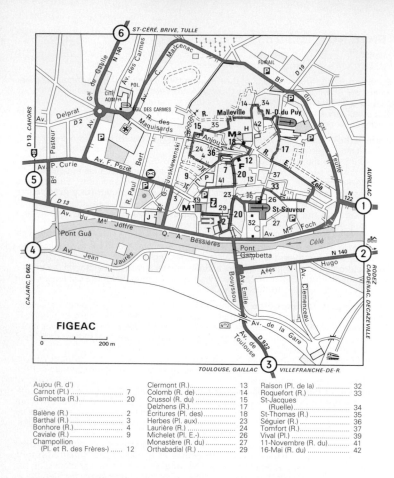

FIGEAC

0   200 m

★OLD FIGEAC *time: 1 hour 30 min*

The old quarter, surrounded by boulevards which trace the line of the former moats, has kept its medieval town plan with its narrow and tortuous alleys.

The buildings, built in elegant beige sandstone, exemplify the architecture of the 13, 14 and 15C. Generally the ground floor was opened by large pointed arches and the first floor had a gallery of arcaded bays. Underneath the flat tiled roof was the *soleilho,* an open attic, which was used to dry laundry, store wood, grow plants etc. Its openings were separated by columns or pillars in wood or stone, sometimes even brick, which held up the roof. Other noticeable period architectural features to be discovered during your tour of the old quarter are: corbelled towers, doorways, spiral staircases and some of the top storeys, which are half-timbered and of brick.

★Mint (Hôtel de la Monnaie) (M¹) – *Tourist information centre.*

This late 13C building, restored in the early 20C, exemplifies Figeac's secular architecture with its *soleilho,* pointed arches on the ground floor and the depressed arched windows placed either singly, paired or grouped in the façade. It is interesting to compare the façade, overlooking the square, which was rebuilt with the elements of the former consul's house of the same period, with the other plainer façades. The octagonal stone chimney was characteristic of Figeac construction at one time, but very few examples remain.

The name *Oustal dé lo Mounédo* owes its name to the Royal Mint created in Figeac by Philip the Fair. It has since been established that the stamping workshop was located in another building and that this handsome edifice was the place where money was exchanged.

The Mint contains a **museum** ⊘ which includes sculpture from religious and secular buildings (the door of the Hôtel de Sully), sarcophagi, grain measurements, old coins and town seals originating from the period when the town had its seven consuls.

Take Rue Orthabadial and turn right into Rue Balène.

Rue Balène (2) – At no 7 stands the 14C **Balène Castle** (Château de Balène), which houses the community hall. Its medieval fortress-like façade is lightened by an ogive doorway and chapel windows with decorated tracery. Exhibitions are held in ogive vaulted rooms.

At no 1, the 15C **Hôtel d'Auglanat,** which housed one of the king's provosts, is decorated with a lovely basket-arched doorway and battlemented turret.

Rue Gambetta (20) – This is the old town's main street. The houses at nos 25 and 28 are half-timbered, with decorative brickwork, and have been beautifully restored.

Continue via Rue Gambetta and Place aux Herbes to Place Edmond-Michelet.

St-Sauveur – This used to be an abbey church, the oldest parts of which date from the 11C. It has kept its original cross plan: a high nave with 14C chapels off the aisles. The nave is unusual for the lack of symmetry between its north and south sides. The south side includes: in the lowest section, rounded arcades; in the middle section, a tribune with twinned bays within a larger arch; and in the upper section, 14C clerestory windows.

On the north side, rebuilt in the 17C (as was the vaulting), the tribune was destroyed during the Wars of Religion.

The chancel, surrounded by the ambulatory, was rebuilt in the 18C. Four Romanesque capitals, remnants of the earlier doorway, support the baptismal font.

★**Notre-Dame-de-Pitié** ⊘ – This former chapter-house became a place of worship after the departure of the Protestants in 1623. A sumptuous carved and painted **wooden décor**★ was added to it, apparently the work of the Delclaux, a family of master painters from Figeac. To the right of the altar there is a striking panel depicting the infant Jesus asleep on the cross, dreaming of his future Passion.

Between the church and the Célé river is the Place de la Raison, on the site of the conventual buildings which were destroyed in the Revolution. The main feature of this square is the obelisk dedicated to Champollion.

Rue du Roquefort (33) – The house with the bartizan on a carved corbel belonged to Galiot de Genouillac, Grand Master of the Artillery of François I *(see Assier)*.

Rue É.-Zola – The oldest street in the town still has ogival arcades and an interesting sequence of Renaissance doorways from nos 35-37.

Rue Delzhens (17) – At no 3, the **Provost's House** (Hôtel du Viguier) has a square keep and a watch turret. Restoration is currently underway to convert it into a hotel.

Église Notre-Dame-de-Puy – The church is on a hill which gives a good view of the town and its surroundings. The Protestants used it as a fortress, strengthening the façade with a watch room.

This Romanesque building underwent many alterations between the 14C and the 17C; it has an enormous altarpiece carved in walnut dating from the end of the 17C, which frames two pictures representing the Assumption and the Coronation of the Virgin.

Go back down the hill along St-Jacques lane (ruelle).

Rue Maleville – This road is blocked by a covered passageway painted with the coat of arms of the Hôtel de la Porte.

Rue St-Thomas (35) – This also passes under a covered passageway, featuring corbelled galleries under the eaves (*soleilhos*).

Rue du Crussol (15) – The courtyard of the 16C **Hôtel de Crussol**, now a terrace-bar, is decorated with two superimposed balconies.

Take Rue Laurière then Rue Bonhore to get to Place Carnot. At the far end of Rue Caviale, opposite no 35 (l'Hôtel d'Ay-de-Lostanges), is the **King's House** (Maison du Roi), so-called because Louis XI is supposed to have stayed there in 1463.

Place Carnot (7) – Formerly Place Basse, this was headquarters to the wheat exchange, which was closed down in 1888. In the northwest corner, with a small side turret, is the **house of Pierre de Cisteron**, Louis XIV's armourer.

From Place Carnot, after crossing the narrow, medieval-looking Rue Séguier (36), go through a porch to get to Place des Écritures.

★**Place des Écritures** (18) – Set amidst a group of medieval architecture, this square has an enormous (14m by 7m - 46ft by 23ft) **replica of the Rosetta Stone** covering the whole of its floor. This was sculpted in black granite from Zimbabwe by the American conceptual artist Joseph Kossuth. Unveiled in 1991, this significant contemporary work of art is also worth being viewed from the hanging gardens overlooking the square. The French translation of the inscriptions is carved on a glass plaque kept in a small neighbouring courtyard. An archway gives access to the Champollion Museum.

★**Champollion Museum (M²)** ⊘ – A collection of documents in Champollion's birthplace traces the life history of this local hero, while original objects or reproductions evoke the use of Egyptian writing and the rites and customs of Ancient Egypt. On the first floor the

Place des Écritures, Figeac

Salle de l'Écriture displays in particular a casting of the Rosetta Stone, the original being in the British Museum in London, also carved steles, a large statuette in black granite of the architect Djehouty (15 BC) and a scribe's palette (an essential writing tool which was included in the mortuary equipment). On the second floor, striking exhibits include a mummy and various sarcophagi from the Thebes necropolis, canopic vases, one of which still contains the deceased person's entrails, an offertory table carved with images of food (that it was believed would be turned into the real thing by magic) and two pieces of porcelain; a mummy's costume decoration and the splendid bust of a worker, in a vivid blue underlaid with black.

Place Champollion (12) – The 14C infirmary of the Knights Templars has beautiful Gothic windows on the second floor.

Return along Rue Gambetta.

Commandery of the Knights Templars ⊘ – *No 41 Rue Gambetta.*
Around 1187 the Order of the Knights Templars, which was expanding rapidly, came to establish itself at Figeac. It built this commandery, and the Gothic façade certainly brightens up Rue Gambetta. In the 15C, another building closed off the elegant **courtyard**. A remarkable 15C wooden staircase leads to the first floor where the guard room, the chapter-house and the chapel are to be found. The latter are connected by oratory hatches. On the second floor a restored wooden balcony links the monks' dormitory with the Commander's residence in which there is also a private chapel. The watchtower at the top of the building has had a 15C timber frame added to it.

EXCURSIONS

Domaine du Surgié ⊘ – This large leisure centre (14ha - 35 acres) is situated north-east of Figeac, on the banks of the Célé river.

Needles of Figeac (Aiguilles de Figeac) – These two octagonal-shaped obelisks to the south and west of town measure (base included) respectively 14.50m – 47ft and 11.50m – 38ft. It is believed that there were four "needles" and that they marked the boundaries of the land over which the Benedictine abbey had jurisdiction.
One of the needles – **Meander Needle** (Aiguille du Cingle), also known as Aiguille du Pressoir (Press Needle) – can also be seen from the D 922, south of Figeac.

Cardaillac – Pop 475. *11km – 7 miles northwest of town. Leave Figeac by ⑥ on the N 140 and then take the D 15 to the right.*
This town is the home territory of the Cardaillacs, one of the most powerful Quercy families.
The section with the fort stands on a rocky spur above the town. Of this triangular-shaped fortification, dating from the 12C, there remain two square towers: the Clock or Baron's Tower and Sagnes Tower. Only the latter is open to visitors. The two tall rooms with their vaulted ceilings are reached by a spiral staircase. From the platform there is a lovely view of the Drauzou Valley and the surrounding countryside.

Musée Éclaté ⊘ – This museum consists of several different sites scattered *(éclaté)* around the village in a determined effort to integrate evidence of the past firmly into the modern life of the village. Exhibits represent the village school, local crafts and the rural way of life. A study of the manufacture of wine-growers' baskets, once a speciality of Cardaillac, is given pride of place.

★ FOISSAC CAVES (Grottes de FOISSAC)

Michelin map 🟥🟥 fold 10 or 🟥🟥🟥 folds 11 and 15 – 13km – 8 miles south of Figeac

Discovered in 1959, **Foissac Caves** ⊘ have a total of 8km – 5 miles of galleries. An underground stream, which drains the caves, is a tributary of the Lot, which it joins near Balaguier. During the visit note the gleaming white stalactites and the lovely rock formations in the Obelisk Chamber (Salle de l'Obélisque); and the reflections, the stalagmites and ivory tower-like formations in the Michel Roques Gallery. In one gallery, Cave-in Gallery (Salle de l'Éboulement), there is a roof covered with round mushroom-like formations, thus proving that the stalactites were in the gallery well before earthquakes changed the aspect of the cave. These bulbous stalactites known as "the onions" (Oignons) are also worth noting.
These caves were occupied by man during the Copper Age (2700-1900 BC), when they were used as quarries, caves and a cemetery, and evidence of man's daily existence is apparent throughout: the "hearth", copper utensils and large rounded pieces of pottery. Also visible are human skeletons, some of which are accompanied by offerings suggesting some sort of ritual burial, and the imprint of a child's foot, fixed here in the clay 4 000 years ago.

GAVAUDUN

Michelin map **79** fold 6 or **235** fold 9 – 12km – 7.5 miles northwest of Fumel

Gavaudun lies in a picturesque **setting★** in the narrow, winding valley of the Lède.

Keep (Donjon) ⊙ – A massive (six storey) 12-14C crenellated keep towers at the top of a rock spur overlooking the river and the village. The keep is reached by a staircase cut into the rock.

EXCURSIONS

St-Sardos-de-Laurenque – Pop 260. *2km – 1 mile to the north.*
The 12C **church** ⊙ has an interesting carved doorway: the capitals are adorned with animals and human figures and there is a frieze decorated with fish. Note the outstanding capitals in the Romanesque nave.

St-Avit – Pop 164. *5km – 3 miles to the north.*
The pleasant road winds along the Lède Valley to the hamlet of St-Avit. Here, the church, its round east end roofed with *lauzes*, and several old houses lie in a pastoral setting overlooking the valley.
Bernard Palissy was born here (1510-90). He is remembered as a glass-blower and potter. He sought to rediscover the formula of a certain glaze and invented a ware halfway between Italian and glazed earthenware. He produced rustic-wares, which were dishes made to resemble little ponds with the appropriate animals – lizards, snakes, fish – and colours – greens, greys, browns.

Sauveterre-la-Lémance – Pop 685. *19km – 11.5 miles northeast.*
Edward I of England (reigned 1272-1307), also Duke of Aquitaine, had this **fortress** ⊙ built in the late 13C to defend his land from Philip III the Bold. A massive keep, two towers and a curtain wall *(no railings)* are all that remains.

★ GOURDON

Michelin map **75** fold 18 or **235** fold 6 – Facilities

Gourdon is the capital of the green undulating countryside called Bouriane *(qv)*. The town, situated on the borders of Quercy and Périgord, is arranged in tiers up the flank of a rocky hillock, upon which the local lord's castle once stood.
Follow the circular route of avenues which have replaced the old ramparts for pleasant views of the hills and valleys of Bouriane.

GOURDON

Briand (Bd A.-) 2
Cardinal-Farinié (R. du) 4
Cavaignac (Av.) 5
Dr-Cabanès (Bd) 7
Gaulle (Pl. Ch.-de-) 8
Gourdon (R. B. de) 9
Hôtel-de-Ville (Pl. de l') 10
Libération (Pl. de la) 12
Mainiol (Bd) 14
République (Allées de la) 17
Zig-Zag (R.) 18

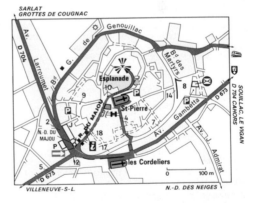

SIGHTS

★Rue du Majou – The fortified gateway, Porte du Majou, and, on the left, the chapel of Notre-Dame-du-Majou lead into the street of the same name.
This picturesque and narrow street was once the high street; all along it there are old houses with overhanging storeys and ground floors with large pointed arches. Just after no 24, there is a good view, to the right, of the old-fashioned Rue Zig-Zag. No 17, Anglars Mansion, has pretty mullioned windows.

Town Hall (Hôtel de Ville) (H) – This former 13C consulate, enlarged in the 17C, has covered arcades which are used as a covered market.

Church (Église St-Pierre) – The church (dedicated to St Peter) was begun in the early 14C and used to be a dependency of Le Vigan Abbey *(see Excursions below)*. The chancel is supported by massive buttresses. The door in the west face is decorated with elegant archivolts and is framed by two tall asymmetrical towers. The large rose window is protected by a line of machicolations, a reminder of former fortifications. The vast nave has pointed vaulting; 17C wood panels, carved, painted and gilded, decorate the chancel and the south transept.

Go round the left of the church outside and go up the staircase and then the ramp, which leads to the esplanade where the castle once stood.

Esplanade – A **panorama★** unfolds from the terrace *(viewing table)*: beyond the town and its roofs, which can be seen in tiers below the massive roof of the church (St-Pierre) in the foreground, one can see the churchyard, a forest of cypress trees, then the plateaus stretching out around the valleys of the Dordogne and the Céou.

Return to Place de l'Hôtel de Ville and go round the outside of the church starting from the right.

There are some old houses opposite the east end, including one with a lovely early-17C doorway.

Opposite the south door of the church take the Rue Cardinal-Farinié which goes downhill and contains old houses with mullioned windows and side turrets. This will bring you back to the Place de la Libération.

Franciscan Church (Église des Cordeliers) ⊙ – The church which used to be part of the Franciscan monastery is worth a visit, despite being slightly marred by a massive belfry porch which was added in the 19C. The slender lines of the nave, restored in 1971, are characteristic of early Gothic; the fine septilateral apse is lit by 19C stained-glass windows.

At the entrance, in the middle of the nave, stands a remarkable **font***. On the outside Christ the King and the twelve Apostles (14C) are depicted on the thirteen trefoiled blind arcades.

EXCURSIONS

★Cougnac Caves – *3km – 2 miles north on the D 70. See Cougnac Caves.*

Chapel (Chapelle de Notre-Dame-des-Neiges) ⊙ – *1.5km – 1 mile to the southeast.* Set in the small valley of the Bléou, this 14C chapel, a pilgrimage centre which was restored in the 17C, has a 17C altarpiece. A "miraculous spring" flows through the chancel.

Le Vigan – Pop 922. *5 km – 3 miles east on the D 673.*
A Gothic **church** ⊙, which is the remains of an abbey founded in the 11C, became a regular chapter for canons in the 14C. The church's east end is overlooked by a tower rising from the transept crossing. There is fine pointed vaulting over the nave and the spectacular east end, in which defensive turrets are tucked in between the apsidal chapels.

Henri-Giron Museum ⊙ – *In the area called Les Prades.* This museum contains about forty oil paintings and sketches by the master from Brussels, Henri Giron. His works unite classical heritage, in particular that of the Flemish primitives, with a remarkable modernity of atmosphere and subject, and include some disturbing female figures.

★ GRAMAT CAUSSE

Michelin map **75** folds 18 and 19 and **79** folds 8 and 9 or **235** folds 6, 7, 10 and 14

The Gramat Causse, which stretches from the Dordogne Valley in the north to the Lot and Célé Valleys in the south, is the largest – and wildest – *causse (qv)* in Quercy. It is a vast limestone plateau which lies at an average altitude of 350m – 1 148ft and contains a variety of natural phenomena and unusual landscapes.

Autumn is the time to cross the *causse*, when the trees are donning their seasonal colours and shedding a golden light on the grey stones and rocks, with the maples adding a splash of deep red.

OUTING ON THE CAUSSE

Route from Cahors to Souillac - 140km - 87 miles - allow one day - local map opposite

★★Cahors. – *See Cahors. Facilities.*
Leave Cahors by ②, *the D 653.*

The road runs along the north bank of the Lot, past **Laroque-des-Arcs** and **Notre-Dame-de-Vêles Chapel** (*see Lot Valley: Cliffs and Promontories*), and then climbs the charming Vers Valley, which in some places widens out into meadowland and in others cuts between tall grey cliffs.

St-Martin-de-Vers – Pop 126. In this small village the houses with brown-tiled roofs cluster round the old priory church and its asymmetrical belltower.

Take the D 10 and the D 71 to arrive at the **Braunhie** "desert", the most arid part of the plateau. Here, dry-stone walls stretch seemingly never-ending into the distance, and the scrubby vegetation includes oaks, maples and stunted walnut trees, or stony heathland with junipers and thorn bushes. To get the most out of this region, continue along the D 71 to Quissac, and then back to Caniac-du-Causse on the D 146 and the D 42. Old sheep and goat tracks have been cleaned up and now offer tempting opportunities to stroll around and discover the various nooks and crannies caused by water infiltrating the limestone (*see Introduction: Caves and Chasms*). Besides attractive farmhouses, the village of **Quissac** has conserved its working methods using teams of oxen, at one time common throughout the communities of the plateau.

Caniac-du-Causse – Beneath the church, the **crypt** ⊙ was built by the monks of Marcilhac-sur-Célé in the 12C to shelter the relic of St Namphaise, an officer in the army of Charlemagne who became a hermit and whom the inhabitants of Braunhie held in great esteem. He was supposed to have hollowed the so-called "St Namphaise's lakes" out of the rocks himself; the sight of these underlines the aridity of the area. This minute crypt has an unusual vault and an attractive central colonnade.

Labastide-Murat – *See Labastide-Murat.*

Beyond Labastide-Murat, the D 677 crosses the east side of the *causse* and then wends its way down to Gramat.

Just before the Gramat railway station turn right and take the D 14 for 1km – 0.5 mile.

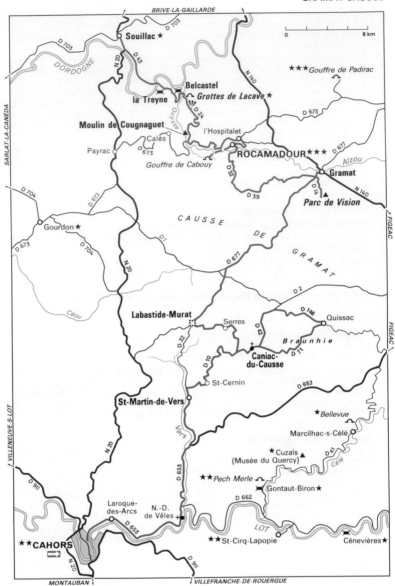

Gramat Nature Park (Parc de Vision de Gramat) ⊘ – This park extends over 38ha – 94 acres. It was acquired by the local authorities so that animals and plants could be visited in their natural environment.

A botanical park is home to trees and shrubs from the *causse* (durmast oak, dogwood, ash etc.).

The animal park contains mainly European species living in semi-captivity in their natural habitat. Some of these animals – wild ox, Przewalski's horses, ibexes, bison – are species which existed during prehistoric times.

A collection of farmyard animals includes a variety of domestic fowl, pigs etc.

Follow the signposted itinerary over 3km – 2 miles for an enjoyable and informative outing.

Take the D 677 which leads to Gramat.

Gramat – Pop 3 526. Facilities. Capital of the *causse* that bears its name, Gramat is also a great town for fairs (sheep).

It is the ideal starting point for visits to Padirac, Rocamadour and the area that lies between the Lot and the Dordogne.

It was here that the French Police Dog Handler Training Centre (Centre de formation des maîtres de chien de la Gendarmerie) ⊘ was established in 1945.

Return to the D 677 and almost immediately take the D 39 to the right; at the point where it joins the D 32, turn right.

The D 32 reaches the edge of the plateau from where there are lovely views of Rocamadour, before it crosses Alzou Canyon. Enter Rocamadour by the narrow ogive gateways.

★★★ Rocamadour – *See Rocamadour.*

L'Hospitalet – *See Rocamadour: L'Hospitalet.*

At L'Hospitalet join the D 673 towards Calès.

The pleasant road drops down through the deep Alzou and Ouysse valleys. The GR 6 below, a wide, well-maintained track, makes an easy walk (*time: 1 hour Rtn*) along the meanders of the river as far as the yawning Cabourg **chasm**, resurgence of the river Ouysse.

Cougnaguet Mill (Moulin de Cougnaguet) ⊘ – The rounded arches of this fortified mill span a derivation of the Ouysse in a cool, lush and charming **setting.** The mill was built in the 15C at the foot of a sheer cliff, on the site of a mill to which the water rights were granted in 1279. In the Middle Ages grain and flour, both highly sought-after commodities, needed to be particularly well-defended, as is illustrated by the impressive defence system here. The opening of the sluice gates hurled assailants towards the penstocks, in which a terrible, watery fate would engulf them. The mill has four millstones; one of which is still in working order.

Continue along the small road which climbs up to the D 247 and turn left. There are splendid **views★** along this road of the Dordogne Valley and of Belcastel Castle at its most attractive.

★Lacave Caves – *See Lacave Caves.*

Take the D 43 on the left, and follow it past the foot of Belcastel Castle.

Belcastel Castle – *See Dordogne Valley* ⒈.

Château de la Treyne – *See Dordogne Valley* ⒈.

Beyond Château de la Treyne the road cuts across a bend in the Dordogne before reaching Souillac.

★Souillac – *See Souillac. Facilities.*

*Make life easier by using **Michelin Maps** with your **Michelin Guide.***

★★ HAUTEFORT CHÂTEAU

Michelin map 🔢 fold 7 or 🔢 fold 44

Hautefort Château dates from the 17C and has been the property of the Bastard family since 1929. Its proud outline dominates the skyline, reminiscent more of the royal palaces of the Loire Valley than of the fortresses of Périgord. The château was badly damaged by fire on the night of 30-31 August 1968. Restoration was begun in 1969 and was excecuted with great care, adhering closely to the design of the original building.

Bertrand the Troubadour – The first castle of Hautefort was built by the Limousin family of Las Tours. In the 12C it passed by marriage to the house of De Born, of whom Bertrand, the very same mentioned by Dante in the *Divine Comedy*, is the most well-known member. **Bertrand de Born**, the famous troubadour who was much admired in the courts of love *(see Introduction: Intellectual and Literary Life)*, became a warrior-knight when the need arose to defend the family castle against his brother Constantine. With the support of Henry Short Coat *(qv)*, he succeeded in having Henry II acknowledge his rights in 1185 in spite of all Constantine's efforts, which were supported by Richard the Lionheart. However, in 1186 Constantine returned to Hautefort and razed the castle to the ground. Renouncing everything, Bertrand withdrew to take monastic orders.

Marie de Hautefort – Marie, also known as Aurore, daughter of the first Marquis of Hautefort, lady-in-waiting to Anne of Austria, is said to have possessed great beauty and a spotless reputation. She is best remembered for the deep admiration and platonic love she inspired in Louis XIII (1610-43). In 1646 she married the Duke of Halluin. She reigned over literary circles and *Salons des Précieuses* (Society drawing rooms) until her death in 1691 at 75 years of age.

Château de Hautefort

TOUR *time: about 1 hour*

The strategic position of the Hautefort site on a hill in the middle of an immense amphitheatre was certainly exploited very early on: in the 9C the viscounts of Limoges are known to have built a stronghold here. During the Middle Ages several castles succeeded one another, leaving some traces (the courtyard's west corner tower). The defensive position of the castle was strengthened in the 16C (barbican flanked by two crenellated bartizans and equipped with a drawbridge) during the tumultuous years of the Wars of Religion.

Complete reconstruction of the castle was instigated by Jacques-François de Hautefort (c1630). This lasted some forty years; the plans are attributed to the architect Nicolas Rambourgt, who kept the former living quarters but made considerable alterations elsewhere. The pavilions set at opposite ends were not completed until the 18C.

The harmonious combination of architectural styles – Renaissance and classical – contributes to the building's original and elegant appearance.

Walk – Go round the perimeter of the beautiful park (40ha - 99 acres) to the terraces, planted with flowers and cypress trees, which overlook the village and offer views of the park.

To reach the entrance to the château go to the end of the esplanade and cross the drawbridge over the moat, which is now decorated with flowers and boxwood. The main courtyard is a vast square open on one side to the village, which nestles at the foot of the castle walls, while on the other three sides it is surrounded by the living quarters. To the south are two round towers topped with domes and lantern turrets.

Interior ⊘ – The extensive restoration has recreated several rooms in their original finery and has repaired the great staircase, very badly damaged in the 1968 fire. The gallery houses two marble busts of the 16 and 18C (Seneca and Marcus Aurelius, respectively) and two vases in Toro stone; the doors are exact replicas of the originals. The tapestry gallery includes three 16C Flemish wall-hangings and another from Brussels, which depicts scenes from the Old Testament. The dining room contains 17C paintings and the state room's walls are covered with Cordoban leather.

Inside the southeast tower is a 17C chapel containing 16C paintings on leather and the altar from Charles X's coronation.

The southwest tower has beautiful chestnut **timberwork★★**, the work of the Compagnons du Tour de France guild. It also contains the museum of Eugène Le Roy (1836-1907) *(qv),* who was born at Hautefort, in the château itself, and wrote *Jacquou le Croquant (see L'Herm Castle below).* Another room contains objects saved from the fire.

Church (Église) – Built on a vast square south of the château, the church used to be the chapel of an almshouse founded by the Hautefort family. It has a fine slated dome topped by a lantern turret.

L'HERM CASTLE

Michelin map **75** fold 6 or **233** fold 43

In Barade Forest, at the heart of Périgord Noir, stands L'Herm Castle.

The **castle** ⊘ was built in 1512 by Jean III of Calvimont, president of the Parliament of Bordeaux and ambassador to Charles V in 1526. A series of violent crimes cast a bloody pall over the castle's history. Jean III was killed here. Then his daughter Marguerite was murdered in 1605 by her husband François d'Aubusson, who married Marie de Hautefort immediately afterwards. This couple commited about ten murders between them. In 1682 the castle was bought by another Marie de Hautefort *(see Hautefort Château above),* the first Marie's niece. Finally it was abandoned.

Recollection of these tragic events gave Eugène Le Roy *(qv)* the idea of making the castle the setting of the bloodier part of his novel *Jacquou le Croquant.*

The ruins of the castle with the powerful crenellated towers protrude from the surrounding forest. Access to the hexagonal staircase tower is through a doorway in essentially Flamboyant style, yet already influenced by the Renaissance style. The second archivolt, decorated with crockets, has a very tall pinnacle. On either side of the door the carved figures of men-at-arms are badly in need of repair. Inside, rising in a single sweep, the remarkable **spiral staircase★**, with a centre pillar decorated with rope moulding, is roofed with quadripartite vaulting. The intricate network of liernes and tiercerons creates a lovely palm tree effect. From the tower's windows there are bird's-eye views of the monumental chimneys decorating all three floors. These bear the Calvimont coat of arms; the coat of arms of the third floor chimney is held by two angels.

ISSIGEAC   Pop 638

Michelin map **75** fold 15 or **235** fold 5

The little town of Issigeac, lying in the Banège Valley southeast of the Monbazillac vineyards, has an interesting church, a castle and picturesque half-timbered and corbelled houses.

Church (Église) – The church was built by Armand de Gontaut-Biron, Bishop of Sarlat, at the beginning of the 16C and is a good example of late Gothic architecture. A belfry porch, supported by large buttresses, features a doorway with a tympanum decorated with twisted recessed arches.

Bishops' Castle (Château des Évêques) – The castle was built by another Bishop of Sarlat, François de Salignac, in the second half of the 17C. It now houses the town hall. The building is vast and is flanked by two square towers each with a corbelled turret of brick and stone on its north side. Fénelon (*qv*) stayed here in 1681.

EXCURSION

Château de Bardou – *7km – 4 miles to the east on the D 25, turning right after 5.5km – 3 miles.*
This interesting château (15-17C), now restored, is set in beautiful parkland.

LABASTIDE-MURAT   Pop 610

Michelin map 🗷 fold 18 or 🗷 fold 10 – Local map under GRAMAT CAUSSE – Facilities

Labastide-Murat, which stands at one of the highest points on the Gramat Causse *(qv)*, was originally called Labastide-Fortunière, but changed its name to Murat in honour of the most famous of its sons.
The modest house in which Joachim Murat was born, on the southwest of the town, as well as the château that he had built for his brother André, preserve the memory of one of the French Empire's (1804-14) most valiant soldiers.

The miraculous destiny of Joachim Murat – Murat was born in 1767, the son of an innkeeper. He was destined for the Church, but at twenty-one decided instead to be a soldier. The campaigns in Italy and Egypt enabled him to gain rapid promotion under Napoleon, whose brother-in-law he became by marrying the First Consul's sister, Caroline; he was promoted to Marshal of the Empire, Grand Duke of Berg and Cleves and King of Naples. The phenomenal bravery he displayed on all the battlefields of Europe and his influence over his troops, at whose head he unhesitatingly charged into battle, made him a legendary hero.
His glory faded with that of his master, whom he abandoned in the dark days of the Empire. His miserable end in 1815 was in keeping with the diversity in his life: after the Bourbons had returned to Naples, he tried to reclaim his kingdom, but was taken prisoner and shot.

Murat Museum (Musée Murat) ⊘ – The museum is in the house where Murat was born *(alleyway to the left of the church)*. The 18C kitchen, the inn's saloon and a large genealogical tree on which 10 European countries and several royal families are represented are on display to visitors. On the first floor there are mementos of the King of Naples and of his mother.

EXCURSIONS

Soulomès – Pop 129. *3km – 2 miles to the southeast on the D 17.*
There is a Gothic **church** ⊘ with a square chevet and a Romanesque belfry porch in this small village on the Gramat Causse. The church was once part of a commandery of the Order of the Knights Templars. Interesting 14C frescoes have been uncovered in the chancel. They illustrate scenes from the life of Christ: Jesus and Mary Magdalene, the Doubting of St Thomas, the Entombment and the Resurrected Christ appearing to a Knight.

Vaillac – Pop 84. *5km – 3 miles to the northwest on the D 17.*
The outline of a massive feudal castle overlooks this modest little village built on the *causse*.
The castle was built in the 14 and 16C and consists of a keep and a huge main building flanked by five towers. Another building, which formed part of the outbuildings, was used as a stable for as many as 200 horses.

LACAPELLE-MARIVAL   Pop 1 201

Michelin map 🗷 folds 19 and 20 or 🗷 fold 7 or 🗷 fold 39 – Facilities

The town has kept many buildings that bear testimony to its age and importance as the fief of Lacapelle-Marival which was held from the 12 to 18C by the Cardaillac family.

Castle – The massive, square, machicolated keep with watch towers at each corner was built in the 13C. The adjacent living quarters, separated by massive round towers, were added in the 15C.
The Gothic church, an old town gateway and the 15C covered market, supported on stone pillars and roofed with round tiles, make a charming sight together with the castle.

EXCURSION

Round tour of 27km – 16.5 miles – *Allow about 1 hour. Leave Lacapelle-Marival on the D 940 to the south.*

Le Bourg – Pop 222. The church is all that is left of a former priory. The transept and chancel are decorated with Romanesque arcades and fine capitals.
 Turn right onto the N 140.

Rudelle – Pop 155. Founded in the 13C by Bertrand de Cardaillac, the lord of Lacapelle-Marival, the fortified **church**, the most striking in Quercy, is in fact a feudal bastion, in which the oval-shaped lower level has been converted into a chapel. From the churchyard *(access by an alleyway to the right of the church)*, there is a view of the east end and the building as a whole.

The upper storey is reached up a wooden staircase to the gallery, then up a ladder, through a trap-door and finally up a stone staircase. This refuge, which now contains the bells, is lit by narrow loopholes.

To reach the terrace, which also provided refuge, another ladder and stone staircase have to be climbed. There is a good view of the village from the rampart walk, to which bartizans were later added.

Behind the church, the small chapel decorated with a scallop is a reminder that one of the pilgrim routes to Santiago de Compostela ran along its east end.

Follow the N 140 to Thémines, then take the D 40 to the right.

Aynac – Pop 604. Aynac Castle, set amidst woods and meadows, is now a riding centre. Its crenellated corner towers topped by domes are built tight up to the keep.

The D 940 returns to Lacapelle-Marival.

★ LACAVE CAVES (Grottes de LACAVE)

Michelin map **75** fold 18 or **235** fold 6 – Local maps under DORDOGNE VALLEY **1** and GRAMAT CAUSSE

Near the valley of the Dordogne as it makes a deep cut through the Gramat Causse a series of **caves** ⊙ was discovered in 1902 by Armand Viré, a student of the geographer and speleologist E A Martel, at the foot of the cliffs beside the river.

The galleries open to visitors are a mile long *(on foot Rtn)* and divide into two groups, which are visited one after the other. The shapes of the concretions in the caves look like people, animals, buildings and even whole cities. Delicate stalactites hang from the ceilings.

The first group of galleries contains a fascinating collection of stalagmites and stalactites.

In the second group underground rivers run in between natural dams *(gours)* and flood out into lakes in which beautiful reflections play. In the Lake Chamber (Salle du Lac) the natural fluorescence of the concretions makes the parts which are still growing glow in the dark. The Hall of Wonders (Salle des Merveilles) contains some beautiful eccentrics.

Flints and prehistoric tools and weapons made of bone and horn were discovered, while the caves were being arranged to accommodate visitors.

★ LANQUAIS CHÂTEAU

Michelin map **75** fold 15 or **235** fold 5 – Local map under DORDOGNE VALLEY **5**

The 14 and 15C main building, with all the defensive characteristics of a **fortified castle**, had a **Renaissance building** ⊙ added to it during the Wars of Religion.

On the outermost façade, where the impact of cannon-balls (traces of a skirmish in May 1577 during the Wars of Religion) are still visible, the only openings in the first floor are loopholes.

Facing the courtyard, there is Renaissance elegance in the harmonious **façades★**, which are divided into vertical registers, underlined horizontally by moulding and stone string courses marking the entablatures and lit by triangular pedimented windows. The dormer windows in particular catch the eye because of their rustic work, open gables and carved niches.

Inside, the two finely carved **chimneys★** and a flint collection are not to be missed.

The barn at the foot of the castle became a Protestant church in the 16C.

LARAMIÈRE   Pop 251

Michelin map **79** fold 19 or **235** fold 15 – 16km - 10 miles west of Villefranche-de-Rouergue

In the midst of the dolmens and *caselles (qv)* which dot the Limogne Causse, the little village of Laramière is to be found, along with the remains of its lovely priory.

Priory (Prieuré de Laramière) ⊙ – The priory was founded in 1148 by Bertrand de Grifeuille, a monk of the Augustinian Order, who also founded the priory at Espagnac-Ste-Eulalie *(qv)*.

The buildings, built in the 12 and 13C, formed a quadrilateral, however some of them were destroyed during the Wars of Religion. The Jesuits arrived in the mid-17C and built the bailiff's house.

Chapter-house

A tour of the restored buildings includes viewing the chapel vaulting, the Romanesque hall, in which the pilgrims of Santiago de Compostela were welcomed, and in particular the **chapter-house** with its walls and vaulting painted with geometric motifs and its capitals bearing carved effigies of St Louis and Blanche de Castille. On the church's south wall, funerary niches harboured the donors' tombs (Hugues de la Roche and his wife).

EXCURSION

Beauregard – *Take the D 55 west.*

Dolmen de la Borie du Bois – *On the left.* One of Quercy's finest dolmens.

   Continue along the D 55.

Beauregard – Pop 184. *6 km – 3.5 miles west.* This *bastide (qv)* still has its original street plan (streets at right angles). The 17C **covered market**, with a roof of *lauzes (qv)*, has grain measures carved into the rock. On the church's parvis there is a lovely 15C cross.

LARROQUE-TOIRAC CASTLE

Michelin map 🔲 fold 10 or 🔲 fold 11 – 14 km – 8.5 miles southwest of Figeac – Local map under LOT VALLEY: Cliffs and Promontories

The **castle** ⊘, clinging to a high cliff face, overlooks the village and the Lot Valley. This fortress was built in the 12C and belonged for many years to the Cardaillac family, who championed Quercy resistance against the English during the Hundred Years War. The castle, captured again and again by the English, was finally burnt down at the end of the 14C, but was rebuilt from its ruins during Louis XI's reign.

Starting from the church parvis *(car park)* a path leads to a round tower built at the beginning of the Hundred Years War as defence against artillery attack. It continues to the part of the castle which was the servants' quarters and then through to the courtyard. The huge keep, which was once 30m-98ft high but was razed to only 8m-26ft in 1793 on the orders of the Commissioners of the Convention, is pentagonal in shape, as this made it better able to withstand the blows of rocks hurled down at it from the cliffs above. A spiral staircase in a Romanesque tower abutting on the main building leads to the different storeys. The guard room has a fine Romanesque chimneypiece, that in the main hall is Gothic; the upper floors contain furnishings from the time of Louis XIII to the Directoire period (early 17 to late 18C).

LASCAUX CAVE

Michelin map 🔲 fold 7 or 🔲 fold 44 – Local map under VÉZÈRE VALLEY

Lascaux Cave ranks as number one among the prehistoric sites of Europe by dint of the number and quality of its paintings.

The cave was discovered 12 September 1940 by four young boys looking for their dog, which had fallen down a hole. With a makeshift lamp, they discovered an extraordinary fresco of polychrome paintings on the walls of the gallery they were in. The teacher at Montignac was immediately told of the discovery, and he just as quickly notified Abbé Breuil *(qv)*. The abbot arrived and examined the paintings with meticulous care, baptising the cave the "Sistine Chapel of Périgord".

In 1948 the cave was officially opened to the public. Over fifteen years more than a million people came to admire the famous Lascaux paintings. But, unfortunately, in spite of all the precautions taken (weak lighting, air conditioning, airlock), the carbon dioxide and the humidity resulted in two damaging effects: the "green" effect (the growth of moss and algae) and the "white" effect (less visible but much more serious as it leads to a build-up of deposits of white calcite).

In 1963, in order to preserve such a treasure, it was decided to close the cave to the public. Ten years later, in an attempt to alleviate such cultural deprivation of the public, a project was put forward to build a replica; Lascaux II was opened in 1983, under the care of the Dordogne *département*'s Tourist Administration.

An exceptional group of paintings – The cave, carved out of the Périgord Noir *(qv)* limestone, is a relatively small cavity, 150m-492ft long. It is made up of four galleries, the walls of which are covered with more than 1 500 representations, either engraved or painted. These works were created between 17 000 and 15 000 years ago, during the Magdalenian Culture *(qv)*.

The Great Black Bull from Lascaux Cave

At that time the cave was open to the outside air. Sometime after the cave artists had decorated the cave, the entrance collapsed and a flow of clay tightly closed off the cave.

The airtight entrance and the impermeable ceiling are the reasons for the lack of concretions and the perfect preservation of the paintings fixed and authenticated by a thin layer of natural calcite.

The cave includes the Bulls' Hall, which extends into an axial gallery *(see Lascaux II)*; these two areas hold 90% of the cave paintings.

To the right of the Bulls' Hall a passage leads to the apse, which extends into the nave and the Feline Gallery. To the right of the apse the Well Gallery opens up; its lower section is decorated with a simplified scene of a wounded bison chasing a man, one of the rare representations of a human figure *(a reproduction can be seen at Le Thot Centre of Research and of Prehistoric Art)*. Such narrative paintings are unique in the history of prehistoric art.

A wide range of fauna is depicted on the cave walls; the cavemen used the wall contours to give relief to the subject matter. There are reproductions of the animals hunted during the early Magdalenian Period: aurochs, horses, reindeer, bison, ibexes, bears and woolly rhinoceroses appear side by side or superimposed, forming part of extraordinary compositions.

The seemingly disorganised paintings (drawings superimposed onto previous drawings or figures apparently illustrated with a sense of hierarchy leave researchers perplexed) and the absence of all landscape form (ground, plants, small animals) suggest the paintings are more a ritual form of expression than a narrative. The geometric signs and enigmatic drawings accompanying the fauna (lines, points, grill-like forms, ovals, sticks) raise the question of the possible existence of a sanctuary.

The Lascaux style – There is a definite Lascaux style: lively animals with small, elongated heads, swollen stomachs and short legs, and fur illustrated by dabs of coloured pigment. The horns, antlers and hoofs are often drawn in three-quarter view – at times even full face – while the animal itself is drawn in profile; this procedure is known as the "turned profile".

★★Lascaux II ⊘ – Located some 200m-219 yds from the original cave, the facsimile reconstitutes two galleries from the upper part of the cave; the Bulls' Hall and the Axial Gallery, which contain the majority of the cave paintings at Lascaux. "Museographical airlocks" forming the antechamber retrace the cave's history. The recreation of the unique atmosphere of the original cave has been made possible purely by real technological prowess and rigid scientific discipline. A detailed description of how the facsimile was made can be found at Le Thot Centre of Research and of Prehistoric Art *(see under Le Thot)*, a worthwhile follow-up visit to Lascaux.

As early as 1966, The National Geographic Institute (Institut Géographique National – IGN) had accomplished a photogrammetric survey of Lascaux using three-dimensional scenes of the cave and stereo images. This survey enabled a shell to be constructed in reinforced concrete (as in shipbuilding) in an opencast quarry.

Once the cave walls were reproduced, the painter Monique Peytral copied the cave paintings using slides and the results from numerous surveys she had made. She used the same methods and materials (pigments, tools etc.) as the cave artists.

Two small rooms, reproducing the original airlock, display the history of Lascaux Cave, items discovered in the cave's archaeological strata — tallow lamps, coloured powders, flints used by the engravers — a model of the scaffolding used, a copy of a panel of the bisons back to back, the dating methods, and the flint and bone industries.

Of the Bulls' Hall only the upper part of the wall and the vaulting, covered with calcite, have been used. The graphic composition here is wonderful. The second animal, the only imaginary animal figure painted at Lascaux, has been nicknamed the "unicorn" because of the odd-looking horns above a bear-like muzzle, on a body not unlike that of a rhinoceros. Among the other animals represented there are some magnificent black bulls, one of which is 5m – 16.5ft long, red bison, small horses and deer.

The Axial Gallery (Diverticule Axial) contains a vault and walls covered with horses, bovidae, ibex, bison and a large deer. A charming frieze of long-haired ponies, a great black bull and a large red pony, seeming to sniff at some sort of branch, bear witness to a very developed art style.

Régourdou – *1km – 0.5 mile east.* On this **prehistoric site** ⊘ discovered in 1954 numerous objects and bones were brought to light (a skeleton of Régourdou man, 70 000 years old and now displayed in the Périgord Museum in Périgueux). All these discoveries are representative of the Mousterian industry. In the cave, now open to the air, near the burial ground of Régourdou man, a pile of bear bones was found, which some specialists have interpreted as evidence of a bear burial ground.

A small museum contains bones (a cast of Régourdou man's jawbone) and tools.

LAUZERTE
Pop 1 529

Michelin map 🔢 fold 17 or 🔢🔢 fold 18

This *bastide (qv)* was built in 1241 by the Count of Toulouse and was occupied at one time by the English.

Upper Town – The pale grey stone houses with their almost flat roofs are clustered round the church of St Bartholomew and a square, Place des Cornières.

This square, named after its covered arcades *(cornières)*, contains a half-timbered house. There are several old houses in Rue du Château, some half-timbered, some Gothic in style with twin windows and some Renaissance with mullioned windows. There are extensive views of the gentle, rolling countryside of hills and small valleys.

The QUERCY BLANC

Round tour of 77km - 48 miles – allow 3 hours – photograph p 165

Lying between the Lot and Tarn valley, the Quercy Blanc region, so-called because of its white, chalky soil, has a soothing relief, with vast undulating white landscapes (*planhès*), divided into long, narrow ridges (*serres*) separated by the fertile valleys. The landscape is more like that of the nearby Garonne region; red-brick buildings, almost flat rooftops covered in pale pink Roman tiles, specialised cultivation of vines (to produce the well-known Moissac chasselas), plum trees, peach trees and melons on the hillsides and tobacco, sunflowers and maize in the valleys.

Montcuq – Pop 1 189. *13km – 8 miles northeast of Lauzerte on the D 953.* Main town of a castellany to which Raymond VI, Count of Toulouse, granted a charter of customary law in the 12C, Montcuq was the centre of many a bloody battle during the Albigensian Crusade, the Hundred Years War and the Wars of Religion. All that remains of this once fortified village is a tall castle keep (12C), on a hillock overlooking the Barguelonnette River. The view stretches over the surrounding hills and valleys.

Castelnau-Montratier – *See Castelnau-Montratier.*

Église de Saux (Church) – *See Montpezat-de-Quercy: Excursion.*

★**Montpezat-de-Quercy** – *See Montpezat-de-Quercy.*

LIZONNE VALLEY

Michelin map **75** fold 4 or **233** folds 30 and 41

The limits of Périgord and Angoumois (the region around Angoulême) are marked by the Lizonne River, a natural boundary which has figured more than once in the region's history. The Petrocorii *(qv)* had already used it all those centuries ago to establish the limits of their land; during the early Middle Ages, their descendants defended it by building wooden strongholds perched on large man-made earth **mounds** (Grésignac, Bourzac and as a last defensive post, La Tour-Blanche).
The Lizonne is also the linguistic boundary between the north and south; on the Périgord side the people still speak the Oc language *(langue d'oc)*, while on the opposite bank they speak the Oïl language *(langue d'oïl)*. Oïl and Oc were the words used for "yes" in the north and south, respectively.
The old Bourzac castellany was established around a feudal fortress. The undulating countryside extends north to Fontaine and south to St-Paul-Lizonne and is characterised by the abundance of its crops and the beauty and tranquility of its villages, which are often huddled around fortified, Romanesque churches.

BOURZAC COUNTRY

Round tour of 37km – 23 miles leaving from Lusignac – allow 3 hours

Lusignac – Pop 192. Built on a ridge, the village has a harmonious appearance with its 15C fortified **church** ⊘ built on the foundations of a 12C domed nave (17C carved wood altarpiece), its old houses and a 15-17C manor-house.
    Take the D 97ᴱ north to Bouteilles-St-Sébastien, then turn left on the D 97 and then immediately right.

St-Martial-Viveyrol – Pop 267. The austerity of the Romanesque church, which has two domes and a belfry-keep, is emphasised by its narrow bays. The defence chamber set above the vaulting is pierced by large openings each surrounded by four holes; in time of attack it was possible to add an extra floor, supported on props set in the holes.
    Continue northeast.

Cherval – Pop 313. This village has one of the loveliest **domed churches** of the region (restored by the Historic Buildings Commission). Four domes follow on from each other: three over the nave and one over the chancel. They are all held up by large pointed arches which take on the shape of the pendentives. The chancel vaulting is decorated with diamond-pointed rustication.
    Take the D 2ᴱ north.

Champagne-et-Fontaine – Pop 415. In the village of Champagne the church was fortified some time after it was built. Inside, the twin nave had pointed vaulting added in the 16C; outside the porch has recessed arches.
Several fine houses and the 16C Chaumont Manor-house (restored) complete the scene.
    Take the road to Vendoire.

Vendoire – Pop 185. The village château, enhanced by a semicircular central pediment, was built under Louis XIV. East of the château, the small Romanesque church has a polygonal apse. The west façade, in great need of repair, still has its first tier of arcades, showing the Saintonge influence.

Peat Museum (Écomusée de la Tourbe) ⊘ – *3km - 2 miles west of Vendoire (route is indicated) along the banks of the Lizonne.* Extensive peat bogs have evolved in the valley formed by the high-water bed of the Lizonne. An area of 22ha-52 acres has been converted into a centre of study of this particular eco-system. Activities include observation of flora and fauna with the aid of an explanatory leaflet sold on site and boat trips along the networks of waterways. In the building there are displays to explain the visit in more detail.
    Head south.

Nanteuil-Auriac – Pop 275. The **church** has clearly had a succession of features added to it over the centuries. It is Romanesque in origin, as the fine capitals of the apse and the domed chancel indicate; fortifications – a belfry porch and a raised apse – were added later; then in the 16C the church was equipped with side aisles and pointed vaulting – the corbels of this can still be seen. The entrance porch is typically Renaissance.

Keep heading south.

Bouteilles-St-Sébastien – Pop 214. The church is a fine example of the trend, which sprang up in this area during the Hundred Years War, of fortifying Romanesque churches. Here, the apse was made higher to form an unusual keep with the belltower.

Go west on the D 97, then turn left towards St-Paul-Lizonne.

St-Paul-Lizonne – Pop 347. The fortified **church** ⊘ contains a **painted ceiling**★ and a late 17C altar.

LOC DIEU ABBEY

Michelin map **79** fold 20 or **235** fold 15 – 9km – 5.5 miles west of Villefranche-de-Rouergue

On the borders of Rouergue and Quercy, **Loc Dieu Abbey** ⊘ *(Locus Dei* means "divine place") was built in 1123 by Cistercian monks from the abbeys of Dalon and Pontigny. Restored and renovated in the 19C by Paul Goût, the monastic buildings were transformed into a castle half-feudal, half-Renaissance in appearance.

The cloisters and chapter-house, destroyed during the Hundred Years War, were rebuilt in the 15C. Only three of the galleries in the 15C cloisters remain and these were restored in the 19C. The chapter-house, also 15C, is supported by two elegant octagonal columns with fine mouldings.

★**Church (Église)** – The church was built between 1159 and 1189 using sandstone of many shades, but with ochre and yellow predominating; the completed building is a wonderful example of the Cistercian style, simple and unadorned, well-proportioned and pure of line. The nave, which is more than 20m - 66ft high, is flanked by narrow aisles. Most Cistercian churches end in a flat east end, but this one has five radiating chapels. The transept crossing is roofed over with a square lantern tower, and four transept chapels lead off the transept; one of them *(first chapel in south arm)* contains a 15C **triptych**★, in carved and painted wood, framing a Virgin and Child. The church has quadripartite vaulting but its vertical elements are Romanesque in character.

★★ LOT VALLEY

Michelin map **79** folds 5 to 10 or **235** folds 9 to 11 and 14 and 15

The River Lot is at its most beautiful where it cuts across the Quercy *causses (qv)*. The river flows at the foot of rocks thickly wooded with chestnut trees and promontories on which old villages are perched; elsewhere the waters flow in great loops around picturesque towns and cities.

From the Cévennes Mountains to the Agenais region – The Lot is a tributary of the Garonne. It rises in the Cévennes on the slopes of Le Goulet Mountain at an altitude of 1 400m - 4 600ft and flows right across the southern part of the Massif Central.

It follows the winding course of an uninterrupted series of meanders or loops, *cingles*, circling tongues of land, some only a couple of hundred yards across. As it flows between the tall limestone cliffs of the Quercy *causses*, its thousand curves provide a never-ending variety of magnificent views. The valley is attractive both in its wilder, unspoiled sections and its brighter, cultivated ones. The Lot leaves Quercy before Libos and, after flowing a further 480km - 300 miles, enters the Garonne in the Agenais Plain.

Scenes from the past – Before the advent of railway, the Lot was an important navigational route. The river was initially adapted by Colbert and was later equipped with dams and even canals to cut across the promontories of the wider bends, as at Luzech *(qv)*.

A whole fleet of barges, known as *sapines* or *gabares (qv)*, used to travel down the Lot to Bordeaux, carrying cheeses from Auvergne, coal from Decazeville and wine from Cahors.

The Lot vineyards – The slopes of the valley of the Olt – the Occitan name for the Lot, which is still found in such place names as St-Vincent-Rive-d'Olt and Balaguier-d'Olt – have long been famous for their vineyards. Quercy wines, with their high alcoholic content, have played a great part in making Cahors and the Olt Valley famous.

In 1C AD the Roman Emperor Domitian punished Cahors for revolting by destroying its vineyards; after two centuries of teetotalism, Probus revoked the ban on wine. Despite the boycott by Bordeaux, through which the wine was shipped, wines from the Lot Valley were preferred by the English for many centuries. Eleanor of Aquitaine brought Quercy to the king of England as part of her dowry; in 1287 letters patent were granted by the king in favour of these wines. The wine was exported to Poland, to Russia – where only the wine of Cahors could entice the Tsar Peter the Great from vodka – and even to Italy. Legend has it that popes insisted on serving this wine at mass.

Two men of Quercy, the poet Clément Marot *(qv)*, and Galiot de Genouillac *(qv)*, gave the wine to François I to taste, and the king's palate delighted in its velvet smoothness. Later, vines from the Lot were transported at great cost to Fontainebleau to create the Royal Vine Arbour.

★★CLIFFS AND PROMONTORIES

From Figeac to Cahors

115km – 71.5 miles – allow 1 day – local map right

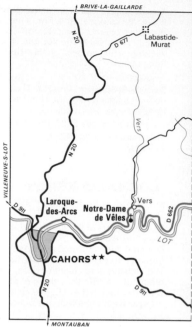

As it crosses Quercy, the Lot flows at the foot of slopes, or often sheer cliffs. Leaving Rouergue, the river hurls itself against the spur on which the old town of Capdenac stands, and then forces its way between the cliff walls of the *causses*. Sometimes the cliffs enclose the river, and from their tops, there are lovely views of the valley.

★★**Figeac** – *See Figeac. Facilities.*

Leave Figeac southeast.

Capdenac – *See Capdenac.*

After Capdenac-Gare, take the D 86, which runs along the south bank of the river and soon provides pretty views of Capdenac. The river makes a wide bend in the centre of an alluvial plain on which crops are grown. Beyond St-Julien-d'Empare, this picturesque road offers a good view of the Capdenac amphitheatre. After Pont-de-la-Madeleine the road runs beside the Lot through rocky countryside with dense undergrowth. Shortly after Balaguier-d'Olt cames St-Pierre-Toirac.

St-Pierre-Toirac – Pop 145. This small village, on the north bank of the Lot, contains an interesting **church** ⊘ of the 11 and 14C. The Romanesque apse alone belies the fortified appearance of this building which served as a defence point with its massive crenellated keep and upper floor. The short nave has cradle vaulting and primitive style capitals. The chancel has trefoil arches, and saw-toothed arches surround the stained-glass windows of the apse. Recently discovered Merovingian sarcophagi have been placed behind the church.

Larroque-Toirac Castle – *See Larroque-Toirac Castle.*

Many delightful villages are to be seen on the north bank which is overshadowed by high rocks and vertical cliffs. As the valley walls open out, the Lot itself widens out into a great expanse of water with rows of poplars, and cultivated tobacco and cereals growing along its banks.

Montbrun – Pop 45. The village of Montbrun rises in tiers on a rocky promontory encircled by steep cliffs. It looks down on the Lot and faces the Saut de La Mounine *(see below)*. Towering above the village are the ruins of a fortress that belonged to one of Pope John XXII' s brothers, and then to the powerful Cardaillac family.

Cajarc – Pop 1 033. Facilities. The town was brought into the public eye when President Pompidou had a house here.

Near the church, the Hébrardie Mansion with Gothic windows is all that remains standing of a 13C castle.

Inaugurated in 1989, the **Georges Pompidou Art Gallery** (Maison des Arts) organises important retrospectives of the works of contemporary European artists. Exhibitions of Hartung, Bissière and Soulages promoted Cajarc to rank among the foremost centres of contemporary art in the region.

There is a very nice reservoir on the Lot here.

Cross the river at Cajarc and follow the D 127 up the south bank as far as Saut de La Mounine. The road overhangs the Lot to start with, then immediately after Saujac rises and winds round to overlook a wooded gorge, before reaching the top of the *causse*.

★**Saut de la Mounine** – There is a good **view**★ of the valley from the top of this cliff. The end of the spur overlooks a wide bend in the river as it encircles a mosaic of arable fields. Over on the left, on the far bank, stands Montbrun Castle.

The curious name, *Saut de la Mounine* – the little monkey's leap, comes from a rather strange legend. The lord of Montbrun decided to punish his daughter for her love of another lord's son and ordered her to be hurled from the top of the cliff; a hermit, appalled at this cruel idea, disguised a small blind monkey (*mounine* in the Oc language) in women's clothes and hurled it into the air. When he saw the object falling the father immediately regretted his brutal action; on seeing his daughter alive and well he was so overjoyed that he forgave her.

Return on the D 127 to the river's north bank. From here the road climbs rapidly and passes near a chapel (Chapelle de la Capellette). This was built in the 12 and 13C and is known as the "little chapel" (thus *capellette*). The apse is all that remains. From this spot there is a sweeping view of the valley.

Calvignac – Pop 194. This old village, where a few traces of its fortress may still be seen, is perched on a spur on the river's south bank.

Staying on the same bank take the D 8 which leads to Cénevières.

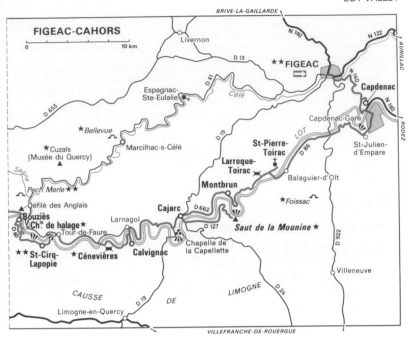

★ Cénevières Castle – *See Cénevières Castle.*

From Tour-de-Faure admire St-Cirq-Lapopie in its remarkable setting on the river's south bank.

★★ St-Cirq-Lapopie – *See St-Cirq-Lapopie.*

Beyond St-Cirq-Lapopie, the D 40, which is built into the cliff, has been designed as a tourist route. There is a good **view★** of the confluence of the Lot and the Célé from a small viewpoint. From the same spot a wide bend of the Lot can be seen curving between white and yellow cliffs; magnificent poplars and fields enhance the beauty of the landscape.

Bouziès – Pop 77. Facilities. On the bank opposite the village, the **Englishmen's Gorge** (Défilé des Anglais) is the most famous of the "fortified gullies" constructed during the Hundred Years War in cave-like openings which could only be accessed by a rope-ladder.

★ Towpath along the Lot (Chemin de halage) – *Take the footpath GR 36 off to the right of the carpark by the moorings.*

500m - 547yds further on, the spectacular towpath comes into view, carved out of the rock because of the extent to which the cliff juts out over the river. In sections such as this, the barges coming up the Lot with their cargoes of salt, dried fish, spices or

Towpath along the River Lot

111

plaster could not be towed by the usual teams of horses or oxen, but had to be pulled along by teams of volunteers, on the whole bad-tempered gangs of people who led a miserable existence. This pathway is now a marvellous walk. At the top of the first lock there is a 15m - 9ft long bas-relief, the work of contemporary artist D Monnier, decorating the limestone wall with fish and shellfish.

Immediately after Bouziès, cross the Lot and take the D 662 again. This runs close beside the river in an attractive, sometimes wooded, cliff setting. In several places the road has been cut out of the rockface itself. After Vers the valley broadens out, cliffs give way to wooded hills, and the alluvial soil is put to arable farming.

Notre-Dame-de-Vêles – This small pilgrimage chapel was built in the 12C and has a lovely square belltower and a Romanesque apse.

Laroque-des-Arcs – Pop 375. This village's name is a reminder of the aqueduct which crossed the Francoulès Valley and supplied water to Cahors. A three-tiered bridge bore the aqueduct which transported water over 20km – 12 miles from Vers to Divona (ancient Cahors). The consuls of Cahors had it demolished in 1370. An old tower perched on a rock beside the Lot enabled guards to watch the river traffic and exact tolls.

★★Cahors – See Cahors. Facilities.

THE MEANDERS OF THE LOT'S LOWER REACHES

From Cahors to Bonaguil

61km – 38 miles – about 4 hours – local map below

From Cahors to Puy-l'Évêque, the Lot winds in a series of meanders – *cingles* – through Quercy *causses*; beyond this, it flows into a flatter region and the valley broadens out.

★★Cahors – See Cahors. Facilities.

Leave Cahors by ① on the D 911 which overlooks the Lot.

Mercuès – Pop 768. Facilities. Once the property of the count-bishops of Cahors, the château is now a hotel. It occupies a remarkable site overlooking the north bank of the Lot. In 1212 the château was a fortified castle, it was then enlarged in the 14C, besieged several times during the Hundred Years War and the Wars of Religion, altered in the 15C and converted in the 16C into a château with terraces and gardens. It was not restored completely until last century. There is an outstanding **view★** of the valley from the château.

From Mercuès take the D 145.

West of Mercuès the road leaves the valley for a short distance to cross a flourishing countryside of vineyards and orchards; then the road returns to the river, following it closely.

Luzech – See Luzech.

Follow the south bank (*on the D 8*), there are good views along the valley.

Albas – Pop 507. This village has narrow streets lined with old houses.

Anglars-Juillac – Pop 329. A Crucifixion adorns the church's Renaissance doorway.

Bélaye – Pop 220. Once the fief of the bishops of Cahors, Bélaye stands on top of a hill. An extensive **view★** of the Lot Valley unfolds from the top of the spur and from the upper square of this little village.

Grézels – Pop 243. Overlooking the village is the **feudal castle of La Coste** ⊙, which has been razed and rebuilt on several occasions. The bishops of Cahors possessed a fief which extended over the Lot Valley from Cahors to Puy-l'Évêque, and Grézels marked the limits of their territory; therefore, a stronghold was built to defend the entrance to their fief.

During the Hundred Years War, it was transformed into a fortress. It was severely damaged during the different wars, then restored in the 14 and 16C. After the Revolution it was abandoned.

The curtain wall and crenellated corner towers are the oldest parts of the castle.

Puy-l'Évêque – See Puy-L'Évêque.

Take the D 911.

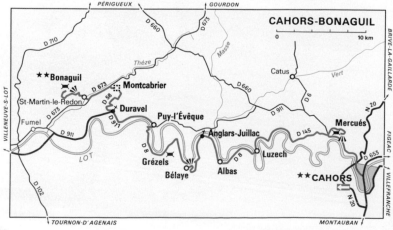

The terraces and hillsides are covered with vines, and the wide alluvial valley is carpeted with fields.

Duravel – Pop 894. The 11C church has historiated capitals decorating the chancel. There is an archaic crypt supported by columns with rough-hewn capitals. The bodies of Saints Hilarion, Poémon and Agathon lie buried at the back of the apse. The *ostension*, or solemn exhibition of relics to the faithful, is held every five years.

From Duravel take the D 58 to Montcabrier.

Montcabrier – Pop 403. The *bastide (qv)* was founded in 1297 by Guy de Cabrier, who gave it his name. It was granted a charter of franchises by Philip the Fair. Overlooking the square, several old houses (including the 16C house of the king's court) are laid out in the regular pattern of the original plan. The church, partly rebuilt in the 14C, has a Flamboyant doorway (restored) surrounded by a fine open-bayed belltower. Inside, a plain 14C statue of St Louis, the parish's patron saint, is surrounded by ex-votos. This statue was the object of a local pilgrimage.

Take the D 673 southwest.

St-Martin-le-Redon – Pop 208. This charming village is known for the St-Martial source water, which was reputed to cure skin ailments.

Take the Route Touristique de Bonaguil.

Shortly after St-Martin-le-Redon there is a lovely **view★** of the fantastic outline of Bonaguil Castle *(qv)*, surrounded by woods.

★★**Bonaguil Castle** – *See Bonaguil Castle.*

LUZECH   Pop 1 543

Michelin map 79 fold 7 or 235 fold 14 — Local map opposite

Luzech has grown up on the narrowest part of a tongue of land almost completely encircled by a loop in the Lot River. The isthmus at this point is some 100m (just over 100 yds) wide. The town is crowned by the old castle keep. To the north lies the Roman city of Impernal and to the south the Pistoule Promontory, washed by the waters of the river as it sweeps round the bend. A reservoir has been formed by the construction of a dam upstream from the peninsula, and a watersports centre has been set up there.

Impernal Hill – Impernal Hill was a natural defence which has been inhabited since prehistoric times; recognising its potential, the Gauls transformed the plateau into a powerful stronghold. A citadel, of which the square keep can still be seen, was built below it in the Middle Ages. In 1118, Richard the Lionheart was master of the citadel. Luzech became the seat of one of the four baronies of Quercy and was much sought as a prize by the English in the Hundred Years War. Nevertheless, the town resisted all their attacks and became an important central strongpoint. During the Wars of Religion, it remained a faithful bastion of Catholicism under the bishops of Cahors. Excavations of the Impernal site have revealed walls and traces of buildings dating from the Roman and Gaulish periods.

★**Viewpoint** (**Point de vue**) – From the top of Impernal Hill, the view encompasses Luzech clustered at its foot, as well as Pistoule Promontary, slicing through the wide alluvial plain like a ship's prow, and the Lot winding between rich and fertile crops.

Old town – In the old Barry Quarter, picturesque alleyways link Rue du Barry-del-Valat with the quays.
Around Place des Consuls, on the other side of Place du Canal, several examples of medieval architecture are still to be seen: Penitents' Chapel (12C), Capsol Gateway with its brick pointed arch and Consuls' House with its elegant paired windows.

Armand Viré Archaeological Museum (Musée archéologique Armand-Viré) ⊘ – *In the Consuls' House.*
Set up in the fine vaulted cellar, the museum retraces the history (from the Palaeolithic Age to the Gallo-Roman times) of the site of Luzech. The items displayed (excavated from the Impernal site and the cave found on the hillside) include the exceptional **reduced model of Trajan's column★**, a feature widespread throughout the Roman Empire in the early 2C AD, and the unusual Gallo-Roman **hinged spoon**, of bronze and iron.

Keep (Donjon) – *Entrance via Place des Consuls.*
The entrance used to be through the small pointed-arched doorway opening onto the first floor. From the terrace of the 13C keep there is a bird's-eye view onto the brown-tiled roofs of the town, tucked amidst meadows and crops with a row of hills along the horizon.

Notre-Dame-de-l'Ile – The chapel, set in a calm landscape of vineyards and orchards against a backdrop of hills along the course of the Lot, stands at the furthest point of the isthmus. This Flamboyant Gothic sanctuary is a pilgrimage centre, which dates back to the 13C.

EXCURSION

Cambayrac – Pop 109. *8km – 5 miles to the south.*
The hamlet possesses an odd-looking church identifiable from afar by a wall belfry shaped like a French policeman's hat. Inside, the Romanesque apse and the side chapels were recovered in the 17C with an unusual marble and stucco décor in the classical style.

★ LA MADELEINE SITE

Michelin map 75 fold 16 or 235 fold 1 – Local map under LES-EYZIES-DE-TAYAC

The location of La Madeleine Site *(access via Tursac and the bridge to l'Espinasse)* stands out very clearly, from the point where the wooded plateau meets the Vézère's alluvial plain below. The terrain is formed by the river's narrowest and most distinctly shaped meander (80m-88yds at its source expanding to 2.2km-1 mile). On the rock above stand the remains of a medieval castle, dating from the mid-15C.

Midway up the hill, and protected by a rock overhang, is an old **troglodyte village** ⊙, which was probably occupied from the end of the 10C (Viking invasions) to the 19C. The village consists of some 20 dwellings carved out of the rock near a spring and protected by a narrow fortified entrance; about 100 people could live there during troubled times, or even all the time. A chapel consecrated to St Mary Magdalene, which was enlarged and had ogive vaulting added to it in the 15C, gave the site its name.

At the foot of the cliff, beneath the village, lies the **prehistoric deposit** which established the characteristics of the Magdalenian Culture *(qv)*, which predominated during the last 60 centuries of the Upper Palaeolithic Age (15 000 to 9 000 BC). The richness and quality of the items discovered by Lartet and Christy in 1863 (for example the ivory plaque of an engraved mammoth) enabled Mortillet, six years later, to propose a classification of the diverse epochs of prehistory based on the products (bone, flint) of human industry *(see pp 18-19)*. The majority of the objects are exhibited in the museums at Les Eyzies and St-Germain-en-Laye, west of Paris.

MARCILHAC-SUR-CÉLÉ   Pop 196

Michelin map 79 fold 9 or 235 fold 11 – Local map under CÉLÉ VALLEY

Marcilhac is built rather attractively in the centre of an amphitheatre of cliffs in the cheery Célé Valley. Interesting old houses surround the ruins of a Benedictine abbey.

The legal jungle – In the 11C the modest sanctuary of Rocamadour was under the care of Marcilhac Abbey, which let it fall into ruins. Noticing this negligence some monks from Tulle installed themselves in the sanctuary. However, in 1166 the discovery of the body of St Amadour *(qv)* turned the sanctuary into a rich and famous pilgrimage centre. Marcilhac recalled its rights and expelled the Tulle monks. Soon afterwards the Abbot of Tulle threw out the Marcilhac monks and again occupied Rocamadour. Lawsuit began to follow lawsuit. The case was acrimonious, and the Bishop of Cahors, the papal legate, the Archbishop of Bourges, even the Pope himself, were all called on to give judgment, but avoided reaching a decision; finally, after a hundred years of squabbling, Marcilhac accepted an indemnity of 3 000 sols and relinquished its claim to Rocamadour.

Marcilhac Abbey flourished until the 14C, but during the Hundred Years War it was virtually destroyed by marauding bands of Englishmen and French mercenary troops. After the Reformation, the abbey, now only a ghost of its former self, fell into the hands of the Hébrards of St-Sulpice; the monks had to give up the monastic way of life and be put up in local people's homes. The abbey church was secularised in 1764.

SIGHTS

Abbey – The ensemble is made up of two very distinct parts.

Romanesque part – The west porch and the first three bays of the nave are open to the sky. They are flanked by a tall square tower, which was probably fortified in the 14C. A round-arched door on the south side is topped by sculpture forming a **tympanum** and depicting the Last Judgment: Christ in Majesty, with figures on either side, thought to be representing the sun and the moon, appears above two thick-set angels with open wings, St Peter and St Paul. These carvings are archaic in style, obviously reflecting the décor of gold- and silverwork, and would appear to date from the 10C. Go through this doorway and enter the church to the right.

Gothic part – This part of the church, closed to the west from the fourth bay on, dates from the 15C and is built in the Flamboyant style. The chancel has stellar vaulting and is encircled by an ambulatory. A baroque pew decorated with the Hébrard family crest has a fabulous **miserere** carved with the head of an angel. A chapel on the left of the chancel has 15C frescoes: Christ giving Blessing with the twelve Apostles; under each Apostle is his name and a phrase which characterises him. The coat of arms in the centre of each triad is that of the Hébrards of St-Sulpice.

On leaving the church, turn right (from the second Romanesque bay) onto the path to the chapter-house, which has very delicate Romanesque capitals alternately made of grey-blue limestone and rose-coloured stalagmitic stone. Go towards an esplanade shaded by plane trees; a round tower marks the site of the abbot's house. By the banks of the Célé *(right)*, the line of the rampart wall is interrupted by a postern.

★**Bellevue Cave (Grotte de Bellevue)** ⊙ – *1.5km – 1 mile to the northwest*. The route leading up to the cave is a *corniche* road overlooking the Célé Valley and giving fine **glimpses** of the village and abbey. After following a series of four steeply climbing hairpin bends, branch off to the left in the direction of the hamlet of Pailhès. *Car park further along on the left.*

This cave was opened to the public two years after it was discovered in 1964. The cave contains a remarkable variety of concretions: stalactites, stalagmites, frozen falls, columns of different widths and vast flows of white calcite striped with ochre or dark red. Its large chamber is wonderful; the very varied eccentrics seem to flower like coral, forming different shapes in every direction.

The particularly delicate stalagmites resemble slim church candles. The regularity of Hercules' Column (Colonne d'Hercule), reaching from the floor to the ceiling, is striking. It is 4m – 13ft high with a circumference of 3.50m – 11 ft. Its upper part is made up of a disc at an angle of 45° to the top of the column.

Michelin map **75** fold 18 or **235** fold 2 – Facilities

Martel, built on the Upper Quercy *causse* to which it has given its name (Martel Causse, *qv*), is known as the "town of the seven towers". It still contains many medieval buildings. Today it is a busy centre for the nut trade and the canning of local products.

The three hammers – After stopping the Saracens at Poitiers in 732, **Charles Martel** chased them into Aquitaine. Several years later he struck again and wiped them out. To commemorate this victory over the infidels and to give thanks to God, Charles Martel had a church built on the spot; soon a town grew up around the church. It was given the name of Martel in memory of its founder and took as its crest three hammers, which were the favourite weapons of the saviour of Christianity.

Martel and the viscounty of Turenne – The founding of Martel by the conqueror of the infidels is probably based more on fiction than on fact. However, it is known that the viscounts of Turenne *(qv)* made Martel an important urban community as early as the 12C. In 1219, Viscount Raymond IV granted a charter establishing Martel as a free town – exempt from the king's taxes, and with permission to mint money. However the town stayed faithful to the king. Very quickly Martel established a town council and consulate and became the seat of the royal bailiwick and of the sene-schalship. It became a real court of appeal which handled all the region's judicial matters; more than fifty magistrates, judges and lawyers were employed. It reached its peak at the end of the 13 and beginning of the 14C; however, as in other parts of the region, the town suffered during the Hundred Years War – batted backwards and forwards between English and French rule – and during the Wars of Religion – pillaged by the Huguenots. In 1738, when the rights of Turenne were sold to the king *(see Turenne)*, Martel lost its privileges and became a mere castellany.

The rebellious son – At the end of the 12C, Martel was the scene of a tragic series of events which brought into conflict **Henry Plantagenet**, King of England and lord of all Western France, his wife Eleanor of Aquitaine and their four sons. The royal house-hold was a royal hell. Henry could no longer stand the sight of Eleanor, who had already been renounced by the king of France, Louis VII. He therefore shut her up in a tower. The sons thereupon took up arms against their father, and the eldest, **Henry Short Coat**, pillaged the viscounty of Turenne and Quercy. To punish him, Henry Plantagenet gave his lands to his third son, Richard the Lionheart, and stopped the allowance paid to his eldest son. Henry Short Coat found himself penniless, surrounded and in an altogether desperate situation: to pay his foot-soldiers he plundered the treasure houses of the provincial abbeys. He took from Rocamadour the shrine and the precious stones of St Amadour, whose body was profaned, and he sold Roland's famous sword Durandal. But as he was leaving Rocamadour after this sacrilegious act, the bell miraculously began to toll: it was a sign from God.
Henry fled to Martel and arrived there with a fever; he felt death to be upon him and was stricken with remorse. He confessed his crimes while Henry II was sent for to come and forgive his son on his death bed; Henry II was at the siege of Limoges and sent a messenger with his pardon. The messenger found Henry Short Coat lying in agony on a bed of cinders, a heavy wooden cross upon his chest. Shortly afterwards he died, a last farewell to his mother Eleanor on his lips.

TOUR *time: 1 hour*

Former perimeter walls – Wide avenues, the Fossé des Cordeliers and the Boulevard du Capitani, have been built on the site of the old ramparts (12 and 13C). The machicolated **Tournemire Tower (B)**, which used to be the prison tower, and the Souillac and Brive Gateways (found at the end of Route de Souillac and Rue de Brive; *not on town plan*) hark back to the time when Martel was a fortified town, well protected by double perimeter walls. The second perimeter wall, built in the 18C, enclosed the suburbs.

> *Leave the car in the car park along the north wall. Pass between the post office and the Tournemire Tower to enter the old town.*

Rue du Four-Bas – There are still some old houses along this street, which is spanned by an ogival archway.

Church (Église St-Maur) – This Gothic church (13C-16C) has some interesting defensive features; huge buttresses converted into defence towers, machicolations protecting the flat east end and a 48m-157ft high belltower which looks more like a keep.
Beneath the porch is a fine historiated Romanesque **tympanum** depicting the Last Judgment. It shows Christ seated, His head adorned with a cruciform halo, His arms stretched wide to show His wounds; two angels hold the instruments of the Passion while two others sound the trumpets of the Resurrection. The width of the nave is striking. The chancel with its stellar vaulting is lit by a large 16C **stained-glass window** showing God the Father, the four Evangelists and scenes from the Passion.

Rue Droite –There are old town houses all along this road, one of which, Hôtel Vergnes-de-Ferron (**D**), is adorned with a lovely Renaissance door.

Hôtel de Mirandol – This town house features a great square tower with an adjoining round turret.

★**Place des Consuls** – In the centre of the square is the 18C **covered market**. The timbering is supported on great stone pillars. On one side the old town measures can be seen.

★**Hôtel de la Raymondie** – Once the fortress of the Turenne viscounts, built around 1280, this building was converted into a Gothic mansion in the 14C. It is topped by corner turrets, and its most striking feature is a belfry. The **façade**★ overlooking the

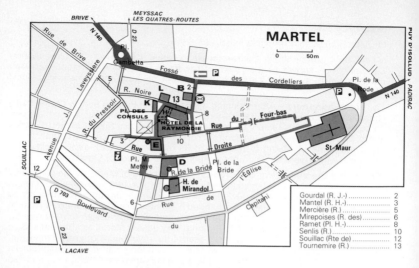

Rue de Senlis has remarkable apertures; a row of ogive arches on the ground floor is surmounted by seven quatrefoil rose windows. The main entrance on the Place des Consuls is decorated with the town's coat of arms, a shield with three hammers. Having been law courts for a while, the mansion now houses the town hall.

In the first floor rooms note the two carved wooden chimneypieces and the Renaissance low relief. In the keep's upper room a small **museum** ⊙ contains items found at the Puy d'Issolud excavations *(see below)*.

Fabri Mansion (Maison Fabri) (E) – The tower, called after Henry Short Coat since he died here in 1183, has windows with frontons decorated with balls at the intersections of their cornices on all five floors.

Rue Tournemire (13) – This attractive little street leads off to the left of the Hôtel de la Raymondie. The 13C Hôtel de la Monnaie **(K)** with intersecting turrets used to mint coins (*écus* and *deniers*) for the Turenne viscounty. The 16C **Grey House** (Maison Grise) **(L)** is decorated with a carved bust and a heraldic shield with three hammers.

EXCURSION

★ Puy d'Issolud – *14km – 9 miles. Leave Martel to the east.*

The plateau near Vayrac, of which the highest point is Puy d'Issolud with an altitude of 311m – 1 020ft, is bordered by steep cliffs overlooking little tributaries flowing into the Dordogne.

Puy d'Issolud was surrounded, at the time of the Gauls, by such solid earthworks and dry-stone defences that it was one of the most redoubtable oppidums of Quercy, and is said to have been the former Uxellodunum, site of the last Gaulish resistance to Caesar after Alesia, led by Drapes and Lucterius of the Caduici. Some historians place Uxellodunum at Capdenac *(qv)* or Luzech *(qv)*, but archaeological research suggests that it is more likely to be the Puy d'Issolud.

The battle, led by the Roman legion-aries, was waged with unbelievable ferocity and, after a spring had been diverted through underground caverns, causing those defending Uxellodunum to believe that their gods had deserted them by cutting off their water supply, ended with another defeat for the Gauls. Caesar, angered at the resistance put up by the besieged Gauls, is said to have ordered that each prisoner's right hand be cut off.

Items discovered during excavations are on display in the museum of the Hôtel de la Raymondie in Martel *(see above)*.

From the plateau there is an extensive, although broken **view★** of the Dordogne.

At Vayrac take the D 15 to get to Curemonte (10km - 6 miles away), a pretty fortified village on a hillside (see Michelin Green Guide in French to Berry-Limousin).

★ MONBAZILLAC CHÂTEAU

Michelin map **75** folds 14 and 15 or **234** fold 8 – Local map under BERGERAC: Excursions

Monbazillac Château ⊙ stands proudly amidst a sea of vines on the edge of a limestone plateau overlooking the Dordogne valley. It is owned by the Monbazillac Wine Cooperative, which restored and refurbished it.

This relatively small château was built in 1550 and is surrounded by a dry moat. Its elegant silhouette is eye-catching, being of an architectural style half-way between military buildings and the Renaissance. There are machicolations and a crenellated watchpath around the main building, which is flanked at each corner by a massive round tower. The façade is pierced by a double row of mullioned windows and a doorway with Renaissance style ornamentation. Two tiers of dormer windows can be seen above the machicolations. The grey patina of the stone tones in well with the brown tiled roofs of the turrets and the pavilions.

From the north terrace there is a good view of the vineyard and of Bergerac in the distance.

Interior – The **Great Hall**, its painted ceiling decorated with gilt foliated scrolls, has a monumental Renaissance chimneypiece, 17C furnishings and two beautiful Flemish tapestries of the same period. In an adjoining room rustic furniture from the Périgord region is on display. There are also interesting documents tracing the history of Protestantism in France in another room.

Several rooms are open on the first floor; note in particular the Viscountess of Monbazillac's **bedroom** furnished in Louis XIII style.

The castle cellars house a small **wine museum** displaying harvesting and wine-making equipment used in the past.

★ MONPAZIER   Pop 531

Michelin map 🔢 fold 16 or 🔢🔢 fold 9

Monpazier was one of the *bastides (qv)* built to command the roads going from the Agenais region to the banks of the Dordogne. The square, surrounded by arcades, the *carreyrous* (alleyways), the old houses, the church and the ruined fortifications make it the best preserved of all the Périgord *bastides*.

A difficult start – The *bastide* of Monpazier was founded on 7 January 1285 by **Edward I**, King of England and Duke of Aquitaine. This *bastide* was designed to complete the process of defence and colonisation of Périgord begun in 1267 with the founding of Lalinde, Beaumont, Molières and Roquépine. To this end Edward I allied himself with Pierre de Gontaut, Lord of Biron. However difficulties soon arose: delays in the building, disagreements between the lord of Biron and the people of Monpazier and renewed hostilities between the King of England and Philip the Fair. The situation soon became complicated, and during the Hundred Years War the *bastide* was assaulted and pillaged as often by the English as by the French.

Monpazier receives royalty – The Reformation, in which the Marshal of Biron played a prominent part, marked the beginning of a violent era. On 21 June 1574, the town was betrayed and fell into the hands of the well-known Huguenot leader, Geoffroi de Vivans, who later won fame with the capture of Domme.

Jeanne d'Albret, who was going to the wedding of her son Henri IV de Navarre to Margaret of Valois, stayed at Monpazier. In her honour "the streets and squares were scrubbed and the dunghills were taken away". Despite such homage to the most militant Calvinist the town did not hesitate to lay on an equally grand display soon afterwards, to receive the Duke of Anjou – the future Henry III of France – leader of the Catholics.

Buffarot the Croquant – After the Wars of Religion were over, the peasants rose again in revolt. The rebels, who were known as the *croquants (qv)*, held a great gathering at Monpazier in 1594. The revolt flared up again in 1637; led by Buffarot, a weaver from the neighbouring town of Capdrot, 8 000 peasants rampaged through the countryside plundering the castles.

The soldiers of the Duke of Épernon pursued them and, after some difficulty, captured Buffarot. He was brought back to Monpazier and, as leader of the revolt, was broken on the wheel in the main square.

SIGHTS

The general layout of the *bastide* is still in evidence, as are three of its original six fortified gateways. Several houses still have their original appearance.

The town is in the shape of a quadrilateral 400m x 220m – 1312ft x 722ft, the main axis orientated north-south. Streets run from one end to the other, parallel with the longer sides, and four transverse roads run east to west, dividing the town into rectangular blocks. Originally all the houses had the unique characteristic of being of equal size and separated from each other by narrow spaces or *androns*, to prevent the spread of fire.

★**Place du 19-mars-1962** – The picturesque main square is rectangular like the *bastide* itself. On the south side stands a covered market housing the old measures. Round the edge, the arcades or covered galleries are supported on arches, some of which are pointed, and have angle irons (*cornières*).

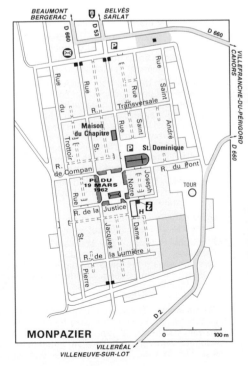

MONPAZIER

Church (St-Dominique) – The church façade has been restored at various times; the doorway decorated with archivolts, the rose window and the gable were all rebuilt in c1550. The wide single aisle has pointed vaulting and extends into a polygonal east end.

Chapter-house (Maison du Chapitre) – This 13C house stands near the church and Place du 19-mars-1962. It was used as a tithe barn. Paired windows light the upper floor.

★★ MONTAL CASTLE

Michelin map **75** fold 19 or **235** fold 7 or **239** fold 39 – 3km – 2 miles west of St-Céré – Local map under ST-CÉRÉ: Excursions

Montal Castle is a harmonious group of buildings with pepper-pot roofs on a wooded knoll on a hillside near the charming Bave Valley.

The wonder of a mother's love – In 1523 **Jeanne de Balsac d'Entraygues,** widow of Amaury de Montal, Governor of Haute-Auvergne, had a country mansion built on the site of a feudal stronghold for her eldest son, Robert, who was away fighting in Italy for François I. The chatelaine had the best artists and workmen brought from the banks of the Loire to Quercy, and by 1534 the masterpiece begotten of a mother's loving pride was there for all to see.

"Hope is no more" – Everything was ready to welcome home the proud knight. But days, then years passed; Marignano, Pavia, Madrid are far away; the mother waited day after day for her eldest son's arrival. Alas, Robert's body was all that returned to the castle. The beautiful dream crumbled. Jeanne had the high window from which she had watched for her son blocked up and she had carved beneath it the despairing lament "Hope is No More" (plus d'espoir).
Jeanne's second son, Dordé de Montal, a church dignitary, was absolved from his ecclesiastical duties by the Pope in order that he might continue the family line; he subsequently married and had nine children.

Death and resurrection – Montal was declared a national asset but became uninhabitable as a result of the depredations it suffered during the Revolution; finally in 1879 it fell into the hands of a certain Macaire. This adventurer, permanently short of cash, made a bargain with a demolition group and divided the palace into lots; 120 tons of carved stone were parcelled up and sent to Paris. The masterpieces of Montal were then auctioned and dispersed throughout the museums and private collections of Europe and the United States. In 1908 Montal rose from its ruins; a new and devoted owner set about finding and buying back at ransom prices all the Montal treasures, until he had refurnished the castle. He donated it to the state in 1913.

TOUR ⊘ time: allow 45 min

Exterior – Steeply pitched lauzes roofs and massive round towers with loopholes give the castle its fortress-like appearance. But this forbidding exterior accentuates the contrast with the inner courtyard, designed with all the graceful charm of the Renaissance.
Montal consists of two main wings set at right angles and linked at the corner by a square tower containing the staircase. A two-storey gallery, also set at a right angle to complete the square, was planned for the other two sides of the courtyard but was never built. The façade of the main building with all its rich decoration is one of the castle's most glorious features.

The frieze – Above the ground floor windows and doors runs a 32m – 105ft long frieze. It is a marvel of ornamental diversity: cupids, birds and dream-like figures appear beside shields and a huge human head. There are also the initials of the founder and her sons: I (Jeanne), R (Robert) and D (Dordé).

The busts – On the first floor mullioned windows alternate with false bays with intricately carved pediments, which contain seven busts in high relief, all masterpieces of realism and taste. Each statue is a likeness of a member of the Montal family; from left to right they are: Amaury with a haughty air, wearing a hat; Jeanne, his wife and the founder of the castle, who has an almost conventual expression apparently transfixed in eternal sorrow; Robert, the eldest son killed in Italy, wears a plumed hat in the style of François I; Dordé, the second son, is shown as a young page; Jeanne's parents, Robert de Balsac with a Louis XII-style hat and Antoinette de Castelnau, and, as the last descendant of the line, Dordé de Béduer who was abbot of Vézelay.

The dormers – There are four, and their decoration brings to mind those of Chambord; the dormer gables have small supporting figures on either side and the niches contain statues.

Interior – The entrance is at the corner, where the wings meet, through a door flanked by pilasters and topped by a lintel supporting several niches.

★★Renaissance staircase – The staircase is built in the fine gold-coloured stone from Carennac, beautifully proportioned and magnificently decorated. Admire the fine carving beneath the stairs: ornamented foliage, shells, imaginary birds, initials and little figures from a ceiling, with decoration which completes that of the lierne and tierceron vaulting of the vestibules. This masterpiece of sculpture combines elegance with fantasy.

The apartments – The guard room, vaulted with basket-handled arches, and containing a lovely chimneypiece, the Stag Room (Salle du Cerf) and the other rooms which contain old pieces of furniture (mainly in the Renaissance and Louis XIII styles), retables, paintings and plates attributed to Bernard Palissy (qv), as well as tapestries from Flanders and Tours constitute a marvellous collection.

★ MONTFORT

Michelin map **75** fold 17 or **239** fold 37 – Local map under DORDOGNE VALLEY **3**

Occupying an advantageous site on the Dordogne River, Montfort has given its name to one of Périgord's most famous meanders.
The tiny *lauze*-roofed village nestles at the foot of the castle, perched on a rock pitted with holes.

★**Montfort Meander (Cingle de Montfort)** – A bend built into the rock along the D 703 (*car park*), offers a lovely **view**★ of a river Dordogne meander below, encircling the Tursac peninsula and its walnut tree plantations, while the castle clings to its promontory.

★**Montfort Castle** – The castle stands in a grandiose **setting**★. Its exceptional site aroused the envy of those who wished to rule Périgord; its history consisted of a long series of sieges and battles. Belonging to the lord of Cazenac, the castle was seized by the formidable **Simon de Montfort** *(qv)* in 1214, who razed it to the ground. It was rebuilt and then later destroyed three times – during the Hundred Years War (1337-1453), under Louis XI (1461-83), and again by order of Henri IV (1562-1610) – only to be rebuilt each time. The renovation work carried out in the 19C – the addition of Italian-style loggias and "Germanic" skylights – has added to the castle's charms and made it look like something out of a light opera.

MONTIGNAC   Pop 2 938

Michelin map **75** fold 7 or **233** fold 44 – Local maps under PÉRIGORD NOIR and VÉZÈRE VALLEY – Facilities

Lying along the banks of the Vézère River, Montignac consists of a group of houses around a tower, a last reminder of the fortress which once belonged to the counts of Périgord. In only a few years, this pleasant town became an important tourist centre due to the discovery of Lascaux Cave.
Eugène Le Roy *(qv)*, the well-known Périgord writer, lived in Montignac.

Eugène Le Roy Museum (Musée Eugène-Le-Roy) ☉ – Housed in the tourist information centre, this museum is in part devoted to the author of *Jacquou le Croquant*; the room where Le Roy wrote the story of a peasant revolt has been reconstructed.
Other rooms are devoted to ancient crafts no longer practised and reconstructions of scenes from local history. There is also a small prehistoric collection.

EXCURSIONS

Fanlac – Pop 158. *7 km – 4 miles to the west.*
The novelist Eugène le Roy set part of his most famous work *Jacquou le Croquant* in this very attractive village.The magnificent houses in pale limestone with wildly crooked roofs, and the well and multifoil cross in front of the Renaissance façade of the small church make a very pretty sight.

★**Tour of Périgord Noir** – *56km – 35 miles from Montignac to Sarlat. See Périgord Noir.*

★**St-Amand-de-Coly** – *9km – 5.5 miles on the D 704 and then a small road to the left. See St-Amand-de-Coly.*

★**Ans Country** – *Round tour 86km – 53.5 miles. See Ans Country.*

La Grande Filolie – *4km – 2.5 miles on the D 704 and then a small road to the right. See Périgord Noir.*

Lascaux Cave, ★★Lascaux II – *1 km – 0.6 miles to the south. See Lascaux Cave.*

★**Le Thot, Cro-Magnon Centre** – *5 km – 3 miles along the D 706. See Le Thot.*

★ MONTPEZAT-DE-QUERCY   Pop 1 411

Michelin map **79** fold 18 or **235** fold 18

On the edge of Limogne Causse, this picturesque small Lower Quercy town with its covered arcades and old half-timbered or stone houses owes its fame and its artistic treasures to the munificence of the Des Prés family.

The Des Prés family – Five members of this family from Montpezat became eminent prelates.
Pierre Des Prés, Cardinal of Préneste (now Palestrina in Italy), founded the Collegiate Church of St Martin, which he consecrated in 1344; his nephew, Jean Des Prés, who died in 1351, was Bishop of Coïmbra in Portugal and then of Castres in France. Three other members of the family were consecrated bishops of Montauban: Jean Des Prés (1517-39), who gave his famous Flemish tapestries to the collegiate church at Montpezat, Jean de Lettes (1539-56) and Jacques Des Prés (1556-89). Jacques was a warrior-bishop, an committed persecutor of the Huguenots. He fought on for 25 years, his diocese being one of the most ardent Protestant strongholds, and was killed in an ambush at Lalbenque, some 15km – 10 miles from Montpezat.

COLLEGIATE CHURCH OF ST MARTIN

(COLLÉGIALE ST-MARTIN) *time: 30 min*

This church, dedicated to St Martin of Tours, was built in 1337 by an architect from the papal court at Avignon. It is comparatively small in size and has many of the characteristics of a Languedoc building: a single nave with no side aisles and chapels separated by the nave's interior buttresses.

Tapestry representing St Martin dividing his cloak

Nave – Unity, simplicity and harmony make a striking impression as visitors enter the nave. Its pointed vaulting has hanging keystones painted with the founder's coat of arms. The side chapels contain several notable religious objects: a 15C Virgin of Mercy in multicoloured sandstone (first chapel on the south side), three 15-16C Nottingham alabaster altarpiece panels depicting the Nativity, the Resurrection and the Ascension (second chapel on the south side), a 14C alabaster Virgin and Doves (second chapel on the north side), and 15C wooden caskets with gold inlay work (fourth chapel on the north side).

★★Tapestries – These 16C tapestries, which were specially made to fit the sanctuary, are nearly 25m – 82ft in length and 3m – 6ft in height. They were woven in workshops in the north of France and consist of five panels, each divided into three scenes. The excellent condition of these tapestries, the vividness and richness of their colouring and the fact that they are still hanging in the exact spot for which they were designed all contribute to their outstanding interest value.

Sixteen scenes depict the best-known historic and legendary events in the life of St Martin, including the dividing of his cloak, many of the various cures performed by the saint and his victorious struggle with the devil.

Each scene is accompanied by a quatrain in old French woven at the top of the panel.

★Recumbent figures – Although the body of Cardinal Pierre Des Prés lies beneath the paving before the chancel, his statue and tomb carved in Carrara marble were placed on the right of the chancel entrance in 1778. Opposite, making a pair, lies the recumbent figure of his nephew Jean Des Prés, which is a masterpiece of funerary statuary.

EXCURSION

Saux – *4km – 2.5 miles. Leave Montpezat to the west.*
This **church** ⊘, once the centre of a large parish, now stands isolated in the middle of the woods. The plain interior consists of three domed bays decorated with beautiful 14 and 15C **frescoes**. The best preserved are in the chancel and show Christ in Majesty with the symbols of the four Evangelists, the Crucifixion and scenes from the Childhood of Jesus. In the south chapel the legend of St Catherine is depicted; and in the north chapel, the legend of St George.

MUSSIDAN   Pop 2 985

Michelin map **75** fold 4 or **233** fold 41 – Local map opposite – Facilities

This old Huguenot city on the banks of the Isle river was laid to siege on several occasions during the Wars of Religion. The siege in 1569, which was particularly bloody, provoked Montaigne to write his essay *L'heure des Parlements dangereuse.*

André Voulgre Museum of Périgord Local Arts and Traditions (Musée des Arts et Traditions Populaires du Périgord André-Voulgre) ⊘ – Displayed in the lovely Périgord mansion where Doctor Voulgre lived, this collection is rich and varied; it includes furniture, objects and tools collected by the doctor during his lifetime.

A handsomely furnished 19C bourgeois interior – kitchen, dining room, drawing room, bedrooms – has been reproduced in several of the museum's rooms.

Workshops (cooper's shop, sabot maker, blacksmith) have also been reconstituted. A collection of agricultural machinery and tools is set up in the barn: a 1927 steam engine, a still, a tractor (1920) built with the tracks of tanks used in World War I, and a reaper-binder.

In a large exhibition hall, brass, pewter, glazed earthenware *(faïences)* and stuffed animals are displayed.

CASTLES OF THE LANDAIS REGION
Round trip of 43km – 27 miles – allow 3 hours – local map below

To the south of the Isle valley, the Landais countryside reveals itself to be not unlike that of the Double region. As in the Double, the sand and clay torn from the Massif Central covered the limestone during the Tertiary Era. However, the forest here is less dense than in the Double, there are fewer lakes, and the more fertile land is occupied by castles, manor-houses and country estates.

Château de Montréal ⊙ – This half-feudal, half-Renaissance building, surrounded by attractive outbuildings, stands at the top of a hill overlooking the Crempse. In the 18C drawing room there are some Louis XVI medallion-backed chairs upholstered with the Fables of La Fontaine.

In the outbuildings is a 12C staircase roofed with a row of barrel vaults, themselves forming steps which lead to the cellars; these are an extension of a natural cave adorned with small concretions.

Legend has it that the town of Montreal on the St Lawrence owes its name to the lord of Montréal, Claude de Pontbriand, one of Jacques Cartier's companions on his second voyage to Canada.

A chapel was built in the 16C to shelter the reliquary of the Holy Thorn found on Talbot's body at the Battle of Castillon *(see Introduction: Historical Table).*

Château-Manoir de la Ponsie – *(St-Jean-d'Estissac).* The rectangular residence of this country mansion and its adjoining polygonal tower are visible from the road near St-Jean-d'Estissac. Ponsie was place of birth to J B de Salignac, a very devout and generous man who became chaplain to Queen Marie-Antoinette and guardian of the "little chimney-sweeps" in Paris (the name denoted a variety of child labourers, from chimney-sweeps to side-show operators). He went to the Guillotine during the Reign of Terror.

Montagnac-la-Crempse – The **hamlet** (Hameau de la Grange) ⊙ here contains several traditional Landais houses, little white-walled "workshops".

Villamblard – Pop 813. In the centre of town stand the ruins of a **fortress**, which was one of the most important fortifications in the Périgord region during the Hundred Years War, and which housed Calvin at one point during the 16C. It has lovely window mouldings and an interesting doorway topped by an ogee arch.

Grignols Castle ⊙ – This fortress, which belonged to the Grignols and Talleyrands, defended the road between Périgueux and Bordeaux. Perched on a rocky crest overlooking the Vern valley, the fortress is set on a triangular terrace between two moats. The buildings (built between the 13 and 17C) overlap one another and are overlooked by a square keep. Most of them were taken down during the Fronde (1648-52) *(qv)*. The 13C lords' room contains lovely chimneypieces adorned with rosettes. Other furnished rooms in the castle can be visited.

Cross the Vern River and take the D 44 towards Neuvic-sur-l'Isle.

The road follows the poplar-lined river on its way to Neuvic-sur-l'Isle, an industrial town (large shoe factory).

Château de Neuvic ⊙ – This castle was built during the first half of the 16C, in a style typical of the Early Renaissance. The machicolations on the outside of its rampart walk are more decorative than protective, since they break off to give way to bays in which there mullioned windows. Inside, some of the rooms are decorated with frescoes. It has become a teaching hospital run by nuns of the Order of St Martha.

Fratteau Castle ⊙ – Recently restored, this fortress now houses a **Pottery Museum**. The neighbouring village of Beauronne was once an important centre of production for this craft.

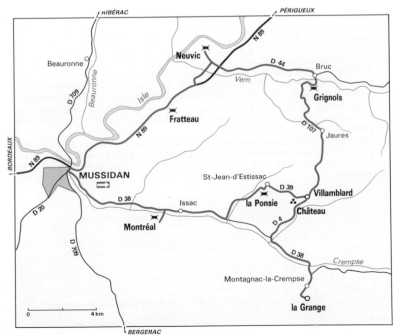

★★★ PADIRAC CHASM (GOUFFRE DE PADIRAC)

Michelin map **75** fold 19 or **235** fold 7 or **239** folds 38 and 39 – Facilities (Padirac)

The Padirac Chasm provides access to wonderful galleries hollowed out of the limestone mass of Gramat Causse *(qv)* by a subterranean river. A visit into the vertiginous well and a tour of the mysterious river and the vast caves adorned with limestone concretions leave visitors with a striking impression of this fascinating underground world.

From legend to scientific exploration – The Padirac Chasm was a source of superstitious terror to the local inhabitants right up to the 19C, as people believed that the origin of this great hole was connected with the devil.

St Martin, so the tale went, was returning from an expedition on the *causse* where he had been looking unsuccessfully for souls to save. All at once his mule refused to go on; Satan, bearing a great sack full of souls which he was taking to hell, stood in the saint's path. Jeering at the poor saint Satan made the following proposition: he would give St Martin the souls he had in his sack on condition that St Martin make his mule cross an obstacle that he, Satan, would create on the spot. Whereupon he hit the ground hard with his foot, and a gaping chasm opened up. The saint coaxed his mule forward and the beast jumped clear with such force that its hoofprints are still visible. Satan, defeated, retreated to hell by way of the hole he had created.

The chasm served as a refuge for the people living on the *causse* during the Hundred Years War and the Wars of Religion, but it would appear that it was towards the end of the 19C, following a violent flooding of the river, that a practicable line of communication opened between the bottom of the well and the underground galleries. The speleologist, **Édouard A Martel**, was the first to discover the passage in 1889. Between 1889 and 1900 he undertook nine expeditions and in 1890 reached the Hall of the Great Dome.

Padirac was opened for the first time to tourists in 1898. Since then, numerous speleological expeditions have uncovered 22km-13.5 miles of underground galleries.

The 1947 expedition proved by fluorescein colouring of the water that the Padirac River reappears above ground 11km-7 miles away where the Lombard rises and at St George's spring in the **Montvalent Amphitheatre** *(qv)* near the Dordogne.

During the expeditions of 1984 and 1985, a team of speleologists, paleontologists, prehistorians and geologists discovered a prehistoric site, 9km-5.5 miles from the mouth of the hole, on an affluent of the Joly, with bones of mammoths, rhinoceroses, bisons, bears, cave-dwelling lions and deer, all of which were found to date from between 150 000 and 200 000 years ago. Amidst the bones found were chipped flints dating from between 30 000 and 50 000 years ago. Copies of some of the bones are exhibited in the chasm's entrance hall.

TOUR ⏱ *time: allow 1 hour 30 min*

Two lifts and some staircases lead into the chasm, which is 99m-325ft in circumference, and to the pyramid of rubble, debris of the original caving-in of the roof. From the bottom of the lift (75m-247ft), there is a striking view of walls covered by the overflow from stalagmites and by vegetation and of a little corner of the sky at the mouth of the hole. Stairs lead down to the underground river, 103m-338ft below ground level. At the bottom, the 2 000m-1.25 mile underground journey begins, 700m-0.5 mile of which is by boat.

Gallery of the Spring (Galerie de la Source) – This chamber is at the end of an underground canyon, the roof of which gets gradually higher and higher; it is 300m-984ft long and follows the upper course of the river that hollowed it out. At the far end is the landing-stage.

Smooth River (Rivière Plane) – A flotilla of flat-bottomed boats offers an enchanting journey over the smooth and astonishingly translucent waters of the river. The depth of the river varies from 50cm to 4m (20in to 13ft), but the water temperature remains constant at 10.5°C (51 °F). The height of the roof increases progressively to reach a maximum of 78m-256ft; the different levels of erosion corresponding to the successive courses of the river can be seen from the boat.

At the end of the boat trip admire the **Great Pendant** (Grande Pendeloque) of **Rainfall Lake** (Lac de la Pluie). This giant stalactite, the point of which nearly touches the water, is simply the final pendant in a string of concretions 78m-256ft in height.

Crocodile Path (Pas du Crocodile) – A narrow passage between high walls links the underground lake and the chambers to be visited next. Look to the left at the **Great Pillar** (Grand Pilier), 40m-131ft high.

The Hall of the Great Natural Dams (Salle des Grands Gours) – A series of pools separated by *gours*, natural limestone dams, divides the river and the lake into superb basins, beyond which can be seen a 6m-20ft waterfall. This is the end of the area open to tourists.

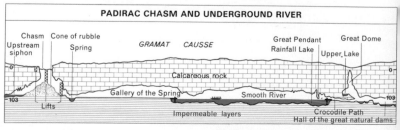

PADIRAC CHASM AND UNDERGROUND RIVER

Upper Lake (Lac Supérieur) – This lake is fed only by water infiltrating the soil and falling from the roof; its level is 20m-66ft above that of the Smooth River. *Gours* ring the lake's emerald waters.

Hall of the Great Dome (Salle du Grand Dôme) – The great height of the roof (91m-295ft) is most impressive in this, the largest and most beautiful of the Padirac caverns. The viewpoint, built half-way up, enables visitors to appreciate the rock formations and the flows of calcite decorating certain parts of the walls. The return trip (to the landing-stage) offers interesting views of the Great Pillar and the Great Pendant. From the end of the Gallery of the Spring, four lifts (to avoid the walk up 455 steps) lead back to the entrance.

ADDITIONAL SIGHT

Zoo le Tropicorama ⊙ – Located on a lovely green site, this zoo has a Bonzaï garden, cacti, rare tropical plants and the zoo, housing a large collection of exotic birds (parrots, horn bills, toucans, birds of prey etc) and an interesting selection of mammals (rare monkeys, lemurs, ocelots etc). Some of the animals are at large.

PAUNAT   Pop 246

Michelin map **75** fold 16 or **235** fold 5 – 7km – 4 miles northeast of Trémolat

Paunat is tucked in a small valley near the confluence of the Dordogne and the Vézère. It possesses an impressive Romanesque church which formed part of a monastery once attached to the powerful Abbey of St-Martial at Limoges.

Church (Église St-Martial) – Built of beautiful ochre stone, this 12C church was modified to incorporate fortifications in the 15C. Its bare walls and high, flat buttresses give it a rather forbidding appearance from the outside.
The solid belfry-porch consists of two floors, each vaulted with a dome.The highest of these is in the archaic style. A design such as this is unique in the Périgord region. The transept crossing is also vaulted with a dome, supported by broken arches. Excavations at ground level have uncovered the foundations of previous buildings by the north pillar.
In the square in front of the church, next to the river, there is a strange penthouse construction incorporating two boilers which were used to heat up animals' feeds during fairs.

★★ PECH MERLE CAVE (Grotte du PECH MERLE)

Michelin map **79** fold 9 or **235** fold 14 – Local map under CÉLÉ VALLEY

Prehistoric man performed religious rites in this cave, which was only rediscovered thousands of years later in 1922. Not only is its natural decoration interesting *(photograph p 163)*, there are also wall paintings and carvings which are of great documentary value to prehistorians.

The underground explorers – Two boys of fourteen were the heroes of the Pech Merle Cave rediscovery.
Inspired by the expeditions and discoveries made throughout the region by Abbé **Lemozi**, the priest from Cabrerets who was a prehistorian and speleologist, the boys explored a small fault known only to have served as a refuge during the Revolution. The two friends ventured forward, creeping along a narrow, slimy trench pitted with wells and blocked by limestone concretions. After several hours their efforts were rewarded by the sight of wonderful paintings.
Abbé Lemozi, who soon afterwards explored the cave scientifically, recognised the importance of the underground sanctuary. It was decided to open it to tourists. In 1949 the discovery of a new chamber led to the finding of the original opening through which men had entered the cave about 10 000 to 20 000 years ago.

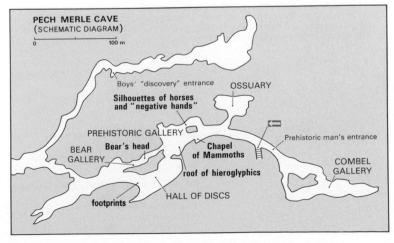

PECH MERLE CAVE
(SCHEMATIC DIAGRAM)
0   100 m

Boys' "discovery" entrance   OSSUARY
Silhouettes of horses and "negative hands"
PREHISTORIC GALLERY   Prehistoric man's entrance
BEAR GALLERY   Bear's head   Chapel of Mammoths
roof of hieroglyphics   COMBEL GALLERY
footprints   HALL OF DISCS

TOUR ⊘ *time: allow 1 hour 45 min*

In addition to the interest it offers lovers of speleology who can marvel at the caverns of vast size communicating with each other through wide openings and decorated with beautiful concretions, the Pech Merle Cave offers prehistorians the sight of highly advanced paintings and engravings and material traces of prehistoric man's sojourn there.

Visitors may, at present, walk through 1 200m – 1 mile of chambers and galleries. The upper level of the Prehistoric Gallery (Salle Préhistorique) is called the **Chapel of Mammoths** (Chapelle des Mammouths) or the black frieze; it is decorated with drawings of bison and mammoths outlined in black and forming a frieze 7m – 23ft long by 3m – 10ft high.

The Hall of Discs (Salle des Disques) is patterned with many strange concretions that look like discs; the origin of their formation remains a mystery. The footprints made by a prehistoric man can be seen, petrified for ever in the once wet clay of a *gour* (natural dam).

Further on are huge, impressive columns, eccentrics with delicate protuberances that defy the laws of gravity and cave pearls, with colours ranging from the shining white of pure calcite to red-ochre caused by the presence of clay and iron oxide in the limestone.

Go down a narrow passageway, which contains an engraving of a bear's head, to the lower level of the Prehistoric Gallery, where one wall is decorated with the **silhouettes of two horses**, with dots patterning them and the surface around them, mysterious symbols and outlined hand prints, known as "negative hands" *(illustration p 19)*. These prints were made by stencilling in different pigments around the hands placed flat against the rock. The horses are depicted with distorted silhouettes (similar to those at Lascaux): a huge body and a tiny head. These prints and the roof of hieroglyphics once decorated a sanctuary older than that of the Chapel of Mammoths.

In the last cave to be visited, Combel Gallery (Salle de Combel), are the bones of cave bears and the roots of an oak tree that bored down into the cave in search of moisture.

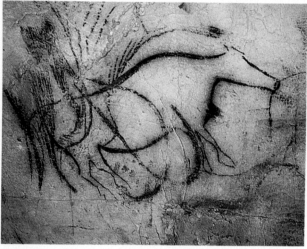

Cave wall horses

Amédée Lemozi Museum (Musée Amédée-Lémozi) ⊘ – This is a research and information centre on prehistory in Quercy. On the lower floor, which is open to the public, there is an attractive and informative display of bones, tools, weapons, utensils and works of art from 160 different prehistoric sites, dating from the Lower Palaeolithic to the Iron Age. In an adjoining room photographs of the decorated caves in the region (in particular Pech Merle and Cougnac) are exhibited. The museum visit ends with a film on palaeolithic art in Quercy.

Join us in our never-ending task
of keeping up to date.
Send us your comments and suggestions,
please.

MICHELIN TYRE Public Limited Company
Tourism Department
The Edward Hyde Building
38 Clarendon Road
WATFORD Herts WD1 1SX

PENNE

Michelin map **79** fold 19 or **235** fold 22 – Local map under ST-ANTONIN-NOBLE-VAL

The old village, overlooked by its castle ruins, perches in a remarkable **setting★**, clinging to a rocky spike which rises sheer above the left bank of the Aveyron in the prettiest part of its course *(see St-Antonin-Noble-Val: Excursions)*. There is a good view from the D 33 to the north of the village and from the D 133 to the south.

The complex outline of the powerful medieval fortress with its jagged walls, in some cases poised on the very edge of the rock and seeming to defy all the laws of gravity, rises above the flat roofs of the village houses.

Village – *Leave the car on the D 9, at the entrance to the village.* A narrow street leads to the church, whose belltower encompassing a pointed arch marks the entrance to the fortified village. The chancel lost its bastion-like appearance in the 17C, when the church's main entrance was opened.

From the belltower, a picturesque street lined with old houses leads up to the castle, then down to Peyrière Gate on the opposite side of the village.

The 17C plague cross, harking back to the scourge that hit Penne on several occasions, indicates the path which leads to the tower ruins.

Castle – The castle's location kept it well in the limelight during the history of Quercy. At the time of the Albigensian Crusade, it became the stake in the bloody wars fought by the lord of Penne, rallying to the cause of the "heretics", and the followers of Simon de Montfort *(qv)*. Later, during the Hundred Years War, the English and the local troops seized and reseized it from each other time after time. It finally fell into ruins last century.

From the tip of the promontory, there is a good **view★** of the towers and jagged walls of the castle, of Penne and of the Aveyron Valley.

★ PÉRIGORD NOIR

Michelin map **75** folds 7 and 17 or **235** folds 2 and 6

Périgord Noir, a vast cretaceous plateau carved by the Vézère River to the west and the Dordogne River to the south, overruns into the Sarladais region.

Périgord Noir means Black Périgord and the word "black" refers to the dark colour of the forest cover consisting mainly of oaks, chestnut and sea pines.

The houses, castles, châteaux, manor-houses and churches have walls of golden-coloured local limestone and steeply-pitched roofs covered with *lauzes* or small flat tiles in a warm brown hue. These architectural elements, combined with the rolling, wooded countryside, make a harmonious picture.

Part of Périgord Noir is described in the itinerary of the Dordogne Valley from Souillac to Limeuil *(see Dordogne Valley* **2**, **3** *and* **4** *)*, the other part in the Vézère Valley itinerary from Montignac to Limeuil *(see Vézère Valley)*, while the itinerary described below completes the third side of the triangle formed by the Vézère and Dordogne Rivers.

FROM MONTIGNAC TO SARLAT

56km – 35 miles – allow 3 hours – local map overleaf

Montignac – *See Montignac.*

> Leave Montignac on the D 704 towards Sarlat. After 4km – 2.5 miles turn right towards La Grande Filolie.

La Grande Filolie – Set in the hollow of a small valley, this charming castle *(photograph below)* dating from the 14 and 15C consists of a group of overlapping buildings and towers linked together. This building, part-castle, part-farm, is built in golden-coloured limestone and covered with *lauzes*. The castle includes the nobles' residence, a 15C quadrangular building flanked at each end by a square machicolated tower, a Renaissance wing, a gatehouse with a bartizan, and a chapel, which has at one end a round tower with a very pointed roof.

> *Return to the D 704 and take the first road on the left towards St-Amand-de-Coly.*

★ **St-Amand-de-Coly** – *See St-Amand-de-Coly.*

> From St-Amand take the D 64 and go south.

La Grande Filolie

★St-Geniès – Pop 736. This is one good example of the Périgord Noir's many beautiful villages with its golden limestone houses covered in *lauzes (qv)*, the ruins of a Romanesque keep and the 15C castle next to the church. Access to the church is through a fortified belfry-porch, which was added in the 16C. Above the pentagonal east end there is an arched cornice supported on brackets carved with faces. Located at the top of a mound behind the Post Office, the **Chapelle du Cheylard**, a small Gothic chapel, is decorated with lovely 14C **frescoes★** depicting the Life of Christ and lives of popular saints. The road, on the left after a wayside cross, leads down through a cool valley to St-Crépin-et-Carlucet.

St-Crépin-et-Carlucet – Pop 321. St-Crépin and Carlucet form one *commune*. The charming **La Cipière Manor-house** (Manoir de la Cipière) ⊘ at St-Crépin was built at the end of the 16C on the spot where a fortified building had once stood. The square main building is entirely roofed in *lauzes* and framed by turrets.

The Romanesque **church**, further down, was altered during the Gothic period. Continue winding along this narrow country road through the valley to Carlucet.

Carlucet – The church of Carlucet has an unusual 17C cemetery. Some of the tombs have been set in carved recesses in the curtain wall.

Join the D 60 and turn right.

Salignac-Eyvigues – See Salignac-Eyvigues.

Eyrignac Manor-house – See Salignac-Eyvigues.

Take the D 61 south. At Simeyrols take the D 47 towards Sarlat.

Ste-Nathalène – Leave the village, taking the road to Proissans for 1.5km-1 mile. The 16C **La Tour watermill** ⊘, driven by the flow of the river Enea, continues the traditional manufacture of walnut and hazelnut oils. There used to be many grain mills in Périgord which were also adaptable for the production of walnut oil during the winter. The mechanism of this mill is 150 years old. The tour of the mill explains the different stages of the production process.

Return to Ste-Nathalène and take the D 47 towards Sarlat. Go straight on at Croix d'Alon.

Temniac – The chapel of Notre-Dame, set on a hill overlooking Sarlat, offers a good **view★** of that city.

Once a pilgrimage centre, this 12C structure has certain Romanesque Périgord School characteristics *(qv)*: a nave vaulted with two domes and a pentagonal chancel. A black Virgin, the object of pilgrimages, is to be found in the crypt, which has archaic-style ogive vaulting.

Near the chapel stands the curtain wall of a castle (now in ruins), which was once a commandery of the Knights Templars before it became the residence of the bishops of Sarlat.

★★★Sarlat – See Sarlat-la-Canéda. Facilities.

THE WARS OF RELIGION IN PÉRIGORD

Religious strife still exists, and yet it is hard to imagine Périgord during the Wars of Religion. Religious ideals turned this lovely, harmonious region into a battlefield.

Imagine this region ravaged for some thirty years (1562-94) by eight military campaigns. Towns and cities were constantly changing hands (Sarlat, Périgueux, Mussidan, Cahors, Domme, Villefranche-du-Périgord), and people were massacred, most often at the fall of a town (Mussidan, Sarlat) or in revenge (La Chapelle-Faucher).

Those mighty castles, some of which had been used during the Hundred Years War, were once again ideal strongholds for their cause (Catholic: Bourdeilles, Puymartin, Hautefort, Mareuil; Protestant: Les Bories, Montfort, Cardaillac).

Military men made a reputation defending their beliefs: Montluc for the Catholics and De Coligny and Vivans for the Protestants.

Today as you drive through the region, there are still a few reminders of the Huguenots. Often a cluster of trees and a tombstone will indicate a Protestant family tomb; most towns have a temple, the Protestant place of worship.

Built in the fertile valley of the River Isle, Périgueux is an ancient town. Its long history can be traced in its urban architecture and its two distinctive districts, each of which is marked by the domes of its sanctuary: the Cité District, overlooked by St Stephen's tiled roof, and Puy St-Front District, with the Byzantine silhouette of the present cathedral bristling with pinnacles.

There is a good overall view of the town from the bridge beyond Cours Fénelon to the southeast.

The wonderful Vésone – The town of Périgueux derives from the sacred spring known as the Vésone. It was near the stream, on the Isle's south bank, that the Gaulish **Petrocorii** (Petrocorii, which meant the "four tribes" in Celtic, gave its name both to Périgueux and Périgord) built their main oppidum (defensive town). After siding with Vercingetorix against Caesar, the Petrocorii finally had to accept Roman domination but in fact benefited greatly from the *Pax Romana*, which enabled the city to become one of the finest in all Aquitaine. Vesunna, as the town was then called, spread beyond the bend in the Isle; temples, a forum, basilicas and an arena were built and an aqueduct over 7km – 4 miles long was constructed to carry water to the baths. But in 3C AD the city's prosperity was destroyed by the Alemanni, who sacked this town as well as seventy other towns and villages throughout Gaul.

The unfortunate town – To avoid further disaster the Vesunnians shut themselves up in a narrow fortified enclosure; stones from the temples were used to build powerful ramparts, the arena was transformed into a keep.

In spite of all these precautions, the town suffered the alternate depredations of fire and pillaging by barbaric invaders such as the Visigoths, Franks and Norsemen. Such misfortune reduced Vesunna to the status of a humble village and finally even its name died; it was known as the "town of the Petrocorii" or more simply still as the "Cité".

St Front later established the town as an episcopal seat and, in the 10C, it became the unassuming capital of the county of Périgord.

The ambition of Puy St-Front – A little sanctuary containing the tomb of St Front, apostle of Périgord, was built not far from the Cité. Initially the object of a pilgrimage, the sanctuary became a monastic centre. A busy market town, Puy St-Front, grew up round the monastery, soon eclipsing the Cité in size.

The townspeople of Puy St-Front joined the feudal alliances against the English kings, established an emancipated consular regime and then sided with Philip Augustus against King John of England.

Little by little, the expanding Puy St-Front annexed the Cité's prerogatives; there were more and more squabbles between the rivals. The Cité, unable to win against a neighbour who was under the protection of the king of France, was forced to accept union. On 16 September 1240, an act of union established that the Cité and Puy St-Front would now form one community governed by a mayor and 12 consuls.

The municipal constitution was established in 1251 and the two towns united under the name of Périgueux. Nevertheless, each town kept its distinctive characteristics; the Cité belonged to the clerics and aristocrats while Puy St-Front belonged to the merchants and artisans.

Loyal Périgueux – "My strength lies in the trust of my fellow citizens" is Périgueux's proud motto. The town, independent of France under the *Treaty of Brétigny* in 1360, was the first to answer the call of Charles V to take up arms against the English. It was in Périgueux that Du Guesclin planned the famous campaigns which enabled him to drive the English from the land.

Soon afterwards, bribed by the English, Count Archambaud V openly committed treason against the king and rode roughshod over the consuls. Hostilities broke out in earnest between the loyal townsfolk and their wicked overlord. When eventually royal troops arrived, Archambaud V fled and the parliament claimed Périgord on behalf of the crown.

During the Fronde (1648-52) the loyalty of Périgueux was unexpectedly put to the test by Condé. The Fronde supporters laid siege to the town; the churches of St Front and St Stephen were badly damaged. The leaders, their patience exhausted, forced the people to revolt; the garrison was rendered useless and soon afterwards the king's men entered the town in triumph.

Périgueux becomes Préfecture – In 1790, when the Dordogne *département* was created, Périgueux was chosen over Bergerac *(qv)* as *Préfecture*. The town, which had slowly become dormant, having encountered no upheavals in the 18C but the construction of the Allées de Tourny (by the administrator of the same name), suddenly found itself the object of a building boom. The old quarters were enhanced by the addition of avenues and new squares.

Périgueux today – A small regional capital in the centre of an agricultural region, Périgueux is first and foremost a market town. Its gastronomic specialities, with truffle and *foie gras* occupying prize position, have become famous around the world.

Its functions are essentially administrative and commercial, however there is some industry, mainly repair workshops for railway equipment and a stamp printing plant. The transfer of the latter activity from Paris to Périgueux in 1970 was one of the earliest implementations of the government's policies of decentralisation and national development. It includes the production of postal stamps (more than 3.5 billion per year!) for France and a dozen or so other countries, as well as tax stamps, vehicle road tax discs and other types of supplementary taxes, postal cheques and money orders.

★DOMED CHURCHES *time: 1 hour*

★**St Stephen's Church (Église St-Étienne-de-la-Cité) (BZ)** ⊘ – Built in the 12C on the site of the ancient temple of Mars, this church, the town's first Christian sanctuary, was consecrated by St Front to the martyr Stephen and was the cathedral church until 1669.

It included a row of four domed bays, one after the other, preceded by an imposing belfry porch. When the town was occupied in 1577, the Huguenots demolished all but the two east bays. The episcopal palace, nearby, was also destroyed. Restored in the 17C, ravaged again during the Fronde, secularised during the Revolution, St Stephen's was reconsecrated at the time of the First Empire.

The church as it now stands is a good example of the pure Périgord-Romanesque style. Still visible outside are the beginnings of a ruined bay and the vestigial foundations of a dome.

Inside, it is interesting to compare the architecture of the two bays built within a fifty-year interval. The first is archaic, primitive, short and dark. The arches serve as wall ribs and the 11C dome, the largest in Périgord, being 15m-49ft in diameter, is illuminated by small windows which open onto the top of the dome. The second bay is more elongated. Its dome rests on pointed arches held up by square pillars, made less heavy in appearance by twinned columns. Moulded windows with small columns throw light onto an elegant blind arcade with columns which supports an open passage.

This part was greatly damaged by the Huguenots; when it was rebuilt in the 17C, scrupulous attention was paid to reproducing the original.

Against the south wall of the first bay is an impressive 17C **altarpiece** in oak and walnut built for the seminary. Facing it is a carved arcade, part of the tomb of Jean d'Astide, bishop of Périgueux (1160-69), which now frames the 12C baptismal font.

A modern Stations of the Cross is the work of the painter J-J Giraud.

★**St Front's Cathedral (Cathédrale St-Front) (DZ)** – This cathedral, dedicated to St Front, first bishop of Périgueux, is one of the largest in southwest France and one of the most curious. Built in the purest Périgord style, it was largely reconstructed by Abadie from 1852 onwards in the style of Second Empire pastiche. He was to use this restoration later as the inspiration for the design of the Sacré Cœur Basilica in Paris. A chapel was first built on the site of the saint's tomb in the 6C. The origin of the abbey established around the sanctuary is either Augustinian or Benedictine. In 1047 a larger church was consecrated. This second building was almost completely destroyed by fire in 1120, whereupon it was decided to construct an even bigger church by extending the damaged building.

This third basilica, completed about 1173, was Byzantine in style, with a dome and with a ground plan in the form of a Greek cross. This architecture, which is uncommon in France, brings to mind St Mark's in Venice and the Church of the Apostles in Constantinople. This was the first domed church to be built on the Roman road, which was still used in the Middle Ages by those travelling from Rodez to Cahors and on to Saintes.

In 1575, during the Wars of Religion, St Front's was pillaged by the Huguenots, the treasure was scattered and the saint's tomb destroyed. A substantial amount of restoration work was carried out with little regard for the original design. The complete reconstruction, undertaken 1852-1901 under the supervision of the architects Abadie and Boeswillwald, included the destruction of the conventual buildings. Only the cloisters remain standing.

Exterior – *Stand in Place de la Clautre to have an overall view.* Before the restoration the domes, covered in stones and tiles, had small amortizements. The façade overlooking the Place de la Clautre and the open bays were part of the 11C church. The beautiful tiered belltower is all that remains of the 12C church, and is preserved more or less as it was originally. Abadie drew on its lantern as inspiration for the tall pinnacles which adorn the new domes.

The domes of St Front's Cathedral

Interior – Enter the cathedral by the north door. In order to respect the chronological order of the building's construction, visitors should first of all see, near the base of the belltower, the remains of the 11C church; two bays covered with domes perched on tall column drums.

From its prestigious Romanesque model, the church redesigned by Abadie appropriated its dimensions, the boldness of its domes on pendentives and the strength of its odd-looking pillars carved in places in the shape of a cross.

Adorning the back of the apse is a monumental **altarpiece★★** in walnut; this masterpiece of baroque sculpture, from the Jesuit College, depicts the Dormition and the Assumption of the Virgin. The 17C stalls are from the old Benedictine abbey of Ligueux.

Admire the **pulpit★**, a fine example of 17C craftsmanship, where Hercules is holding up the stand while two atlantes carry the sounding board. The five monumental brass candelabra, hanging at each of the bays, were designed by Abadie.

Cloisters – The cloisters date from the 12, 13 and 16C and are of a half-Romanesque, half-Gothic architectural style. The chapter-house is covered with groined vaulting resting on columns. The enormous pine-cone-like mass in the centre of the cloisters once crowned the belltower; during the Revolution it was replaced by a weathercock which was later replaced by Abadie's angel. On display in the cloisters' galleries are architectural elements of St Front's before its restoration.

★① PUY ST-FRONT DISTRICT *time: 2 hours*

The old artisans' and merchants' district has been given a face-lift. A conservation program for safeguarding this historic area was set up, and the area has been undergoing major restoration. Its Renaissance façades, courtyards, staircases, elegant town houses and shops have been brought back to life; the pedestrian streets have rediscovered their role as commercial thoroughfares.

Place du Coderc and Place de l'Hôtel de Ville are colourful and animated every morning with their fruit and vegetable market, while Place de la Clautre is where the larger Wednesday and Saturday market is held. During the winter, the prestigious truffle and *foie gras* markets attract hordes of connoisseurs. In the summer, the restaurants, overflowing onto the pavements, serve high quality Périgord cuisine in an atmosphere of days past...

Start at the Mataguerre Tower opposite the tourist office (syndicat d'initiative).

Mataguerre Tower (Tour Mataguerre) (CZ B) ⊘ – This round tower (late 15C) is crowned by a machicolated parapet and pierced by arrowslits. It was part of the defensive system which protected Puy St-Front in the Middle Ages. On the side of Rue de la Bride part of the ramparts can be seen. The name Mataguerre is believed to have come from an Englishman who was imprisoned in the tower.

From the top is a view of the old district with its tiled roofs, the towers of the noblemen's town houses, the domes of St-Front's and the neighbouring hills, one of which is the well-known Écornebœuf Hill (*écorner*: to break the horns of an animal; *bœuf*: ox) so named because the hill was so steep that the oxen broke their necks... and lost their horns.

Go up Rue de la Bride and Rue des Farges.

Rue des Farges (CZ) – At nos 4 and 6 stands the **House of the Women of Faith**. The medieval (13C) layout of its façade is still visible in spite of its damaged state: pointed arches on the ground floor, rounded arches on the upper storey and a loggia beneath the eaves. A small bell turret set in one corner brings to mind the fact that in the 17C the building was a convent, whose congregation gave the house its name.

It is said that the building housed Du Guesclin during the Hundred Years War.

Rue Aubergerie (CZ 9) – At no 16, the **Hôtel d'Abzac de Ladouze** consists of a main building, preceded by a great round arch, an octagonal tower and a corbelled turret, all characteristic of 15C architecture.

At nos 4 and 8 the **Hôtel de Sallegourde**, also 15C, has a polygonal tower surmounted by a machicolated watchpath.

Rue St-Roch (CDZ 48) – At no 4 a small arcaded loggia is decorated with diamond-work.

Rue de Sully (DZ 51) – The houses in this attractively restored street are half-timbered.

Rue du Calvaire (DZ 16) – The condemned, on their way to be executed on Place de la Clautre, came up this street, their "road to Calvary". At no 3 there is a lovely door ornamented with nailheads beneath a Renaissance porch.

Place de la Clautre (DZ 26) – There is an interesting view of the imposing St Front's Cathedral from here. Tombs are concealed underneath the square.

Place du Thouin (DZ 54) – The two bronze cannon with the inscription "Périgueux 1588" were excavated at Place du Coderc in 1979 on the site of the armoury in the old consulate.

Daumesnil's Birthplace (Maison Natale de Daumesnil) (DYZ D) – *7 Rue de la Clarté*. This house has an 18C façade. **General Pierre Daumesnil** was born here on 27 July 1776. This soldier followed Napoleon to Arcola, to Egypt and to Wagram, where he lost a leg. In 1814, while governor of the Vincennes fortress, he gave the enemy, who were laying siege and urging him to give up, the response: "I'll surrender Vincennes when you give me back my leg" *(see Michelin Green Guide to Paris)*.

Place de l'Hôtel-de-Ville (CZ 37) – The town hall is located in the 17 and 18C **Hôtel de Lagrange-Chancel (CZ H)**. The 15C house at no 7 has a polygonal staircase tower characteristic of the period. Its machicolations, as well as the small shop opening directly onto the street, are neo-Gothic.

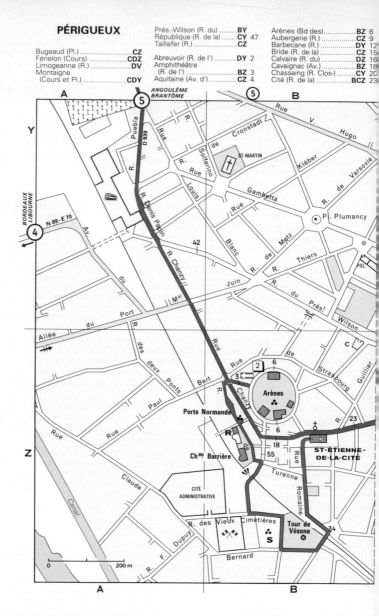

PÉRIGUEUX

Place du Coderc (DY 27) – Originally a field for keeping pigs, this square has become the geographic and administrative centre of the Puy St-Front District. In the early 19C the old consulate, the heart of municipal and legislative life, still had its old square belfry, some 600 years old. The covered market was built on this site in c1830.

Rue de la Sagesse (CDY 50) – At no 1, the **Hôtel de Lestrade** (CDY E) ◷ contains an elegant **Renaissance staircase★**, of a square groundplan and decorated with a coffered ceiling depicting mythological scenes, one of which recounts Venus putting down her weapons, symbolising the young wife entering the household. The intertwined H and S represent the initials of the Hauteforts and Solminihacs.

Place St-Louis (CDY) – This square is known locally as Foie Gras Square, as it is here that the *foies gras (qv)* are sold in late autumn.
It features a modern fountain, decorated with a bronze sculpture by Ramon.

The **Maison Tenant or Maison du Pâtissier** (F) opposite used to be the Talleyrands' town house; it consists of a square residential part with an adjoining corbelled turret. The corner door, oddly enough, has a double squinch above it. A machicolated parapet runs around the small inner courtyard. The façade on the Rue Eguillerie has a marvellous Gothic window.

Rue Lammary (DY 38) – No 9 has an unusual superposition of mullioned corner windows.

★**Rue Limogeanne** (DY) – In the past, this street led to Limogeanne Gate (Porte Limogeanne), which opened onto the Limoges road. The large pedestrian street is lined by numerous stores and several elegant Renaissance town houses.
In the courtyard of the **Hôtel de Méredieu** (no 12) there is a 15C carved doorway decorated with a coat of arms, which was added in the 17C.
At no 7, note the initials A C in the centre of the wrought-iron impost; these denote Antoine Courtois, the famous 18C caterer, whose partridge pâtés were the talk even of the Court of Prussia. His headquarters were in the cellars of this town house.

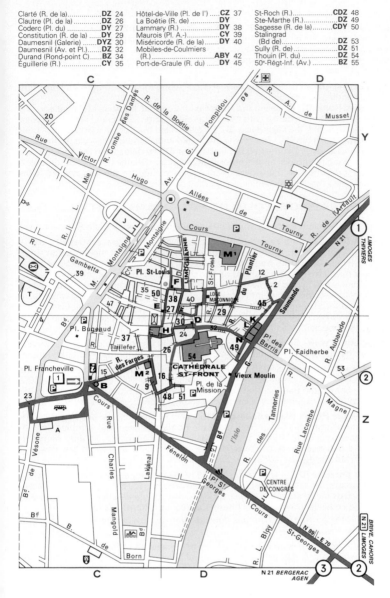

The elegant Renaissance façade of the **Estignard Mansion** (no 5) is embellished with highly ornate dormers, mullioned windows and pilaster capitals decorated with heads of men, animals and other motifs.

The Regional Department of Architecture is to be found at no 3. Behind the heavy balustrade above the doorway, the inner courtyard has a lovely door decorated with grotesques on the lintel and François I salamanders on the tympanum. The huge staircase leads into a permanent exhibition on the restoration of the buildings in Périgueux.

Lapeyre House (no 1), which is at the corner of Place du Coderc, has a corbelled corner turret.

★**Galerie Daumesnil** (**DYZ 30**) – This leads off Rue Limogeanne, opposite no 3. It consists of a network of courtyards and small squares linked together by alleyways. The buildings, which were grafted onto each other over the centuries, have been demolished, creating open spaces and revealing the fine 15, 16 and 17C façades.

The arcade ends on Rue de la Miséricorde, beneath an attractive doorway with a broken pediment.

Walking along Rue St-Front, made in the 19C, notice on the left the unusual Masonic Lodge (Loge Maçonnique) perforated by openings like arrow-slits. The sculptures on the façade represent masonic emblems.

Rue de la Constitution (**DY 29**) – At no 3 is the **doorway of the Hôtel de Crémoux** with a crocketed arch between tall pinnacles.

At no 7, the **Hôtel de Gamanson** consists of two 15C wings set at right angles, linked by a staircase tower, flanked by a corbelled turret and perforated by mullioned windows. A 17C well is sheltered by a Moorish dome.

Rue du Plantier (**DY**) – Beyond the crossroads with Rue Barbecane is the Mint (no 24) with its very steep crocketed gable, which dates the building to the 16C.

Rue du Port-de-Graule (DY 45) and Rue Ste-Marthe (DZ 49) – These two roads still have a medieval air about them with their large uneven paving stones, their low doors and the little staircase-alleyways that lead off them. In 1967, several scenes from the film of *Jacquou le Croquant* (based on local author Eugene le Roy's novel) were shot here.

The quays (Boulevard Georges-Saumande) (DYZ) – Along the river there are several fine houses standing side by side.

The **Lambert House (DZ K)**, called the House with Columns because of its gallery, is a fine Renaissance town house with two wings set at a right angle and lit by mullioned windows. Next to it, the **Cayla House (DZ L)**, also called the Consul's House, was built on the ramparts in the 15C. The roof is decorated with Flamboyant-style dormers. At the corner of Avenue Daumesnil, the **House of Lur (DZ N)** dates from the 16C.

Continue along the quays; on the other side of Avenue Daumesnil the half-timbered building, corbelled over the fortress wall, is a remainder of the **barn attached to the cathedral**, called the old mill, which once jutted out over the river.

② CITÉ DISTRICT: TOUR OF LOCAL ANTIQUITY *time: 1 hour*

On the site of ancient Vesunna, this district contains numerous Gallo-Roman ruins.

Arena (Arènes) (BZ) – A pleasant public garden occupies the space where the arena once stood. Built in the 1C, this elliptical amphitheatre, one of the largest in Gaul, (153m x 125m-502 x 410ft) had a capacity for 20 000 people. Great blocks of stone still mark the stairwells, the vomitories and the vaulting, but all of the lower part of the building is still buried below ground. Demolition of the arena began in 3C, when the amphitheatre was turned into a bastion and became part of the city ramparts. In the 11C a count of Périgord built a fortress in the arena, which was then dismantled after Archambaud V's betrayal in 1391. The arena was next transformed into a quarry, its stone being used to build houses in the town.

Gallo-Roman wall – Several buildings have been put up on the old elliptical defence works of the 3C, which were destroyed once and for all during the Wars of Religion.

Viking Gate (Porte normande) (BZ) – This is the most interesting monument in this group. There is some disagreement over whether it was built in the 3C or the 10C. The story behind the name is that the gate is supposed to have played a part in the defence of the city against the Vikings who came up the river Isle in the 9C.

Romanesque House (Maison Romane) (BZ R) – This 12C rectangular building is neighbour to the vestiges of a tower from the Gallo-Roman defence wall, jumbled up with bits of capitals, column drums and other architectural elements. An altar on which bulls were sacrificed was discovered here; it is now on display in the Périgord Museum *(see Périgueux: Additional Sights below)*.

Château Barrière (BZ) – This castle has a 12C keep rising above one of the towers on its ramparts. It was altered during the Renaissance period but kept the lovely main entrance door in the staircase tower. Its Flamboyant style and decoration with pinnacles and crockets bring to mind l'Herm Castle *(see L'Herm Castle)*.

Turn right on Rue de Turenne, towards the railway bridge which leads into Rue des Vieux-Cimetières.

From the bridge there is an interesting view of the ancient wall.

Turn left into Rue des Vieux-Cimetières.

Domus du Bouquet, known as "Villa de Pompeius" (BZ S) ⊘ – The ruins of this *domus* (detached town house) were discovered in 1959 during the early stages of a building project.

The excavations uncovered the base of this luxurious Gallo-Roman residence. Its rooms overlook a square court enclosed by a peristyle. The *domus* had every comfort with a hypocaust (a heating system: hot air circulated through brick pipes), baths, a cold plunge *(piscina)* and individual baths. There were also workshops for the smith and potter. There are plans to develop the site, which is not very appealing at the moment.

Vesunna's Tower (Tour de Vésone) (BZ) ⊘ – This tower, 20m – 65.5ft high and 17m – 56ft in diameter, is all that remains of the temple dedicated to the titular goddess of the city. The temple, which was built in the heart of the forum in the old Cité when the Antonines were in power in the 2C AD, originally had a peristyle, was surrounded by porticoes and framed by two basilicas. The tower is still impressive despite being damaged.

ADDITIONAL SIGHTS

★**Périgord Museum (Musée du Périgord) (DY M¹)** ⊘ – The museum, located on the Allées de Tourny, on the site of what was an Augustinian convent, was created to house the Gallo-Roman finds of ancient Vesunna, including also the wealth of objects uncovered in the numerous prehistoric sites in the region. It is today one of the most important museums of prehistory in France. An ethnography collection completes the museum's display. The collections are described in order of the tour.

Prehistoric Section – The Maurice Féaux Gallery is devoted to the Lower Palaeolithic Era and displays mainly flint bifaces and stone tools. On display in a special case is the Neanderthaloid skeleton from Régourdou (*c* 70 000 BC) found near Montignac *(qv)*.

The Michel Hardy Gallery is concerned with the Upper Palaeolithic and Mesolithic Ages as shown by the massive carved blocks from Castel-Merle, the painted flat stones from Mas d'Azil and in particular the skeleton of the Chancelade man (15 000 years old) which was found in the Raymonden shelter, among his belongings. The skeleton of the Combe-Capelle man discovered at St-Avit-Sénieur (designated burial place from the Lower Gravettian era, 25 000 BC) is a casting.

The Henri Breuil Gallery illustrates evolution from the Neolithic Era to the Iron Age, using as examples the sandstone used to polish the flint, polished axes, earthenware, bronze axes and jewellery, as well as some relics of the "Barbarian Years".

The hall before the "Vesunna Petrucorum" display room is decorated with a reproduction of a fresco in Pompeian style and contains two exceptional exhibits; a perfectly preserved wooden **water pump** found in Périgueux, and a **funerary tiara★** in very delicately worked gold, made in Magna Graecia in the 3C.

"Vesunna Petrucorum" room: Gallo-Roman Archaeology – For the most part, this collection (mosaics, steles, funerary cippuses, glassware and earthenware) has been formed with the finds from the excavations of the ancient town of Vesunna.

Note the **altar**, found near the Viking Gate *(see above)*, dedicated to Cybele (a goddess who personified Earth), which was used for the sacrifice of animals. Carved on one of its sides note a bull's head wreathed with a narrow band from which the sacrificial knife, hook (to rip out the animal's entrails), pitcher and libatory cup are hung.

The altar dedicated to Apollo also comes from Vesunna; the **ground mosaic** with a central motif depicting a stag and a doe has been transferred here from a 4C villa near Terrasson.

Room L – The magnificent enamelled terracotta **roof finial** *(photograph p 161)* from Thiviers once adorned the roof of the Château de la Borde. It depicts its maker, Christophe Joumard, in the costume of a 16C foot soldier. On the walls are caricatures by the satirical illustrator of Parisian high society **Sem** (Georges Goursat, 1863-1934), born in Périgueux.

Octogonal Room – This contains a collection of medieval exhibits, in particular the **Rabastens diptych** – 13C illuminated manuscripts on large pieces of parchment, a small, beautifully detailed 15C stone Pietà and a Christ giving Blessing in polychrome wood, a 15C German work of art.

Painting Department – Note among the pictures the portrait of Fénelon by F Bailleul. Beautifully carved furniture is also on display, including a 15C liturgical cupboard which used to belong to Chancelade Abbey.

Cloisters – These galleries house the lapidary collection which covers all periods: Gallo-Roman inscriptions, funerary steles, Renaissance sculptures, architectural elements from St Front's including an altarpiece representing the Death of the Virgin (12C)

Périgord Military Museum (Musée Militaire du Périgord) (CZ M²) ⊘ – Arms and weapons of all sorts, standards and uniforms evoke the military history of Périgord from the Middle Ages to today. The great military men of the region are also honoured: Bugeaud, Deputy of the Dordogne, and General Daumesnil *(qv)*. Particularly honoured is the 50th Infantry Regiment stationed in Périgueux since 1876; note one of the regiment's flags, which Colonel Ardouin wrapped around his body to prevent it from falling into enemy hands after the surrender of Sedan.

EXCURSIONS

Beauronne Valley – *Round tour of 45km - 28 miles north of Périgueux - allow 2 hours.*

★ **Chancelade Abbey** – *See Chancelade Abbey.*

Merlande Priory – *See Chancelade Abbey: Excursion.*

Château-l'Évêque – The town took its name from the episcopal castle. This has been altered several times since the 14C. It consists of an asymmetrical main building. The façades facing the Beauronne Valley have mullioned windows, and a machicolated watchpath runs around the line of the roof.

The parish church is where St Vincent de Paul, founder of missionary organisations to help the poor, was ordained by Monsignor François de Bourdeille in September 1600 at the early age of twenty.

Agonac – *See Agonac.*

Caussade Castle (Château de Caussade) – *10km – 6 miles northeast.*
Standing in a clearing of the Lanmary Forest, this noble fortress represents on a small scale all the characteristics of a 15C stronghold. Its polygonal curtain wall, surrounded by a moat (half-filled), is flanked by square towers.

★ PUYGUILHEM CHÂTEAU

Michelin map 75 fold 5 or 233 fold 31 – 10km – 6 miles west of St-Jean-de-Côle

Puyguilhem Château ⊘ was built at the beginning of the 16C by Mondot de la Marthonie, first President of the Parliaments of Bordeaux and Paris, and resembles many of the Loire Valley châteaux which were built during the reign of François I. It was bought by the Fine Arts Department in 1939.

The main building is flanked on one side by a massive round tower joined to an octagonal turret, and on the other by an asymmetrical tower with cant walls, containing the main staircase. Overall the decoration is uniform and harmonious in style. The pierced balustrade at the base of the main building's roof, the dormer windows, the finely carved chimneys, the mullioned windows and the decorated machicolations on the great round tower all contribute to the building's elegance.

Inside note the carved **chimneys★**, especially the one in the guard room with its mantelpiece ornamented with foliage and medallions. On the first floor note the chimney, part of which is modern, illustrating Hercules' Labours. Its uprights are adorned with shell-shaped niches, and six of the Labours are depicted on the entablature.

The chestnut timber-work of the ceiling in the great hall on the second floor and the carved main staircase are also fine examples of their kind.

PUY-L'ÉVÊQUE

Pop 2 209

Michelin map **79** fold 7 or **235** fold 14 – Local map under LOT VALLEY: Meanders of the Lower Reaches – Facilities

This small town, which took its present name (*évêque* = bishop) when it came under the overlordship of the bishops of Cahors, occupies one of the most picturesque sites in the valley downstream from Cahors. The old houses in golden stone are overlooked by the church and the castle keep. The river bank opposite, at the entrance to the suspension bridge, gives the best **view** of the whole town.

Church (Église) ⊘ – The church was built on the northeast side of the town, at the furthest point in the defence system of which it was itself a part. In front of the church stands a massive belfry porch flanked by a turret and buttresses. The doorway, surmounted by an ogee-arched pediment, is embellished with statues including figures of the Virgin and St John at the feet of Christ on the Cross. The nave was built in the 14 and 15C and ends in a polygonal apse. In the churchyard there are many old tombs, and on the left of the church stands a wayside cross ornamented with archaic-style sculpture.

Keep (Donjon) – The keep, all that remains of the episcopal castle, dates back to the 13C. An extensive view of the Lot Valley is revealed from the Truffière esplanade adjoining the keep and the town hall.

PUYMARTIN CASTLE

Michelin map **75** fold 17 or **235** fold 2 – 9km – 5.6 miles northwest of Sarlat-la-Canéda

Built in golden stone and roofed with *lauzes*, the **castle** ⊘ stands on a steep hill in the heart of Périgord Noir. Constructed in the 15 and 16C (restored in 19C), it comprises several main buildings, linked by round towers and girt by curtain walls. During the Wars of Religion it was a Catholic stronghold against the Protestants of Sarlat.

Inside, the **decoration★** and **furnishings★** are sumptuous. The state room is hung with 18C Aubusson *verdures* in fresh green tones. The next room is adorned with interesting *grisaille* mural paintings on mythological themes. The main hall has a chimney decorated in *trompe l'œil* and a ceiling with beams painted in the 17C; note in particular a set of six Flemish tapestries illustrating the Trojan War, a table and chairs in Louis XIII style, a Regency chest of drawers and a Louis XV writing desk.

The tour includes a visit to a hexagonal defence chamber with stellar vaulting, and then to the attic rooms before it ends on the ground floor in the old guard room adorned with furnishings, tapestries and paintings.

RIBÉRAC

Pop 4 118

Michelin map **75** fold 4 or **233** fold 41 – Facilities

The small capital of the Ribérac region, which was a sub-prefecture *(sous-préfecture)* until 1926, is one of the most active agricultural markets in Aquitaine, renowned for the rich produce of its fairs.

A poet much admired – Ribérac castle, destroyed in the 18C, was birthplace in around 1150 to the troubadour Arnaut Daniel; this virtuoso of Occitan lyric poetry won the admiration of Petrarch as well as of Dante, the latter paying him homage by including him in his *Divine Comedy*.

Ribérac Collegiate Church of Our Lady (Collégiale Notre-Dame) – The chancel of this church is topped with a dome on pendentives. The church has now become an exhibition centre and concert hall, having been completely restored.

DOMED CHURCHES OF THE RIBÉRAC REGION

Round tour of 102 km – 63 miles – allow half a day – local map right

The furthest outpost of Occitania before the regions of the "langue d'oïl" around Angoulême and the Charente begin, the Ribérac region stands out amidst its Périgord setting by dint of its wide open countryside, which sets off more strikingly the crinkles of the ploughed furrows on its whitish hills. To the charm of its natural features this area adds the appeal of its attractive country towns and an unusually large number of domed Romanesque churches, which are most densely congregated in the sunny **Dronne valley**.

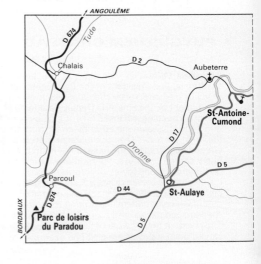

St-Martin-de-Ribérac – Pop 607. The 12C church has two domes in which the calottes were made higher in the 19C. Guy de Larigaudie, a leading figure in French scouting between the two World Wars, was born in this town in 1908. He was killed in action in 1940.

After crossing the Tocane-St-Apre bridge, the route continues east along the north bank of the Dronne.

Montagrier – Pop 397. Near a terrace from which there is a superb view of the valley stands the church of Montagrier, once the chapel for a priory which was a dependency of Brantôme, but which has now disappeared. All that remains of the 12C building are the square area of the transept, the dome on pendentives above it and the **trefoil apse** with two apsidal chapels attached to it, a design unique in the Périgord region. Notice the reintegration of a **bas-relief** chrisma dating from the 6C above the triumphal arch.

Grand-Brassac – Pop 488. This small village has an interesting **fortified church** ⊙. From the 13C onwards, fortifications were added to the church so that it might serve as a refuge for the villagers. The crenellations, defensive galleries and narrow openings, more like loopholes than window bays, give the building a forbidding appearance. The north doorway's **carved decoration** brings together sculpture of different periods; an arch adorned with fine foliated scrolls and containing statuettes which formed part of a group depicting the Adoration of the Magi, and above this five 16C statues sheltered by a overhanging porch roof. Among the figures are Christ between St John and the Virgin, and lower down, St Peter and another saint. Inside the church, the narrowness of the nave increases the impression of immense height.

Villetoureix – Pop 779. Situated on the banks of the Dronne 1km-0.6 miles upstream of the village, the Manoir de la Rigale has a tower dating from the Gallo-Roman era, almost certainly once the cella of temple. It is comparable with, although slightly smaller than, the Vesunna tower at Périgueux. In the village itself there is a Romanesque church with a dome.

St-Antoine-Cumond – Pop 394. The 12C domed church has a wonderful **porch** with nine arches and capitals carved with geometric patterns. The apse is also subtly decorated, both inside and out.

A quick detour for a glimpse of the magnificent monolithic church at Aubeterre in Charente can be made from St-Antoine *(2km – just over 1 mile, see Michelin Green Guide in French to Poitou-Charentes)*. To continue this tour, take the D 17 to St-Aulaye for the best views of the river Dronne.

St-Aulaye – Pop 1 531. St Eulalie's church, which has a beautiful façade in the Saintonge style, no longer has a dome over its transept crossing. The elegant 16C mansion which houses the town hall once belonged to the Chabot family. One of the sons, Guy Chabot de Jarnac, lord of St-Aulaye, was the originator of the well-known "Jarnac thrust"; thanks to a secret lunge technique he picked up from an Italian fencing master, he won a dual against King Henry II's favourite swordsman.

Parc de Loisirs du Paradou ⊙ – *(Parcoul)*. In an area of 15 ha – 37 acres around a lake, Paradou Park has a large number of recreational activities on offer (mini-golf, far-west train, tennis etc.). Perhaps the most spectacular of all are the enormous water slides.

Take the D 44 back to St-Aulaye, and then the D5 east.

St-Privat-des-Prés – *See St-Privat-des-Prés.*

Vanxains – Pop 665. Several lovely houses dating from the 16C to 18C have been preserved in this town, as well as a fortified Romanesque **church**. Inside this, the spacious rectangular chancel is lit by a triple bay and decorated with blind arcading and a richly carved stringcourse. Above the prechancel is a dome with elegant capitals. Both these features mark the Romanesque origins of this otherwise much-altered building. In the north aisle of the 15C Gothic part of the church there is a 17C carved wooden altarpiece. The heavy belfry-porch dates from the 16C.

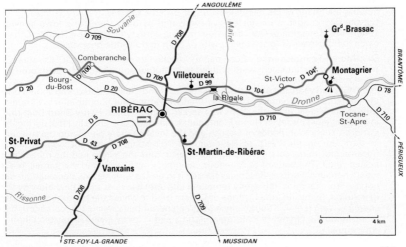

Michelin map 📖 folds 18 and 19 or 📖 fold 6 or 📖 fold 38 – Local map under GRAMAT CAUSSE – Facilities

Rocamadour *(photograph p 39)*, with its slender castle keep towering above it, comprises a mass of old dwellings, oratories, towers and precipitous rocks on the rugged face of a *causse* cliff rising 150m – 492ft above the Alzou Canyon.

★★★**The site** – The best way to arrive in Rocamadour is on the L'Hospitalet road *(see below)*. From a terrace there is a marvellous **view** of Rocamadour: the Alzou winds its way between fields at the bottom of a gorge, while some 500m – 1 640ft above, clinging to the cliff face, can be seen the extraordinary profile of this village; such an incredibly daring construction appears to defy the force of gravity. The ecclesiastical city rises above the village, and the whole scene is crowned by the castle ramparts. Morning, when the sun shines full upon the rock, is the best time of all for looking at the view. There is another striking view of Rocamadour from the D 32, the Couzou road, going down from the plateau past a road off to the left.

ROC AMADOUR, CENTRE OF MEDIEVAL CHRISTIANITY

The enigmatic St Amadour – The identity of St Amadour, who gave his name to the sanctuary village, has never been firmly established. A 12C chronicler reported that in 1166 "as a local inhabitant had expressed the wish to be buried beneath the threshold of the Chapel of the Virgin, men began to dig a grave only to find the body of a man already buried there. This body was placed near the altar so that it might be venerated by the faithful and from that time onwards miracles occurred".

Who was this mysterious person whose tomb appeared to be so old? Conflicting theories have been put forward: some contend that he was an Egyptian hermit, others that it was St Silvanus.

The most widely accepted theory, since the 15C, is that the body was that of the publican Zaccheus, a disciple of Jesus and husband of St Veronica, who, when she saw Christ on His way to Calvary, wiped the blood and sweat from His face with her veil. Both Zaccheus and Veronica were obliged to flee Palestine. They took a boat and were guided on their journey by an angel. They set up home in Limousin. On the death of Veronica, Zaccheus retired to the deserted and wild Alzou Valley to preach. All this is hearsay, but one thing is certain; there was a hermit, and he knew the rock well as it often sheltered him.

The *Langue d'Oc* expression – *roc amator* (he who likes the rock) – was adopted as the name of this village sanctuary, later becoming Roc Amadour and finally Rocamadour.

The fame of Rocamadour – From the time that the miracles began until the Reformation, the pilgrimage to Rocamadour was one of the most famous in Christendom. Great crowds would gather there. 30 000 people would come on days of major pardon and plenary indulgence. Since the village was too small to house all the pilgrims, the Alzou Valley was transformed into a vast camp. Henry Plantagenet, King of England, was miraculously cured and among the first to kneel before the Virgin; his example was followed during the Middle Ages by the most illustrious people including St Dominic, St Bernard, St Louis and Blanche of Castille, Philip IV the Fair, Philip VI and Louis XI. Veneration of Our Lady of Rocamadour was established at Lisbon, Oporto, Seville and even in Sicily; the Rocamadour standard, flown at the Battle of Las Navas at Tolosa, put the Muhammadans to flight and gave victory to the Catholic kings of Spain.

Pilgrimage and penitents – Ecclesiastical, and in some cases, lay tribunals used frequently to impose the pilgrimage on sinners. It was a considerable penance, inflicted especially on Albigensian heretics, who were said to hate the Mother of God. On the day of their departure, penitents attended mass and then set forth dressed in clothes covered with large crosses, a big hat upon their head, a staff in their hand and a knapsack on their back. On reaching the end of their journey, pilgrims stripped off their clothes, climbing the famous steps on their knees in only a shirt with chains bound round their arms and neck. On being brought before the altar to the Black Virgin in this humiliating condition they pronounced their *amende honorable*. A priest recited prayers of purification and removed the chains from the penitents, who, now forgiven, received from the priest a certificate and a kind of medal in lead bearing the image of the miraculous Virgin, called a **sportelle**.

But the pilgrimages were not always motivated by piety; lords and town consuls sought the protection of Our Lady when making a treaty or signing a charter. Others came to Rocamadour to see the crowds or even to do a little business.

Decline and renaissance – Rocamadour reached its zenith in the 13C. Favours not even granted to Jerusalem were granted to it; money poured in, but wealth brought covetousness with it.

For a hundred years the Abbeys of Marcilhac *(qv)* and Tulle disputed who should own the church at Rocamadour; Tulle was finally awarded the honour after arbitration. During the Middle Ages, the town was sacked several times: Henry Short Coat *(qv)*, in revolt against his father Henry Plantagenet, pillaged the oratory in 1183; during the Hundred Years War, bands of English and the local soldiery plundered the treasure in turn; during the Wars of Religion the Protestant Captain Bessonies seized Rocamadour to desecrate it and lay it to waste; only the Virgin and the miraculous bell escaped. The body of St Amadour, still intact, was thrown to the flames, but it would not burn! Furious, Bessonies hacked it to pieces with his axe. Rocamadour did not rise from its ruins; the abbey remained idle until it was dealt its final blow by the Revolution. In the 19C, the bishops of Cahors tried to revive the pilgrimage, and the churches were rebuilt. Though much of its splendour has vanished, Rocamadour has found again the fervour of its former pilgrims and is today a very respected pilgrimage centre.

THE VILLAGE *time: 30 min*

The village and the ecclesiastical city are pedestrian zones. They can be accessed from the plateau (car park) on foot or by lift, or from the Alzou valley (car parks) on foot or by a small train (there is a charge) which runs to the village, and then from here to the ecclesiastical city either by the flights of stairs up the Via Sancta or by lift.

Once a fortified town, Rocamadour still retains many features which bear witness to its past. Go through **Figuier Gateway** (Porte du Figuier) (**AZ**), which was a gateway to the town as early as the 13C, and enter the main street which is now cluttered with souvenir shops. The narrow street, clinging to the living rock, is overlooked by a towering tiered arrangement of houses, churches and the castle.

Beyond the Salmon Gate (Porte Salmon), which is crowned by a two-storey tower, the town hall can be seen to the right.

Town Hall (Hôtel de Ville) (**BZ H**) ⊘ – The town hall is located in a 15C house (restored), known as the Couronnerie or the House of the Brothers. In the council chamber there are two fine **tapestries★** by Jean Lurçat which portray the flora and fauna of the *causse*.

Rue de la Couronnerie passes under the 13C Hugon Gate (Porte Hugon) and, as far as the Low Gate (Porte Basse), it goes through a picturesque quarter where small houses descend the slope to the banks of the Alzou.

Nearby stands the old fortified mill, known as the Mill of Roquefrège (Moulin de Roquefrège).

THE ECCLESIASTICAL CITY *time: 1 hour 30 min*

Climb the 223 steps of the Great Stairway *(Via Sancta)*. Pilgrims often make this ascent, kneeling at every step.

The first 141 steps lead, in five flights, to terraces on which buildings for the canons to live in once stood. These have now been converted into shops and hotels.

The fort (**BZ B**) – This vast building of military appearance, which used to be the palace of the bishops of Tulle, stands at the base of the huge cliff face. It was here that important pilgrims were lodged. Built in the 14C, it was extensively restored in the 19C.

This terrace is called Place des Senhals because of the pilgrims' insignia called *senhals* or *sportelles* that were made there; coming out onto the square is the small Rue de la Mercerie.

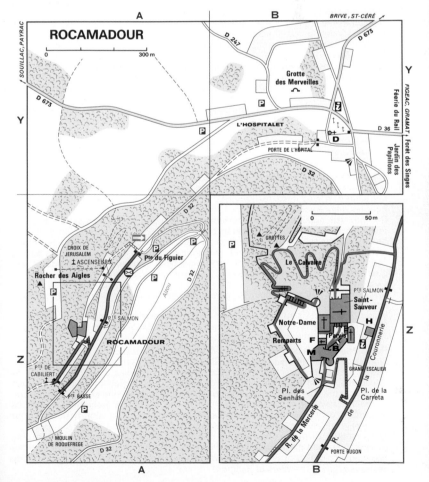

Rue de la Mercerie (BZ) – There are terraced gardens all along this, the oldest street in Rocamadour. The street ends at the 13C Cabiliert Gate (Porte de Cabiliert), once flanked by a defensive tower.

The **Fort Gateway** (Porte du Fort), which opens under the palace perimeter wall, leads to the sacred perimeter wall. Seventy-five steps lead up to the parvis surrounded by its churches.

Churches' parvis (BZ) – The parvis, which is also known as Place St-Amadour, is fairly small and has seven churches: St Saviour's Basilica opposite the stairway, St Amadour's Crypt below the basilica, the Chapel of Our Lady or Miraculous Chapel on the left, the three chapels of St John the Baptist, St Blaise and St Anne on the right and the Chapel of St Michael standing on a terrace to the left.

St Saviour's Basilica (Basilique St-Sauveur) – This 11-13C Romanesque-Gothic sanctuary has two naves of equal size, each of which has three bays divided by massive columns. One of the basilica walls is made out of the cliff's living rock, upon which the arches of the third bay are supported. The mezzanine was added in the last century to enlarge the basilica during the great pilgrimages.

Above the altar stands a fine 16C **Christ**, in polychrome wood, with a cross which resembles a lopped off tree.

St Amadour's Crypt (Crypte St-Amadour) ⊘ – It is a sanctuary which lies below the basilica. It consists of a flat chevet and two bays with quadripartite vaulting. It used to be a place of worship: the body of St Amadour was venerated here.

Chapel of Our Lady (Chapelle Notre-Dame) (BZ) – From the parvis, 25 steps lead to the Miraculous Chapel or Chapel of Our Lady, considered the "Holy of Holies" of Rocamadour. It is here that the hermit is believed to have hollowed out an oratory in the rock.

In 1476 the chapel was crushed by a rock-fall; it was rebuilt in the Flamboyant Gothic style. This new chapel, sacked during the Wars of Religion and the Revolution, was restored last century.

On the exterior façade, to the right of the Flamboyant doorway, part of the 13C fresco remains, illustrating the dance of death of the "three living and three dead men": three menacing skeletons are ready to bury or kill their victims.

On the altar, in the semi-darkness of the chapel blackened by candle smoke, is the miraculous Virgin, also called **Black Madonna★**. This rustic-style reliquary statue, carved in walnut, dates from the 12C. It is small in size (69cm – 27in). The rigidly-seated Virgin holds the Infant Jesus, who has the face of an adult, on Her left knee, without touching Him. It was covered with silver plating of which several fragments, blackened by candle smoke and oxidation, remain.

The interior is adorned with many votive offerings: ex-votos and chains worn by the penitents during certain ceremonies of repentance.

Difficult to see in the darkness, the miraculous **bell**, made of jointed iron plates and most likely dating from the 9C, hangs from the roof. It rang out of its own accord to foretell miracles, for example when sailors lost at sea invoked Our Lady of Rocamadour.

As early as the 11C the pilgrimage to Rocamadour was very popular with Breton sailors, and a chapel dedicated to Our Lady of Rocamadour was built at Camaret-sur-Mer (see Michelin Green Guide to Brittany). This explains the presence of the small ship figures among the ex-votos.

On leaving the chapel, stuck in the cliff face above the doorway, one can see a great iron sword, which legend identifies as **Durandal**, Roland's famous sword. The story goes that Roland, surrounded by the Saracens and unable to break his sword to prevent it falling into enemy hands, prayed to the Archangel Michael and threw him his sword, which in a single stroke implanted itself in the rock of Rocamadour, far from the Infidels.

St Michael's Chapel (Chapelle St-Michel) (BZ F) ⊘ – This Romanesque chapel is sheltered by a rock overhang. The apse, which houses a small oratory, juts out towards the square. It was used for services by the monks of the priory, who had also installed a library there.

On the wall outside are two frescoes representing the Annunciation and the Visitation; the skill of the composition, the richness of colour – ochre, yellow, reddish-brown, and the royal blue background, protected from condensation and, therefore, well preserved – and the grace of movement all seem to point to the works having been painted in the 12C. They may well have been inspired both by Limousin reliquaries (note the figures in relief in the background) and Byzantine mosaics (note the swarthy complexions).

Below them, a 14C fresco depicts an immense St Christopher, patron saint of travellers and thus of pilgrims.

Inside, the chancel is adorned with paintings (not as well preserved as those outside): Christ in Majesty is surrounded by the Evangelists; further down a seraph and the Archangel Michael are weighing souls.

Francis-Poulenc Museum of Sacred Art (BZ M) ⊘ – The museum is dedicated to the famous composer Francis Poulenc (1899-1963), who, having received a revelation during a visit to Rocamadour in 1936, composed Litanies à la Vierge Noire de Rocamadour. The museum displays an important collection of sacred art which came from the churches' treasuries, donations and from several churches in the Lot.

In the hallway various documents recount the history of Rocamadour and its pilgrimage, with the help of maps and a statue of St James as a pilgrim (Rocamadour was a pilgrims' stop on the way to Santiago de Compostela).

The vestibule displays objects from the sanctuary: 13C stained glass (the only remaining stained glass from the basilica), showing the death of St Martin, and the 17C reliquary casket of St Amadour, which contained the relics of the saint's body destroyed during the Wars of Religion.

The first gallery contains objects (ex-votos, paintings and items in carved wood) dating for the most part from the 17C. A naïve panel (1648) shows St Amadour hailing the Virgin with the *Ave Maria*; next to it, a baroque statue of Flemish origin represents the prophet Jonas as an old man writing.

The treasury contains fine items which came from the once fabulous treasure collection of the sanctuary. **Limoges reliquary caskets** from Lunegarde and Laverhne (both 12C) and Soulomès (13C), ornamented with enamelwork, demonstrate the craftsmanship of the Limousin artist. Among the other works displayed note the reliquary of St Agapit, in the form of a head, the silver reliquary monstrance surmounted by a Crucifixion with the Virgin and St John on either side, a 15C silver processional cross and a 12C seated Virgin in wood. The next gallery contains 17, 18 and 19C religious paintings.

> *On leaving the museum take the gallery, known as "the tunnel", which passes beneath St Saviour's Basilica and comes out on a terrace overlooking Alzou Canyon.*

THE PLATEAU *time: 45 min*

Calvary (Calvaire) (BZ) – A shaded Stations of the Cross winds up towards the ramparts. After passing the caves *(grottes)* of the Nativity and the Holy Sepulchre, visitors will see the great Cross of Jerusalem (Croix de Jérusalem), brought from the Holy Land by the Penitential Pilgrims.

Ramparts (Remparts) (BZ) ⊘ – These are the remains of a 14C fort which was built to block off the rocky spur and protect the sanctuary. Leaning against the fortress, the residence of the chaplains of Roc-Amadour was built in the 19C. From the ramparts, which tower above a sheer drop, there is an unforgettable **panorama★★★** of the *causse*, the site of Rocamadour and the rock amphitheatre surrounding it.

Eagles' Rock (Rocher des Aigles) (AZ) ⊘ – This is a breeding centre for birds of prey.

> *To return to the village, go back to an esplanade which is on the same level as the Ecclesiastical City and take the lift to the main street near Salmon Gate (Porte Salmon).*

L'HOSPITALET

The name of this village, clinging to Rocamadour's cliff face, comes from the small hospital founded in the 11C by Hélène de Castelnau to nurse the pilgrims on the pilgrim road from Le Puy (Auvergne) to Santiago de Compostela. Only a few ruins of this hospital remain; the Romanesque **chapel (BY D)**, which is set in the middle of the churchyard, was remodelled in the 15C.

L'Hospitalet is very popular with visitors for its viewpoint which overlooks the site of Rocamadour. There is a large tourist information centre *(syndicat d'initiative)*.

Cave of Wonders (Grotte des Merveilles) (BY) ⊘ – Discovered in 1920, this small cave, only 8m – 24ft deep, has some lovely formations: stalactites, stalagmites and natural limestone dams *(gours)* into which are reflected the cave roof and its concretions.

On the walls are cave paintings dating back, most likely, to the Solutrean Period (*c*18 000 years ago), depicting outlined hands, black spots, a few horses, a cat and the outline of a deer.

Model Railway (Féerie du rail) ⊘ – Sixty model trains wind around a giant **model track★** (70sq meters – 754sq feet) with scenes of city, mountain and country life complete with accessories, lights and sound.

Butterfly Garden (Jardin des papillons) ⊘ – In a vast greenhouse (climatic control) butterflies of all sizes and colours live at complete liberty. These ephemeral beauties, whose life span lasts about 2 weeks, come from all over the world (Malaysia, Madagascar, United States, South America...).

Monkey Forest (Forêt des Singes) ⊘ – Living at liberty on 10ha – 25 acres of woodland are 150 monkeys in an environment similar to the upper plateaux of North Africa from where they originated. These monkeys are Barbary apes *(see Gibraltar in Michelin Green Guide to Spain)* and macaques, a species which is becoming extinct.

★★ LA ROQUE-GAGEAC

Michelin map **75** fold 17 or **235** fold 6 – Local map under DORDOGNE VALLEY **3** – Facilities

The village of La Roque-Gageac, huddled against a cliff which drops vertically to the River Dordogne, occupies a wonderful **site★★** – one of the finest in this part of the valley, in which Domme, Castelnaud and Beynac-et-Cazenac are all within a few miles of each other.

La Roque-Gageac

★★View – The best view of La Roque-Gageac is from the west: the late afternoon sun highlights the tall grey cliff face covered with holm-oaks, while the houses, with their stone slab *(lauzes)* or tile roofs, are reflected in the calm waters of the river below.
In the foreground the outline of the Château de la Malartrie can be seen; at the other end of the village, at the foot of the sheer rock-face, is the charming Tarde Manor-house.

The village – Attractive little streets, in which the humble homes of peasants and craftsmen nestle side by side with the grander residences of the gentry, run tightly along the rocky bluff. One of them, leading off to the right of the Belle Étoile hotel, climbs through luxuriant plant life towards the small church (beautiful view of the Dordogne) and then to the Tarde manor-house.

Tarde Manor-house (Manoir de Tarde) – Two pointed gabled buildings, with mullioned windows, stand next to a round tower. This charming manor-house is associated with the Tarde family, the most famous members of which are the canon Jean Tarde, a 16C local humanist, historian, cartographer, astronomer, mathematician, etc. and Gabriel Tarde, a 19C sociologist.

At the top of the cliff there are clear traces to remind visitors of the tragic night in 1957 when a huge block of rock came away from the cliff-face, crushing the homes and their sleeping residents below.

Château de la Malartrie – A castle built in the early 20C, greatly influenced by the 15C style.

ROUFFIGNAC

Michelin map **75** fold 6 or **235** fold 1

The church is all that escaped when the Germans set about burning the town in March 1944 as a reprisal; the town has been rebuilt.

Church (Église) – The entrance is through an interesting belfry-porch containing a doorway built in the style of the Early Renaissance. It was constructed in about 1530 and is decorated with Corinthian capitals and surmounted by a finely carved lintel; the somewhat irreligious decoration – mermaids, busts of women – is surprising, under the circumstances.
The church's main body has three aisles of equal height built in the Flamboyant style; the pointed vaulting is supported by round pillars reinforced by remarkable engaged twisted columns.

EXCURSIONS

★Rouffignac Cave (Grotte de Rouffignac) ⊘ – *5km – 3 miles to the south.*
This dry cave, which is also called the Cro de Granville, was known about as early as the 15C. The galleries and chambers extend for more than 8km – 5miles. The tour (4km – 2.5 miles), which is made by electric railway, takes in all the principal galleries. In 1956 Professor L R Nougier called attention to the remarkable group of paintings marked with black lines and **engravings★** produced during the Middle or Upper Magdalenian Period (some 10 - 13 000 years ago). These engravings are of horses, ibexes, rhinoceroses, bison and a great number of mammoths, among which may be seen the "Patriarch" and an amazing frieze depicting two herds locked in combat. There is an outstanding group of drawings on the ceiling of the last chamber (unfortunately disfigured with graffiti).

L'Herm Castle – *6km – 3.5 miles northwest. See L'Herm Castle.*

★ ST-AMAND-DE-COLY   Pop 312

Michelin map ▨ fold 7 or ▨ fold 25 – Local map under PÉRIGORD NOIR

Tucked away in the fold of a small valley off the Vézère Valley is St-Amand-de-Coly, its old *lauze*-roofed houses clustering round the impressive abbey church.

★★Church (Église) – This church of fine yellow limestone is perhaps the most amazing of all Périgord's fortified churches. The Augustinian abbey of which it was once part saw its spiritual activity reduced during the Hundred Years War – by 1430 there were only two monks left. It transformed itself into a fortress, as documents of that period illustrate by their references to "St-Amand fort". The highly elaborate defence system was designed to keep enemies at a distance, but also to drive them away should any forays be made into the church. The Huguenots occupying the church in 1575 were able to hold out for 6 days against 20 000 soldiers of the Périgord seneschal, who had powerful artillery backup.

Exterior – An impression of tremendous strength is created by the **tower-keep**, indented by the enormous pointed arch of the doorway which supports a defence room intended to prevent anyone approaching. A wooden hoarding was added to the corbels, still visible, on its upper wall. A narrow, paved passageway, protected by a defence-work perforated with strong-rooms, runs around the east end. The harmony of the apsidal chapels is a contrast to the severity of the high walls of the nave and transept. These are made to seem even heavier by the defensive balconies resting on the gabled ends of the transept arms. A rampart walk runs around the building beneath the *lauze*-covered roof.

Interior – Purity of line and simplicity of decoration, both of which are usually to be found in Augustinian architecture, contribute to the beauty of the lofty space inside. There is an archaic-style dome on pendentives above the transept crossing. The chancel, raised by eight steps and roofed with ribbed vaulting, ends in a flat east end. The concern for protection also affected the interior design; remains of the defence system include a narrow passage enclosing the chancel and some of the transept arms, small lookout posts in the pillars of the transept area and the loopholes in the base of the dome.

Opposite the church, in the **former presbytery** ⊘, there is an audio-visual show (Diaporama) on the church and its history.

The village and its church

*Travel with the **Michelin Sectional Map Series** (1:200 000).*
These maps are revised regularly.

St-Antonin, an old city on the borders of Quercy, of Albi and of Rouergue, faces a vertical cliff of rocks known as the Anglars Rocks (Roc d'Anglars) on the far side of the Aveyron Valley. The houses, with virtually flat roofs covered in round tiles faded by the sun, rise in tiers on the north bank of the river.

So delightful was the setting of this Gallo-Roman site, forerunner of the present town, that it was given the name of "glorious valley" (Noble-Val). An oratory founded by St Antonin, who came to convert this part of Rouergue, was replaced in the 8C by an abbey.

The town developed rapidly during the Middle Ages, as can be seen by the 13, 14 and 15C houses which were once the residences of rich merchants.

Jordan, singer of "Chivalrous Love" – The viscount of St-Antonin, Ramon Jordan, born in 1150, ranks among the most illustrious troubadours of his age. His poetry quivers with passion, but a pure, chaste version of it in keeping with the idea of the "chivalrous love" he declared to Adelais, the wife of the Lord of Penne. While he was away fighting in the Crusades, unfounded rumours that he had been killed began to spread. The emotional strain on Adelais was so great that she shut herself away in a nunnery. Jordan returned safe and sound, but on learning that he would never be able to see his beloved again, he lost all his joy and animation, all desire to sing and even all interest in horse-riding. He, too, chose to end his life as a recluse.

"Hardly a chance to draw breath" – St-Antonin, which at the beginning of the 13C tended to sympathise with the Cathars and made no secret of its allegiance to the Count of Toulouse, was by no means spared by the Albigensian Crusade, led by Simon de Montfort. The inhabitants, finding themselves surrounded on all sides, made a half-hearted foray, but were vigorously repelled and, as the chronicler Guilhem Peyre (author of *The Song of the Crusade*) drily puts it, "had hardly a chance to draw breath" before their attackers sacked the town. Those of the defeated who had sought refuge in the monastery were not permitted to return to their homes until they had been stripped of all their clothes.

SIGHTS

★**Old Town Hall** (Ancien Hôtel de Ville) – This mansion was built in 1125 for a rich, newly ennobled townsman, Pons de Granolhet, and is one of the oldest examples of civil architecture in France. In the 14C it was the consuls' residence; Viollet-le-Duc restored it in the 19C, adding a square belfry in the Italian Tuscan style with a machicolated loggia on top of it, based on a project he presented in 1845. It now houses a museum.

Adam and Eve

The façade consists of two storeys. The gallery of small columns on the first floor is adorned with two pillars bearing statues of King Solomon and **Adam and Eve**; the second storey is divided into three sets of twin bays.

Museum (Musée) ⊘ – The museum contains a collection on prehistory which is particularly rich in material from the Magdalenian Period. One room covers local traditions and folklore.

Rue Guilhem Peyre –This street leads off from beneath the belfry of the old town hall. It used to be the grand route taken by all processions. On the right there is what used to be the Royal Barracks, known as the "English Barracks", and in a bend in the road a splendid 13-16C residence.

Rue des Grandes Boucheries – The Maison du Roy, now a restaurant, has five ogival arcades on the ground floor, and the same number of twin bays on the first floor, with capitals decorated with youthful faces.

Convent of the Order of St Genevieve (Ancien Couvent des Génovéfains) – Built in 1751, this is now home to the town hall and the tourist office.

Market Calvary (Croix de la Halle) – In front of the solid pillars of the covered market, there is a strange lollipop-shaped 14C **Calvary**, carved on both sides. This unique and original piece of work would once have stood at the entrance to or in the middle of the cemetery.

Rue Pélisserie – There are the sumptuous 13C-14C houses of master-tanners and furriers all along this road.

Rue Rive-Valat – A little canal spanned by bridges flows along by this street; it is one of many tributaries of the river Bonnière which were dug during the Middle Ages to provide a main drainage system and water for the tanneries. These have open top floors similar to *soleilhos (qv),* which are used to store and dry skins etc.

Rue Droite – Two houses stand out because of their carved keystones: the **House of Love** (Maison de l'Amour) dating from the end of the 15C where a man and woman are depicted touching lips in a chaste kiss, and the **House of Repentance** (Maison du Repentir) where, in contrast, two faces are shown turned away from each other. About halfway along the street, there is a beautiful double corbelled façade, decorated with half-timbering, calcareous tufa and wooden mullions.

EXCURSIONS

★⒈ **Aveyron Gorges (Gorges de l'Aveyron)** – *Round tour of 49km – 30 miles – allow 3 hours – local map below. Leave St-Antonin towards the south, cross the Aveyron and take the road on the right, built along a disused railway track.*
After 2.5km – 1.5 miles turn left into a fine **cliff-face road**★★, cut into the rock, which climbs rapidly. Pass through the hamlet of Vieilfour with its round-tiled roofs. Shortly after passing through a tunnel there is a viewpoint, above a sheer drop, from which there is a good view of the Aveyron enclosed by tall rock walls. As the road descends towards the river, Brousses comes into view.

At Cazals cross the river.

The road begins to climb immediately and passes between vineyards, affording views of the meanders in the Aveyron River and the valley floor covered with peach and apple orchards and meadows intersected by lines of poplars.

Penne – *See Penne.*

Leave Penne to the south on the D 9, which gives lovely **views**★ of the village. The road drops down over the edge of the plateau before crossing a region of sparse vegetation with stunted bushes and the occasional vine.
The road then descends once more into the valley where the high, wooded hillsides are often strewn with rocks.

★**Bruniquel** – *See Bruniquel.*

Follow the road along the north bank of the Aveyron from Bruniquel to Montricoux.

Montricoux – *See Bruniquel: Excursion.*

Return to St-Antonin on the D 958.

This road running through the Garrigue Forest (Forêt de la Garrigue) affords glimpses of the Aveyron Gorges below and to the right. Then take a road cut into the rock-face overlooking the Aveyron.

⒉ **Upper Aveyron Valley** – *Round tour of 42km – 26 miles – allow 2 hours – local map below. Leave St-Antonin to the northeast.*

Bosc Cave (Grotte du Bosc) ⊘ – The galleries, once the bed of an underground river which is now dry, go back some 220m - 220yds underneath the plateau between the Aveyron and Bonnette Valleys. Stalactites and eccentrics decorate the cave *(for more details on caves and chasms see Introduction).*
A museum of mineralogy and prehistory has been set up in the reception hall.

Continue along the D 75, then take the D 20 to the right and the D 33 to the left.

★ **Beaulieu-en-Rouergue Abbey** – *See Beaulieu-en-Rouergue Abbey.*

Turn back and follow the D 33.

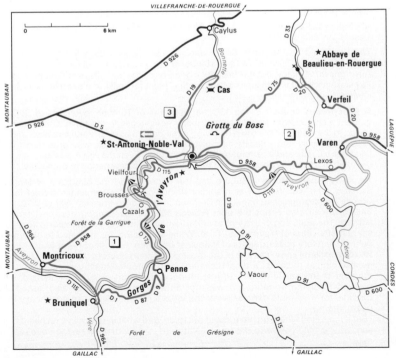

Verfeil – Pop 360. This small but charming bastion lies in the Seye Valley. Its old houses with their flower-bedecked façades surround a covered market rebuilt of stone. In the church, both the high altar in embellished gilt wood and the 17C wood figure of Christ came from the former abbey of Beaulieu-en-Rouergue.

Take the D 20 and then the D 958 to the right.

The road follows the Aveyron, which flows at this point along the wide valley floor carpeted with meadows and crops.

Varen – *See Varen.*

At the entrance to Lexos, the road passes near a large cement works. 2km – 1 mile after Lexos turn right on the D 33, then left on the road signposted "St-Antonin par le coteau".

The road climbs rapidly along the hillside, revealing more and more glimpses of the Aveyron Valley to which it returns after a winding descent. The river, marked by a string of poplars, flows at the foot of tall cliffs covered with sparse vegetation. A little before St-Antonin, the road and river run closely together along the narrow valley bounded by steep rocky sides.

3 **Cas Castle (Château de Cas)** ⊘ – *6km – 3.5 miles north – local map on previous page.*
Built in the 12C, Cas Castle was altered in the 14 and 16C. In the 13C it was a Templar commandery; it then became the property of the powerful Cardaillac family before passing into the hands of the Lastic Saint-Jals.
This solid white limestone building contains a number of furnished rooms.

ST-AVIT-SÉNIEUR
Pop 366

Michelin map 📗 fold 16 or 📗 fold 5

This small village is dominated by a massive church and a few conventual buildings which are the remains of an old Benedictine abbey built in the 11C in memory of Avitus Senior, who was a Périgord soldier under King Visigoth Alaric II, and who later became a hermit.

Church (Église) – The church exterior is austere and rugged; in the 14C the building was fortified, as can be seen from the crenellated brattice above the porch, the tall almost blind walls of the nave and east end, and the towers, linked by a watchpath on either side of the façade.
The interior is currently closed for restoration work.

Conventual buildings (Bâtiments monastiques) – The only traces of the former abbey to be seen are a few arches of the former cloisters and the chapter-house. In the monks' dormitory, above the chapter-house, a **Geology and Archaeology Museum** (Musée de Géologie et d'Archéologie) ⊘ has been set up. It is concerned, for the most part, with the Dordogne Basin.
Excavations have revealed the foundations of the conventual buildings and of a primitive Romanesque church.
To the right, the lovely house with a semicircular doorway and a colonnaded gallery is the castle, which used to belong to the Cugnac family and is now a presbytery.

★ ST-CÉRÉ
Pop 3 760

Michelin map 📗 folds 19 and 20 or 📗 fold 7 or 📗 fold 39 – Local map under Excursions below – Facilities

The lovely old houses of St-Céré cluster in the cheerful Bave Valley, at the foot of St Laurence's Towers. St-Céré stands at the junction of roads from Limousin, Auvergne and Quercy, but has become a good place to stay in its own right because of its pleasant **site★**. It is also an excellent starting-point for walks and excursions in Upper Quercy.

A prosperous town – In the 13C the viscounts of Turenne, overlords of St-Céré, granted a charter with franchises and many advantages to the town. Other charters added to the wealth of the town by giving it the right to hold fairs and establish trading houses. Consuls and officials administered the town, which was protected by St Laurence's Castle and a formidable line of ramparts. Even the Hundred Years War left the town practically unscathed. With the 16C dawned a new period of prosperity.

An early Academician – St-Céré had the honour to be the birthplace of Marshal **Canrobert,** who won renown as a soldier in Algeria, was commander-in-chief in the Crimea and distinguished himself at St-Privat in the Franco-Prussian War of 1870.
The town can also count the poet **François Maynard** *(qv)* among her most famous citizens. The poet, son of a member of Parliament, was born in Toulouse in 1582, but spent many years of his life in St-Céré. While still young, he managed to obtain the post of secretary to Marguerite of Valois, at one time the wife of Henri IV.
He soon became known as one of the most skilful court poets of the period. Malherbe noticed him, as did also Cardinal Richelieu, who honoured him by nominating him a member of the Academy he had just founded. The story goes that Maynard, who enjoyed receiving honours but was not above receiving money also, asked the Cardinal for a tangible expression of the latter's confidence. He sent a cheeky little poem, asking:
"But if I'm asked what you have asked me to do, and what in return I've received from you, what would you have me say?" "Nothing", the Cardinal is said to have replied drily.

Chapou (R.) 2
Dr-Roux (R.) 3
Église (R. de l') 4
Gaulle (Av. de) 7
Hôtel-de-Ville (R. de l') 9
Lagarouste (Passage) 12
Maquis (Av. des) 13
Mazel (R. du) 15
Mercadial (Pl. du) 16
Monzie (Av. A.-de-) 17
Pasteur (R.) 18
Pont-d'Hercule (R. du) 19
Roubinet (R. du) 22
Victor-Hugo (Av.) 23

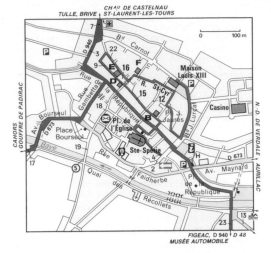

Dismissed by Parisian society, the poet came to live in St-Céré. He devoted himself to versification, frequented literary circles and society and went to the fabulous receptions given at Castelnau-Bretenoux. When he died in 1646, he was buried beneath the chancel of the Church of Ste-Spérie in St-Céré.

Jean Lurçat and St-Céré – Born in 1892 in the Vosges, Jean Lurçat, who was destined to be a doctor, directed his talents instead to painting, decoration of theatrical scenery, mosaics and ceramics. He soon became interested in tapestry as a medium; it is for his work on tapestry design and technique that he achieved world renown.

After a period spent in Aubusson, he participated in the Resistance movement and through this discovered the Lot. He settled in St-Céré in 1945. It was in St Laurence's Towers that he set up his studio, and this is also where he lived until his death in 1966.

Lurçat had the Aubusson tapestry factory weave most of the tapestries for which he had painted the designs (cartoons).

OLD TOWN

The 15, 16 and 17C houses give St-Céré a picturesque character all of its own. Some houses still have their half-timbered corbelled façades and fine roofs of brown tiles.

Place de l'Église – The church of Ste-Spérie, a very old place of worship, was rebuilt in the 17 and 18C in the Gothic style.

The **Hôtel de Puymule** (15C), in the square near the east end, is a turreted town house, with doors and windows decorated with ogee arches.

Cross Rue de la République, a busy shopping street, and turn left onto Rue du Mazel.

Rue du Mazel (15). – This street and the surrounding area form one of the most charming districts in the old town, with old houses and fine doorways. At the corner of Rue St-Cyr, note the 15C **Hôtel Ambert** (B) with its two corbelled turrets and Renaissance doorway.

Further along on the right, the narrow cobblestoned **Passage Lagarouste** (12), with a stream down the middle, is overshadowed by tall corbelled houses.

Place du Mercadial (16). – This was the market square where fishermen brought their catch to be displayed on the *taoulié*, a stone bench beside the 15C **Jean de Séguirier's House** (D) at the corner of Rue Pasteur. From this spot, there is a lovely view of the square surrounded by half-timbered houses against St Laurence's Towers. The **Consuls' House** (E) has an interesting Renaissance façade overlooking Rue de l'Hôtel-de-Ville.

Rue St-Cyr – At the beginning of the street stands a lovely medieval house with three corbelled façades. Further on, to the right, is the 15C **Hôtel de Miramon** (F) flanked with a corner turret. The street, which runs in a semicircle and has old houses all along it, ends in Rue du Mazel.

On leaving Rue du Mazel take Boulevard Jean-Lurçat to the left.

Maison Louis XIII – This fine mansion has an elegant façade adorned with a loggia.

ADDITIONAL SIGHTS

Casino Gallery (Galerie du Casino) ⊘ – In addition to temporary exhibitions, there is a large collection of **Jean Lurçat's tapestries★** on permanent display. The tapestries combine matter, form and colour and depict fantastic animals and cosmic visions.

St Laurence's Towers (Tours de St-Laurent) – *2km – 1 mile to the north.*
Perched on a steep hill which overlooks the town, the two tall medieval towers and curtain wall are a familiar local landmark.

Although the road to the right is private, the restriction is not strictly enforced. A track *(1 hour on foot Rtn)* skirts the ramparts and offers pleasant **views★** of the town, the Bave and Dordogne Valleys and the surrounding plateaus.

★**Jean Lurçat Studio-Museum** (Atelier-musée Jean-Lurçat) ⊙ – In the ground floor rooms (studio, drawing room, dining room) of this c1900 house Lurçat's works (tapestries, designs, paintings, ceramics, lithographs, gouaches, wall paper) are exhibited. Note the copies of the thrones ordered in 1956 by Haile Selassie, Emperor of Ethiopia.

Upper Quercy Motor Museum (Musée automobile du Haut-Quercy) ⊙ – Some thirty vehicles in working order are exhibited here. Several models have become prototypes: the Renault AX Marne Taxi model (1908), the Citroën P 17 Caterpillar (1930), which took part in the Trans-Asian Expedition known as the *Croisière Jaune*, the Volkswagen cross-country vehicle, the amphibian Schwimmwagen (1942), the Citröen ID 19 (1962) and the Citröen 2 CV Sahara (1965), 4-wheel drive and two engines.

EXCURSIONS

★**1 Bave Valley: from St-Céré to Castelnau-Bretenoux** – *25km – 15.5 miles – about 3 hours – local map below. Leave St-Céré westwards.*

The towers of Montal Castle soon come into view on the left, rising above fertile fields and meadows interspersed with lines of poplars.

★★**Montal Castle** – *See Montal Castle.*

The road towards Gramat climbs above the Bave Valley, offering views of St Laurence's Towers.

★**Presque Cave** (Grotte de Presque) ⊙ – The cave consists of a series of chambers and galleries that go back 350m-380yds into the rocks. Concretions, especially strange-shaped stalagmite piles and thousand-faceted frozen falls along the walls, have built up in the Draperies Chamber (Salle des Draperies), the High Chamber (Salle Haute), the Chamber of the Great Basin (Salle de la Grande Cuve) and the Red Marble Hall (Salle de Marbre Rouge). Slender columns of astonishing whiteness stand at the entrance to the Hall of Wonders (Salle des Merveilles).

At Le Boutel turn right to Autoire.

★**Autoire Amphitheatre** (Cirque d'Autoire) – Leave the car in a parking area. Take, on the left of the road, the path that overlooks the Autoire River, which here forms a series of waterfalls (viewpoint).
Cross the little bridge and go up the steep stony path cut in the rocks. Very soon a wonderful **view**★★ of the amphitheatre, the valley and the village of Autoire unfolds.

★**Autoire** – Pop 272. Autoire in its picturesque **setting**★ is typical of the character of the Quercy region. Enchanting scenes are revealed at every street corner: a fountain at the centre of a group of half-timbered houses, old corbelled houses with brown-tiled roofs, elegant turreted manors and mansions.
From the terrace near the church, which has a fine Romanesque east end, there is a good view of the Limargue Mill and the rocky amphitheatre that lies to the south-west.

★**Loubressac** – Pop 449. This old fortified town stands on a rocky spur overlooking the south bank of the Bave River.
From near the church, there is a good **view** of the valley and of St-Céré, marked out by its towers. Walk through the enchanting narrow alleys as they wind between brown-tiled houses to the castle's postern.
This 15C manor-house, which was rebuilt in the 17C, stands on a remarkable **site**★ at the very end of the spur on which the village was built.
The D 118 and then the D 14 from the hamlet of La Poujade descend towards the Bave Valley, giving fine **views**★ of the Dordogne Valley dominated by the impressive outline of Castelnau-Bretenoux Castle.

★★**Castelnau-Bretenoux Castle** – *See Castelnau-Bretenoux Castle.*

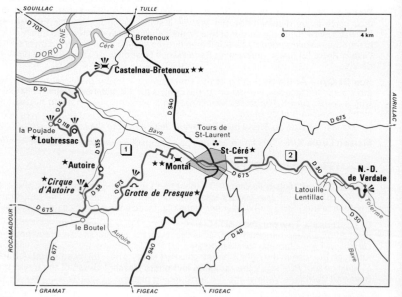

2 **Chapel of Our Lady (Chapelle Notre-Dame de Verdale)** – *10km – 6 miles east plus 1 hour on foot Rtn – local map below opposite.*

The road passes wooded hills and meadows at it goes up the Bave Valley.

Beyond Latouille-Lentillac a narrow road branches off to the left from the D 30; follow this to a hamlet and park the car.

Walk up a path, which runs beside the Tolerme, as it falls in cascades over the rocks. After crossing the stream twice on primitive wooden bridges the path starts to climb steeply, in a hilly setting, and finally leads to the pilgrimage chapel of Our Lady of Verdale which stands perched on a rocky crag. From the crag there is an extensive **view***of the Tolerme Gorges and the chestnut-covered hills.

★★ ST-CIRQ-LAPOPIE   Pop 187

Michelin map **79** fold 9 or **235** fold 14 – Local map under LOT VALLEY: Cliffs and Promontories – Facilities

St-Cirq-Lapopie ("Cirq" pronounced "Sear"), faces a semicircle of white cliffs and is itself perched (80m-262ft) on a rocky escarpment that drops vertically to the left bank of the Lot; it is a remarkable **setting★★**.

St-Cirq-Lapopie

HISTORICAL NOTES

A contested stronghold – This rock commanding the valley has probably tempted would-be occupiers since Gallo-Roman times. The present name of the site commemorates the martyrdom of the young St Cyr, killed with his mother in Asia Minor during the reign of Diocletian; his relics were brought back, it is said, by St Amadour *(qv)*. The La Popies, local lords in the Middle Ages, gave their name to the castle built on the cliff's highest point and, by extension, to the village that grew up at its foot. The history of the fortress is a long series of sieges. In the struggle against Pepin the Short in the 8C, Waïfre, Duke of Aquitaine, pinned his last hopes on this bastion. In 1198 Richard the Lionheart tried in vain to seize the stronghold.
During the Hundred Years War, the English fought bitterly to take St-Cirq from the garrison, commanded by the lord of Cardaillac, who remained loyal to the King of France. In 1471, Louis XI ordered the castle to be demolished but the ruins were still of sufficient strategic importance for the Huguenots to fight for them during the Wars of Religion. In 1580 Henri de Navarre, the future Henri IV, ordered that those walls of the valiant fortress which were still standing be knocked down.

The end of a craft – St-Cirq-Lapopie had a strong guild of wood-turners dating back to the Middle Ages. Even last century, there were a considerable number of craftsmen still to be seen working their primitive lathes; their industry added a characterful note to the old-fashioned village alleyways. The "tap-makers" made taps for the casks, the bushel-makers candlesticks, rosary beads and crossbars for chairs. Their shopfronts set small and large ogive openings side by side. They now house other activities, there being only one woodworker left in St-Cirq.

SIGHTS

It is a perennial pleasure to wander along narrow, steeply sloping streets lined with houses with lovely brown-tiled roofs. The corbelled façades and exposed beams of some of the houses are further ornamented with Gothic windows, or bays with mullioned windows in the Renaissance style. Most of the houses have been carefully restored by artists, particularly painters and craftsmen who have been attracted by the beauty of St-Cirq-Lapopie and the Lot Valley. Among the most famous are the writer André Breton, who lived in the Place du Carol in the old sailors' inn, and the painters Henri Martin and Pierre Daura, the latter of whom lived in the house with carved beams (his own work) in the Ruelle de la Fourdonne.

Church (Église) – This 15C sanctuary stands on a rock terrace overlooking the Lot. A squat belfry-tower, flanked by a round turret, stands at the front end.
Inside, the main body of the church has pointed vaulting and contains several baroque statues. There is a good view from the terrace to the right of the church.

La Gardette Castle – *Also known as Maison Rignault.*
The two main buildings, each flanked by a battlemented turret, house a **museum** ☉ containing the donation of Mr Rignault (painter and collector) to the Lot *département*. Exhibited are old furniture (Renaissance cabinet and sideboard, 14C dowry chest), 14 and 15C statues, lacquerware from China and frescoes dating from the Ming Dynasty.

La Popie – Take the path that starts on the right of the town hall *(mairie)*, to reach the castle ruins and the highest part of the cliff. From the cliff top (telescope), on which once stood the keep of La Popie fortress, there is a remarkable **view★★** right over the village of St-Cirq, with the church clinging to the cliff face, to a bend of the Lot River, encircling a chequerboard of arable fields and meadows delineated by poplars, and to the north, the wooded foothills that border the Gramat Causse.

Le Bancourel – Follow the D 40 towards Bouziès for 300m – 330yds to reach this rock promontory overlooking the Lot. A lay-by esplanade *(car park)* has been built where the D 8 branches off to the left from the tourist road that has been cut *corniche*-fashion into the cliff *(see Lot Valley)*.
There is a **view★** from Le Bancourel of the Lot Valley and St-Cirq, with the rock of La Popie rising up out of the village.

ST-CYPRIEN Pop 1 693

Michelin map **75** fold 16 or **235** fold 5 – Local map under DORDOGNE VALLEY **3** – Facilities

St-Cyprien clings to the side of a hill near the north bank of the Dordogne, in a setting of hills and woodlands characteristic of the Périgord Noir *(qv)*. It is dominated by the massive outline of its church around which are clustered old houses.

Church (Église) – The church, belonging to an abbey for Augustinian canons, was built in the 12C and restored in the Gothic period. Its size is impressive; it still has a Romanesque belfry-keep. Inside, the enormous main body of the church has pointed vaulting. A wealth of 17C furnishings include altarpieces, a pulpit, stalls, an organ loft and a wrought-iron balustrade.

EXCURSION

Chapel (Chapelle de Redon l'Espi) – *7.5km – 4.5km east.*
Lost in the middle of a remote valley, this sober Romanesque chapel is flanked to the south by the ruins of a small monastery; the buildings were ransacked during the Wars of Religion in the 16C. The name of the chapel, Redon Espi, is said to come from the Latin *rotondo spino*, possibly the evocation of a reliquary of the Holy Thorn, preserved for centuries at the nearby St-Cyprien Abbey.

★ ST-JEAN-DE-CÔLE Pop 339

Michelin map **75** fold 6 or **233** fold 32

Old houses and a Gothic bridge give an antique charm to the village, with its unusual church and castle. This charming picture is enhanced by golden stones which blend well with the brown of the small roof tiles. An old, narrow, humpbacked bridge with cutwaters spans the Côle, a tributary of the Dronne.

Church (Église) – This was started in the 11C and used to be the priory chapel. It has several unusual features: a curiously shaped belltower pierced by windows, a nave which is high in proportion to its length, capitals which divide the south chapel and the chancel, sculpture found at roof level and old covered markets built onto the east end.
Inside, note the 17C oak woodwork in the chancel. The nave is covered by a wooden ceiling replacing the dome, which has collapsed although the pendentives can still be seen; on the south side, in a chapel, note the recumbent figure in a niche.

Marthonie Castle ☉ – A gallery houses a collection of old publicity posters and handmade paper. All that remains of the 12C castle is the tower and its foundations (on the square); several mullioned windows remain from the 15 and 16C, when the castle was rebuilt. The basket-arched gallery and the inside staircase, with straight ramps and with eccentric or basket arches, date from the 17C.

EXCURSIONS

★**Puyguilhem Château** – *See Puyguilhem Château.*

★**Villars Caves** – *See Brantôme: The Heart of Périgord Vert.*

Thiviers – *See Brantôme: The Heart of Périgord Vert.*

You will find a selection of touring programmes on pp 6-7
Plan your route with the help of the map of principal sights on pp 4-5

★ ST-LÉON-SUR-VÉZÈRE

Pop 427

Michelin map **76** fold 17 or **233** fold 44 or **235** folds 1 and 2 – Local map under LES-EYZIES-DE-TAYAC

Built in a picturesque loop of the Vézère River, this charming village, overrun by greenery, possesses two castles and one of the finest Romanesque churches of Périgord.

★**Church (Église)** – The church was part of a Benedictine priory which was founded in the 12C and depended upon the Sarlat abbey. It was built on the ruins of a Gallo-Roman villa. The remains of one of the villa's walls can be seen on the river side.

Church

From the square, the apse, the perfectly smooth radiating chapels and the fine square two-storey arcaded belltower form a harmonious unit. The church is roofed with the heavy limestone slabs *(lauzes)* of Périgord Noir. Inside, the transept crossing is vaulted with a dome, while apsidal chapels are connected to the apse by narrow openings, known as *passages berrichons* as they are a feature of churches in the Berry region in particular. The apse and south radiating chapel are decorated with parts of Romanesque frescoes, in which red is the predominant colour.

La Salle Castle – Standing on the square, this small castle built of dry-stone has a fine 14C square keep crowned with machicolations.

Château de Clérans – This elegant 15 and 16C palace, flanked with machicolated towers and turrets, stands on the banks of the river.

Cemetery Chapel (Chapelle du cimetière) – This small 14C chapel is roofed, like the church, with *lauzes*. An inscription in the "*langue d'oc*" above the door harks back to an extraordinary event; in 1233, a servant who had let fly an arrow onto the crucifix guarding the entrance to the cemetery dropped dead on the spot, "with his head turned back-to-front". In 1890, the blasphemer's grave was excavated, and a skeleton with its skull back-to-front was unearthed... The cemetery still has a tall crucifix, and there are six ogival tombs in the defence wall.

---

*Travel with the **Michelin Sectional Map Series** (1:200 000).
These maps are revised regularly.*

ST-MARTIN-DE-GURÇON

Pop 559

Michelin map **75** fold 13 or **234** fold 4

Located in Gurçon Country on the boundary between Périgord and Guyenne, St-Martin possesses an interesting church.

Church (Église) – Its fine façade in the Saintonge style dates from the 12C. The doorway, without a tympanum, opens onto five smooth recessed arches supported by ten columns, with capitals carved with birds and monsters. Above the doorway an arcade of seven rounded arches resting on small columns is edged with a moulding decorated with heads, on top of which is a fine cornice with carved modillions.

Inside, the third bay is roofed with an ovoid-shaped dome.

EXCURSIONS

Montpeyroux – *10km – 6 miles to the southwest.*
This excursion goes through Gurçon Country: a flat countryside of vineyards and outcropping mounds, crowned with limestone tables.

Carsac-de-Gurson – This village, surrounded by vineyards, has a church with a Romanesque façade which displays all the characteristics of the Saintonge style.

Continue towards Villefranche-de-Lonchat, turn left onto the D 32 and then right onto a small road which passes below Gurson Castle.

Gurson Castle – The castle is set on a mound and still has some of its fortifications. Henry III of England, Duke of Aquitaine, made a gift of it to his seneschal Jean de Grailly. It was rebuilt in the 14C.

At the foot of the castle is a lake.

After the castle, turn right, then left into the D 10.

Montpeyroux – Pop 318. The Montpeyroux mound is crowned by a group of buildings which includes the church and château. At the far end of the mound is a lovely view of the region with the low squat houses scattered among the vines.

The Romanesque **church**, surrounded by its churchyard, possesses a Saintonge style façade similar to the one at St-Martin-de-Gurçon. Note the lovely cornice with carved modillions running round the apse, which is covered with a blind arcade made of nine arches.

Near the church stands an elegant 17 and 18C château. It is composed of a main building flanked by two pavilions at right angles, cantoned by round towers. Each opening is surmounted by an *œil-de-bœuf* window.

ST-PRIVAT-DES-PRÉS   Pop 702

Michelin map **75** fold 4 or **233** fold 41 – Local map under RIBÉRAC

This village located on the border of Périgord and Charentes has a lovely Romanesque church which used to belong to a 12C Benedictine priory, a dependent of Aurillac Abbey.

★ Church (Église) – Its main façade is clearly very much influenced by the Romanesque Saintonge style. Its fine doorway includes nine semicircular recessed arches forming an archivolt carved with geometric designs. Above this is blind arcading. Once a shelter for the village, the church has kept some evidence of its role as a fortress: at the east end the extension upwards of the chevet as a defence tower, at the west end the thickness of the façade wall into which a defence corridor was built and on the upper walls traces of merlons. The inside is attractive with its very narrow pointed-barrel vaulted aisles; the dome of the transept crossing was added after the church was built. On either side of the semicircular oven-vaulted apse, both tiny chapels (extensively restored) contain a 17C wooden **altarpiece**. At the entrance is a fine Romanesque baptistry.

Museum of Village Life and Tools (Musée de l'outil et de la vie au village) ⊙ – Located near the church, the museum has assembled a variety of objects recalling the traditional way of life of this region. A grocer's shop, artisans' workshops and a cobbler's have been reconstructed. Also exhibited are different items from a 19C school room (maps, benches...), clothes, tools, etc. An annexe exhibits wooden **models★** of castles, châteaux and cathedrals found in France.

ST-ROBERT   Pop 331

Michelin map **75** fold 7 or **239** fold 25 – 5km – 3 miles northwest of Ayen

This pretty village is situated on the top of a *puy (qv)*, on the boundaries of the Corrèze and the Dordogne. It was used as the setting for a French television series *Des Grives aux Loups*, taken from local author Claude Michelet's *(qv)* historical novels of country life of the same name.

From the terrace of the town hall, there is a good **view** of the church's east end and of the surrounding countryside.

★ Church (Église) – Only the transept, supporting an octagonal belltower at the crossing, and the well-proportioned chancel remain of the original 12C building. The turret and square tower which flank the east end are evidence of the defences in the 14C.

The chancel is lit by a clerestory and is divided from the ambulatory by six columns topped by interesting embellished capitals; the capitals attached to the ambulatory wall are carved in a more archaic manner – note the two old men pulling at their beards. On the left stands a figure of **Christ** in wood (13C) by the Spanish School.

STE-FOY-LA-GRANDE   Pop 3 218

Michelin map **75** folds 13 and 14 or **234** fold 8

Alphonse de Poitiers, brother of Saint Louis, founded this *bastide (qv)* in 1255 on the south bank of the Dordogne. It is now an animated market town selling regional products (fruit, flowers, tobacco) as well as a wine centre.

Ste-Foy is also the home town of the surgeons **Jean-Louis Faure** (1863-1944), **Paul Broca** (1824-80) founder of the school of anthropology, **Élie Faure** (1873-1937) art critic and historian whose writings were important in the study of art history and the Reclus brothers.

Reclus brothers – Among the famous family of five brothers – four writers and one surgeon – there were **Élisée** (1830-1905), who wrote the monumental work *Géographie Universelle* and was obliged to leave France in 1851 for his republican ideas, **Élie** (1827-1904), **Onésime** (1837-1914), **Armand** (1843-1927) and the youngest, **Paul** (1847-1914), not a writer but a surgeon, whose name has been given to Reclus disease (cysts in the breasts).

Town – An atmosphere of days past permeates the town from Place de la Mairie (Place Gambetta), surrounded by covered arcades and old houses (medieval, Renaissance, 17C) to the tall spire (62m – 203ft) of the neo-Gothic church overlooking the town.

In Rue de la République note no 53, a house flanked by a corner turret, no 94, a carved half-timbered 15C house and no 102, also with a corner turret.

The path along the river, flowing below the ramparts, makes a lovely walk.

SALIGNAC-EYVIGUES

Michelin map **75** folds 17 and 18 or **235** fold 2 – Local map under PÉRIGORD NOIR – Facilities

In Artaban country – The small region dominated by Salignac has come to be called Artaban country, after a character created by Gauthier de Costes, known familiarly as *La Calprenède* (after the land he owned) and born at Toulgou Manor. The novelist was very successful during the 17C and was greatly admired by all the *précieuses* who ran literary salons, but his success was not long-lived. Although the author has fallen into obscurity, however, the expression "proud as Artaban" is still in modern usage.

Salignac village – The market square, which is overlooked by the façade of the 13C convent (Couvent des Croisiers), and the neighbouring streets, in particular Rue Sainte-Croix, are a charming sight, just a few yards away from the entrance to the castle.

Castle ⊘ – There is a good overall view from the D 60, east of the village, of this medieval fortress wich still belongs to the family of the Archbishop of Cambrai, François de Salignac de la Mothe-Fénelon *(qv)*.
The castle, which was built between the 12 and 17C, is still encircled by ramparts. Mullioned windows lighten the façade of the main building, which is flanked by round and square towers. The whole building is enhanced by the warm colour of the stone and the lovely stone slab *(lauzes)* roofs.
Go up a Renaissance spiral staircase to visit several rooms with interesting furnishings, mainly in the Renaissance and Louis XIII styles.

Eyrignac Manor-house (Manoir d'Eyrignac) ⊘ – Lovely 18C French- and Italian-style **gardens★** (avenues of greenery, with parterres of yew, boxwood and hornbeam) surround an elegant 17C manor-house of the Sarlat region.
The chapel, located in a square pavilion near the entrance, is decorated with a tiny balustraded gallery.

*For hotels with private tennis courts, gardens, swimming pool,
or equipped beach look in the current **Michelin Red Guide France**.*

★★★ SARLAT-LA-CANÉDA

Michelin map **75** fold 17 or **235** fold 6 – Local maps under DORDOGNE VALLEY **2** and **3** and PÉRIGORD NOIR – Facilities

At the heart of Périgord Noir, Sarlat-la-Canéda (Sarlat for short) was built in a hollow surrounded by wooded hills. Its charm lies in its preservation of the past; it still "feels" like a small market town – the home of merchants and clerks during the Ancien Régime (period before the Revolution) – with narrow medieval streets, restored Gothic and Renaissance town houses *(hôtels)* and the famous **Saturday market**.

HISTORICAL NOTES

From abbey to bishopric – Sarlat grew up around a Benedictine abbey founded in the 9C and to which the relics of St Sacerdos, Bishop of Limoges, and of his mother, St Mondane, had been entrusted under Charlemagne.
The abbots were all powerful until the 13C when internal strife and corruption caused their downfall. In 1299 the *Book of Peace*, an act of emancipation signed by the community, the abbey and the king, stated that the abbot might continue in his role of lord but that the consuls should be given all administrative power concerning the town itself. In 1317, however, Pope John XXII divided the Périgueux diocese and proclaimed Sarlat the episcopal see of an area which extended far beyond the Sarladais region. The abbey church therefore became a cathedral, and the monks formed a chapter.

Sarlat's golden age – The 13 and early 14C had been a prosperous time for this active market town, but the Hundred Years War left it weakened and depopulated. Therefore, when Charles VII bestowed numerous privileges (new revenues and certain tax exemptions) upon Sarlat and its population to thank them for their loyalty and strong resistance against the English (despite Sarlat's having been ceded to the English with the *Treaty of Brétigny* in 1360), the people of Sarlat began reconstruction. Most of the town houses to be seen were built between 1450-1500. This has created an architectural unity which is appreciated by the townspeople and tourists alike.
The magistrates, clerks, bishops, canons and merchants formed a comfortable bourgeois class which included such men of letters as Étienne de La Boétie.

The true and faithful friend – Étienne de La Boétie, who was born in Sarlat in 1530 in a house that can still be seen *(see below)*, became famous on many counts. He proved himself to be a brilliant magistrate in the Bordeaux Parliament as well as an impassioned writer – he was only eighteen when he wrote the compelling appeal for liberty, *Discourse on Voluntary Subjection* or *Contr'un (Against One)*, which inspired Jean-Jacques Rousseau when he came to write the *Social Contract*. He formed a friendship with **Michel de Montaigne** that was to last until he died and which has been immortalized by posterity. Montaigne was at La Boétie's bedside when the young man died all too early in 1563; with his friend in mind, Montaigne wrote his famous *Essay on Friendship* in which he formulated the excellent sentiment: "If I am urged to explain why I loved him, I feel I can only reply: because he was himself and I am myself..."

Sarlat's secular architecture – Sarlat's old district was cut into two in the 19C by the "Traverse" (or Rue de la République), separating it into a more populated western section and a more sophisticated eastern section.

The town houses are quite unique: built with quality ashlar-work in a fine golden-hued limestone, with interior courtyards; the roofing, made of heavy limestone slabs *(lauzes)*, necessitated a steeply pitched framework so that the enormous weight $(500kg/m^2 - about 102lb/ft^2)$ could be supported on thick walls. Over the years new floors were added: a medieval ground floor, a High Gothic or Renaissance upper floor and classical roof cresting and lantern turrets.

This architectural unit escaped modern building developments in the 19 and 20C because of its distance from the main communication routes. It was chosen in 1962 as one of the new experimental national restoration projects, the goal of which was to preserve the old quarters of France's towns and cities. The project, begun in 1964, has allowed the charm of this small medieval town to be recreated.

★★★OLD SARLAT *time: 1 hour 30 min*

Start from Place du Peyrou.

★La Boétie's House (Maison de la Boétie) **(Z)** – This house was built in 1525 by Antoine de La Boétie, a criminal magistrate in the seneschal's court at Sarlat, and is the birthplace of Étienne de La Boétie *(qv)*.

A large arch on the ground floor used to shelter small shops; the two upper floors of Italian Renaissance style have large mullioned windows, framed by pilasters carved with medallions and lozenges. The steeply pitched gabled roof is decorated with crockets, and on the left side there is a heavily ornamented dormer window *(photograph p 31)*.

On the left of the house is Passage Henri-de-Ségogne *(see below)*.

Former bishopric (Ancien Évêché) **(Z T)** – To the right of St Sacerdos' Cathedral, is the former bishopric. Its façade has windows in the Gothic style on the 1st floor, Renaissance on the 2nd floor and an Italian Renaissance loggia above, added by the Italian bishop Nicolo Goddi, friend of Catherine de' Medici. The interior has been converted into a theatre.

St Sacerdos' Cathedral (Cathédrale St-Sacerdos) **(Z)** – St Sacerdos' Church was built here in the 12C. In 1504 the Bishop Armand de Gontaut-Biron had the church razed, in order to build a cathedral.

However, when the bishop left Sarlat in 1519, the construction work ceased for more than a century. Although the present church was built during the 16 and 17C, the base of the west front's tower is Romanesque. Of its three storeys, the lowest is formed of blind arcading, the second has open bays, while the third is a 17C addition.

La Boétie's House

Inside, the most striking features are the elevation and harmonious proportions of the nave. Among the furnishings are an 18C organ loft and an organ by Lépine (a well-known 18C organ maker).

Leave by the south door.

The first courtyard is bordered by the **Chapel of the Blue Penitents** (Chapelle des Pénitents Bleus), a pure Romanesque building (12C) which is a vestige of the Benedictine abbey. From here notice the south side of the cathedral supported by flying buttresses, the side chapels built between the buttresses and the bulbous-shaped lantern crowning the belltower.

Continue into the **Cour des Fontaines** and then turn left into the second courtyard, the **Cour des Chanoines (3)**, which is closed in on its north side by the Chapel of the Blue Penitents.

Go round the chapel, by the right, to reach the east end of the cathedral, which is adjoined by buildings with *lauzes* roofs.

Former cemetery (Ancien Cimetière) (Z) – Excavations around the east end have enhanced the funerary niches carved into the retaining wall and have permitted the creation of a terraced cemetery garden using 12-15C tombstones found in the earth recovered from the site.

Lantern of the dead (Lanterne des Morts) (Z) – Built at the end of the 12C, this mysterious cylindrical tower topped by a cone and split into tiers by four bands contains two rooms. The room on the ground floor has domical vaulting held up by six pointed arches; the other room is in the cone part of the tower and is inaccessible to people.

A number of hypotheses have been put forward concerning the lantern's function: was it a tower built in honour of the visit of St Bernard in 1147 (he had blessed bread which miraculously cured the sick); or a lantern of the dead (but it is difficult to imagine how the lantern was lit because the top room was inaccessible); or a funerary chapel.

Lantern of the dead

From the garden near the lantern, there is a fine **view** of the cathedral's east end and its various courtyards.

Take the alley opposite the garden.

At the corner of the dead end (where the old rest-stop for post-horses can be seen) and Rue d'Albusse stands the **Hôtel de Génis**, a massive, plain 15C building with an overhanging upper storey supported by seven stone corbels.

Go down Rue d'Albusse and turn into Rue du Présidial.

Presidial (Présidial) (Y) – This building was the seat of the royal court of justice created in 1552 by Henri II.

It is possible to get a glimpse through the gate of the 16C façade with its two large openings, one above the other, and the heavy stone slab *(lauzes)* roof. Note the odd octagonal lantern turret (added in the 17C), with a roof in the form of a bell and propped up by supports.

Turn around and go along Rue de la Salamandre.

Hôtel de Grézel (Y) – Built at the end of the 15C, the town house straight ahead has a half-timbered façade with a tower and a lovely Flamboyant Gothic ogee-arched doorway.

The skill and artistry of the carpenter and roof-layer can be admired by looking further down onto several of the roofs: the fine layout of the *lauzes*, following the line of the roof perfectly down to where the roof widens and levels out (this is achieved by furring: nailing thin strips of board under the line of the roof; a technique used to compensate for the thickness of the walls).

Place de la Liberté (Y) – Animated by cafés, Sarlat's main square has on its east side the 17C **town hall** (Hôtel de Ville – **Y H**) and on its north side the old, secularised **church** (Église Ste-Marie – **Y D**); the chancel of this was destroyed, leaving a space which is used today as the stage set for the summer Sarlat Theatre Festival. Note the *lauze* roof of this church and several of the nearby roofs which have small dormer-like windows; these small triangular openings were used for the airing of the attic. Behind the "set" and used as a backdrop is the **Hôtel de Gisson** (16C), two buildings joined by a hexagonal staircase tower with a remarkable pointed *lauze* roof.

★**Place des Oies (Y)** – Appropriately called Goose Square, this is the place where on Saturdays from November to March people come from far and wide to haggle over the price of geese and, of course, of delicious goose liver *(foie gras)*.

The square is an elegant architectural collection of turrets, pinnacles and corner staircases.

★**Rue des Consuls (Y 4)** – The town houses in this street are beautiful examples of Sarlat architecture from the 14-17C.

Hôtel de Vassal (Y) – Located on a corner of Place des Oies, this 15C town house consists of two buildings at right angles flanked by a twin battlemented turret.

★**Hôtel Plamon (Y)** – As identified by the shield on the pediment above the doorway, this town house belonged to the Selves de Plamon family, members of the cloth merchants' guild. Because it is made up of a group of buildings built in different periods, it is a particularly interesting illustration of the evolution of the different architectural styles used in Sarlat construction.

The 14C ground floor opens through two large pointed arches. The first floor has three Gothic windows ornamented with High Gothic tracery, and the second floor has 15C mullioned windows.

Left of the town house is the very narrow Plamon Tower with windows which get smaller the higher up they are; this architectural ruse makes the tower seem much taller than it is.

On the corner of the street is a rounded overhanging balcony supported by a squinch.

Go into the courtyard to admire the elegant 17C wooden **staircase★**.

Fountain (Fontaine Ste-Marie) (Y) – Opposite the Hôtel de Plamon, the fountain plays in a grotto.

Follow Rue Albéric-Cahuet. In a small square, take the vaulted passage on the left, which cuts through the Hôtel de Maleville.

★Hôtel de Maleville (Y) – This town house is also known as the Hôtel de Vienne after the man who built it, Jean de Vienne. Born of humble parents in Sarlat in 1557, he successfully climbed the social ladder to become Financial Secretary under Henri IV. Later, the town house was bought by the Maleville family; a member of this same family, Jacques de Maleville *(see Domme),* helped write the *Code Civil.*

Three existing houses were combined in the mid-16C to form an imposing mansion. In front of the tall, narrow central pavilion is a majestic tower, is a terrace under which opens the arched main doorway surmounted by medallions depicting Henri IV and Maria de' Medici. It is flanked by a corbelled turret which joins it to the left wing.

The right wing, overlooking Place de la Liberté, has a gable which very much resembles one at La Boétie's House *(see above),* although it is in a later Renaissance style with bays surrounded by small columns supporting entablature and pediment.

Passage Henri-de-Ségogne (Z 21) – Between Hôtel de Maleville and La Boétie's House, this alleyway leads visitors through an arch, a passageway and a covered pasaggio.

Picturesque half-timbered buildings have been restored and, in summer, artisans can be seen selling their crafts.

ADDITIONAL SIGHTS

Western Section – The area west of the "Traverse" is a maze of narrow, twisting, sloping alleys in which some of the houses are being restored, while in other cases demolition is the only solution.

Rue des Trois-Conils (des Trois Lapins) (Z 22) – This street bends sharply left around the foot of a house flanked by a tower, which once belonged to consuls.

Executioner's Tower (Tour du Bourreau) (Z) – This tower, which was part of the ramparts, was built in 1580.

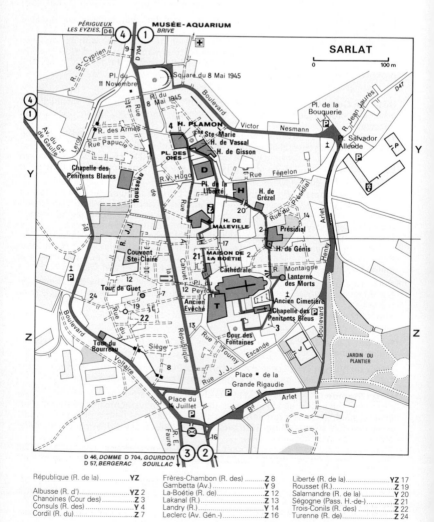

République (R. de la)	**YZ**	Frères-Chambon (R. des)	**Z** 8	Liberté (R. de la)	**YZ** 17
		Gambetta (Av.)	**Y** 9	Rousset (R.)	**Z** 19
Albusse (R. d')	**YZ** 2	La-Boétie (R. de)	**Z** 12	Salamandre (R. de la)	**Y** 20
Chanoines (Cour des)	**Z** 3	Lakanal (R.)	**Z** 13	Ségogne (Pass. H.-de-)	**Z** 21
Consuls (R. des)	**Y** 4	Landry (R.)	**Y** 14	Trois-Conils (R. des)	**Z** 22
Cordil (R. du)	**Z** 7	Leclerc (Av. Gén.-)	**Z** 16	Turenne (R. de)	**Z** 24

Watch Tower (Tour du Guet) (Z) – Overlapping the buildings, the watch tower is crowned by 15C machicolations and flanked by a corbelled turret.

Rue Jean-Jacques Rousseau (Y) – In this mysterious district of convents and walled gardens, the battlemented turret at the corner of Rue de La Boétie marks the site of **St Clare's Convent**, a vast L-shaped 17C building.

Chapel of the White Penitents (Chapelle des Pénitents Blancs) (Y) – This 17C building, once a chapel, has a classical doorway surrounded by columns.
It now houses a **Museum of Sacred Art** (Musée d'Art Sacré) ⊘. Most of the exhibits date from the 16 to 18C. There are several *Pietà* (including a 17C one in the glass case), a 16C tabernacle in multicoloured wood, sections of magnificent wooden baroque retables and a particularly lovely statue of an Angel in Adoration.

★ Museum-Aquarium (Musée-Aquarium) ⊘ – *Access via Avenue Gambetta and* ① *on the town plan, then follow the signposts.*
The objective of this museum is to describe the Dordogne River and everything related to it: fishing, fishing vessels, navigation, construction of dams, etc.
About thirty freshwater species from the region can be seen swimming about in vast aquariums. Anadromous fish (Atlantic salmon, lamprey, shad) and non-migratory species (pike, perch, barbel, bleak) live side by side.
Fishing techniques are explained on panels and illustrated with displays of nets and a *gabare* (flat-bottomed boat - *qv*). The most original fishing technique used was the seine: an immense net was dropped, extending from one bank of the river to the other, which caught a large quantity of migrating fish swimming up river to spawn. This type of fishing has practically disappeared due to the damming up of rivers.
A film shows the large-scale management measures used to attract the migrating fish in spite of the dams: collecting the fish, fishing ladders. Other audio-visual displays supplement this presentation of river life.

EXCURSIONS

Temniac – *3km – 2 miles north. See Périgord Noir.*

Puymartin Castle – *9km – 5.5 miles northwest. Leave Sarlat by* ④. *See Puymartin Castle.*

St-André-d'Allas, archéosite de Breuil (archaeological site of Breuil hamlet) ⊘ – *12 km – 7.5 miles to the northwest. Route signposted along the D 25 leaving from St-André-d'Allas.*
Breuil hamlet has the richest collection of the little shepherds' shelters known as *caselles (qv)* in Périgord; there are a dozen or so huts, some of which are semi-detached, with domed roofs and gable windows.

Dry-stone huts

SORGES   Pop 1 074

Michelin map ⁊⁵ fold 6 or ²³³ fold 43 – Facilities

Sorges, a pleasant town famous as a truffle market at the turn of the century, is situated on the road from Périgueux to Limoges, not far from the valley of the Isle, as the plateaux rise gently from Périgord Blanc to Nontronnais.

Church (Église) – This Romanesque building with a dome has a massive square bell-tower with twin windows and a fine Renaissance doorway.

Truffle Centre (Maison de la Truffe) ⊘ – Truffles are an important Périgord speciality. A museum, housed in the tourist information centre, features this product with the help of tables, maps, photographs, films and literary passages. *For more on truffles see the Introduction: Dordogne's Homegrown Gastronomy.*
A walk to the truffle beds marked "A la découverte des Truffières" has been mapped out 2km – 1 mile from Sorges.

Michelin map **75** fold 18 or **235** fold 6 – Local maps under DORDOGNE VALLEY **1** and **2** and GRAMAT CAUSSE – Facilities
Town plan in the current Michelin Red Guide France

At the confluence of the Corrèze and the Dordogne, in the centre of a fertile region, of an abundance greatly in contrast with the poverty of the *causses (qv* – limestone plateaux) of Martel and Gramat, Souillac is a small town bustling with trade and tourists. It developed in the 13C, growing up around the abbey which was a dependency of the Benedictine Monastery at Aurillac; today, the town is bisected by the N 20.

When the Benedictines settled in the plain of Souillès – so-called after the local word *souilh*, meaning bog or marshland where wild boar wallow – story has it that they replaced the community established there previously by St Eligius. The monks drained the land continuously, transforming the marsh into a rich estate. Souillac Abbey was plundered and sacked several times by the English during the Hundred Years War, but rose from its ruins each time thanks to the tenacity of its abbots. Greater disasters, however, befell it during the Wars of Religion: in 1562 Huguenot bands pillaged the monastery; ten years later the monastery buildings were set ablaze and only the abbey church, protected by its domes, escaped the flames. The abbey was rebuilt in the 17C and attached to the Maurist Congregation, but it then ceased to exist during the Revolution. Its buildings now house a tobacconist's.

Abbey Church – *Time: 30 min.* Dedicated to Mary, Mother of Christ, this church became a parish church to replace the church of St Martin, which was destroyed during the Wars of Religion. The disfigured belltower, which is all that remains of St Martin's, is now the town hall belfry.

Built in the 12C, the church is related to the Romanesque cathedrals of Angoulême, Périgueux and Cahors with their Byzantine inspiration, but it is more advanced in the lightness of its columns and the height of its great arcades than these are. From Place de l'Abbaye it is possible to admire the attractive east end with its five pentagonal apsidal chapels, three of which radiate out from the apse, while the other two are in line. At the front of the interior is a tower decorated on its lowest tier with carved brackets, which was part of a previous building and dates from the 10C or perhaps the beginning of the 11C. It is the equivalent of the tower-porches which usually formed the narthex of Romanesque churches. Inside, the pure lines of the nave are covered with a row of three tall domes on pendentives. In the first bay on the left there is a 16C polyptych painted on wood, depicting *The Mysteries of the Rosary.*

★**The back of the doorway** – This composition consists of the remains of the old doorway, which was badly damaged by the Protestants and had been placed inside the nave of the new church, when it was erected in the 17C.

Prophet Isaiah

Above the door, framed by the statues of St Peter on the right and St Benedict on the left, is a low relief relating episodes in the life of the Monk Theophilus, Deacon of Adana in Cilicia: a new abbot, misled by false reports, removes Theophilus from his office of treasurer of the monastery of Adana; Theophilus, out of resentment, signs a pact with the devil to regain his office *(left).* Repenting of his sins, Theophilus implores forgiveness and prays to the Virgin Mary *(right)* who appears before him in his sleep, accompanied by St Michael and two angels who guard her; they bring him the pact he made with the devil, and she shows how she has had his signature annulled and has obtained his pardon. The engaged pillar on the right, which was originally the central pillar of the doorway, is richly decorated. The right side depicts concupiscence during the various stages of life; on the main facet monstrous animals grip and devour one another. The left side proclaims the remission of sin through the sacrifice of Isaac. The hand of Abraham is stayed by the messenger of God. On either side of the door are fine low reliefs, in boldly decorative attitudes, of the prophet **Isaiah**★★ *(right)*, striking in its expression, and the patriarch Joseph *(left)*. Beneath the narthex is a crypt containing primitive sarcophagi.

★**National Museum of Automata and Robotics (Musée national de l'automate et de la robotique)** ⊘ – *Enter by the parvis of the abbey church (abbatiale St-Pierre).*
The museum contains some 3 000 objects, including 1 000 automata donated by the **Roullet-Decamps** family, who for four generations were leaders in the field. In 1865 Jean Roullet created his first mechanical toy: a small gardener pushing a wheel barrow. In 1909 he created the first Christmas window display for the Bon Marché department store.

The collection illustrates the evolution of automata from Antiquity to the present-day. These mechanical objects were considered precious enough to offer to nobility; they were also offered as sophisticated toys and even used as publicity items.

Note especially the **Jazzband** (1920), a group of electric automata with black musicians performing a concert; or the lovely fairy-like **Snow Queen** (1956), based on the tale by Hans-Christian Andersen. The impressive robotic brain which controls the movements of the automata and the new collection of "robots of the year 2000" both reflect the extent of the amazing developments that have been made in this field on the eve of the 21C.

EXCURSION

Lanzac Viewpoint (Belvédère de Lanzac). There is a wide view from the left of the N 20 *(car park)* of the Dordogne Valley, where Château de la Treyne can be seen standing out to the east and the dovecot of Le Bastit Castle to the southeast.

★ LE THOT

Michelin map 75 fold 7 or 235 fold 2 – 7km – 4 miles south of Montignac – Local map under VÉZÈRE VALLEY

Le Thot Cro-Magnon Centre (Espace Cro-Magnon) ⊙ – Created in 1972, this centre offers an initiation into prehistoric art, and is also a good introduction to the many sites in Périgord, especially that of Lascaux II, the reproduction of the Lascaux Cave *(see Lascaux Cave)*

The **museum** displays a large overview of the expression of prehistoric man through painting, sculpture, graffitti etc., of his position in the history of mankind, his evolution and his motivation.These topics are developed with the aid of modern technology; facsimiles, enormous slide shows, audiovisual presentation, film and so on.

The **gardens** are situated in a protected spot and offer a glimpse of the animals with which the Cro-Magnon man came into contact and which he painted on the rocky faces of caves: animals still in existence, such as the wild oxen, European bison and Przewalski's horses, or animated lifesize reproductions of species that are now extinct, such as the mammoth and the woolly rhinoceros.

Several, often spectacular, reconstructions of camps and scenes from the everyday life of the Upper Palaeolithic Age all contrive to make a most enjoyable visit.

TOURTOIRAC   Pop 756

Michelin map 75 fold 7 or 233 fold 44 – Facilities

This small market town, tucked amidst the greenery on the banks of the Auvézère, was the seat of a royal abbey in the 12C. The cemetery contains the tomb of an extraordinary character.

Orélie-Antoine I, King of Araucania and Patagonia – Antoine Orélie de Tounens was born in Périgord in 1825. By 1858 he was practising as a lawyer in Périgueux, but was largely unknown. Suddenly he was seized by the ambition to live on a scale larger than life. He had become convinced that a bold man could subdue the backward tribes of South America and establish a powerful kingdom on the borders of Chile and Argentina. He borrowed a large sum of money and set sail for Chile, where he was greeted by the Indians as a liberator, and in 1860 he proclaimed himself King of Araucania under the title of Orélie-Antoine I. He raised an army and promulgated a constitution. Chile became distrustful of what was going on and arrested and imprisoned the *Libertador*. The "king", repatriated to France, did not lose heart but gathered funds for a second expedition. In 1869 he landed secretly in Patagonia. After fantastic adventures, he was once more repatriated. Two further attempts were equally unsuccessful and in 1878 this comic opera character, who nearly gave France a kingdom, died at Tourtoirac, where he had retired.

Abbey (Abbaye) ⊙ – The remains of a Benedictine abbey, founded in the 11C, stand in the gardens of the presbytery. To the right, there is a small priory chapel with barrel vaulting and amphora-like objects set in the wall for the purpose of improving the acoustics, side by side with the monk's bread oven and the watchpath. Of the trefoil-shaped abbey church, only the transept, surmounted by a powerful square belltower, remains. The apse was destroyed during the Revolution. Note the fine capitals, carved at the beginning of the 12C, and the dome on pendentives. The much altered nave is now used for worship. The chapter-house under the presbytery has been restored, revealing remarkable Romanesque twin capitals. It gives access to the ruins of the cloisters.

★ TURENNE   Pop 740

Michelin map 75 fold 8 or 239 fold 26 – Local map under BRIVE-LA-GAILLARDE: Excursions

An old French dictum stated that of Pompadour, Ventadour and Turenne, Turenne was king – this is a good reflection of the pride of the capital of the old viscounty as well. Here the houses form a picturesque crescent round the castle ruins.

HISTORICAL NOTES

The small town with a great past – The incapability of the last Carolingians of governing the whole of their territories and the aptitude of the lords of Turenne for resisting Viking invasion seems to have been the root of the fief's emancipation from royal power. As early as the 11C, a fortress was set on the outlier of the Martel Causse. In the 15C, Turenne held sway over a third of Lower Limousin, Upper Quercy and the Sarladais region or 1 200 villages and a number of abbeys. The viscounty, in its heyday, enjoyed enviable privileges; like the king of France, the viscounts ruled absolutely, ennobling subjects, creating offices and consulates, minting money and levying taxes.

The La Tour d'Auvergne-Turenne families – The name Turenne became famous through the family of La Tour d'Auvergne. In the 16C, Henri de la Tour d'Auvergne was leader of the Limousin Huguenots and the most valiant supporter of the Reformation. As a reward for his zeal, Henri IV allowed him to marry the heiress to the Duchy of Bouillon, Charlotte de la Marck; the Turennes then went to live in Sedan and administered their viscounty, which remained sovereign, at a distance. Charlotte died three years after her marriage, leaving the titles of Duke de Bouillon and Prince of Sedan to her husband Henri, who remarried Elizabeth of Nassau. His youngest son, also a Henri, was to become the Great Turenne. His eldest son, who inherited the viscounty and title of Duke de Bouillon, participated in the Fronde (an aristocratic rebellion against Mazarin with which Turenne had associated himself in its early days – 1648). In 1650 he welcomed two supporters of the Fronde, the Princess of Condé and her son the Duke of Enghien. The meeting was celebrated with such pomp and magnificence that it was baptised "Turenne's wild week" and in consequence the people of Turenne were taxed for two years to refill the impoverished coffers. This meeting helped restore the young Turenne to favour with the Queen-Regent in 1652.

Henri de Turenne (1611-75), France's marshal-general was a brilliant military man, who helped end the Thirty Years War due to his great skill during his campaign in Germany (1643-48), and who also played an important role (1652-53) in the suppression of the Fronde, preventing the young Louis XIV from being captured by the rebels.

Louis XIV ordained that the Great Turenne be buried beside the French kings and Du Guesclin at St-Denis. Napoleon considered him the greatest soldier of modern times and had him moved to the Invalides in Paris in 1800 *(see Michelin Green Guide to Paris).*

The golden age of the viscounty – The inhabitants living in the reflected glory of their lord's prowess in battle passed their days quietly within their small state and were envied since they were exempt from the tithes which fell so heavily on other French peasants. But this golden age had to end. In 1738, the last member of the La Tour d'Auvergne dynasty, the ninth viscount, who no longer had a single sou to his name, sold the viscounty to Louis XV for 4 200 000 livres, ending the quasi-complete independence of this French state. Once united to the French kingdom, the taxes of the former viscounty were multiplied by ten!

TOUR

time: 1 hour 30 min

Lower town – At the foot of the hill is the Barri-bas Quarter, the old part of town.

On **Place du Foirail** (**6**), the Hôtel Sclafer (**B**), with a loggia, was a residence for notaries in the 17C.

Opposite it is a small shop (15C) (**D**) with a large arcade.

Rue du Commandant-Charollais goes into **Place de la Halle**.

The town houses around this square reflect the wealth of its inhabitants, especially the **Vachon House**, the residence of the consuls of Turenne in the 16 and 17C.

Between two town houses, the narrow **Rue Droite** climbs towards the castle.

The street is lined with old

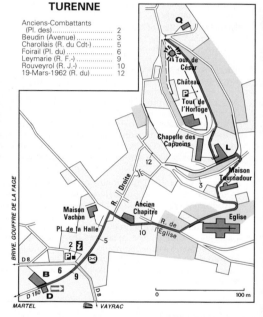

TURENNE

Anciens-Combattants	
(Pl. des)	2
Beudin (Avenue)	3
Charollais (R. du Cdt-)	5
Foirail (Pl. du)	6
Leymarie (R. F.-)	9
Rouveyrol (R. J.-)	10
19-Mars-1962 (R. du)	12

houses with overhanging upper storeys and small shops. Turn right onto Rue Joseph-Rouveyrol and note the **House of the Old Chapter-house**, the tower of which is decorated with a lovely Flamboyant-Gothic-style doorway.

Church (**Église**) – The construction of the church was decided upon by Charlotte de La Marck in 1593, the year Henri IV converted to Catholicism.

After Charlotte's death, Elizabeth of Nassau took over the project; and yet it was not consecrated until 1668. The church is in the form of a Greek cross, and has an unusual ornamentation – a yellow and white mosaic forming a network of prismatic ribbing. The 17 and 18C furnishings include stalls and a high altar surmounted by a carved and gilded wood altarpiece depicting the Passion of Christ. The *trompe l'œil* decoration between the twisted columns was added later on.

Just above the church, a vast building, the **Tournadour Mansion** was once the town's salt storehouse.

Upper town – Access is through the **fortified gateway** of the second of the three curtain walls which protected the castle. On the right the Seneschal's House (**L**) has an elegant tower. On the left the **Capuchin's Chapel** (Chapelle des Capucins) (1644) houses exhibitions.

Go round the castle from the right. A series of manor-houses, roofed with slate and flanked by squat towers have names which evoke their past purpose – the Gold Foundry (**Q**), for example.

Castle ⊙ – The castle was demolished by the king once the viscounty was sold to the crown. Only the Clock and Caesar's Towers, at each end of the promontory, were spared. The **site**★ is remarkable. Imagine this promontory occupied by the castle, its outbuildings and chapel (behind the Clock Tower).

Clock Tower (Tour de l'Horloge) – The keep's (13C) guard room with pointed barrel vaulting is open to visitors. Objects recalling Turenne's past are on display. Above it is the mint or treasury.

Caesar's Tower (Tour de César) – This round tower with irregular stone bonding seems to date from the 11C. A staircase goes up to the top, from where there is a vast **panorama**★★ of the region. In the foreground below are the village's slate roofs, in the distance, beyond a green and valleyed landscape, appear the Monts du Cantal to the east and the Dordogne Valley directly southwards *(viewing table)*.

Return to Place du Foirail via the fortified gateway and Rue Droite.

EXCURSION

★**La Fage Chasm (Gouffre de la Fage)** ⊘ – *7km – 4 miles northwest. Local map under Brive-la-Gaillarde: Excursions.*

The underground galleries form two separate groups, which can be visited successively. A staircase leads into the chasm, which was created by the collapse of the roof section. The first group of chambers, to the left, contains fine draperies in the form of jellyfish in beautiful rich colours. In the Organ Hall (Salle des Orgues), the concretions are played like a xylophone.

The second group, with many stalagmites and stalactites, also has a forest of needle-like forms hanging from the roof. In the last chamber excavations are underway to uncover bones from prehistoric times.

The cave is occupied by a very large colony of bats, including six different species.

VAREN   Pop 870

Michelin map 🎗🎗 fold 19 or 🎗🎗🎗 fold 19 – 16km – 10 miles east of St-Antonin-Noble-Val – Local map under ST-ANTONIN-NOBLE-VAL: Excursions

The charming and picturesque old town of Varen stands on the north bank of the Aveyron, its houses clustered round the Romanesque church, which is protected by large-scale defences.

Enter the old part of town from the south. The old fortified gateway, the Porte El-Faoure, leads to narrow streets lined by half-timbered and clay houses with overhanging upper storeys and flat roofs covered with round tiles.

Castle – This is a massive keep topped by a machicolated watchpath and flanked by a corbelled turret. The Lord-Prior of Varen shut himself up in this castle when he challenged the decisions of the Bishop of Rodez and wished to prove his complete independence. In 1553 the Council of Trent replaced the monks in the Benedictine priory by a more tractable college of 12 canons.

★**Church (Église St-Pierre)** – The church, part of the town's defence, was built at the end of the 11C. Its west face was included in the perimeter wall – the side door was opened in 1758 and the present doorway was opened in 1802, when the moats were filled in. The doorway, which was walled-up in the 16C, once led to the old town via the east end; two archaic capitals still remain, representing St Michael slaying the dragon *(left)* and Samson opening the lion's jaws *(right)*. A plain square belltower rises above the flat chancel and two semicircular apsidal chapels. The north aisle is supported by huge flying buttresses and has several openings.

The main part of the building is pure Romanesque in style and consists of a long nave of nine bays separated from the aisles by square pillars. The chancel and apsidal chapels are adorned with 17C stalls and interesting capitals with plant motifs, tracery, animals and cherubs surrounding the Tree of Life.

★★ VÉZÈRE VALLEY

Michelin map 🎗🎗 folds 7 and 8 and 16 and 17 or 🎗🎗🎗 folds 25 and 26 and 🎗🎗🎗 folds 1, 2 and 5

This valley, classified as part of the world's heritage by UNESCO, is a tourist route remarkable both for the beauty of the countryside it passes through and for its fascinating prehistoric sites, particularly around Montignac and Les Eyzies-de-Tayac, a region inhabited for approximately the past 100 000 years *(see notes on prehistory in the Introduction)*.

To enable visitors to get the most from their visit, devices for dispensing information have been set up all along the valley. These consist of two "gateways" placed at either end of the area covered by the Vézère map (at Terrasson and la Brique) and four telematic posts at Terrasson, Montignac, Les Eyzies and the Bugue.

THE PÉRIGORD STRETCH OF THE VÉZÈRE

From Brive to Limeuil

108km – 67 miles – allow 1 day – local map overleaf

Swollen by the waters of the Corrèze, the Vézère, flowing from the north, suddenly changes course and flows westwards to run through a typically Périgord countryside where willows, poplars and roughly hewn cliffs make up a harmonious landscape.

Brive-la-Gaillarde – *See Brive-la-Gaillarde.*

Leave Brive westwards.

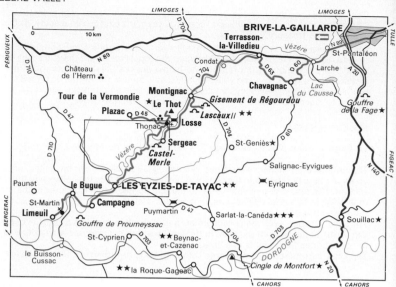

The N 89 crosses the Brive Basin, the centre of market gardening and fruit growing, and joins the Vézère near St-Pantaléon.

Between Larche and Terrasson the road leaves the valley on the D 60, which climbs onto the plateau.

Chavagnac – Pop 301. At the limit of the Corrèze *causse (qv)* and Périgord, this village is dominated by a powerful keep topped with corbels, the remains of a 13C castle. The 12C church has kept its dome.

The picturesque D 63 winds through walnut tree plantations. On the way down to Terrasson, notice slopes thick with vineyards.

Terrasson-la-Villedieu – Pop 6 004. Terrasson, built beside the Vézère, has old districts stretching in tiers up the side of a hill overlooking the left bank of the river, across from La Villedieu. It is a busy little town with a prosperous trade in truffles and walnuts.

The **church** was built in the upper part of the old town in the 15C and has undergone many bouts of restoration. The single aisle, transept and chancel have pointed vaulting.

From the terrace, on the north side of the church, there is a view of the site of Terrasson: on the left, the slate roofs of the houses of the upper town spill down the hillside to the Vézère, spanned by two bridges; in the distance beyond the part of the town built on the right bank is the Périgord countryside with its characteristic lines of poplars, walnut plantations and rich arable land, slowly making room for poplars. The old bridge, Pont Vieux, was built in the 12C and is complete with cutwaters.

Between Terrasson-la-Villedieu and Condat, the road follows the valley floor before crossing to the right bank of the river. 3km – 2 miles after Condat, the river cuts through wooded slopes.

Montignac – *See Montignac.*

★★Lascaux II; Régourdou – *See Lascaux Cave.*

From Montignac to Les Eyzies the road closely follows the course of the river, which is lined with magnificent poplars. This is the most attractive part of the valley.

From the D 65, shortly after Montignac, the elegant outline of the Château de Losse can be seen towering above the Vézère between the trees.

Château de Losse ⊙ – This elegant 16C building set amidst greenery is perched high on a rock above the right bank of the River Vézère. A terrace adorned with a balustrade, supported by a fine basket-handled arch, projects in front of the main building, which is flanked by a round tower at one corner. Inside, there are splendid furnishings (16C Italian cupboards and coffers, Louis XIII furniture) and in particular **tapestries.** Note the fresh colours of the Flemish tapestry in the tower room and the Florentine tapestry depicting the *Return of the Courtesan* in the main chamber; both are 17C.

Sergeac – Pop 156. This village is pleasantly situated beside the Vézère at a spot where tall cliffs follow the line of the valley.

The village of Sergeac, which has an interesting and delicately carved 15C cross standing at its entrance, also contains old houses roofed with *lauzes* and a turreted manor-house, the remains of a commandery, which once belonged to the Order of St John of Jerusalem. The restored Romanesque **church**, despite its porch of fine ochre-coloured stone and recessed arches, still retains a fortified appearance with its loopholes, machicolations and belltower. A rounded triumphal arch supported by twinned columns opens onto the chancel, which has a flat east end, and is adorned with archaically carved capitals.

Castel-Merle – This site, which is well-known to the specialists, was for a long time closed to the public. Some of the finds – bones, flints, head-dresses – discovered are exhibited in the museums of Les Eyzies, Périgueux and St-Germain-en-Laye (west of Paris).

Near the site, a small local **museum** ⊘ exhibits a number of interesting artefacts from the Mousterian Age to the Gallo-Roman era. Note the handsome necklaces, found during the excavations, made of stone and bone beads, teeth and shells.

Several **shelters** *(abris)* ⊘ can be visited, one of which contains wall sculptures (bison, horses) of the Magdalenian Age. In the Souquette shelter a section of strata is shown with the different levels from the Aurignacian Age to the modern era.

The so-called **Fort of the English**, upstream, is a fine shelter under rock, rearranged in the Middle Ages, entered by a staircase carved into the rock. This is an astounding example of a troglodyte dwelling with living quarters, stables... Its location enabled its inhabitants, who occupied it during troubled times, to watch the Vézère.

★ **Le Thot** – *See Le Thot.*

Thonac – Pop 257. In the church there an emotive **Virgin in Majesty**★, made locally from polychrome wood *(photograph p 29)*.

La Vermondie Tower (Tour de la Vermondie) – This curious leaning tower, which, it is said, was demolished by the Saracens in 732, stands near a 15C manor-house on a hillside overlooking the Vézère. A delightful legend tells how, long ago, a young prince was held prisoner in the tower; every day his fiancée passed below; moved by the young people's misfortune, the tower leaned so low one day that the lovers were able to exchange kisses.

Plazac – Pop 543. The Romanesque church, in the centre of a churchyard planted with cypress trees, stands on a hillock overlooking the village. The 12C belfry-keep is roofed with *lauzes* and embellished with blind arcades resting on Lombard bands.

> *Return to Thonac. For this section of the itinerary between Thonac and Les Eyzies-de-Tayac see local map and text under Les Eyzies-de-Tayac.*

After Thonac, the road gives a succession of very pleasant views of typical Périgord landscapes: a background of meadows, a line of poplars or willows mirrored in smooth waters and tall, eroded white and grey cliffs, scattered with scrub and evergreen oaks. These caves, in some cases hanging over the road, served as shelters for prehistoric man. Such scenery is often to be found south of St-Léon-sur-Vézère, as for instance at St-Christopher's Rock, at Rusac and near Les-Eyzies-de-Tayac, with castles and manor-houses adding a touch of elegance.

★ **St-Léon-sur-Vézère** – *See St-Léon-sur Vézère.*

★ **St Christopher's Rock** – *See Les-Eyzies-de-Tayac: Sights: Along the Vézère River.*

Le Moustier – *See Les-Eyzies-de-Tayac: Sights: Along the Vézère River.*

Tursac – *See Les-Eyzies-de-Tayac: Sights: Along the Vézère River.*

★★ **Les Eyzies-de-Tayac** – *See Les-Eyzies-de-Tayac.*

Beyond Les Eyzies, the valley widens, the slopes become more gentle, and crops interspersed with plantations of walnut trees become more widespread.

Campagne – Pop 281. Facilities. At the opening of a small valley stands a small Romanesque church preceded by a belfry.

The **castle** of the lords of Campagne, built in the 15C, was restored in the 19C. The towers with crenellations and machicolations which flank the living quarters and the neo-Gothic elements give the castle the appearance of an English manor-house. The last Marquis de Campagne gave the castle to the state in 1970.

Le Bugue – *See Le Bugue.*

The D 703 in the direction of Bergerac and the D 31 towards Trémolat lead to the delightful country **chapel** (Chapelle St-Martin-*qv*), built at the end of the 12C.

Limeuil – *See Dordogne Valley* ④.

Terracotta figures (16C) used as finials
on roof cresting from the Château
de la Borde at Festalemps –
in the Périgord Museum, Périgueux

Practical
Information

Pech Merle Cave

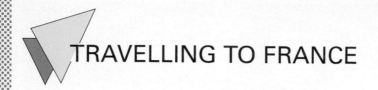

TRAVELLING TO FRANCE

Passport – Visitors entering France must be in possession of a valid national **passport** (or in the case of the British, a Visitor's Passport). In case or loss of theft report to the embassy or consulate and the local police.

Visa – An **entry visa** is required for Canadian and US citizens (for a stay of more than 3 months) and for Australian citizens in accordance with French security measures. Apply to the French Consulate (visa issued same day; delay if submitted by mail).
US citizens should obtain the booklet "Your Trip Abroad" ($1) which provides useful information on visa requirements, customs regulations, medical care etc for international travellers. Apply to the Superintendent of Documents, Government Printing Office, Washington DC 20402-9325.

Customs – Apply to the Customs Office (UK) for a leaflet ("A Guide for Travellers") on customs regulations and the full range of duty-free allowances. The US Treasury Department (☎ 202 566 8195) offers a publication "Know before you go" for US citizens. There are no customs formalities for holidaymakers bringing their caravans into France for a stay of less than 6 months. No customs document is necessary for pleasure boats and outboard motors for a stay of less than 6 months but the registration certificate should be kept on board.

By air – The various national and other independent airlines operate services to **Paris** (Charles de Gaulle and Orly). There are also package tour flights with a rail or coach link-up as well as Fly-Drive schemes. Information, brochures and timetables are available from the airlines and from travel agents.
The domestic network (Air Inter) operates frequent services covering the whole country. There are transfer buses to town terminals and to rail stations. Roissy-Rail and Orly-Rail operate fast rail links to the centre of Paris.

By sea – There are numerous **cross-Channel services** (passenger and car ferries, hovercraft, SeaCat) from the United Kingdom and Eire. For details apply to travel agencies or to:

P&O European Ferries, Channel House, Channel View Road, Dover CT17 9TJ; ☎ 0304 203388. Ticket collection: Russel St, Dover, Kent CT16 1QB.
The Continental Ferry Port, Mile End, Portsmouth, Hampshire PO2 8QW; ☎ 0705 827677.
Sealink, Charter House, Park Street, Ashford, Kent TN24 8EX; ☎ 0233 647047.
Hoverspeed, International Hoverport, Marine Parade, Dover, Kent CT17 9TG; ☎ 0304 240241.
Maybrook House, Queen's Gardens, Dover CT17 9UQ; ☎ direct line from London 554 7061, Birmingham 021 236 2190 or Manchester 061 228 1321.
Brittany Ferries, Millbay Docks, Plymouth, Devon PLI 3EW; ☎ 0752 221321.
The Brittany Centre, Wharf Road, Portsmouth, Hampshire PO2 8RU; ☎ 0705 827701.
Sally Line, 81 Piccadilly, London WIV 9HF; ☎ 071 409 2240.
Argyle Centre, York St, Ramsgate, Kent CT11 9DS; ☎ 0843 595522.

By rail – British Rail offers a range of services to the Channel ports, and French Railways operates an extensive network of lines including many high speed passenger trains and motorail services throughout France. There are rail passes (France Vacances Pass) offering unlimited travel and group travel tickets offering savings for parties. Eurorail Pass, Flexipass and Saver Pass are options available in the US for travel in Europe and must be purchased in the US – ☎ 212 308 3103 (information) and 1 800 223 636 (reservations). Tickets bought in France must be validated (*composter*) by using the orange automatic date-stamping machines at the platform entrance.
Information and bookings from French Railways, 179 Piccadilly, London WIV OBA; ☎ 071 409 3518 and from principal British and American Rail Travel Centres and travel agencies.
Baggage trolleys (10 F coin required-refundable) are available at main line stations.

By coach – Regular coach services are operated from London to Paris and to large provincial towns:

Hoverspeed, Maybrook House, Queens Gardens, Dover CT17 9UQ; ☎ 0304 240241.
Euroways/Eurolines, 52 Grosvenor Gardens, Victoria, London SWIW OAU; ☎ 071 730 8235.

MOTORING IN FRANCE

Documents – Nationals of EC countries require a valid national **driving licence**; nationals of non-EC countries require an **international driving licence** (obtainable in the US from the American Automobile Club).
For the vehicle it is necessary to have the **registration papers** (log-book) and a **nationality plate** of the approved size.

Insurance – Insurance cover is compulsory and although an International Insurance Certificate (Green Card) is no longer a legal requirement in France it is the most effective proof of insurance cover and is internationally recognised by the police and other authorities.

Certain UK motoring organisations (AA, RAC) run accident insurance and breakdown service schemes for members. Europ-Assistance (252 High St, Croydon CRO 1NF) has special policies for motorists. Members of the American Automobile Club should obtain the brochure "Offices to serve you abroad". Affiliated organisation for France: Association Française des Automobile-Clubs, 9 Rue Anatole-de-la-Forge, 75017 Paris. ☎ (1) 42 27 82 00.

Highway code – The minimum driving age is 18 years old. Traffic drives on the right.
It is compulsory for the front-seat passengers to wear **seat belts**; all back seat passengers should wear seat belts where they are fitted. Children under the age of ten should be on the back seat.
Full or dipped headlights must be switched on in poor visibility and at night; use sidelights only when the vehicle is stationary.
In the case of a **breakdown** a red warning triangle or hazard warning lights are obligatory.
Drivers should watch out for unfamiliar road signs and take great care on the road. In built-up areas **priority** must be ceded to vehicles joining the road from the right. However, traffic on main roads outside built-up areas and on roundabouts has priority. Vehicles must stop when the lights turn red at road junctions and may filter to the right only where indicated by an amber arrow.
The regulations on **drink-driving** and **speeding** are strictly enforced – usually by an on-the-spot fine and/or confiscation of the vehicle.

Speed limits – Although liable to modification these are as follows:
– toll motorways 130kph-80mph (110kph-68mph when raining);
– dual carriage roads and motorways without tolls 110kph-68mph (100kph-62mph when raining);
– other roads 90kph-56mph (80kph-50mph when raining) and in towns 50kph-31mph;
– outside lane on motorways during daylight, on level ground and with good visibility – minimum speed limit of 80kph (50mph).

Parking Regulations – In town there are restricted and paying **parking zones** (blue and grey zones); tickets must be obtained from the ticket machines (*horodateurs* – small change necessary) and displayed (inside windscreen on driver's side); failure to display may result in a heavy fine.

Route Planning – For 24-hour road traffic information: dial 48 94 33 33 or consult Minitel 3615 Code Route.
See page 3 for the **Michelin maps** covering the Dordogne region.
The road network is excellent and includes many motorways, mostly toll-roads (*autoroutes à péage*). The roads are very busy during the holiday period (particularly weekends in July and August) and to avoid traffic congestion it is advisable to follow the recommended secondary routes (Bison Futé-itinéraires bis).

Car Rental – There are car rental agencies at airports, air terminals, railway stations and in all large towns throughout France. European cars usually have manual transmission but automatic cars are available on demand. An **international driving licence** is required for non-EC nationals.
Fly-drive schemes are operated by major airlines.

TRAVELLING TO THE DORDOGNE

By road – Use Michelin Motoring Atlas France, or see page 3 for which Michelin maps cover the region (scale 1:200 000).

By rail – Fast inter-city service from Paris to Périgueux on the TGV Paris-Angoulême, then take the express coach service from Angoulême to Périgueux (four daily return trips, total journey time: 4 hours). From Paris to Cahors, daily fast train connection "Le Capitole" (journey time: 5 hours).

By air – Three daily return trips from Paris to Périgueux (flight time: 1 hour 15 min), two from Paris to Bergerac (flight time: 1 hour 25 min) and from Paris to Brive (flight time: 1 hour 15 min).

Quercy Blanc countryside around Lauzerte

ACCOMMODATION

Places to stay – The map of places to stay (*p 8*) indicates recommended places for over-night stops and may be used in conjunction with the **Michelin Red Guide France. Loisirs Accueil** is an officially-backed booking service which has offices in most French *départements*. For information contact Réservation Loisirs Accueil, 2 Rue Linois, 75015 Paris; ☎ 40 59 44 12.

The '**Accueil de France**' tourist offices, which are open all year, make hotel bookings for a small fee for personal callers only. The head office is in Paris (127 Avenue des Champs-Élysées; ☎ 49 52 53 54 for information only) and there are offices in many large towns and resorts.

The brochure 'Logis et Auberges de France' is available from the French Government Tourist Office.

Rural accommodation – Apply to Maison des Gîtes de France, 35 Rue Godot-de Mauroy, 75009 Paris, (☎ 47 42 20 20), or 178 Piccadilly, London W1V OAL (☎ 071 493 3480), or Maison du Périgord, 6 rue Comboust, 75001 Paris, (☎ 47 03 42 57), or the Service Loisirs-Accueil of the local *(département)* tourist offices for a list of relevant addresses.

Bed and Breakfast – Gîtes de France (*see above*) publishes a booklet on bed and break-fast accommodation (*chambre d'hôtes*).

On a local scale, "country farmhouse breaks" (*vacances vertes*) are organised by a number of local tourist offices (*syndicats d'initiative*) and other associations:

"Bienvenue à la ferme en Sarladais", Maison de l'Agriculture, place de la Grande Rigaudie, 24200 Sarlat-la-Canéda, ☎ 53 59 41 56.

"Bienvenue à la ferme à Ribérac et dans la riante vallée de la Dronne" (syndicat d'initia-tive de Ribérac, ☎ 53 90 03 10) etc.

Youth Hostels – There are many youth hostels (*auberges de jeunesse*) throughout France. Holders of an International Youth Hostel Federation card should apply for a list from the International Federation or from the French Youth Hostels Association, 38 Boulevard Raspail, 75007 Paris. ☎ 45 48 69 84.

Members of American Youth Hostels should call ☎ 202 783 6161 for information on budget accommodation.

Camping – There are numerous officially graded sites with varying standards of facili-ties throughout the Dordogne region. The **Michelin Guide Camping Caravaning France** lists a selection of camping sites. An International Camping Carnet for caravans is useful but not compulsory; it may be obtained from the motoring organisations or the Camping and Caravanning Club (11 Lower Grosvenor Place, London SW1).

Those in search of the outdoor life (walking, pony-trekking, cycling, canoeing etc.) should consult the guidebook (in French) *Gîtes et Refuges, France et Frontières*, by A and S Mouraret, pub La Cadole, BP 303, 75723 Paris Cedex 15.

GENERAL INFORMATION

Electricity – The electric current is 220 volts. Circular two pin plugs are the rule – an electrical adaptor may be necessary.

Medical treatment – First aid, medical advice and chemists' night service rota are avai-lable from chemists (*pharmacie* – green cross sign).

It is advisable to take out comprehensive insurance cover as the recipient of medical treatment in French hospitals or clinics must pay the bill. Nationals of non-EC countries should check with their insurance companies about policy limitations. Reimbursement can then be negotiated with the insurance company according to the policy held.

American Express offers a service, "Global Assist", for any medical, legal or personal emergency – call collect from anywhere ☎ 202 554 2639.

British citizens should apply to the Department of Health and Social Security for **Form E 111**, which entitles the holder to urgent treatment for accident or unexpected illness in EC countries. A refund of part of the costs of treatment can be obtained on appli-cation in person or by post to the local Social Security offices (Caisse Primaire d'Assurance Maladie).

Currency – There are no restrictions on the amount of currency visitors can take into France. To facilitate the export from France of currency in foreign banknotes in excess of the given allocation visitors are advised to complete a currency declaration form on arrival.

Banks – Banks are open from 0900 to 1200 and 1400 to 1600 and are closed on Monday or Saturday (except if market day); some branches open for limited transactions on Saturday. Banks close early on the day before a bank holiday. A passport is necessary as identification when cashing cheques in banks. Commission charges vary and hotels usually charge more than banks for cashing cheques for non-residents.

Most banks have cash dispensers which accept international credit cards.

Credit Cards – American Express, Carte Bleue (Visa/Barclaycard), Diners Club and Eurocard (Mastercard/Access) are widely accepted in shops, hotels and restaurants and petrol stations.

Post – Post Offices open Monday to Friday 0800 to 1900, Saturday 0800 to 1200. Postage via air mail to: UK letter or postcard 2.80 F; US aerogramme 5.00 F; letter (20g) 4.30 F; postcard 4.00 F. Stamps are also available from newsagents and tobacconists.

Poste Restante mail should be addressed as follows: Name, *Poste Restante*, *Poste Centrale*, *département* postal code followed by town name, *France*. The **Michelin Red Guide France** gives local postal codes.

Telephone – Public phones using pre-paid phone cards (*télécarte*) are in operation in many areas. The cards (50 or 120 units), which are available from post offices, tobacconists and newsagents, can be used for inland and international calls. Calls can be received at phone boxes where the blue bell sign is shown.

Internal calls – When calling within either of the two main zones (French provinces and Paris and its region) dial only the 8 digit correspondent's number. From Paris to the provinces dial 16 + 8 digit number. From the provinces to Paris dial 16 + 1 + 8 digit number. The French ringing tone is a series of long tones (slightly longer than those of the British engaged tone); the French engaged (busy) tone is a series of short pips.

International calls – For Paris dial the country code 33 + 1 + 8 digit number. For the provinces the country code 33 + 8 digit number.

When calling abroad from France dial 19, wait until the continuous tone recurs, then dial the country code and dialling code and number of your correspondent. For international enquiries dial 19 33 12 + country code.

Telephone rates from a public telephone at any time are: Paris-London: about 5.60 F for 1 minute; Paris-New York: 10.30 F for 1 minute. Cheap rates with 50 % extra time are available from private telephones on weekdays between 2230 and 0800, at weekends starting at 1400 on Saturdays.

Shopping – The big stores and larger shops are open Monday to Saturday, 0900 to 1830-1930, Smaller, individual shops may close during the lunch hour. Food shops – grocers, wine merchants and bakeries – are open from 0700 to 1830-1930; some open on Sunday mornings. Many food shops close between 1200 and 1400 and on Mondays. Hypermarkets usually open until 2100-2200.

Public holidays – The following are days when museums and other monuments may be closed or may vary their hours of admission:

New Year's Day	France's National Day (**14 July**)
Easter Sunday and Monday	Assumption (**15 August**)
May Day (**1 May**)	All Saint's Day (**1 November**)
V E Day (**8 May**)	Armistice (**11 November**)
Ascension Day	Christmas Day
Whit Sunday and Monday	

National museums and art galleries are closed on Tuesdays whereas municipal museums are closed on Mondays.

In addition to the usual school holidays at Christmas and in the spring and summer, there are long mid-term breaks (10 days to a fortnight) in February and early November.

Embassies and Consulates

Australia	Embassy	4 Rue Jean-Rey, 75015 Paris, ☎ 40 59 33 00.
Canada	Embassy	35 Avenue Montaigne, 75008 Paris, ☎ 44 43 32 00.
Eire	Embassy	4 Rue Rude, 75016 Paris, ☎ 45 00 20 87.
New Zealand	Embassy	7 ter Rue Léonard-de-Vinci, 75016 Paris, ☎ 45 00 24 11.
UK	Embassy	35 Rue du Faubourg St-Honoré, 75008 Paris, ☎ 42 66 91 42.
	Consulate	16 Rue d'Anjou, 75008 Paris, ☎ 42 66 38 10 (visas).
		9 Avenue Hoche, 75008 Paris, ☎ 42 66 38 10.
USA	Embassy	2 Avenue Gabriel, 75008 Paris, ☎ 42 96 12 02.
	Consulate	2 Rue St-Florentin, 75001 Paris, ☎ 42 96 14 88.

Every year

*the **Michelin Red Guide France***
revises its selection of stars for cuisine (good cooking)
accompanied by a mention of the culinary specialities and local wines
and proposes a choice of simpler restaurants offering
a well-prepared meal, often with regional specialities, for a moderate price.

TOURIST INFORMATION

French Government Tourist Offices – For information, brochures, maps and assistance in planning a trip to France travellers should apply to the official tourist office in their own country:

Australia

Sydney – Kindersley House, 33 Bligh St, Sydney, New South Wales 2000. ☎ 612 231 52 44.

Canada

Toronto – 1 Dundas St, West Suite 2405 Box 8, Toronto, Ontario M5G IZ3. ☎ 416 593 47 23.

Montreal – 1981 Ave McGill College, Suite 490, Montreal, Quebec H3-A2 W9. ☎ 514 288 42 64.

Eire

Dublin – c/o 38 Lower Abbey St, Dublin. ☎ (01) 300 777.

United Kingdom

London – 178 Piccadilly, London WIV OAL. ☎ 071 499 6911 (24-hour answering service with recorded message and information) or 071 491 7622 (urgent enquiries only).

United States

Toll-free number – Dial 900 420 2003 for information on hotels, restaurants and transportation.

Middle West: Chicago – 645 North Michigan Avenue, Suite 630, Chicago, Illinois 60611. ☎ 312 337 6301.

East Coast: New York – 610 Fifth Avenue, Suite 222, New York 10020-2452. ☎ 212 757 1125.

West Coast: Los Angeles – 9454 Wilshire Boulevard, Suite 303, Beverly Hills, California 90212. ☎ 213 272 2661.

South: Dallas – 2305 Cedar Spring Road, Suite 205, Dallas, Texas 75201. ☎ 214 720 4010.

Département Tourist Offices – Fédération Nationale des Comités Départmentaux de Tourisme, 2 rue Linois, 75015 Paris. ☎ (1) 45 75 62 16.

Office Départemental du Tourisme de Dordogne, 16 rue Wilson, 24009 Périgueux, ☎ 53 53 44 35.

Comité Départemental du Tourisme du Lot, Chambre de Commerce, 107 quai Cavaignac, 46001 Cahors Cedex, ☎ 65 35 07 09.

Office Départemental du Tourisme de Corrèze, Maison du Tourisme, Quai Baluze, 19000 Tulle, ☎ 55 26 39 99.

Office Départemental du Tourisme du Tarn-et-Garonne, Hôtel des Intendants, Place du Maréchal-Foch, 82000 Montauban, ☎ 63 63 31 40.

Tourist Information Centres – The addresses and telephone numbers of the tourist information centres (syndicats d'initiative) of most large towns and tourist resorts may be found among the Admission Times and Charges at the end of this section and in the **Michelin Red Guide France**. They can supply large scale town plans, timetables and information on local entertainment facilities, sports and sightseeing.

Minitel – The French Telecom videotex service offers a wide variety of information and can be consulted at post offices, libraries etc. (*fee charged: 1.27 F/min*). Minitel terminals are installed in hotel chains and certain petrol stations throughout the country. Listed below are some of the telematic services offered:

3615 PERIGORD	local tourist information (in French)
3615 QUERCY	
3615 TCAMP	camping information
3615 METEO	weather report
3615 or 3616 HORAV	general airline information and flight schedules
3615 BBC	BBC news
3615 LIBE	USA TODAY
3615 MICHELIN	Michelin tourist and route information

Local radio – These usually give frequent updates on traffic, local demonstrations or other disturbances, as well as information on local cultural events. Listed below are some of the stations available on FM:

Radio-France Périgord; 89.1 at Sarlat, 94.6 at Périgueux, 99.0 at Bergerac.

Radio-Vicomte (Brive); 103.9.

Radio-Emeraude (Périgord Vert); 104.1.

Tourism for the Disabled – Some of the sights described in this guide are accessible to handicapped people. They are listed in the publication 'Touristes quand même ! Promenades en France pour les Voyageurs Handicapés' published by the Comité National Français de Liaison pour la Réadaptation des Handicapés (38 Boulevard Raspail, 75007 Paris, ☎ 45 48 90 13). This booklet covers nearly 90 towns in France and provides practical information for people who suffer reduced mobility or visual or aural impairment.

The **Michelin Red Guide France** and the **Michelin Camping Caravaning France** indicate hotels and camping sites with facilities suitable for physically handicapped people.

RECREATION: NEW DISCOVERIES

There are all sorts of "original" travel opportunites open to those visitors who are not pressed for time, which allow the best possible appreciation of the wealth of local art, life and countryside in the Dordogne.

Trips with a theme – Some tourist offices have worked out tourist routes based on particular themes; they also provide information to enable visitors to take advantage of such trips under their own steam:
Promenades littéraires en Périgord (Literary trips in Périgord), Office départemental de tourisme de la Dordogne, 16 rue Wilson, 24009 Périgueux Cedex, ☎ 53 53 44 35.
Circuit Jacquou le Croquant (On the trail of Jacquou le Croquant), Syndicat d'initiative de Périgueux, Rond-point de la Tour Mataguerre, 26 place Francheville, ☎ 53 53 10 63.
Route historique des Mille et un Châteaux du Périgord (Historical trip round the Dordogne's 1 001 castles), same address as above.
Route du tabac, de Bergerac à Sarlat (The tobacco trail; from Bergerac to Sarlat), Centre de formation et de perfectionnement des planteurs de tabac, avenue Paul-Painlevé, 24100 Bergerac, ☎ 53 57 49 33.
Route du vin de Cahors (Cahors wine route), Comité départemental du tourisme du Lot, 107 quai Cavaignac, 46001 Cahors Cedex, ☎ 65 35 07 09.
Route historique des Marches de Quercy (Historical trip round the marchlands of Quercy), same address as above.
Circuit des églises à coupoles du Ribéracois (Tour of domed churches around Ribérac), Syndicat d'initiative de Ribérac, ☎ 53 90 03 10.

Down on the farm – There are guided tours of farms (take own car) organised by the following *syndicats d'initiative*:
Ribérac (Tuesday afternoons 15 June-15 September, ☎ 53 90 03 10)
Brantôme (Wednesday afternoons July-August, ☎ 53 05 80 52)
Saint-Astier (Friday afternoons 12 July-30 August, ☎ 53 54 13 85)
Maison de l'Agriculture, place de la Grande Rigaudie, **Sarlat** (July-August, ☎ 53 59 41 56)
These visits sometimes include the chance to taste local farm produce.

Bus trips – These half-day or day trips avoid taking the more popular routes, in favour of undertaking interesting voyages of discovery, on themes such as old villages, the Dordogne people and their roots etc. Contact the tourist office at **Sarlat** (☎ 53 59 27 67) or at **Les Eyzies** (☎ 53 06 97 05) for further information.

Riding – Rides with or without a guide leave from **Festalemps**, **Monpazier** or **Alles-sur-Dordogne**, staying overnight in two-star hotels (about 4 500 F per week) or in guest rooms/holiday cottages (about 3 500 F per week). Information available from the Dordogne Tourist Office, 16 rue Wilson, 24009 Périgueux Cedex, ☎ 53 53 44 35.
The Dordogne Tourists' Riding Association (*L'Association de Tourisme équestre de la Dordogne*, Chambre d'Agriculture, 4-6 place Francheville, 24000 Périgueux, ☎ 53 09 26 26) and its equivalent in the Lot *département* (BP 7, 46002 Cahors Cedex, ☎ 65 35 07 09) have further addresses. The Lot association has a regional map (*Carte Départementale de la Randonnée*, which is also available in bookshops, showing the route of GR (*Grande Randonnée*) footpaths and bridle paths on a scale of 1:200 000.

Horse-drawn carriages – Day trips are offered by the following companies; Périgord en calèches (24550 Mazeyrolles-près-Monpazier, ☎ 53 29 98 99), Relais de Bellemire (46200 Lacave, ☎ 65 37 05 85) and Tourisme Attelé Diffusion (46120 Aynac, ☎ 65 38 93 16).

Caravans – Visit the Dordogne in a fully-equipped (bunk-beds, basic kitchen facilities), horse-drawn caravan! These trips cover about 15-20km or 9-12 miles a day, leaving from "Beauvignière" (at **Quinsac**, in the **Périgord Vert**) and "Faurilles" (at **Issigeac**, in the **Bergerac region**). Average price in high season is 4 500F. Further information from the Dordogne Tourist Office, 16 rue Wilson, 24009 Périgueux Cedex, ☎ 53 53 44 35.
In Quercy, contact Roulottes du Quercy (46700 Sérignac, ☎ 65 31 96 44).

Rambling – There are many GR footpaths crisscrossing the Dordogne region: GR 6 (Alps-Atlantic Ocean), GR 65 (Le Puy-Santiago de Compostela), GR 36 (Channel-Pyrénées), GR 46 (Limousin and Quercy regions), to name but a few.
The Topo-guides to the GR footpaths are published by the *Fédération Française de la Randonnée pédestre-Comité National des sentiers de Grande Randonnée* and can be bought from the Information Centre, 64 rue de Gergovie, 75014 Paris, ☎ 45 45 31 02.
There is a collection of seven small guides to walks in the Quercy region (*Promenades et Randonnées*), each describing 20-30 short walks: From Lot to Célé, Ségala Garden, Gramat Causse, Bouriane, Lower Quercy, Lower Lot Valley and Dordogne Valley. They are available from bookshops or from the Lot tourist authorities (BP 7, 46001 Cahors Cedex, ☎ 65 35 07 09), which also produces an interesting leaflet on the Lot river paths (*Le Lot – les chemins de la rivière*) which gives a selection of walks leaving from moorings.
Many local districts restore, create and maintain footpaths and produce information to enable tourists to take full and independent advantage of them (St-Antonin-Noble-Val and Montignac, for example). Contact the local tourist offices or town halls for information.

An off-beat idea – How about a walk with a donkey for company (and to carry the bags)? Contact Picotin and Constant (St-Avit-Vialard, 24260 Le Bugue, ☎ 53 07 15 40) or the Fédération Nationale Anes et Randonnées (Ladevèze, 49090 Coux, ☎ 65 31 42 79).

Cycling – There may not be any actual cycle paths in the Dordogne, but there are great stretches of roads and footpaths which have been salvaged in the face of increasing density of traffic and set aside for the exclusive use of cyclists. Local tourist offices have lists of addresses of cycle hire outlets, which include the SNCF railway stations at Bergerac, Le Bugue, Cahors, Gourdon, Gramat, Rocamadour-Padirac, Sarlat and Souillac. The pamphlet *Cyclotourisme en Périgord* (available from Dordogne Tourist Office, 16 rue Wilson, 24009 Périgueux Cedex, ☎ 53 53 44 35) contains suggested routes for the Dordogne region, as does *Connaître et savourer le Périgord* by Claire Gérardin (available from kiosks or Gérardin Books, BP 2056, 24002 Périgueux Cedex). The Topo-guide *Cyclotourisme en Quercy* is also available from bookshops, tourist offices of the Lot *département*, as well as from the Comité départemental de cyclotourisme du Lot, avenue de la Dordogne, 46600 Martel.

Canoeing – The peaceful waters of the rivers in the Dordogne region are ideally suited for visitors to explore the beautiful castles and other sights spread along the region's valleys by canoe. Sailing bases welcome beginners and experienced canoeists alike (hire of a canoe for two costs 50-90F per hour, or 130-200F per day). The bases listed below are affiliated with the French Canoeing Association (*Fédération française de Canoë-Kayak*):

On the Dordogne; bases at **Vézac** (SNCF bridge, ☎ 53 29 54 27) and **Bergerac** (AOL Canoë-Kayak, promenade Pierre-Loti, ☎ 53 27 20 05).
On the Vézère; at **Montignac** (Nouveau Pont, ☎ 53 51 91 14).
On the Célé; at **Liauzu** (Les Amis de Célé, 46300 Orniac, ☎ 65 31 32 17).
On the Lot; at **Caïx** (CPL, 46140 Luzech, ☎ 65 20 11 30).
Topo-guides: *Descente du Célé, Descente de la Dordogne* and *Descente du Lot*. All available from bookshops and tourist offices in the Lot *département*, or from the Comité départemental du tourisme du Lot, 107 quai Cavaignac, 46001 Cahors Cedex, ☎ 65 35 07 09.

Dordogne Valley at Belcastel

House-boats – Add a little more zest to a visit to the Quercy region by spending a few days on the river Lot in a house-boat (no need for a special licence; cost for four people for a week in high-season is 7 000-10 000F). As a further incentive, a section of the Lot's locks has recently been opened to boat traffic.
House-boats can be hired from the following companies:
Blue Line (Le Grand Bassin, BP 21, 11400 Castelnaudary, ☎ 68 28 17 51, base **Douelle**)
Locaboat Plaisance (quai du Port-au-Bois, 89300 Joigny, ☎ 86 91 72 72, base **Luzech**)
Babou Marine (Port-St-Mary, 46000 Cahors, ☎ 65 30 08 99, base **Cahors**)
Safaraid (46140 Albas, ☎ 65 36 23 54, base **Bouziès**)
Details of **boat sight-seeing trips** up the Lot, Dordogne and Dronne rivers are given in the Admissions Times and Charges section of the guide.

Swimming – There are beaches along the rivers, but beware of the currents, which can be quite strong. Several new water sports centres have sprung up quite recently, with water chutes, wave machines and so on. The main ones are given in the Admission Times and Charges section of the guide.

Sailing and Wind-surfing – Some stretches of water allow these activities, notably the Jemaye Lake in the Double region, the Causse lake near Brive, the Tauriac, Trémolat and Mauzac reservoirs on the Dordogne and the Cajarc and Luzech reservoirs on the Lot.

Caving and Pot-holing – The Dordogne region with its limestone relief pitted with caves and caverns is a speleologist's paradise.

Lot: contact the Comité départemental de spéléologie, J R Broqua, 46230 Bach, ☎ 65 31 70 81

Dordogne: contact Randonnée Dordogne, Le Port de Domme-Cénac, 24250 Domme, ☎ 53 28 22 01.

Fishing – Beautiful stretches of river in categories one and two are open to anglers of all levels. Further information can be obtained from local angling associations (*Fédérations départementales des associations agréées de pêche et de pisciculture*; in the **Lot**: 182 quai Cavaignac, 46000 Cahors, ☎ 65 35 50 22, in the **Dordogne**: 2 rue Antoine-Gadaud, 24000 Périgueux, ☎ 53 53 44 21, in the **Corrèze**: 1 avenue Winston-Churchill, 19000 Tulle, ☎ 55 26 11 55).

Courses in local cookery – These take place between October and April (without exception) and last for a weekend. Those who wish to learn how to make *confits*, *foies gras* and traditional desserts can do this at farms while staying in guest rooms (average cost: 700-1 000F). The following list of addresses is not exclusive:

Maison du Plein-Air et de la Randonnée, 16 rue Fénelon, 24000 Sarlat, ☎ 53 31 24 18 (Périgord cuisine).

M Alard, La Maurinie, 24330 Eyliac, ☎ 53 07 57 18 (traditional cuisine with duck).

MJ Archer, La Barabie, route de St-Alvère, 24520 Lamonzie-Montastruc, ☎ 53 23 22 47 (how to cook *foie gras*, *confit* and with truffles).

D and G Dubois, Peyrenègre, 24120 La Dornac, ☎ 53 51 04 24 (courses all year round; how to cook duck, introduction to truffle beds).

E Coustatie, Boyer, 24240 Meyrals, ☎ 53 29 24 83 (one-week courses available; how to cook duck).

Loisirs-Accueil Lot, 5 rue Bourseul, BP 162, 46003 Cahors Cedex, ☎ 65 22 19 20 (courses in Quercy regional cuisine: *foies gras*, *confits*, desserts, at Moncabrier or Marcilhac-sur-Célé).

Still life

FAIRS AND MARKETS

Not to be missed during a visit to the Dordogne are some of the fairs and specialist agricultural markets, which are worth seeing for their originality, the quality of their produce and their lively embodiment of local traditions.

Main Fairs

Beginning of January
Brive .... Epiphany Fair
Périgueux .... Epiphany Fair

Last Sunday in March
Latronquière .... Wood Fair

30 April/1 May
La Latière (St-Aulaye) .... Horse Fair
Aubazine .... Goat Fair

1 May
Calès .... Flower Fair

7 June
Souillac .... Rag-tag and Bobtail Fair

Whit Sunday
Rocamadour .... Cheese Fair

23 July
Martel .... Wool Fair

First Monday in August
Hautefort .... Turkey Fair

Beginning of August
Lalinde .... Wine Fair

15 August
Duravel .... Wine Fair

SPECIALIST AGRICULTURAL MARKETS

Walnut, chestnut and mushroom markets tend to be held around October and November, *marchés aux gras* (fattened up poultry, *foies gras* etc.) between November and March, truffle markets between December and March and strawberry markets between April and November. The main markets are listed in the Admission Times and Charges section of the guide and on the map (*see Introduction: Dordogne's Homegrown Gastronomy*).

A traditional festival: the Félibrée

Every year in July a different town in Périgord hosts the Félibrée, a meeting of a society of poets and writers set up in the late 19C with the aim of preserving the Provençal language. The chosen town is decorated with thousands of multi-coloured paper flowers around all the windows and doors and brightening up trees and shrubs to form triumphal arches. The people of Périgord flock from all corners of the département decked out in traditional costume; lace head-dresses, embroidered shawls and long skirts for the women, huge black felt hats, full white shirts and black velvet waistcoats for the men.

The queen of the Félibrée, surrounded by a member of the Félibrige society committee and the guardians of the local traditions, receives the keys to the town and makes a speech in the local dialect. Then the assembled gathering files off in procession to Mass, accompanied by the sound of hurdy-gurdies, before sitting down to a sumptuous feast. Traditionally the meal begins with chabrol, a soup of wine and clear stock typical of the southwest, which is drunk from plates made especially for the occasion and bearing the name and year of the Félibrée. Everyone present keeps these plates as a souvenir, and they can be seen hanging in numerous homes or in museums of local art such as that at Mussidan (qv).

CALENDAR OF EVENTS

End May
Sarlat .... Fête de la Ringueta, traditional games (every two years: 1993, 95, etc.) ☎ 53 59 27 67

First fortnight in June
Cahors .... Springtime for photography ☎ 65 22 07 32

Mid-June to mid-September
Beaulieu-en-Rouergue .... Contemporary Art Exhibition ☎ 63 67 06 84
Cajarc .... Contemporary Art Exhibition ☎ 65 40 71 50

July
Terrasson .... Puppet Festival ☎ 53 36 42 17
Sarlat .... Festival of Symphonic Music ☎ 53 31 53 34
Rocamadour .... Theatre Festival
Brive .... Folklore Festival ☎ 55 24 06 44
Bergerac .... Foodlovers' Festival, "Cyrano's Table"

Mid-July
Allas-les-Mines .... Grand Thresher Festival
Cahors .... Blues Festival ☎ 65 35 09 56
Souillac .... "Sim Copans" Jazz Festival ☎ 65 37 04 93

End July to beginning of August
Domme .... Medieval Spectacular: "The Great Art of Minstrelsy"
Montignac .... Folklore and Friendship
Sarlat .... Theatre Festival ☎ 53 31 10 83

July to August
Brantôme .... Concerts of Classical Music
Gourdon .... Summer Encounters (theatre and concerts)
Périgord Noir .... Music Festival in abbeys, churches and castles ☎ 53 50 18 39
Ribérac .... Festival of Words and Music from the Ribérac region ☎ 53 90 03 10
Brive and Brive area .... Vézère Festival

Mid-July to mid-August
St-Céré .... Festival of Music and Opera ☎ 65 38 29 08
St-Robert .... Concerts of Classical Music ☎ 55 25 11 05

First fortnight in August
Bonaguil .... Music Festival ☎ 53 71 13 70
Périgueux .... "Mimos" Mime Festival ☎ 53 53 55 17

Mid-August
Rocamadour .... Festival of the Assumption, Torch-lit Procession
St-Amand-de-Coly .... Horn Concert and St Hubert Mass

August
Aubazine .... Concerts of Sacred Music
In the Quercy region .... Quercy Blanc Music Festival ☎ 63 02 07 64

First fortnight in September
Notre-Dame-du-Capelou .... Annual Pilgrimage
Rocamadour .... Annual Pilgrimage
Rocamadour .... Festival of Poetry in the French language

End September to beginning of October
Meyrals .... Wine Harvest Festival
Périgueux .... "Sinfonia en Périgord"

First weekend in November
Brive .... Book Fair ☎ 55 92 39 39

Christmas Eve
Lacapelle-Cabanac .... Midnight Mass in Occitan, live Nativity Crib

ADMISSION TIMES AND CHARGES

As times and charges for admission are liable to alteration, the information below is given for guidance only.

The information applies to individual adults. However, special conditions regarding times and charges for parties are common and arrangements should be made in advance. In some cases admission is free on certain days, eg Wednesdays, Sundays or public holidays.

Churches do not admit visitors during services and are usually closed from 1200 to 1400. Tourists should refrain from visits when services are being held. Admission times are indicated if the interior is of special interest. Visitors to chapels are accompanied by the person who keeps the keys. A donation is welcome.

If facilities for the disabled are available at a particular sight, this is indicated below by the symbol ♿ under the sight.

Some towns organise guided tours regularly during the tourist season. This is mentioned below with the details of each town for which this is the case. Visitors should apply to the local tourist office for details.

When guided tours are indicated, the departure time of the last tour of the morning or evening will be up to an hour before the actual closing time. Most tours are conducted by French-speaking guides, and in some cases the term "guided tours" may cover group visits with recorded commentaries. Some of the larger and more frequented sights may offer guided tours in English or other languages. Enquire at the ticket office or bookshop. There are often other aids available for foreign visitors, such as notes, leaflets or audio-guides.

When parking your car in unattended car parks or isolated places, please make sure to leave no valuables in the car.

Every sight for which there are specific admission times and charges is followed by the symbol ⏲ in the main part of the Guide.

A

AGONAC

Église St-Martin – Guided tours in July and August Monday to Friday from 1630 to 1800; contact the incumbent *(M. le Curé)*.

ALLASSAC

Discover the Yssandon Region

Perpezac-le-Blanc Astropole – Open July and August daily; observation of the sky until 0200-0300.

ANS COUNTRY

Round tour

Auriac-du-Périgord Bee Museum – Open April to October daily from 1000 to 1200 and from 1430 to 1900; admission free.

LES ARQUES

Zadkine Museum – 15 June to 15 September open daily from 1000 to 1900; otherwise weekends and public holidays only from 1400 to 1800; 15F; ☎ 65 22 83 27.

Église St-Laurent – Open summer from 1000 to 1900; otherwise afternoons only.

Église St-André-des-Arques – Guided tours July and August Tuesdays and Fridays from 1500 to 1800.

ASSIER

Castle – Guided tours (45 min) July and August daily from 0930 to 1830; April to June and in September daily (except Tuesdays) from 0900 to 1200 and from 1400 to 1800; otherwise open daily from 1000 to 1200 and from 1400 to 1700, closed Tuesdays, 1 January, 1 May, 1 and 11 November, 25 December; 20F; ☎ 65 40 40 99.

AUBAZINE

Conventual Buildings – Guided tours (45 min) July and August Tuesdays to Sundays at 1100, 1530 and 1630; in June and September at 1100 and 1600; otherwise at 1600; closed Mondays and in January; 15F; ☎ 55 84 61 12.

B

BEAULIEU-EN-ROUERGUE

Abbey – Guided tours (30 min) from Palm Sunday to end September daily (except Tuesdays) from 1000 to 1200 and from 1430 to 1800; closed 1 May; 20F; ☎ 63 67 06 84.

BELVÈS

Walnut Market – October to mid-December on Wednesdays.

Castrum Museum – Open July and August daily (except Tuesdays); 30F; ☎ 53 29 12 43.

BERGERAC

🛈 97, rue Neuve d'Argentan, ☎ 53 57 03 11

Guided tours of the town – Apply to the tourist office (at least 10 people).

Boat trips on the Dordogne – May to October daily leaving every half hour from the Old Port.

Tobacco Museum – ♿ Guided tours (45 min) Tuesdays to Saturdays from 1000 to 1200 and from 1400 to 1800; Sundays from 1430 to 1830; closed Mondays; 15F; ☎ 53 63 04 13.

Museum of Urban History – Same admission times and charges as for Tobacco Museum above; ☎ 53 57 80 92.

Recollects' Cloisters and Wine Centre – Guided tours July and August daily (except Sundays) from 0900 to 1200 and from 1300 to 1800; 10F; ☎ 53 57 12 57.

Wine, Shipping and Cooperage Museum – ♿ Open Tuesdays to Fridays from 1000 to 1200 and from 1400 to 1730, Saturdays from 1000 to 1200; closed Sundays, Mondays and public holidays; 5F; ☎ 53 57 80 92.

Museum of Sacred Art – Open during spring and summer school holidays (guided tours available) daily (except Monday) from 1500 to 1830; otherwise Wednesdays and Sundays only; 10F; ☎ 53 57 33 21.

Excursions: Caudau Valley

Vergt Strawberry Market – Mid-April to mid-November on Fridays.

BESSE

Excursion

Villefranche-du-Périgord Chestnut and Mushroom Market – September to November on Saturdays.

Villefranche-du-Périgord Chestnut Tree, Chestnut and Mushroom Centre – Open June to September daily from 0900 to 1200 and from 1500 to 1900 (mornings only on Sundays and Mondays); otherwise Saturdays from 0900 to 1200; 20F; ☎ 53 29 98 37.

BEYNAC-ET-CAZENAC

🛈 La Balme, ☎ 53 29 43 08

Guided tours of medieval village – July and August evenings; contact the tourist office.

Barge trips on the Dordogne – June to October daily from 1000 to 2000; departures every half hour from the car park.

Castle – Guided tours (50 min) May to September daily from 1000 to 1200 and from 1430 to 1800; in March, April and October from 1000 to 1200 and from 1430 to 1730; 1 to 15 November from 1400 to 1630; dogs admitted; ☎ 53 29 50 40.

Museum of Proto-History and Archaeological Park – Open July and August daily from 1000 to 1900; combined ticket 25F; ☎ 53 29 51 28.

BIRON

Castle – Guided tours (1 hour) 1 July to 7 September daily from 0900 to 1200 and from 1400 to 1900; February to June and 8 September to mid-December daily (except Tuesdays) from 1000 (0930 April to June and 8 September to mid-October) to 1200 and from 1400 to 1700 (1800 April to June and 8 September to mid-October); 25F; ☎ 53 63 13 39.

BONAGUIL

Castle – Guided tours (1 hour 30 min) June to August daily from 1000 to 1745; 16 February to 31 May and September to November from 1030 to 1430 and from 1530 to 1630; 25F; ☎ 53 71 05 22.

Les BORIES

Castle – Guided tours (30 min) July to September daily from 0900 to 1200 and from 1400 to 1900; April to June and in October by appointment only; ☎ 53 06 00 01; donations at visitors' discretion.

BOURDEILLES

Castle – Guided tours (45 min) 1 July to 7 September daily from 0900 to 1200 and from 1400 to 1900; February to June and 8 September to mid-December daily (except Tuesdays) from 1000 (0930 April to June and 8 September to mid-October) to 1200 and from 1400 to 1700 (1800 April to June and 8 September to mid-October); 25F; ☎ 53 03 73 36.

BOURIANE

Round Tour

Catus Priory Chapter-house – Open April to September daily from 0900 to 1900; otherwise from 0900 to 1800; admission free.

BRANTÔME
🖪 Pavillon Renaissance, ☎ 53 05 80 52

Guided tours of the town – July and August on Saturdays; contact the tourist office.

Markets – October to November (**walnuts**) and November to February (**marché gras**) on Fridays.

Boat trips on the Dronne – June to September daily; leave from the quay by the Renaissance house.

Belltower – Guided tours 1 July to 15 September daily (except Tuesdays) from 0900 to 1900; otherwise from 1000 to 1200 and from 1400 to 1800 (1700 November to March); closed 24 December and 1 January; 18F; ☎ 53 05 80 63; NB large numbers of stairs make this a physically demanding visit.

Fernand-Desmoulin Museum – Same admission times as for the Belltower above; 5F.

Troglodytic Tour – ♿ Same admission times and charges as for the Belltower above.

The Heart of Périgord Vert

La Chapelle-Faucher Castle – Guided tours (45 min) 1 July to 15 September daily from 1000 to 1200 and from 1400 to 1900; 15F; ☎ 53 54 81 48.

Thiviers Market – Marché gras November to March on Saturdays.

Thiviers Goose and Duck Centre – Open Tuesdays to Saturdays from 1000 to 1200 and from 1500 to 1800; 15F.

Villars Caves – Guided tours (45 min) July and August daily from 1000 to 1830; 12 April to 30 June and September to October from 1400 to 1830; 26F; ☎ 53 54 82 36.

Château de Richemont – Guided tours (30 min) 15 July to 31 August daily (except Fridays and Sunday mornings) from 1000 to 1200 and from 1500 to 1800; closed 15 August; 10F; ☎ 53 05 72 81.

BRIVE-LA-GAILLARDE
🖪 Place du 14-Juillet, ☎ 55 24 08 80

Brive-la-Gaillarde Market – Immortalised by the singer Georges Brassens; takes place in Place de la Guierle on Tuesdays, Thursdays and Saturdays; November to February **marché gras** on Saturdays.

Labenche Museum – ♿ Open April to October daily (except Tuesdays) from 1000 to 1830; otherwise from 1000 to 1800; 25F; ☎ 55 24 19 05.

Museum of the Resistance and of Deportation (Musée Edmond Michelet) – Open from 1000 to 1200 and from 1400 to 1800; closed Sundays and public holidays; admission free; ☎ 55 74 06 08.

Excursions: The Corrèze Causse

Noailles Church – Apply to M Delmas next door.

Cause Lake Leisure Centre – Open mid-June to mid-September daily from 1000 to 1930.

BRUNIQUEL

Castle – Guided tours (1 hour) July and August daily from 1000 to 1200 and from 1400 to 1900, starting every half hour; in April to June, September and October apply to the town hall: ☎ 63 67 24 91; 12F.

Maison Payrol – Open 15 June to 15 September daily from 1000 to 1200 and from 1400 to 1800; otherwise by appointment only; 12F; ☎ 63 67 25 18.

Excursion

Montricoux Marcel Lenoir Museum – Open June to October daily from 1000 to 1200 and from 1430 to 1900; 20F; ☎ 63 67 26 48.

LE BUGUE

Périgord Noir Aquarium – ♿ Open May to September daily from 1000 to 1900; otherwise from 1000 to 1200 and from 1400 to 1800; 35F.

Fossil site – Guided tours (40 min) July and August daily from 1000 to 1900; open April to June and September to October daily from 1000 to 1200 and from 1400 to 1900; otherwise daily (except Mondays) from 1400 to 1800; 20F; ☎ 53 04 24 34.

Bara-Bahau Cave – Guided tours (30 min) July and August daily from 0900 to 1900; April to June and 1 September to 11 November from 1000 to 1200; 25F; ☎ 53 07 27 47.

Excursion

Proumeyssac Chasm – Guided tours (45 min) July and August daily from 0900 to 1900; otherwise from 0900 to 1200 and from 1430 to 1730; closed January; 30F; ☎ 53 07 27 47.

C

CADOUIN

Cloisters and Shroud Museum – Open 1 July to 7 September daily from 0900 to 1200 and from 1400 to 1900; February to June and 8 September to mid-December from 1000 (0930 April to June and 8 September to mid-October) to 1200 and from 1400 to 1700 (1800 April to June and 8 September to mid-October); 24F.

Bicycle Museum – Open daily from 0900 to 1200 and from 1400 to 1900; 20F.

CAHORS

🄱 place Aristide-Briand, ☎ 65 35 09 56

Guided tours of the medieval city – July and August; contact the tourist office.

Boat trips on the Lot – April to October daily (except Mondays); leaving from Quai Valentré.

Valentré Bridge – Guided tours (30 min) July and August daily from 0930 to 1215 and from 1430 to 1830; 12F; ☎ 65 35 09 56.

Millboat – Open July and August daily from 1000 to 1900; in September daily (except Mondays) from 1000 to 1800; 20F; ☎ 65 22 14 00.

Chapelle St-Gausbert – Guided tours 15 June to 15 September daily from 1000 to 1300 and from 1500 to 1900; otherwise by appointment only, contact the Service départemental de l'Architecture, place Chapou, 46000 Cahors, ☎ 65 35 12 30.

Roaldès Mansion – Guided tours (30 min) mid-June to 22 September daily from 1000 to 1200 and from 1400 to 1800 (1830 from mid-July to 31 August, 1730 1 to 22 September); Sundays and public holidays open afternoons only; 15F; ☎ 65 35 04 35.

Église St-Barthélémy – Contact the presbytery nearby, 95 rue St-Barthélémy, ☎ 65 35 06 80.

Excursions

Château de Cieurac – Guided tours (45 min) 1 July to 15 September daily (except Thursdays) from 1000 to 1200 and from 1400 to 1800; ☎ 65 31 64 28.

Roussillon Castle – Guided tours (40 min) 1 July to 25 August Wednesdays and Thursdays from 1400 to 1700; 20F; ☎ 65 36 87 05.

CAPDENAC

Keep Museum and Fountain of a Hundred Steps – Guided tours (1 hour 30 min) 15 June to 15 September daily from 1000 to 1200 and from 1500 to 1900; 10F; ☎ 65 34 17 23.

CARENNAC

Cloisters – Open July and August daily from 1000 to 1230 and from 1400 to 1900; April to June from 1030 to 1230 and from 1500 to 1800; September to November from 1100 to 1230 and from 1500 to 1730; 7F (guided tours: 10F).

CASTELNAU-BRETENOUX

Castle – Open July and August from 0900 to 1830; April to June from 0900 to 1200 and from 1400 to 1800; otherwise from 1000 to 1200 and from 1400 to 1700; closed Tuesdays (except July and August), 1 January, 1 May, 1 and 11 November, 25 December; 25F; ☎ 65 38 52 04.

Collégiale St-Louis – Open from Easter to 1 November daily until 1700 (1800 July and August).

CASTELNAUD

Castle – Open April to November daily from 1000 to 1900; 25F; ☎ 53 29 53 99.

CÉNEVIÈRES

Castle – ♿ Guided tours (1 hour) Easter to end September daily from 1000 to 1200 and from 1400 to 1800; in October from 1400 to 1800; 20F; ☎ 65 31 27 33.

CHANCELADE ABBEY

Conventual buildings – Open July and August daily from 1400 to 1900, also major public holiday weekends; 20F; ☎ 53 04 86 87.

COLLONGES-LA-ROUGE

Guided tours of the village – Daily in high season; contact Mme Faucher, le Bourg, ☎ 55 25 42 48.

Mermaid's House – Open Easter to end October daily from 1000 to 1200 and from 1500 to 1800.

COUGNAC

Caves – Guided tours (1 hour) July and August daily from 0900 to 1800; Easter to end June and September to October from 0930 to 1100 and from 1400 to 1700; otherwise by appointment only; 25F; ☎ 65 41 22 25.

CUZALS

Quercy Open-Air Museum – Open June to September daily (except Saturdays) from 1000 to 1900; 12 April to 31 May and in October from 1400 to 1800; 45F; ☎ 65 22 58 63.

D

DOMME

Rampart Walk and Towers' Gateway – Guided tours (30 min) all year by appointment; 20F; ☎ 53 28 37 09.

Caves – Guided tours (30 min) July and August daily from 0930 to 1900; April to June and in September from 0930 to 1200 and from 1400 to 1800; in March and October from 1400 to 1800; otherwise by appointment only; 25F; ☎ 53 28 37 09.

Museum of Folk Arts and Traditions – Open July and August daily from 1000 to 1900; April to June and September to October from 1000 to 1200 and from 1400 to 1800; otherwise by appointment only; 15F; ☎ 53 28 37 09.

DORDOGNE VALLEY

⑴ Quercy Stretch

Belcastel Castle – Apply to the owner directly.

Château de la Treyne – Guided tours (25 min) of the grounds June to September daily (except Mondays) from 0900 to 1200 and from 1400 to 1800; 10F; ☎ 65 32 66 66.

⑵ Périgord Stretch

Fénelon Castle – Guided tours (45 min) July and August daily from 1000 to 1200 and from 1400 to 1900; March to June and September to October daily (except Tuesdays) from 1000 to 1200 and from 1400 to 1800; 30F; ☎ 53 29 81 45.

Château de Veyrignac – Guided tours (45 min) June to September daily from 1000 to 1300 and from 1400 to 1900; otherwise by appointment only; 28F.

⑶ Périgord Stretch

Cénac Church – Open June to September daily from 1000 to 1900; ☎ 53 28 32 73.

Les Milandes Castle – Guided tours Palm Sunday to 1 November daily from 0930 to 1130 and from 1400 to 1830; 30F; ☎ 53 29 54 63.

⑸ Périgord Stretch

Couze-et-St-Front Larroque Mill – Open daily (except Sundays) from 0900 to 1200 and from 1400 to 1700; closed 1 and 8 May, 11 November; 5F; ☎ 53 61 01 75.

E

ESPAGNAC-STE-EULALIE

Church – Guided tours of the interior are included in tours of the village daily from 1030 to 1200 and from 1500 to 1800; ☎ 65 40 06 17.

EXCIDEUIL

Market – Marché gras December to January on Thursdays.

Church – Contact Mme Genouillac, 2 rue Jean-Chanoix.

EYMET

Museum (in Keep) – Guided tours 15 June to 15 September daily from 1500 to 1800; 12 F; ☎ 53 23 92 33.

LES EYZIES-DE-TAYAC　　　　　　　　　　🅱 place du Centre, ☎ 53 06 97 05

National Museum of Prehistory – Open daily (except Tuesdays) from 0930 to 1200 and from 1400 to 1800 (1700 December to March); closed 25 December and 1 January; 18 F; ☎ 53 06 97 03.

Font-de-Gaume Cave – In season the maximum number of visitors per day is 340; the cave is therefore open only to those who have reserved tickets at the ticket office (same day or up to three days in advance); open July and August from 0900 to 1800; April to June and in September from 0900 to 1200 and from 1400 to 1800; otherwise from 1000 to 1200 and from 1400 to 1700; closed Tuesdays, 1 January, 1 May, 1 November, 25 December; 32 F; ☎ 53 06 97 48.

Pataud Shelter – Guided tours (40 min) July and August daily from 0930 to 1930; otherwise daily (except Mondays) from 1000 to 1200 and from 1400 to 1730; closed January; 24 F; ☎ 53 06 92 46.

Église de Tayac – Apply to the presbytery; ☎ 53 06 97 57.

Museum of Speleology – Open 15 June to 15 September daily from 1100 to 1800; 15 F ☎ 53 31 27 30.

Le Poisson Shelter – Open July and August daily (except Tuesdays) from 0900 to 1200 and from 1400 to 1800; otherwise from 1500 to 1600 by appointment only; ☎ 53 06 97 48.

Grand Roc Cave – Guided tours (30 min) June to mid-September from 0900 to 1900; 15 March to 30 May and mid-September to 11 November from 0930 to 1800; 30 F; ☎ 53 06 96 76.

Upper Laugerie Deposit – Guided tours (1 hour) July and August daily (except Tuesdays) from 1400 to 1800; otherwise by appointment only; 20 F.

Carpe-Diem Cave – Guided tours (30 min) mid-March to mid-November daily; 20 F; ☎ 53 06 91 07.

St-Cirq Cave – Guided tours (30 min) April to September daily from 1000 to 1800; otherwise from 1200 to 1600; 16F; ☎ 53 07 14 37.

St Christopher's Rock – Open (guided tours in high season: 45 min) 1 July to 15 September daily from 1000 to 1900; March to June and mid-September to mid-November from 1000 to 1800; 25F; ☎ 53 50 70 45.

Tursac Préhistoparc – Open July to September daily from 0930 to 1900; March to June from 1000 to 1830; 1 October to 11 November from 1000 to 1800; 25F; ☎ 53 50 73 19.

Les Combarelles Cave – The maximum number of visitors per day is 114, so in season it is essential to buy tickets at 0900 for a morning visit and at 1400 for afternoon visits; guided tours (45 min) April to October daily (except Wednesdays) from 0900 to 1200 and from 1400 to 1800; otherwise from 1000 to 1200 and from 1400 to 1600; closed 1 January, 1 May, 1 and 11 November, 25 December; 25F; ☎ 53 06 97 72.

Bernifal Cave – Guided tours (1 hour) July and August daily from 0930 to 1800; in June and September from 0930 to 1200 and from 1400 to 1800; otherwise by appointment only; 20F; ☎ 53 29 66 39.

Cap-Blanc Shelter – Guided tours (30 min) July and August daily from 0930 to 1900; Palm Sunday to end June and September to October from 1000 to 1200 and from 1400 to 1800; 20F; ☎ 53 59 21 74.

F

FIGEAC

🛈 Hôtel de la Monnaie, place Vidal, ☎ 65 34 06 25

Guided tours of the old town – Daily in high-season; contact the tourist information centre.

Mint Museum – Open July to September from 1000 to 1230 and from 1430 to 1900; 12 April to 30 June from 1030 to 1230 and from 1430 to 1730; otherwise Mondays to Fridays from 1430 to 1730; 10F; ☎ 65 34 06 25.

Notre-Dame-de-Pitié – If closed telephone ☎ 65 34 11 63.

Champollion Museum – Open March to October daily (except Mondays) from 1000 to 1200 and from 1430 to 1830; otherwise from 1400 to 1800; closed 1 January, 1 May and 25 December, 20F; ☎ 65 34 66 18.

Commandery of the Knights Templars – Guided tours (30 min) July and August daily from 1000 to 1900; April to June and in September at 1100, 1600, 1700 and 1800; otherwise open on Sundays only or by appointment; 25F; ☎ 65 34 28 00.

Excursions

Domaine du Surgié (Leisure Centre) – Open 18 May to 8 September daily from 1030 to 1900; ☎ 65 34 59 00.

Cardaillac Musée Éclaté – Guided tours in the summer at 1445, 1530, 1615, 1700 and 1745.

FOISSAC

Caves – Guided tours (1 hour) July and August daily from 1000 to 1830; in June and September from 1000 to 1130 and from 1400 to 1800; Easter to end May and in October on Sundays and public holidays from 1400 to 1800; otherwise by appointment only; 25F; ☎ 65 64 77 04.

G

GAVAUDUN

Keep – Open July and August daily from 1000 to 1200 and from 1400 to 1900; March to June and September to November from 1500 to 1800 by appointment; 10F; ☎ 53 40 82 29.

Excursions

St-Sardos-de-Laurenque Church – Contact M Vierge next to the church at Gavaudun.

Sauveterre-la-Lémance Fortress – Contact the town hall for details, ☎ 53 40 68 81.

GOURDON

Guided tours of the town – July and August on Wednesdays and Fridays at 2130; contact the tourist office.

Franciscan Church – Contact the tourist office.

Excursions

Chapelle de Notre-Dame-des-Neiges – Apply to the presbytery (☎ 65 41 12 90) or to the tourist office.

Le Vigan Church – Open July to August from 1000 to 1230 and from 1500 to 1800; otherwise contact the Le Vigan town hall or the Gourdon presbytery; ☎ 65 41 12 46.

Le Vigan Henri-Giron Museum – Open July and August daily; May to June and September to October daily (except Mondays); otherwise by appointment only; 16F; ☎ 65 41 33 78.

GRAMAT CAUSSE

Outing on the Causse

Caniac-du-Causse Crypt – Guided tours, preferably on Wednesdays and at weekends; contact the house opposite the church.

Gramat Nature Park – Open April to November daily from 0900 to 1900; otherwise from 1400 to 1800; 30F; ☎ 65 38 81 22.

Gramat French Police Dog Handler Training Centre – Guided tours (1 hour 30 min) 2nd Thursday in June to 2nd Thursday in September Mondays to Fridays from 1500 to 1700; admission free; ☎ 65 38 71 59.

Cougnaguet Mill – Guided tours (30 min) July and August daily from 0930 to 1200 and from 1400 to 1900; April to June and in September from 1000 to 1200 and from 1400 to 1800; 15F; ☎ 65 32 63 09.

H

HAUTEFORT

Château – Guided tours (45 min) June, July and beginning of September daily from 0900 to 1200 and from 1400 to 1900; March to June and 14 September to 15 November from 0945 to 1200 and from 1400 to 1800; 25F; ☎ 53 50 51 23.

L'HERM

Castle – Open July to September daily from 1000 to 1900 (Sundays from 1400 to 1900); 16F; ☎ 53 05 46 61.

L

LABASTIDE-MURAT

Murat Museum – Guided tours (30 min) 15 June to end September daily from 1000 to 1200 and from 1500 to 1800; 15F.

Excursion

Soulomès Church – Open daily in season.

LACAVE

Caves – Guided tours (1 hour 15 min, access by electric train) 15 July to 25 August daily from 0900 to 1900; 1 June to 14 July from 0900 to 1200 and from 1400 to 1830; April to May and 26 August to beginning of November from 0900 to 1200 and from 1400 to 1800; closed 1 November; 34F; ☎ 65 35 87 03.

LALBENQUE

Truffle Market – November to March Tuesday afternoons.

LANQUAIS

Château – Guided tours (35 min) April to September daily and October weekends only from 1000 to 1200 and from 1500 to 1800; closed Thursdays (except July to August); 20F; ☎ 53 61 24 24.

LARAMIÈRE

Priory – Guided tours (30 min) May to September daily (except Tuesdays) from 1430 to 1730; 14F; ☎ 65 45 36 91.

LARROQUE-TOIRAC

Castle – Guided tours (30 min) 9 July to 9 September daily from 1000 to 1200 and from 1400 to 1800; 20F.

LASCAUX

Lascaux II – *NB! During the summer the ticket office is in Montignac in the Point-Information arcades. Tickets are sold from 0900 until 2 000 tickets (the maximum entries for the day) have been sold – which takes hardly any time in high season.* Guided tours (40 min) July to August daily from 0930 to 1930; February to June and September to December from 1000 to 1200 and from 1400 to 1730; entrance tickets to Lascaux II are valid also for the park and museum at Le Thot; 47F; ☎ 53 51 95 03.

Régourdou – Guided tours (20 min) in summer daily from 0900 to 1200 and from 1400 to 1830; otherwise from 1000 to 1200 and from 1400 to 1630; 20F; ☎ 53 51 81 23.

LIMOGNE-EN-QUERCY

Market – **Marché gras** November to March on Sunday mornings.

Bois-de-Lafont Recreation Park – Open June to September daily and May weekends only from 1000 to 2000; 46260 Varaire, ☎ 65 24 32 70.

LIZONNE VALLEY

Bourzac Country

Lusignac Church – Contact Mme Pervallet; ☎ 53 91 61 17.

Vendoire Peat Museum – Open May to September daily (except Tuesdays) from 1030 to 1230 and from 1430 to 1830; otherwise from 1400 to 1700; 21F; boats for hire and fishing permits on sale.

St-Paul-Lizonne Church – Contact the town hall.

LOC DIEU

Abbey – Guided tours (45 min) 1 July to 10 September daily (except Tuesdays) from 1000 to 1200 and from 1400 to 1830; 20F; ☎ 65 29 51 17.

LOT VALLEY

Cliffs and Promontories

St-Pierre-Toirac Church – Open Easter to 1 November.

Meanders of Lower Reaches

Grézels La Coste Feudal Castle – Guided tours (1 hour 30 min) 1 July to 15 September daily at 1600 and 1700; 20F; ☎ 65 21 34 18.

LUZECH

Boat trips on the Lot – Daily in summer; leave from Caïx sailing base; on Thursdays "Castle Cruise" *(Croisière des Châteaux)* return trip Luzech-Cahors from 0830 to 1930.

Armand Viré Archaeological Museum – Open 15 May to 15 September daily from 0900 to 1200 and from 1500 to 1900; otherwise by appointment only; admission free.

M

LA MADELEINE SITE

Troglodyte Village – Open 1 July to 7 September daily from 0900 to 1200 and from 1400 to 1900; otherwise daily (except Tuesdays) from 1000 (0930 April to June and 8 September to 15 October) to 1200 and from 1400 to 1700 (1800 April to June and 8 September to 15 October); 24F; ☎ 53 06 92 49.

MARCILHAC-SUR-CÉLÉ

Bellevue Cave – Closed temporarily.

MARTEL

Hôtel de la Raymondie Museum – Open July to August daily from 1000 to 1200 and from 1500 to 1800; ☎ 65 37 30 03.

MONBAZILLAC

Château – Guided tours (45 min) June to September daily from 1000 to 1230 and from 1400 to 1930; otherwise from 1000 to 1200 and from 1400 to 1700 (1800 in May); 25F; ☎ 53 57 06 38.

Cooperative Wine Cellars and Bottling Centre – Open from 0900 to 1200 and from 1400 to 1700; closed weekend and public holidays; admission free.

MONPAZIER

🚩 le Bourg, ☎ 53 22 68 59

Guided tours of the bastide – June to August at 1000, 1120, 1500 and 1700, Saturdays at 1500 only, no tours on Tuesday mornings or Sundays; contact the tourist office.

MONTAL

Castle – Guided tours (45 min) Palm Sunday to 1 November from 0930 to 1200 and from 1430 to 1800; in August from 1430 to 1900 only; closed Saturdays (except July and August); 22F; ☎ 65 38 13 72.

MONTIGNAC 🏠 24, rue du 4-Septembre, ☎ 53 51 82 60

Chestnut and Walnut Market – October and November on Wednesdays.

Lascaux II Ticket Office – In summer; see under **Lascaux**.

Eugène Le Roy Museum – Guided tours (35 min) July and August daily from 0930 to 1200 and from 1400 to 1730; otherwise by appointment only; 12F; ☎ 53 51 82 60.

MONTPEZAT-DE-QUERCY

Excursion

Saux Church – Contact the town hall or the presbytery in Montpezat.

MUSSIDAN

André Voulgre Museum of Périgord Local Arts and Traditions – Guided tours (1 hour) June to September daily (except Tuesdays) from 0930 to 1200 and from 1400 to 1800; October to November and March to May from 1400 to 1800; otherwise weekends only from 1400 to 1800; 10F; ☎ 53 81 23 55.

Pottery Workshops – Open July and August daily from 0900 to 1200 and from 1400 to 1800; otherwise daily (except Tuesdays) from 1400 to 1800; ☎ 53 81 18 84.

Castles of the Landais Region

Château de Montréal – Guided tours (45 min) July to September daily from 0930 to 1230 and from 1430 to 1830; otherwise by appointment only; 25F; ☎ 53 81 11 03.

Montagnac-la-Crempse Hameau de la Grange – Open all year by appointment only; ☎ 53 53 44 35.

Grignols Castle – Guided tours (45 min) mid-June to mid-September daily (except Wednesdays) in the afternoon; 20F; ☎ 53 54 25 40.

Château de Neuvic – Open to visitors only on certain days in the year; contact the tourist office for details; ☎ 53 81 52 11.

Fratteau Castle Pottery Museum – Open July and August daily from 1000 to 1200 and from 1500 to 1900; otherwise Wednesdays to Sundays from 1500 to 1800; ☎ 53 81 61 93.

P

PADIRAC

Chasm – Guided tours (1 hour 30 min) daily in August from 0800 to 1900; 10 to 31 July from 0830 to 1830; April to beginning of July and 1 September to 10 October from 0900 to 1200 and from 1400 to 1800; closed mid-October to end March; 36F; ☎ 65 33 64 56.

Zoo le Tropicorama – ♿ Open 8 May to 30 September daily from 0900 until nightfall; 30F.

PECH-MERLE

Cave – Guided tours (1 hour 15 min) April to September daily from 0930 to 1200 and from 1330 to 1730; October to November from 0930 to 1200 and from 1330 to 1645; combined ticket including admission to the Amédée Lemozi Museum: 44F; ☎ 65 31 27 05.

Amédée Lemozi Museum – Same admission times as the Cave; 22F.

PÉRIGORD NOIR

St-Crépin-et-Carlucet La Cipière Manor-house – Open 15 June to 15 September Sundays and Mondays from 1400 and 1800.

Ste-Nathalène La Tour Watermill – Open Mondays to Saturdays from 0800 to 1230 and from 1400 to 2000; demonstrations of mill in action July and August on Mondays, Wednesdays and Fridays.

PÉRIGUEUX 🏠 Rond-Point de la Tour Mataguerre, 26 place Francheville, ☎ 53 53 10 63

Guided tours of the medieval and Renaissance town – July and August Tuesdays to Fridays at 1430; contact the tourist office.

Guided tours of the Gallo-Roman site – Same as above, but departure at 1000.

Markets – **Livestock** (place de la Clautre) and **flower** (place de la Mairie) markets all year on Wednesdays and Saturdays; **marché gras** (place St-Louis) and **truffle** market (place St Silvain) November to March on Wednesdays and Saturdays.

St Stephen's Church – Closed in the afternoon on Sundays and public holidays.

Mataguerre Tower – Guided tours (45 min) July and August Mondays to Fridays; 5F; is also included in the guided tour of the medieval and Renaissance town (see above).

Hôtel de Lestrade – Included in the guided tour of the medieval and Renaissance town (see above).

Domus du Bouquet – Included in the guided tour of the Gallo-Roman site (see above).

Vesunna's Tower – Open daily from 0730 to 2100.

Périgord Museum – Open daily (except Tuesdays and public holidays) from 1000 to 1200 and from 1400 to 1800 (1700 October to March); 10F; ☎ 53 53 16 42.

Périgord Military Museum – Open April to September daily (except Sundays and public holidays) from 1000 to 1200 and from 1400 to 1800; October to December from 1400 to 1800; otherwise Wednesdays and Saturdays only from 1400 to 1800; 20F; ☎ 53 53 47 36.

PUYGUILHEM

Château – Guided tours (45 min) 1 July to 7 September daily from 0900 to 1200 and from 1400 to 1900; April to June and 8 September to 15 October daily (except Tuesdays) from 0930 (1000 16 October to 15 December) to 1200 and from 1400 to 1800 (1700 16 October to 15 December); 24F; ☎ 53 53 85 50.

PUY-L'ÉVÊQUE

Church – Contact Mlle Bessière; ☎ 65 21 38 03.

PUYMARTIN

Castle – Guided tours (45 min) 15 April to 15 October daily from 1000 to 1200 and from 1400 to 1830; 25F; ☎ 53 59 29 97.

R

RIBÉRAC

Domed Churches of the Ribérac Region

Grand Brassac Fortified Church – Contact Mme Lacour, opposite the church; ☎ 53 90 70 61.

Parc de Loisirs du Paradou – Open 15 June to 15 September daily from 1000 to 2200; Easter to 14 June weekends and public holidays only; ☎ 53 91 42 78.

ROCAMADOUR   🚹 Hôtel-de-Ville, ☎ 65 33 62 59

Guided tours of the Ecclesiastical City – June to September and during school holidays daily (except Sundays).

Lifts – These operate May to September from 0800 to 2200; in March, April and October from 0830 to 1830; otherwise from 1400 to 1700.

Evening train ride – Sight-seeing trip by tourist train past the illuminated town by night 1 April to 15 August; departure from in front of the Lion d'Or hotel; 32F.

Light show "Les Lumières du Temps" – 8 to 15 August at 2230.

Town Hall – Open July and August daily from 1000 to 2000; April to June and September to October daily (except Wednesdays) from 1000 to 1200 and from 1500 to 1900; 5F; ☎ 65 33 62 59.

St-Amadour's Crypt – Included in the guided tour of the Ecclesiastical City (see above).

Chapelle-St-Michel – Open in summer Mondays to Fridays from 0900 to 1200 and from 1400 to 1800.

Francis-Poulenc Museum of Sacred Art – Open 1 April to 1 November daily from 0900 to 1200 and from 1400 to 1800; 13F.

Ramparts – Open July and August daily from 0900 to 1900; April to June and September to October from 0900 to 1200 and from 1330 to 1800; 7F.

Eagles' Rock – Open Palm Sunday to 15 November daily from 1000 to 1200 and from 1400 to 1900; demonstrations at 1100, 1430, 1530, 1630, 1730 in July and August, otherwise at 1100, 1500, 1600, 1700; 30F; visitors interested in seeing eagles in free flight are advised to telephone in advance to check that this is included in the demonstration they plan to see; ☎ 65 33 65 45.

L'Hospitalet

Cave of Wonders – Guided tours (30 min) July and August daily from 0900 to 1900; April to June and September to beginning of November from 1000 to 1200 and from 1400 to 1800; 20F; ☎ 65 33 67 92.

Model Railway – Open 13 July to 22 August daily from 0900 to 1200 and from 1400 to 1900 and from 2030 to 2230; Palm Sunday to 12 July and 23 August to 11 November from 1000 to 1200 and from 1400 to 1800; 25F; ☎ 65 33 71 06.

Butterfly Garden – Open July and August daily from 0900 to 1830; 18 April to 30 June and 1 September to 15 October from 1000 to 1200 and from 1400 to 1730; 23F; ☎ 65 33 71 72.

Monkey Forest – Open 15 June to 31 August daily from 0900 to 1900; April to mid-June and September to October from 1000 to 1200 and from 1400 to 1800; 29F; ☎ 65 33 62 72.

LA ROQUE-GAGEAC

Barge trips on the Dordogne – Easter to 1 November daily.

ROUFFIGNAC

Excursion

Rouffignac Cave – *NB Number of admissions is limited*. Guided tours (1 hour) July and August daily from 0900 to 1130 and from 1400 to 1800; April to June and September to October from 1000 to 1130 and from 1400 to 1700; 24F.

When driving through France
*use the **Michelin Motoring Atlas France***
with map coverage at a scale of 1:200 000

S

ST-AMAND-DE-COLY

Diaporama – Shown in the presbytery on request at the town hall; ☎ 53 51 67 50.

ST-ANTONIN-NOBLE-VAL
🏛 Hôtel-de-Ville, ☎ 63 30 63 47

Guided tours of the town – July and August on Saturdays; apply to the tourist office.

Museum – Open July and August daily (except Tuesdays) from 1500 to 1830; otherwise on Thursdays and Fridays 1030 to 1200 and at weekends from 1500 to 1700 (1600 November to December); 8F.

Excursions

Upper Aveyron Valley Bosc Cave – Guided tours (35 min) July and August daily from 1000 to 1200 and from 1400 to 1900; April to June and in September from 1400 to 1800; 24F; ☎ 63 30 62 91.

Cas Castle – Guided tours (1 hour) July and August daily (except Mondays) from 1000 to 1200 and from 1400 to 1900; April to June and September to October weekends and public holidays only; 20F; ☎ 63 67 07 40.

ST-AVIT-SÉNIEUR

Geology and Archaeology Museum – Open July and August daily from 1400 to 1900; ☎ 53 22 32 27.

ST-CÉRÉ
🏛 place de la République, ☎ 65 38 11 85

Casino Gallery – Open Mondays to Fridays from 0930 to 1200 and from 1400 to 1830; on Sundays and public holidays from 1100 to 1230 and from 1430 to 1900; closed Tuesdays out of season and 1 January; no admission charge; ☎ 65 38 19 60.

Jean Lurçat Studio-Museum – Open Palm Sunday to Easter and 14 July to 30 September daily from 0930 to 1200 and from 1430 to 1800; 15F; ☎ 65 38 28 21.

Upper Quercy Motor Museum – *Closed until further notice* (Guided tours (30 min) Easter to end September daily from 1000 to 1200 and from 1400 to 1800 (1900 June to September); 22F) ☎ 65 38 15 72.

Excursion

Presque Cave – Guided tours (30 min) 29 March to 11 October daily from 0900 to 1200 and from 1400 to 1800 (1900 July and August); admission charge not disclosed; ☎ 65 38 0744.

ST-CIRQ-LAPOPIE
🏛 place du Sombral, ☎ 65 31 29 06

La Gardette Castle – Open July and August daily from 1000 to 1200 and from 1400 to 1900; April to June and September to October daily (except Tuesdays) from 1000 to 1200 and from 1400 to 1800; 10F; ☎ 65 31 23 22.

ST-JEAN-DE-CÔLE

Marthonie Castle – Guided tours (30 min) July and August daily from 1000 to 1200 and from 1400 to 1900; 16F; ☎ 53 62 30 25.

ST-PRIVAT-DES-PRÉS

Museum of Village Life and Tools – Open June to September daily from 1500 to 1800; otherwise by appointment only; 10F; ☎ 53 91 22 87.

SALIGNAC-EYVIGUES

Castle – Open 15 June to 15 September daily from 1000 to 1200 and from 1400 to 1800; otherwise by appointment only; 22F; ☎ 53 28 81 70.

Eyrignac Manor-house Gardens – Guided tours (45 min) July to September daily from 1000 to 1230 and from 1430 to 1830; April to June and in October afternoons only; otherwise by appointment only; 25F; ☎ 53 28 99 7.1.

SARLAT-LA-CANÉDA
🏛 place de la Liberté, ☎ 53 59 27 67

Guided tours of the town – In July and August Mondays to Fridays at 1030, 1500 and 2200, Saturdays at 1500 and 2200 and Sundays at 1030 and 2200; 15 July to 15 August extra tour at 1800 (except on Sundays); contact the tourist office.

Coach Service – 1 July to 25 August regular service to Cénac, Domme, La Roque-Gageac and Beynac (departure from Place Pasteur); day-trips by coach to these destinations, for details contact SCETA Voyageurs, 24 rue Aristide-Briand, 87000 Limoges; ☎ 55 77 57 65.

Markets – **Chestnut and Walnut** market October to November on Saturdays; **marché gras** and **truffle** market November to March on Saturdays.

Chapelle des Pénitents Blancs Museum of Sacred Art – Open Easter to 1 November daily (except Tuesdays) from 1000 to 1200 and from 1500 to 1800 (on Sundays and public holidays afternoons only); 10F; ☎ 53 31 19 34.

Museum-Aquarium – ♿ Open 1 June to 15 September daily from 1000 to 1900; 19 April to 31 May and mid-September to end October from 1000 to 1200 and from 1400 to 1800; 27F; ☎ 53 39 44 58.

Excursion

St-André-d'Allas Archéosite de Breuil – Open all year; 10F.

SORGES

Truffle Centre – Open July and August daily from 1000 to 1200 and from 1400 to 1800; otherwise at these times until 1700 and closed on Mondays; 16F; ☎ 53 05 90 11.

Tour of the Truffle Beds – July and August on Wednesdays at 1600 (2 hours); meet at the Truffle Centre; 16F.

SOUILLAC
 boulevard L J Malvy, ☎ 65 37 81 56

Guided tours of the town – July and August on Tuesdays at 0900; contact the tourist office.

National Museum of Automata and Robotics – Open July and August daily from 1000 to 1900; April to June and September to October daily (except Mondays) from 1000 to 1200 and from 1500 to 1800; otherwise Wednesdays to Sundays from 1400 to 1700; 26F; ☎ 65 37 07 07.

Excursion

Parc de Loisirs Quercyland "Les Ondines" – Recreation Park open 15 May to 15 September daily from 1000 to 2200; ☎ 65 37 33 51.

T

LE THOT

Cro-Magnon Centre – Open July and August daily from 0930 to 1900; February to June from 1000 to 1200; otherwise daily (except Mondays) from 1400 to 1730; combined ticket with Lascaux II on sale July and August at Montignac in the Point-Information arcades: 47F; otherwise tickets available on site: 36F; ☎ 53 53 44 35.

TOURTOIRAC

Abbey – Open 15 June to 15 September daily from 0900 to 2000; otherwise contact the town hall.

TURENNE

Castle – Open April to September daily from 0930 to 1200 and from 1400 to 1900; 10F.

Excursion

La Fage Chasm – Guided tours (45 min) mid-June to mid-September daily from 0930 to 1900; 1 April to 15 June and 16 September to 31 October from 1400 to 1830; 20F; ☎ 55 87 12 21.

V

VÉZÈRE VALLEY

Château de Losse – Guided tours (45 min) end June to end September daily from 1000 to 1230 and from 1400 to 1830 (no break for lunch between 2nd weekend in July and 3rd weekend in August); 24F; ☎ 53 50 70 38.

Castel-Merle Museum – Guided tours (45 min) 15 June to 15 September daily from 1000 to 1800; 15F; ☎ 53 50 77 45.

Castel-Merle Prehistoric Shelters – Guided tours (45 min) 15 June to 15 September daily from 1000 to 1830; major public holiday weekends from 1400 to 1800; 20F; ☎ 53 50 79 70.

INDEX

Cahors Lot

Le Roy, Eugène

L.-et-G. Lot-et-Garonne
T.-et-G. Tarn-et-Garonne

Towns, sights and tourist regions followed by the name of the *département* (for abbreviations see below).

People, historical events and subjects.

Isolated sights (caves, castles, château, abbeys, dams...) are listed under their proper name.

Départements where abbreviations have been used.

C

NOTES

ILLUSTRATION ACKNOWLEDGEMENTS

p. 11 MICHELIN, Paris
p. 17 National Museum of Prehistory, Les Eyzies *(above)*
p. 23 Bibliothèque Nationale, Paris
p. 28 S. Bois Prévost/RAPHO, Paris
p. 29 Berthoule/EXPLORER, Paris *(above)*
p. 29 Éditions René, Marsac-sur-L'Isle *(below)*
p. 31 S. Marmounier/CEDRI, Paris
p. 32 After photo by B. Brillion/MICHELIN, Paris *(above)*
p. 32 After photo by MICHELIN, Paris *(centre)*
p. 32 After drawing by R. Bayard/Maisons paysannes de France *(below)*
p. 33 After photo by P. Tétrel/EXPLORER, Paris *(above)*
p. 33 A. Kumurdjian, La Brède *(below)*
p. 36 J.-M. Charles/RAPHO, Paris *(above)*
p. 36 M. Guillard/SCOPE, Paris *(below)*
p. 37 Michel/Bildagentur Schuster, Oberursel
p. 39 J.-D. Sudres/SCOPE, Paris
p. 43 After photo by Bibliothèque Nationale, Paris
p. 48 Tobacco Museum, Bergerac
p. 51 After photo by ZODIAQUE, La-Pierre-Qui-Vire
p. 52 A. Kumurdjian, La Brède
p. 56 Éditions René, Marsac-sur-L'Isle
p. 58 Vincent/VLOO, Paris
p. 62 Labenche Museum, Brive-la-Gaillarde
p. 66 After photo by D. Repérant/SCOPE, Paris
p. 68 R.G. Everts/RAPHO, Paris
p. 74 C. Sappa/CEDRI, Paris
p. 79 R. Cauchetier/PIX, Paris

p. 80 Ph. Chair/Édition La Clé des Champs, Cahors
p. 82 J.-D. Sudres/SCOPE, Paris
p. 83 Pélissier/VLOO, Paris
p. 90 After photo by ARTHAUD, Grenoble
p. 94 Préhistoparc, Les Eyzies
p. 97 A. Kumurdjian, La Brède
p. 102 J.-D. Sudres/SCOPE, Paris
p. 105 J.-L. Nespoulos
p. 106 C.N.M.H.S., Paris © SPADEM
p. 111 A. Kumurdjian, La Brède
p. 120 R. Lanaud/EXPLORER, Paris
p. 122 After document of the Société d'Exploitations Spéléologiques de Padirac
p. 124 R. Delon/CASTELET, Boulogne-Billancourt
p. 125 D. Repérant/SCOPE, Paris
p. 128 D. Cauchoix/PIX, Paris
p. 140 K. Hackett/VLOO, Paris
p. 141 B. Brillion/MICHELIN, Paris
p. 142 Delderfield/IMAGES PHOTOTHÈQUE, Toulouse
p. 147 Novali/IMAGES PHOTOTHÈQUE, Toulouse
p. 149 D. Cauchoix/PIX, Paris
p. 152 Meauxsoone/PIX, Paris
p. 153 J.-D. Sudres/SCOPE, Paris
p. 155 Nimetz/IMAGES PHOTOTHÈQUE, Toulouse
p. 156 After photo by MICHELIN, Paris
p. 161 Périgord Museum, Périgueux
p. 163 R. Delon/CASTELET, Boulogne-Billancourt
p. 165 B. Brillion/MICHELIN, Paris
p. 170 Apa/PIX, Paris
p. 171 J.-D. Sudres/SCOPE, Paris

MANUFACTURE FRANÇAISE DES PNEUMATIQUES MICHELIN

Société en commandite par actions au capital de 2 000 000 000 de Francs

Place des Carmes-Déchaux – 63 Clermont-Ferrand (France)

R.C.S. Clermont-Fd B 855 200 507

© Michelin et Cie, Propriétaires-Éditeurs 1993

Dépôt légal décembre 1993 – ISBN 2-06-132303-0 – ISSN 0763-1383

Printed in France 11-93-15

Composition : NORD-COMPO, Villeneuve-d'Ascq

Impression : I.M.E., Baume-les-Dames – Brochage : S.I.R.C., Marigny-le-Châtel

TRAVELLING COMPANIONS
Michelin tourist Guides and detailed Maps are designed to be used together.